KT-165-922

SCOTLAND'S 100 BEST WALKS

CAMERON MCNEISH

First published in Great Britain in 1999 for Lomond Books
36 West Shore Road, Granton,
Edinburgh EH5 1QD

Reprinted 2001, 2003, 2004, 2005

Produced by Colin Baxter Photography Ltd.

Information used in the creation of the maps was kindly supplied by the
Macaulay Land Use Research Institute in Aberdeen and the Royal Commission on the
Ancient and Historical Monuments of Scotland, Edinburgh.

ISBN 0-947782-66-4

Printed in China

Front cover photograph: Walking in the West Highlands © Paul Tomkins, STB/Scottish Viewpoint 2001
Back cover photograph: Dumgoyne, Stirling Region, from the West Highland Way © David Robertson, Still Moving Pic. Co. 2001
Page 1 photograph: Beinn Dorain and the West Highland Way near Tyndrum

SCOTLAND'S 100 BEST WALKS

CAMERON MCNEISH

PHOTOGRAPHS BY
COLIN BAXTER

LOMOND BOOKS
EDINBURGH • SCOTLAND

Contents

Glen Affric and Loch Affric from the air

SCOTLAND'S
100 BEST WALKS
1 - 16 The Southern Hills and Coast
17 - 28 The Borders and South-West
29 - 49 The Eastern Highlands and Coast
50 - 61 The Central Highlands
62 - 71 The Western Highlands
72 - 87 The Northern Highlands
88 - 100 The Islands
Shetland Islands
Haroldswick
Unst
Yell
Scalloway
Lerwick
Foula
Sumburgh Head
Fair Isle
Orkney Islands
Westray
Sanday
Stronsay
Stromness
Kirkwall
Hoy
Burwick
Pentland Firth
John o' Groats
Thurso
Wick
Durness
Kinlochbervie
Tongue
Scourie
Altnaharra
Lochinver
Loch Shin
Lairg
Helmsdale
Brora
Golspie
Dornoch
Tain
Ullapool
Aultbea
Gairloch
L Maree
Kinlochewe
Shieldaig
Contin
Alness
Invergordon
Dingwall
Moray Firth
Elgin
Buckie
Banff
Fraserburgh
Fochabers
Forres
Keith
Craigellachie
Mintlaw
Peterhead
Western Isles
Port of Ness
Carloway
Stornoway
Lewis
Harris
Tarbert
N Uist
Lochmaddy
Uig
A836
A9
A99
A837
A835
A832
A96
A98
A95

ABERDEEN
Aboyne
Banchory
Stonehaven
Braemar
Kingussie
Kincraig
Aviemore
Dalwhinnie
Clova
Kirriemuir
Montrose
Arbroath
DUNDEE
PERTH
Pitlochry
Dunkeld
Aberfeldy
L Tummel
Loch Rannoch
L Ericht
Loch Tay
Killin
Crianlarich
Lochearnhead
Crieff
Callander
Aberfoyle
STIRLING
Drymen
Kinross
Dunfermline
Falkirk
St Andrews
Crail
Pittenweem
North Berwick
Firth of Forth
Dunbar
EDINBURGH
St Abbs Head
Eyemouth
Berwick on Tweed
Coldstream
Kelso
Melrose
Selkirk
Hawick
Innerleithen
Peebles
Penicuik
Moffat
Lockerbie
Annan
Dumfries
Kirkcudbright
Solway Firth
Castle Douglas
Newton Stewart
Dalmellington
Sanquhar
Lanark
Wishaw
GLASGOW
Largs
Ardrossan
Troon
AYR
Girvan
Cairnryan
Stranraer
Mull of Galloway
Helensburgh
Dunoon
Firth of Clyde
Rothesay
Arrochar
Lochgilphead
Tarbert
Claonaig
Arran
Brodick
Lamlash
Campbeltown
L Awe
Dalmally
Oban
Craignure
Lochaline
Tobermory
Salen
Ballachulish
Fort William
Spean Bridge
Fort Augustus
Loch
Invergarry
Cluanie
L Quoich
Loch Arkaig
Glenfinnan
L Morar
Loch Shiel
Mallaig
Armadale
Broadford
Rum
Coll
Tiree
Mull
Colonsay
Jura
Craighouse
Islay
Bridgend
Port Ellen
Barra
Castlebay
Lochboisdale
Larne
BELFAST
NORTHERN IRELAND
ENGLAND
Motorway
Trunk Road
Other Roads
Rail Network
Vehicle Ferry
Passenger Ferry
Airport
0 10 20 30mls
0 10 20 30 40 kms
© Wendy Price Cartographic Services 2001

Walks List and Distances

SCOTLAND'S 100 BEST WALKS

I think it was the romance and mystery of the Highlands that first inspired me to climb mountains and take to the quieter byways of Scotland. I remember childhood visits to the Kelvingrove Art Gallery and Museum in Glasgow, full of fascinating artefacts, models of steam trains and ocean-going ships, suits of armour and ancient weapons, but I was drawn to the voluminous art galleries where I searched out the Victorian landscapes of Scotland. Here were paintings resonant with the mystery and enigma of that period known as the Celtic Twilight, great wide canvasses full of exaggerated splendour, misty with promise of another world, far removed from that of the city in which I grew up.

I've never been able to fully articulate the powerful emotions those paintings aroused in me, but there was something curiously familiar in those rough, yet sublime, landscapes, something instinctive, a longing perhaps for some desire buried deep within me.

Over forty years on I still retain a childlike fascination for the atmospheres, the colours, and the impressions of wild landscape which have never failed to invoke in me a deep sense of wonder and humility. Even the misty days can make an impact, when the eye shrinks from the wide expansive views to the microscopic: the earth-colours of the lichens, the coarse granular etchings of granite, or gneiss, or schist, the mountain flowers and the shimmering of dewdrops hanging like diamonds.

While years of foreign travel have expanded exploratory horizons, the hills of home still harbour that one single element that isn't to be found in the mountains of the greater ranges, or the varied landscapes of Europe or North America. Put simply, I suspect it's the Celtic love of a homeland, passed down from father to son since time immemorial. It's not jingoistic nationalism, it's not even a particularly patriotic thing, but it is probably genetic. And by far the finest way to explore that homeland, is by walking through it.

A writer whose work has influenced me more than any other is a Welsh-American by the name of Colin Fletcher. He thought up a cardinal rule of travel which I believe is pertinent to everyone who goes walking. Essentially, Fletcher claims you can only come close to the land by walking on it – the less there is between you and the environment, the more you appreciate that environment. It's obvious that you'll feel closer to the land by walking over it than travelling through it in an air-conditioned, 112-seater coach! It's the same in sailing; a solo yachtsman learns more about the sea than a passenger on the *QE2*, and you'll

Glen Luibeg and Monadh Mor, Cairngorms

certainly experience more of the moods of the ocean, the winds and the night stars.

By leaving the car behind and walking along a track you begin to appreciate the detail that turns a pretty countryside into a living, vibrant landscape – but leave that track for a faint footpath and you come even closer to the feel of the land. Almost inevitably, once you leave the footpath for an open hillside, released from any sign of man, you bring other senses into play; you can smell the crushed bog myrtle beneath your feet, you can feel the coarse heather brush against your legs and your attention is immediately taken up with the ground right in front of you. And it's then, and probably only then, that you begin to tune in to the heartbeat of the land.

This then is a book about walking, a simple activity that's become extremely popular in the past few years. Walking has become recognised not only as a major benefit to health, but it's increasingly seen as an activity which allows us to escape the turmoil of urban pressures for an environment which fulfills our mind's need for variety, beauty and reflection. It's also recognised as a sustainable form of green tourism.

Several years ago a survey by Highlands and Islands Enterprise showed that hill walkers and climbers brought over £164M into the Highland economy, a figure well in excess of that produced by forestry, hunting, fishing, shooting and downhill ski-ing. Significantly, that figure didn't take into account low-level ramblers or backpackers such as those who walk the West Highland Way, a long distance trail which supports the equivalent of 168 full-time jobs and brings in some £3.5M to the rural communities it passes through.

But critics see this promotion of walking as encouraging too many people onto the hills and trails, resulting in a destruction of the peaceful ambience that many seek, and the constant and steady erosion of mountain footpaths. Indeed, figures extrapolated from various reports over the past few years and quoted by the National Mountaineering Centre at Glenmore Lodge, suggest that some 70,000 people are climbing Scottish hills each weekend, a considerable number of trampling boots. Not surprisingly the cost of repairing and maintaining footpaths is high.

Such user numbers also reflect a growing political body of opinion, a body that could be crucial when conflicting pressures make demands on Scotland's wild places. Issues like over-coniferisation, access problems, high-level bulldozed roads, inappropriate ski developments and a thousand and one other potential developments constantly threaten the beauty and sanctity of our wild and remote areas, and an increasing number of people are coming to the realisation that such places are vitally important to society. It was the American writer Edward Abbey who said: 'We need wilderness even if we never set foot in it. We need the possibility of escape as surely as we need hope; without it the life of the cities would drive all men into crime, drugs or psychoanalysis. The natural environment has the power to set one's mind at peace and give hope to a sometimes dreary world.'

He's right. Over the last century our increasing urbanisation has ensured a steady divorce of our physical lives from the natural world, so that we no longer consider ourselves a part of it. Many of us have become over rational, over analytical, at the expense of the intuitive, instinctive side of our nature. We have become cut-off from both inner and outer Nature. We've lost trust in the traditional faiths, the spiritual side of our nature has been subdued, and the resultant loss of meaning in the lives of many people is reflected in statistics for depression, suicide and mental illness.

Perhaps one of the reasons walking has become so popular is that many people now crave a simpler life, reminiscent of our aboriginal ancestors, and there's nothing more simple than going for a walk. When you start walking your brain and body operate as one unit, and muscle use, followed by muscle relaxation, produces brain relaxation. It just might be that for your brain to function at its best, your body has to exercise, preferably in natural surroundings. As an old friend, the late and much lamented John Hillaby, once wrote: '...the land of our better selves is surely reached by walking.' And where better than among the mountains, the moors and forest, and the coastline of Scotland.

My author's brief for this book was a simple one – at least in theory. Choose the hundred best walks in Scotland, and write about them. For someone like me to whom walking is a way of life, that should have been a joyous and exciting task, a dream job, but life is rarely that simple. In any such list there have to be certain provisos. There's always a danger in the selection of a list of preferences that omissions may disappoint some folk, perhaps even annoy some. As I'm essentially a mountaineer, my list contains a surfeit of mountain walks, but as I've grown older I've also enjoyed many shorter, low-level walks, particularly where there are wildlife associations or powerful links with history. It's taken me a long time to appreciate that short low-level walks can often be as rewarding as the big hill days, as though maturity and experience have eroded the prejudices of youth.

A well-balanced geographical spread has been an over-riding factor in my choice, and the need for some sort of balance between mountain walks, coastal walks, moorland walks and forest walks. I've also borne in mind a long and protracted discussion some of us enjoyed when trying to nominate Scotland's ten best mountains. No matter how hard we tried we couldn't come to an agreement, so I have little confidence that everyone will agree with my choice of a hundred best walks. Rather, consider the list as self-indulgence on my part, with the corollary that I genuinely hope you enjoy walking the routes as much as I have.

CAMERON McNEISH

THE SOUTHERN HILLS AND COAST

These southern hills extend from the Campsie Fells just north of Glasgow to Glen Lyon. The area's western boundary is the coastline and the most eastern hill covered is Meall nan Tarmachan. This is an area known to many. Some of the walks, like that to The Whangie and The Trossachs tops, are justifiably popular and no less fine for that. Others are less well known, like the low-level walks to Dunstaffnage and the old railway walk in Glen Ogle, just north of Lochearnhead. Of the more challenging routes the Glen Lochay Horseshoe is a fairly arduous day out. Ben More and Stob Binnein, the Cruachan Horseshoe, Beinn Laoigh and The Cobbler are all hillwalking classics.

THE WALKS

1	The Glen Lochay Horseshoe	25km
2	The Tarmachan Horseshoe	10km
3	The Glen Ogle Railway Trail	9km
4	Ben More and Stob Binnein	15km
5	Beinn Laoigh (Ben Lui) – Queen of Scotland's Hills	20km
6	The Cruachan Horseshoe	15km
7	Beinn Lora – Deirdre's Hill	5km
8	Dunstaffnage – In Search of Ancient Kings	8km
9	The Cobbler	15km
10	The Trossachs' Ben A'n	6km
11	Ben Ledi	12km
12	Ben Venue	13km
13	Ben Lomond	12km
14	Conic Hill – West Highland Way	10km
15	The Whangie – The Work of the Devil?	5km
16	The Campsie Fells – Glasgow's Hills	12km

Ben Challum and Glen Lochay, Mamlorn Hills

1 The Glen Lochay Horseshoe

Route Summary

From Badour climb NW to the top of Stob an Fhir-bhogha. From here a broad ridge leads N to the summit of Beinn Heasgarnich. Return to Stob an Fhir-bhogha and follow the SW ridge to the Bealach na Baintighearna. Find the lochan on the bealach which gives a good line for a steep, direct ascent of Creag Mhor. Follow the rim of Coire-cheathaich to Stob nan Clach, drop into Lairig Mhic Bhaidein, cross the spur of Cam Chreag and climb Challum's NW ridge to the summit. Return to Badour by Challum's ENE ridge.

Map: OS Sheets 50 and 51

Access Point: Badour in Glen Lochay, GR431351

Distance: 25km

Approx Time: 8-10 hours

Grade: Strenuous hill walk

These hills of the Mamlorn forest are big and well-muscled but few hill-walkers would include their ascent in a list of favourite walks. Over the years I've enjoyed a number of days in this lonely and comparatively isolated western extremity of Glen Lochay and the combination of all three mountains, Beinn Heasgarnich, 1078m, Creag Mhor, 1047m and Beinn Challum, 1025m, in one outing is both challenging and strenuous. The highest hills in the old hunting forest of Mamlorn, they dominate the head of Glen Lochay and give a big day of 25km with some 1800m of climbing, much of it on trackless, rough terrain.

Beinn Heasgarnich is a great grassy whaleback of a hill and is easily reached from Badour, at the end of the public road in Glen Lochay, via the subsidiary top of Stob an Fhir-bhoga. Hamish Brown suggests it means 'peak of the roaring waterfall of the horses', but Peter Drummond, in *Scottish Hill and Mountain Names*, considers 'peaceful or sheltering mountain' to be more suitable. Take your pick.

From the summit of Heasgarnich return over Stob an Fhir-bhoga and drop down its south-west ridge into the boggy depths of the Bealach na Baintighearna. A small lochan, cradled here in the curve of the col, is useful as a navigational aid to line up the steepish route of ascent, all the way to the summit of the second Munro, Creag Mhor.

Its minor top, Stob nan Clach, is easily reached by following the rim of Coire-cheathaich from where you should drop down steep southerly slopes to reach the Lairig Mhic Bhaidein. Ben Challum can be climbed from here by crossing the south-east spur of Cam Chreag and negotiating the steep slopes of Challum's north-west ridge. Return to Glen Lochay by the east-north-east ridge.

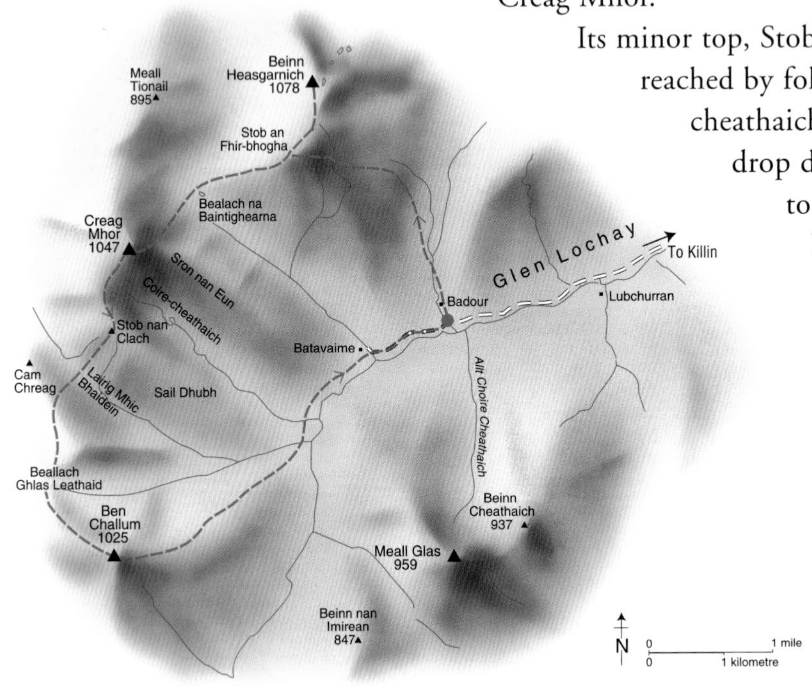

2 The Tarmachan Horseshoe

Meall nan Tarmachan and Beinn nan Eachan, Breadalbane

I've climbed the splendid Meall nan Tarmachan ridge above Loch Tay a number of times and in all seasons of the year. The Munro, Meall nan Tarmachan, lies at the north-east end of a 2km ridge, a twisting promenade above steep craggy corries which crosses three other prominent tops. A fairly short outing, it nevertheless makes for a great day out, especially in wintry conditions when snow adds an Alpine feel to the narrow sections of the ridge.

The normal route, the one described in most of the guidebooks, including my own Munro books, leaves the National Trust for Scotland Visitor Centre on the high pass between Loch Tay and Glen Lyon and with a distinct lack of subtlety simply thrutches up the front of the mountain to the summit cairn. Many folk nowadays just bag the Munro and return the same way, but for those who do go on to traverse the ridge there is always an awareness that the line of tops is carrying you further and further away from where you want to finish. Once the delights of the ridge end, you have to descend a steepish corrie and take a 2km walk back to your starting point by way of a bulldozed track, a soul-destroying climax to what is one of the most exhilarating little ridges in the Southern Highlands.

This mountain deserves a better route, and I'd often looked at the north ridge which bounds Coire Riadhailt on the western slopes of Meall nan Tarmachan. By starting on the Glen Lyon side of the Lochan na Lairig road, close to the upper reaches of the Allt Bail a' Mhuillin, you can reach the crest of this ridge in about 30

Route Summary

Leave the Lochan na Lairige road and head W to gain the N ridge of Meall Glas. Follow this ridge S to Beinn nan Eachan. Bear E and scramble to the summit of Meall Garbh, descend to a broad bealach and climb easy slopes to the summit of Meall nan Tarmachan. Continue N, over four steep noses and the crest of Creag an Lochain. Follow grassy slopes back to the road.

Map: OS Sheet 51

Access Point: Lochan na Lairige road at GR582417

Distance: 10km

Approx Time: 3-5 hours

Grade: Moderate hill walk

Translation: hill of the ptarmigan

Pronunciation: myowl nan tar-mach-an

minutes of climbing heather and tussocky grass. Once this is out of the way the going is on deer-cropped turf which climbs gradually towards an obvious gap in the Tarmachan ridge south-west of the Munro between Meall Glas and Beinn nan Eachan. It's a lovely ridge, narrowing as it climbs higher with rounded grassy slopes giving way to craggy, gully-seared slopes, with the steep western slopes of Meall nan Tarmachan looking increasingly dramatic across the void of Coire Riadhailt. To the west Meall Ghaordie rises impressively out of Glen Lochay and beyond it stretch the great hills of Breadalbane.

Following this easy ridge, things change dramatically when you reach the Tarmachan ridge. A confusion of high-level knolls and rocky knobs abound with the odd crag thrown in for good measure. If it wasn't for the obvious footpath weaving its way in-between it could prove tricky in misty conditions. To the left the path drops down steeply from Meall Garbh and to the right you can, if you wish, wander along the rest of the Tarmachan ridge for as far as you like before retracing your steps to this point. In actual fact the best of the ridge now forms the middle section of our horseshoe walk, steeply up the western crag of Meall Garbh with some good sections of scrambling, over the narrow, airy summit and down to a broad bealach before the final rise to the Munro, Meall nan Tarmachan at 1044m.

To the east rise the big tops of the Ben Lawers group, the highest hills in the Southern Highlands and to the south the rather uninspiring plateau on the south side of Loch Tay. But the real views are to the north, with Schiehallion lifting its head over the Carn Mairg group and the far outline of the Cairngorms. Head north now, over a series of four steep little noses, (the difficulties can be avoided on the left) and over the ridge of Creag an Lochain with good views into Lochan na Lairige. Easy grassy slopes drop you back down to the roadside – a fine horseshoe ridge of some 10km and infinitely more rewarding than the popular route from the National Trust Centre. It's well worth trying.

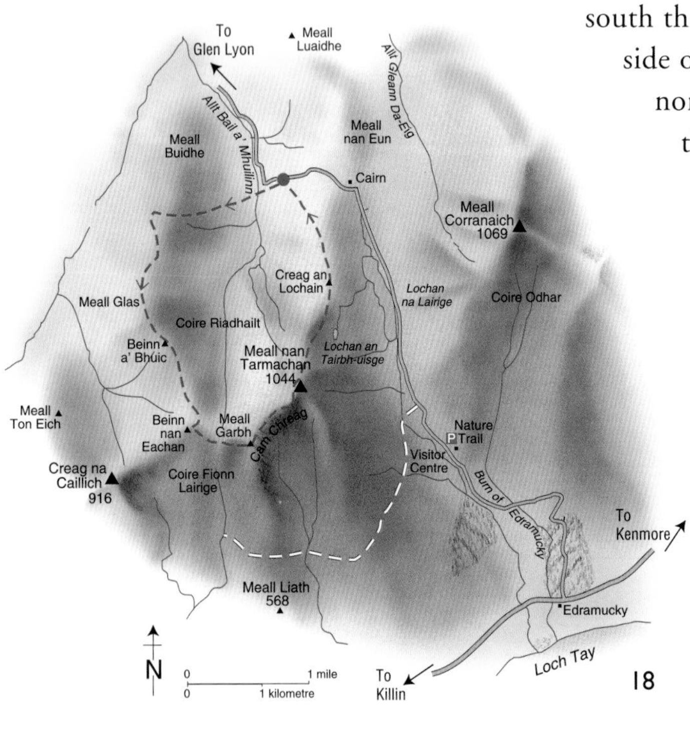

3 The Glen Ogle Railway Trail

Glen Ogle – Looking south towards Lochearnhead, Ben Vorlich and Stuc a' Chroin

Confession time. As a youngster I spent many happy hours watching steam trains, joyously ticking off the names of the trains in my little book – a forerunner of my later inclinations with Munros perhaps? This walk relives memories of that steam railway age as it follows the old railway line past Lochearnhead, up the length of Glen Ogle, the long pass which carries the A85, and over to the Lix Toll.

The route of the railway track makes up part of the Glen Ogle Trail, an imaginative walking route devised by Stirling District Council. Part of the route climbs the length of Glen Ogle from Lochearnhead, following the trackbed of the old Caledonian Railway which once ran north from Stirling, via Callander and Strathyre, then westwards towards its final destination at Oban.

The line was opened in 1880 and was eventually closed in 1965 by the infamous Dr Beeching. I remember the excitement of this train journey and especially one particular view which never failed to enthrall me, even as a child, the view down the length of Loch

Route Summary

Leave the old Lochearnhead railway station, now a Boy Scout headquarters. A footpath climbs up through the trees, over a stile, across a field and up a series of wooden steps. Continue up a series of zigzags before another line of steps takes you onto the old rail trackbed. Follow this across several bridges and a viaduct until you come to a fence and stile. Cross the stile onto a stretch of track, clamber along the right hand side of the rubble for about 100m until you come to a ladder stile. Cross it and drop down to the green track below. This leads down to a hump-backed bridge and a footpath which runs down the glen between the burn and the road. Halfway down the glen cross the road, to where another series of signs and stiles lead you back to Lochearnhead.

Map: OS Sheet 51

Access Point: Lochearnhead

Distance: 9km

Approx Time: 3 hours

Grade: Easy low-level walk

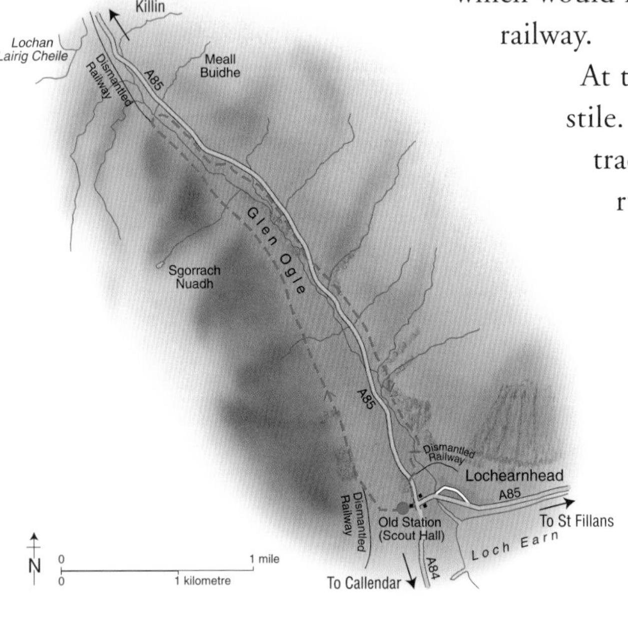

Earn towards St Fillans. It was thought at one time to be the finest view from a railway anywhere in the country and happily it can now be enjoyed by walkers.

The line this route takes up Glen Ogle is an interesting one too, running parallel with the road built originally in the eighteenth century by Major Caulfeild and his troops of navvy soldiers. But travellers had been using Glen Ogle as a gateway to the Highlands long before that and it's thought that Roman legions once tramped this way as well as generations of drovers and travellers.

Start at the old Lochearnhead railway station, now used as the local Boy Scout headquarters. This old building wasn't on the original Caledonian line but was a station on the Crieff-Lochearnhead line which was closed in 1951. Both lines ran together as far as Balquhidder, then the Caledonian line took a much higher route before tackling the long pull up Glen Ogle. The bad news is that you have to climb steeply up to the old Caledonian line from the old station before you can enjoy the leisurely stroll up Glen Ogle.

From the driveway of the Boy Scout building, a footpath climbs up through the trees, over a stile, across a gorse-covered field and up a series of wooden steps. Signposts keep you in the right direction as the path climbs the hill in a series of zigzags before another line of steps takes you onto the old rail trackbed. This offers a fine surface to walk on, even though it is rough in places underfoot. It crosses several old bridges and a well-preserved 12-arched viaduct. Ancient Scots pines line much of the route, trees which would have seen both the coming and the going of the railway.

At the end of the trackbed you'll reach a fence and stile. Cross the stile onto a rather worn stretch of track. Clamber along the right-hand side of the rubble for about 100m until you come to a ladder stile. Cross it and drop down to the green track below, which leads down to a little hump-backed bridge and a lovely stretch of green footpath down the glen between the burn and the road. Halfway down you'll have to cross the road, where signs and stiles lead you back to Lochearnhead, not far from your starting point.

4 Ben More and Stob Binnein

I've driven down the long hill into Tyndrum from Bridge of Orchy countless times and glanced eastwards towards the Crianlarich hills. Often, and particularly in winter, it can be an Alpine spectacle with Cruach Ardrain reflecting the setting sun from the snow-filled gully of its northern corrie. Its ridges make up a fine peak alongside its larger neighbours, Ben More and Stob Binnein, from which it is separated by the long ridge of Stob Garbh.

I always consider Ben More and Stob Binnein to be the Castor and Pollux of the Scottish Highlands, celestial twins joined together by the Bealach-eader-dha-Beinn, a grand-sounding name with a rather prosaic translation – the pass between the mountains. But they're big mountains, 1174m and 1165m respectively, indeed they're the highest peaks in Scotland south of the Tay. While Ben More has a rather bulky profile, rising to a blunt pyramid, Stob Binnein is more shapely, its slopes rising gracefully from its long, sweeping ridge to its truncated summit. I've climbed it from several directions and recall one memorable ascent, on skis, from Inverlochlarig in the south. It was one of those precious days that stands out

Route Summary

Follow the line of the Benmore Burn S as far as the spur of Creagan Liatha. Gain the SSE ridge of Stob Binnein and follow it to the summit. Descend N to the Bealach-eader-dha-Beinn before ascending the S ridge of Ben More. Descend the N slopes of Ben More, taking care to avoid the steep NW corrie.

Map: OS Sheet 51

Access Point: Benmore Farm, GR414257

Distance: 15km

Approx Time: 6-8 hours

Grade: Moderate hill walk

Translation: big hill; hill of the anvil

Pronunciation: byn moar; stop binyin

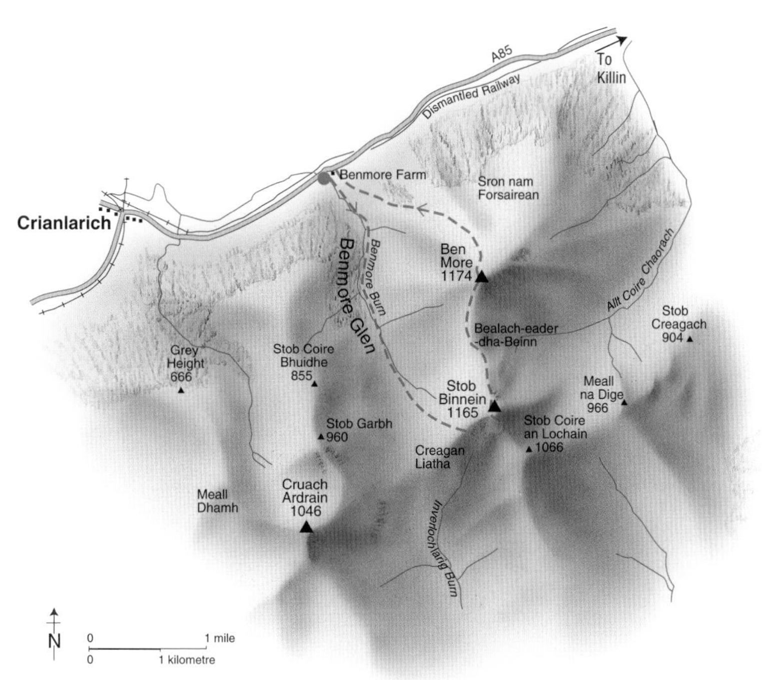

Ben More and Stob Binnein from Strath Fillan

in the memory – a day of white snow and blue skies and we descended under a dimming sky that was burnished yellow, gold and crimson with the setting of the sun.

While Stob Binnein is elegance itself, Ben More is brutish, a big and brash mountain whose northern slopes sweep down virtually in one fell swoop from its summit all the way to Glen Dochart. My longtime friend, Hamish Telfer, co-adventurer in many a teenage mountain ploy, and I once slid almost all the way from the summit down to Benmore Farm in under 45 minutes, whooping and hollaring in delight as we managed, just, to control our direction by the propitious use of our long-handled, wooden ice axes. On a more serious note, a hanging corrie immediately below the summit facing north-west, has a steep upper section which is prone to avalanche and has been the site of a number of fatal accidents, so caution is required here.

While the normal ascent route follows the Sron nam Forsairean ridge almost all the way from Benmore Farm to the summit of Ben More, another route initially follows the Benmore Burn southwards. The main advantage of this route is that it avoids the rather long and tedious climb up the Sron nam Forsairean ridge and adds a little variety; the main disadvantage is that the headwaters of the Benmore Burn take you into wet and boggy ground, but not for long. The spur of Creagan Liatha falls down from Stob Binnein in the south and provides an opportunity to get off the soggy ground and gain some height, and drier ground, before gaining the south-south-east ridge of Stob Binnein, which then climbs steadily to the summit cairn.

A beautifully uniform slope drops northwards to the level Bealach-eadar-dha-Beinn before curving right to climb to Ben More's rocky summit.

The ascent of the two hills makes a memorable day out in all the seasons of the year, with exceptional views southwards towards the other Glen Falloch hills and the lower, brackish hills of the Trossachs. Northwards, on a good day, the landscape poses a massive jumble of high hills, the mountains of Mamlorn leading the eye all the way to the huge hump-back of Ben Nevis itself.

5 Beinn Laoigh (Ben Lui) – Queen of Scotland's Hills

The anthropomorphising of mountains is a risky business. I don't believe it's particularly fanciful to describe Beinn Laoigh, or Ben Lui, as the Queen of Scottish mountains, as many writers have, but in these politically correct times there is always someone willing to challenge your vision of regal comeliness.

That Beinn Laoigh is dramatically beautiful is no exaggeration, and it is no mere fancy to describe the mountain as shapely and elegant. Seen through this writer's eyes, Beinn Laoigh is one of the most beautiful hill shapes in the country, one which is more than capable of stopping me in my tracks to simply stand and stare. In particular, the mountain's east face soars to imposing double tops, the most Alpine-looking feature in the central Highlands with its great bowl of Coire Gaothaich holding snow well into the spring in most years.

My own choice of ascent would be from Dail Righ, or Dalrigh, the King's Field, on the A82 Crianlarich to Tyndrum road, where in 1306 Robert the Bruce escaped down Glen Dochart after battling with the MacDougalls of Lorn. You'll be glad of the escape too, after tussling with the traffic on the busy A82 road. It is always a relief to leave the trucks and the caravans behind for the

Route Summary

Take the private road from Dalrigh, past Cononish Farm to the forestry road which stops close to the Allt an Rudd. Cross this stream and follow the burn which tumbles out of Coire Gaothaich above. Reach the corrie, bear right and climb to the ridge of Stob Garbh. Follow this ridge to the N top, then follow the corrie rim to the summit. Return the same way, or descend SW to the head of the Fionn Choirean where a rough path drops down through the forest to Glen Lochy.

Map: OS Sheet 50

Access Point: Dalrigh on the A82, GR344291

Distance: 20km

Approx Time: 7-9 hours

Grade: Moderate hill walk

Translation: hill of the calf

Pronunciation: byn loo-ee

heady scent of the Caledonian pine forest just across the River Cononish. It may be a long hike up the length of Glen Cononish, and the bulldozed gold-mining activities on the lower slopes of Beinn Chuirn may be less than appealing, but the shapely hill ahead of you does have an imposing presence, even a regal presence, which dominates everything else.

About 8km from the Dail Righ the route crosses the Allt an Rudd and steeply follows the stream which issues from Coire Gaothaich high above. Once you get into the corrie, bear right and scramble up onto the hill's north-east spur, called Stob Garbh on OS maps. Climb this ridge to the north top and then along the rim of the corrie to the true summit.

From this double summit of Beinn Laoigh, twin spurs enclose the round-bottomed Coire Gaothaich, some 300m deep. At the back of the corrie a gully splits the wall, and in winter often forms an enormous, steep snow ramp which offers a glorious romp to the summit ridge. It's a classic snow climb, often topped by an equally classic cornice. A word of warning – it is also a route which is frequently avalanched as I found to my cost many years ago. I had been inspired by a photograph in an ancient climbing book of a figure burrowing through the cornice at the top of the corrie. With a single ice axe each, and no crampons, a pal and I innocently cut

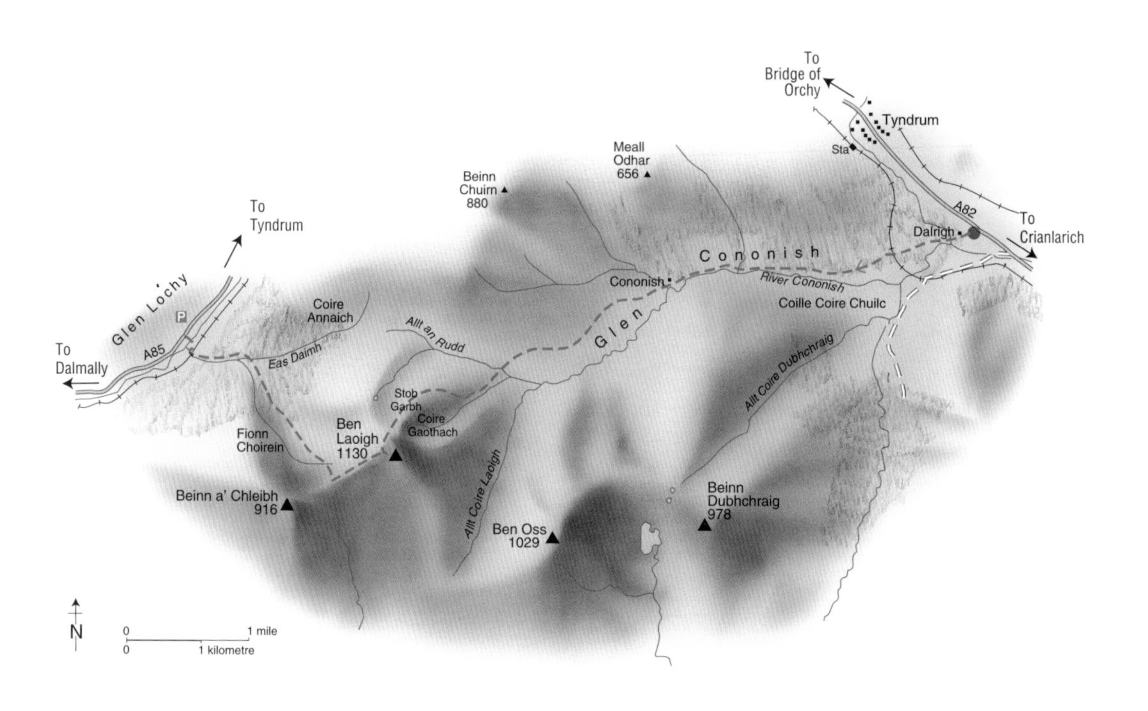

Beinn Laoigh (Ben Lui) from the west

steps up most of the corrie headwall to find soft snow on the top section. Naively we forged our way through it and had just stepped onto the cornice when the whole snowfield suddenly swept away below our feet. It was two very shaken laddies who made their way down into the darkness of Glen Lochy to hitch a lift home.

A shorter route, which appears to satisfy most Munro-baggers intent on simply getting to the summit, leaves the A85 in Glen Lochy at GR239278. Look for some stepping stones to get you across the River Lochy, or you may prefer to walk a kilometre or so downstream to a footbridge. Once across the river, and the railway line, find the muddy path which follows the north bank of the Eas Daimh through the forest. After about 400m cross the burn and follow the path to the stile in the fence which leads to the open hillside. Head eastwards now, climbing steadily to reach the broad north-north-west ridge of Beinn Laoigh, which is followed over some craggy steps to the 1130m summit.

For those who want to bag another Munro, wide slopes lead down to the col at the head of the Fionn Choirein from where another broad ridge leads to the summit of Beinn a' Chleibh, at 916m.

6 The Cruachan Horseshoe

Route Summary

Climb the path beside the Allt Cruachan to the dam access road. Follow the E shore of the reservoir before ascending to Stob Garbh. Continue N, descend slightly, then climb to the summit of Stob Diamh. Follow the W ridge over the Drochaid Ghlas (slightly N of the main ridge) then along a bouldery crest to the summit of Cruachan. Head due S to Meall Cuanail and grassy slopes back to the Cruachan dam.

Map: OS Sheet 50

Access Point: Cruachan Power Station GR078268

Distance: 15km

Approx Time: 6-8 hours

Grade: Moderate hill walk

Translation: stacky hill

Pronunciation: byn kroo-achan

The rocky summit of Drochaid Ghlas perches slightly north of the main Cruachan ridgeline, and abuts the main ridge by means of a tight, scrambly neck of rock. As you approach this short ridge from the east the main route narrows, rich in promise of some scrambling, so it is almost inevitable that you are seduced onto the wrong route, as the rocks carry you 90 degrees off-line. In essence it isn't really a big problem – as the route steepens into an awkward scramble it becomes fairly obvious you're off-route, but for those who are unhappy with steep, rocky terrain it could create difficulties.

But when the weather is clear, the classic Cruachan Horseshoe, a round of the Cruachan peaks that form a high mountain wall around the Cruachan Reservoir above the Pass of Brander, poses little difficulty. With almost 1500m of climbing, a relatively short day of 15km becomes a substantial mountain walk, and takes in no fewer than five tops, with options of another couple.

This high-level circuit follows the skyline above the Cruachan Reservoir which was created in 1965 as part of a huge hydro-electric scheme. Below your feet lies a vast hall, hewn out of the mountain's heart, where an intricate system of tunnels, pipes, turbines and pumps operates what is one of the finest feats of engineering in the country.

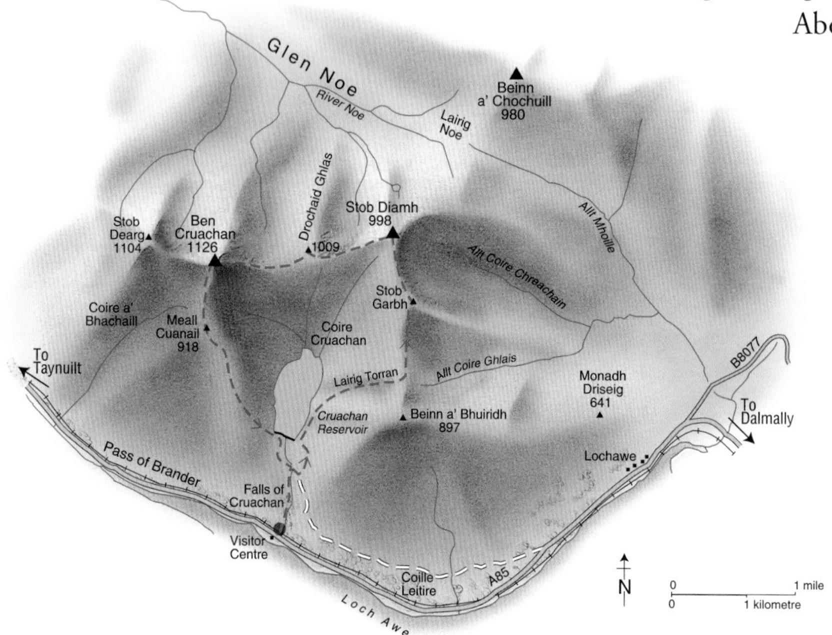

Above the ground, other than the reservoir and its access road, little has changed in centuries. The horseshoe route begins at the Power Station beside the A85 where a minor road runs up to the railway line. Once safely across the rails a footpath climbs steeply uphill beside the Allt Cruachan all the

Ben Cruachan from the west at dusk

way to the Reservoir. The footpath follows the east shore of the loch to where easy slopes lead to the Lairig Torran, an ancient transhumance route from Dalmally. Little could the cattle herders have imagined that one day their grazing grounds in Coire Cruachan would be drowned with waters which were to fuel a hydro-electric pumped storage station! It's maybe as well that while God created us with an ability to remember the past, he didn't think it a good idea to let us see the future. Divine wisdom!

From here it's a straightforward climb onto the south ridge of Stob Garbh. Continuing north, the ridge begins to narrow before a climb to the summit of Stob Diamh, at 998m one of Cruachan's two Munros.

The main ridge sweeps westwards, bounded on the north side by a series of scalloped, craggy corries dropping steeply down towards Glen Noe, past Drochaid Ghlas, then along a narrower bouldery crest with a couple of sections of entertaining scrambling to the main summit of Cruachan, at 1126m.

Such is the hill's proximity to the sea that the coastal views, particularly those across to the Isle of Mull, are superb and that, taken together with spectacular rocky ridges, a series of fine peaks, and some high, imposing corries, makes this one of the finest hills south of Glen Coe.

If you feel fit you can continue along the westwards ridge to a bealach and Stob Dearg. Return to the bealach, re-ascend the main peak for some distance to avoid the slabby face of Coire a' Bhachaill, then head due south to grassy Meall Cuanail and the easy slopes back to the Cruachan dam.

The Firth of Lorn, Mull, Lismore and Rubha Garbh-aird from Beinn Lora

7 Beinn Lora – Deirdre's Hill

Rising just over 300m above the village of Benderloch and the lovely curve of Ardmucknish Bay, known locally as Tralee Bay, Beinn Lora offers one of the finest panoramas in the Southern Highlands, a wonderful viewpoint which is largely accessible by good forestry paths. Surrounding the foot of the hill is an area rich in standing stones, chambered cairns and forts and it's believed that the large mound at the south-east end of the bay was once the site of the fort of ancient warriors from Ulster, Dun MacUisneach, the Fort of the Sons of Uisneach.

An ancient Celtic tale, the *Lay of Deirdre*, tells the story of this young woman who was promised in marriage to the High King of Ulster, Concubar MacNessa. But Deirdre had fallen in love with Naoise, the eldest of the three Sons of Uisneach, hereditary Knights of the Red Branch, and to escape the High King's wrath, they fled from Ulster to Scotland. There are several place names in nearby Glen Etive which recall the story of Deirdre. In the field next to the mound there remains a solitary standing stone.

The summit of Beinn Lora is a magnificent viewpoint – south, across the mouth of Loch Etive to Kerrera and the islands beyond; west to Lismore, Loch Linnhe and the hills of Morvern and Mull; north to upper Loch Linnhe and the hills of Lochaber and Appin, and east to the fine conical Stob Dearg, the peak of Cruachan.

It is not a difficult walk to the summit and is ideal for a good summer's evening. Turn left by the information sign at the back of the car park. Follow the red and blue marker posts along a well-

Route Summary

Follow the footpath at the back of the car park and turn left by the information sign. Follow the red and blue marker posts along a forest path. Go through a gate beyond which lies a Y junction. Take the left fork following the red and blue waymarkers. Follow the path and soon it swings right and begins to climb steeply. At the top of the climb there's a long, flat section with forest on both sides. At the end of this section the path turns slightly to the right and another path bears off to the left. This time the waymarker post is marked in blue only, indicating the route to the summit. Follow it to where another signpost points to the 'Eagles' Eyrie' viewpoint to the left and 'Walk to Beinn Lora' to the right. Visit the Eagles' Eyrie then return to the main path which is followed all the way to a deer fence, with a gate, and a picnic table. The summit of Beinn Lora lies 800m on along an unmade hill path.

Map: OS Sheet 49
Access point: A828, Forest Enterprise car park
Distance: 5km
Approx Time: 2-3 hours
Grade: Easy hill walk

made forest path. Go through a gate beyond which lies a Y-junction. Take the left fork following the red and blue waymarkers. Follow the path and soon it swings right and begins to climb steeply. Almost at the top of this hill there is a bench by the trailside where you can see across to the hills of Ardgour. At the top of the climb there's a long, flat section with forest on both sides. At the end of this section the path turns slightly to the right and another path bears off to the left. This time the waymarker post is marked just in blue indicating the route to the summit.

Already the views become noticeable. Through a clearing you can easily see the hills of Mull. The path begins to climb again, with densely planted conifers on your left and a clear-felled area on the right. The path begins to twist and turn and starts another steep climb. At the end of a particularly steep section a signpost points to the 'Eagles' Eyrie' viewpoint to the left and 'Walk to Beinn Lora' to the right. A further steep path to the left may put you off, but it is worthwhile visiting the Eagles' Eyrie for the magnificent views.

Retrace your steps to the signpost and turn left, climbing again to reach an open area and Lochan nan Ron, a good place to see roe-deer. The path curves its way round and to the right, then climbs again over a rather rough section of track.

Reach a deer fence, with a gate, and a picnic table. This fence marks the boundary of the Forest Enterprise area and the views are southerly, over Connel airfield and west to the Isle of Mull. The summit of Beinn Lora, with its magnificent panorama, lies 800m further on along an unmade hill path which can be very wet and boggy, but the views are well worth wet feet. To return, make your way back to the last red and blue waymarker. The path descends through the forest and bends right into an area of more open deciduous woodland. Soon the path veers off to the left following a line of fence all the way back to the start.

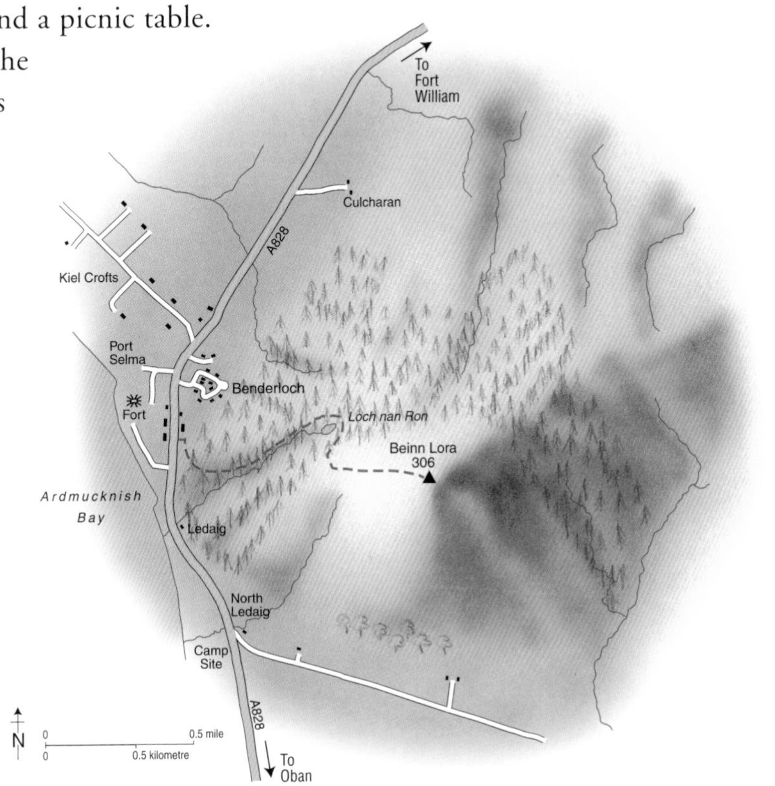

8 Dunstaffnage – In Search of Ancient Kings

Route Summary

Follow the track N from Ganavan car park to a footbridge at the Aonadh Mor, the first of a number of gullies. Further on, another of these gullies, the Slochd a' Bhiorain, the Sharp Cleft, necessitates an easy leap to get across. Continue following the coastline, cross a stile at another break in the cliffs, and cross several bays and promontories to the big bay of Camas Rubha na Liathaig. The footpath curves round the bay and enters the wooded policies of Dunstaffnage Castle. Follow the faint path with care, round the headland to the rear of the castle. A road leads past the pier, past the Marine Research Laboratory buildings and just before it reaches Dunstaffnage Bay, goes through a gate in the fence and crosses the headland back to Camas Rubha na Liathaig.

This area with its combination of sea-cliffs, ancient ruins and extensive seaward views across the islands of Kerrera and Lismore towards the blue hills of the Isle of Mull, is very much the cradle of civilisation in Scotland. The focus of this walk is Dunstaffnage Castle, the erstwhile home of the Stone of Destiny.

The environs of Oban are rich in Iron-Age hill forts and 'duns' and it seems as if almost every hill top and headland is crowned with these remains. These buildings date back to about AD150 and there are other sites in the area which would have been occupied during the Roman invasion of Iron-Age Britain. One of these, the Dun a' Mhonaidh, or Dunavona, is known better these days as Dunstaffnage. Local legend links Dun a' Mhonaidh with a local chieftain called Eoghann who is thought to have been killed while fighting the Romans in AD45. Also killed by the Romans was the great Celtic chieftain Calgacus who died at the battle of Mons Graupius in AD74. It's thought that the remains of both these great leaders lie somewhere in the vicinity of Dun a' Mhonaidh, the 'Old Dun' which lies near the site of the present Dunstaffnage Castle.

It is also believed that the ancient kings of Dalriada were once crowned at Dunstaffnage, seated upon a great block of red sandstone known as the Lia Fail, or Stone of Destiny. Later, when the Picts and Scots were united under Kenneth MacAlpin in 850, the Stone was transferred to the royal palace at Scone, to where many believe it should be returned in these present times.

Dunstaffnage Castle

Retrace your steps to the S shore of the bay, cross a stile then bear left along a stone wall to find the undulating cliff-top track which takes you back to Ganavan.

Map: OS sheet 49

Access Point: Car park at Ganavan Sands, N of Oban

Distance: 8km

Approx Time: 3-4 hours

Grade: Easy low-level walk

Ganavan Bay, to the north of Oban, has a good car park from where a track heads off along the shore to a footbridge at the Aonadh Mor, the first of a number of gullies which break through the line of low-lying conglomerate cliffs. Further on, another of these gullies, the Slochd a' Bhiorain, the Sharp Cleft, necessitates an easy leap in order to get across.

Continue to follow the coastline, cross a stile at another break in the cliffs, and cross a number of attractive bays and promontories to the big bay of Camas Rubha na Liathaig. The footpath curves round the bay and enters the wooded policies of Dunstaffnage Castle.

The path becomes quite faint here but can be followed with care round the headland to the rear of the castle. A road leads past the pier, past the Marine Research Laboratory buildings and just before it reaches Dunstaffnage Bay, go through a gate in the fence and cross the headland back to Camas Rubha na Liathaig. Retrace your steps to the south shore of the bay, cross a stile then bear left along a stone wall to find the undulating cliff top track which takes you all the way back to your starting point at Ganavan.

The Cobbler (Ben Arthur)

9 The Cobbler

Route Summary

From the car park beside the A83 cross the road and follow the path through the forest to a forest road. Turn left, follow the road for 1km to the Buttermilk Burn. Turn right and follow the path on the W bank of the Burn until it clears the trees. Continue N, cross the burn, and follow the path past the Narnain Boulders towards the obvious col between the Cobbler and Beinn Narnain. Before you reach this col, bear left and cross the burn again, climbing up into the corrie below the overhanging prow of the N peak. Climb steeply on an eroded path below the prow onto the summit ridge. Follow the path over slabby rocks and boulders to the N peak. The true summit of the mountain is on the central peak, but involves awkward scrambling moves. Walkers should return to the ridge and descend by the route of ascent.

There are a handful of mountains in Scotland which have the presence and the character to stop me in my tracks with a gasp of amazement. The majestic Buachaille Etive Mor is one, when first seen from that particular bend on the A82 near the White Corries. The Cobbler is another. As you drive into the village of Arrochar from Loch Lomondside its familiar triple-topped outline dominates everything else, and yet unlike the Buachaille, or Liathach or An Teallach, The Cobbler seems more benevolent, more familiar.

Some mountains give a perception of character, of personality, which puts us on our guard, while others appear more benign. To me The Cobbler is outrageous, audacious and impertinent; despite its relatively lowly height of 884m, it's an incredibly rocky mountain, one of the few hills in Scotland that demands a rock-climb to reach its summit. How's that for impudence?

Curiously surrealistic, The Cobbler dominates its neighbours despite its inferior size, and it is the odd shape that gives the commonly used name – some think it resembles a cobbler working at his last. Ben Arthur is its proper, if rarely used, name. It has three distinct tops: the left one formed into a leaning pyramid; the central peak, the true summit, is a flat-topped table; the North Peak is an immense overhanging prow, a remarkable feature which boasts many of the mountain's best rock-climbs.

Map: OS Sheet 56
Access Point: Car park beside the A83
Distance: 15km
Approx Time: 5-7 hours
Grade: Moderate hill walk

Approach The Cobbler from the A83, just across Loch Long from Arrochar where there is a new car park. On the other side of the road a track leads into the woods beside a sign which proclaims the Argyll Forest Park. Follow the path uphill to reach a forest road. Turn left, follow this track for 800m or so to the Buttermilk Burn. Leave the forest track west of the burn and follow a very muddy path uphill until you clear the trees. From here the mountain bares itself in full glory with the most logical route exposed; by the obvious bealach between the north and the central peaks. But first cross the Buttermilk Burn to its east bank and follow the broad muddy path which comes up from Succoth past the Narnain Boulders towards the obvious col between The Cobbler and its eastern neighbour, Beinn Narnain.

Before you reach this col bear left and cross the burn again, climbing up into the rock-strewn corrie below the overhanging prow of the north peak. It's an awesome place where rock dominates. Climb up steeply now on an eroded path below the black prow, and onto the summit ridge. With the hard work over, follow the well-worn path that takes you up through the rocks and boulders to the flat top of the north peak. What an eyrie this is, with sheer drops on three sides.

Many walkers are content with the ascent of this north peak, but the true summit of the mountain is on the central peak, and the route to the top isn't too evident. From the summit ridge you'll see a narrow window in the rock above you. Squeeze through this hole to find a narrow ledge which traverses off to the left. Follow this around the back of the rock, its south aspect, where a couple of easy moves take you onto the summit platform. It's a rock climb, and unless you're badly fazed by exposure, fairly simple. As you stand on the summit, exhilarated by the space around you, I think you'll understand something of the audacious, outrageous character of this, one of the finest mountains in the country.

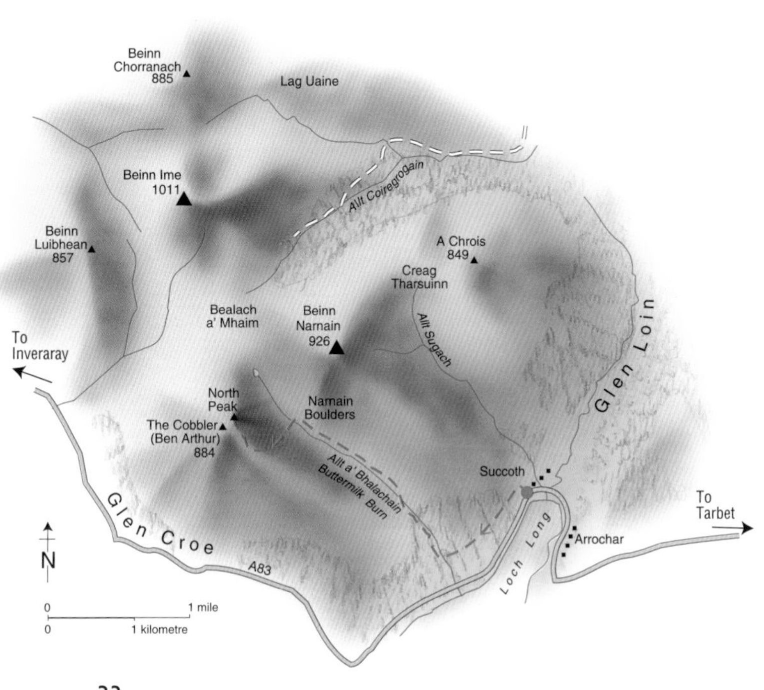

10 The Trossachs' Ben A'n

Route Summary

Cross the road from the car park and follow the footpath steeply up through the forest. After a while a signpost indicates a viewpoint to the left. It offers your first glimpse of Ben A'n. Return to the path and continue uphill. Leave the trees behind and continue to climb up wet and broken ground, contour round the back of the hill, cross some wet, mossy areas, and ascend the final few metres to the rocky summit. Return to the car park the way you came.

Map: OS Sheet 57

Access Point: Forest Enterprise car park near Trossachs Hotel

Distance: 6km

Approx Time: 2-3 hours

Grade: Easy hill walk

Drive over the Duke's Pass from Aberfoyle to the Trossachs and ahead of you a long line of hills fills the horizon. At their western end, standing up like an afterthought, is the shapely peak of Ben A'n.

The height of this hill, 454m, is out of all proportion to its huge character. Not only is it a pleasant afternoon stroll for those who don't mind a steep climb, but the hill's south-facing rocky flanks are also enjoyed by rock climbers, where there are a number of classic routes of all grades.

The old name of this fine little peak is Am Binnein, the Rocky Peak, but it was changed by Sir Walter Scott to Ben A'n and so it has stayed in its modern form. What a summit this is – a fine rocky eyrie with magnificent views towards the west and the north-west. On clear days all the Arrochar hills are clearly seen, from the unmistakable outline of The Cobbler to Ben Vorlich. Further to the right the Crianlarich hills come into view with the twin summits of Ben More and Stob Binnein particularly impressive. Loch Katrine stretches into the heartland of MacGregor country and across the waters below you lies the ancient pass of the Bealach nam Bo at the foot of Ben Venue.

Take time to enjoy this summit, and if you enjoy a challenge, try the 10-Second Slab. This is the boiler-plate rock slab which leads to the summit cairn – it is claimed that good climbers will scale it in 10 seconds. Ordinary walkers will take a little longer!

The route to the summit is straightforward. On the north shore of Loch Achray, close to the turreted grandeur of the newly refurbished Trossachs Hotel, the Forestry Commission have built a car park and erected signposts indicating the Ben A'n walk. Cross the road from the car park and follow the signpost. This initial section of path is steep and is often quite muddy but it does allow you to gain height quickly and directly. After a while the steepness relents considerably, and a signpost indicates

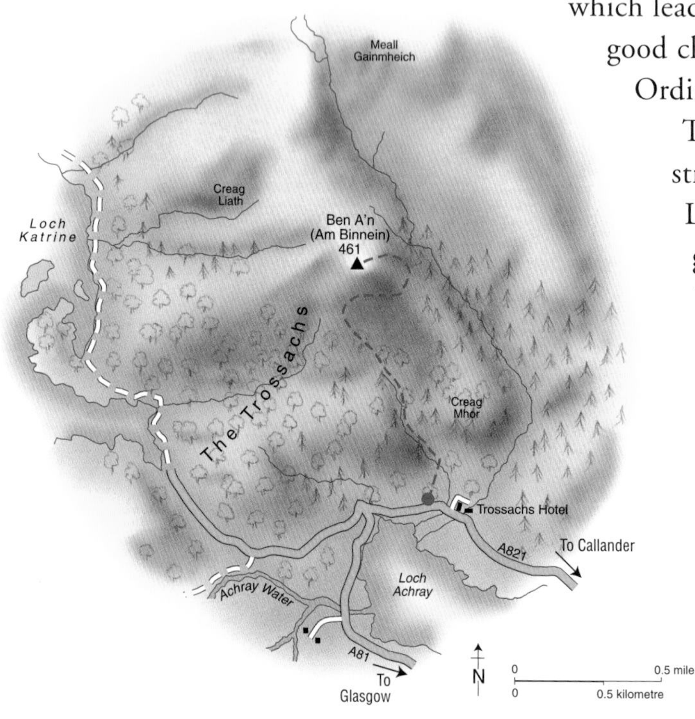

Ben Venue and Loch Katrine from the summit of Ben A'n

a viewpoint to the left. It's well worthwhile visiting this viewpoint as it offers your first glimpse of Ben A'n. It's a good view – framed by spruce and larch it looks steep and exposed and for all the world like a mountain several times its height.

Return to the path and continue uphill. Soon you'll leave the trees behind and the views begin to open up, across to the crags, bluffs and corries of Ben Venue and the long stretch of Loch Katrine. Continue on the path and now you begin to climb again, up wet and broken ground, helped significantly by some good path construction work. Higher up this section of path there is a lot of loose rock and scree and after heavy rain there is always plenty of running water. Climb up over this rough ground, contour round the back of the hill, cross some wet, mossy areas, and then climb up the final few metres to the rocky summit.

There is a descent route from Ben A'n which leads off to the north and west, down through the forest to the north shore of Loch Katrine, but it is an ill-defined and awkward path, often very wet and slippery. Best advice is to return to the car park the way you came.

Ben Ledi from the west near Callander

11 Ben Ledi

Route Summary

From the car park walk N and follow the road to just before the farmhouse at Stank, where a forest track bears off to the left towards the Stank Glen. Follow this zig-zagging track up the glen, past a series of waterfalls and onto an elevation of about 500m where you can leave the main forest for the open, upper glen. The summit route slants half left of Creag na h-Iolaire, the Crag of the Eagles, and continues onto the ridge towards Lochan nan Corp. Once the ridge is reached the route to the summit is straightforward. Turn S and follow a line of old fenceposts to the summit cairn and trig point.

My leanings towards favourite areas of Scotland rarely fall far short of the Trossachs, and I'm in respectable company. Such literary luminaries as the Wordsworths, James Hogg the Ettrick Shepherd and Sir Walter Scott have praised the area highly.

From Ben Ledi you can appreciate the flats of Flanders Moss stretching out towards Stirling with the Pentland Hills a dim outline beyond Edinburgh. Ben Lomond, the beacon hill, stands out, and to its north the unmistakable outline of The Cobbler dominates the higher Arrochar Alps. All the Crianlarich and Glen Falloch hills can be easily identified and to the north-east Ben Vorlich is hidden by its close neighbour, Stuc a' Chroin, and beyond them the great Lawers massif stands out clearly.

The exact derivation of the name Ben Ledi seems to be unknown, the Gaelic being Beinn Lididh. The old *Statistical Account* suggests a possible derivation in the name Ben le Dia, the Hill of God, and that's not unreasonable. Flat stretches of turf on the summit ridge have been associated with the Beltane or May

Day Festival once held annually there. The ceremonies which took place were thought to be a version of a Druidic rite involving human sacrifice to the sun god Baal – however, no stones or artefacts have been found to substantiate this theory.

To heighten further the somewhat grisly aspect of the mountain's history, a small lochan lies about 1.5km north of the summit. This is Lochan nan Corp, or the small loch of the dead bodies! Centuries ago, a cortège of mourners was following an old coffin route across the hill from Glen Finglas to St Bride's Chapel in the Pass of Leny in the depths of winter. As they crossed the frozen waters of the lochan the ice cracked open and several of the mourners died in the bitterly cold water. Such stories can affect your thoughts, for I've always been vaguely apprehensive in the great eastern corrie of Ben Ledi.

The route to the top climbs up through the tree-bound Stank Glen up a steep path to a point where it overlooks a very fine waterfall. Continue on the Stank Glen track to a height of about 450m where you will leave the main forest and step out into the upper glen. The route slants half left up the hill staying left of Creag na h-Iolaire, the Crag of the Eagles.

Continue past the crag onto the ridge and a little way to the north you'll come across Lochan nan Corp. Once on the ridge the way to the summit is straightforward; turn south and follow the line of old fenceposts which once marked the boundary between estates.

The descent continues abruptly down the ridge until the angle eases at some marshy ground. It then swings sharply left to cross a stile at the top of the forest. A path runs through the forest beside a burn, back to the car park.

Descend by continuing down the ridge to the SE until the angle eases, before bending sharply left to reach a stile at the top of the forest. Follow the footpath down through the forest beside a small burn, all the way back to the car park.

Map: OS Sheet 57

Access Point: Car park at Stank, just off the Callander to Strathyre road

Distance: 12km

Approx Time: 4-6 hours

Grading: Easy/Moderate hill walk

Translation: possibly hill of God

Pronunciation: byn leady

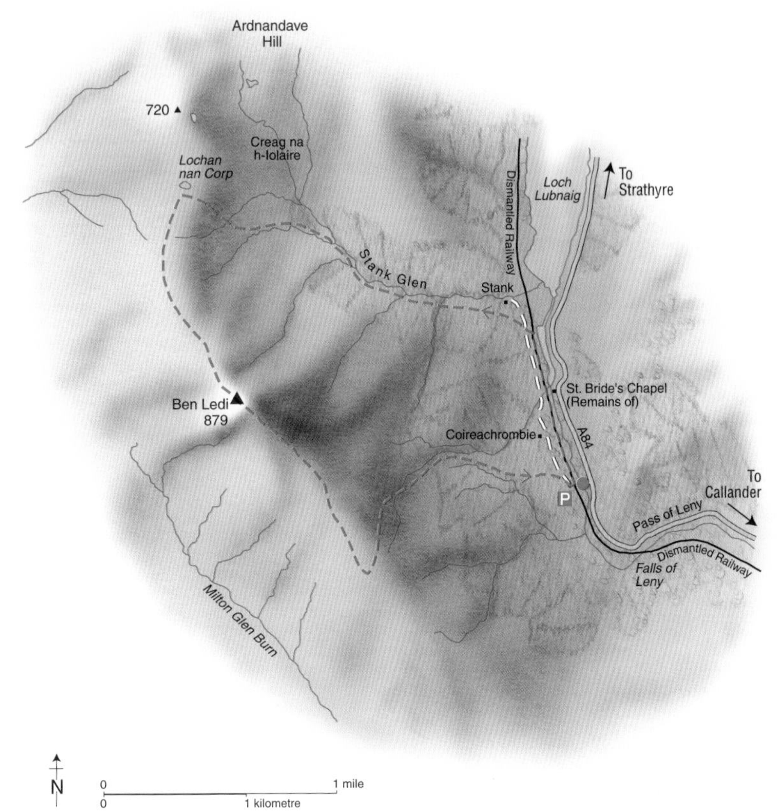

12 Ben Venue

During the 1980s I lived for a short time in Fintry, north of Glasgow, and during that time I became familiar with that wonderfully craggy area known as the Trossachs. Here on Glasgow's doorstep is a tumbled land of small mountains, lochs and forest, a landscape that has inspired poets and artists and was the scene for Sir Walter Scott's *Lady of the Lake*. The Trossachs were Scotland's first tourist destination.

The whole area is dominated by Ben Venue, paradoxically translated as the 'small mountain', from the Gaelic Beinn Mheanbh. Some modern authors have suggested the name means the hill of the caves, but whatever it means it is undoubtedly one of the finest 'wee hills' in the Southern Highlands. With its twin tops, its western outliers, and its rugged mien, it towers above the central craggy landscape of the Trossachs.

The steep, rocky slopes which tumble down towards the shores of Loch Katrine form the wall of the Bealach nam Bo, the Pass of the Cattle, a legendary, possibly mythical, trade route in centuries past for stolen cattle which were secretively whisked back from the Lowlands to the MacGregor strongholds west of Loch Katrine. Close by is Coire na Urisgean, or the Corrie of the Goblins. Sir Walter Scott, who roamed this area and found inspiration for his works, depicted the Goblin's Corrie as a retreat for Ellen Douglas and her father after they had withdrawn from Roderick Dhu's stronghold on Eilean Molach. This was the meeting place of Scotland's Urisks, or goblins, and according to Dr Graham in his *Scenery of the Southern Confines of Perthshire* of 1806, they were a 'sort of lubbery supernatural, who could be gained over by kind attention to perform the

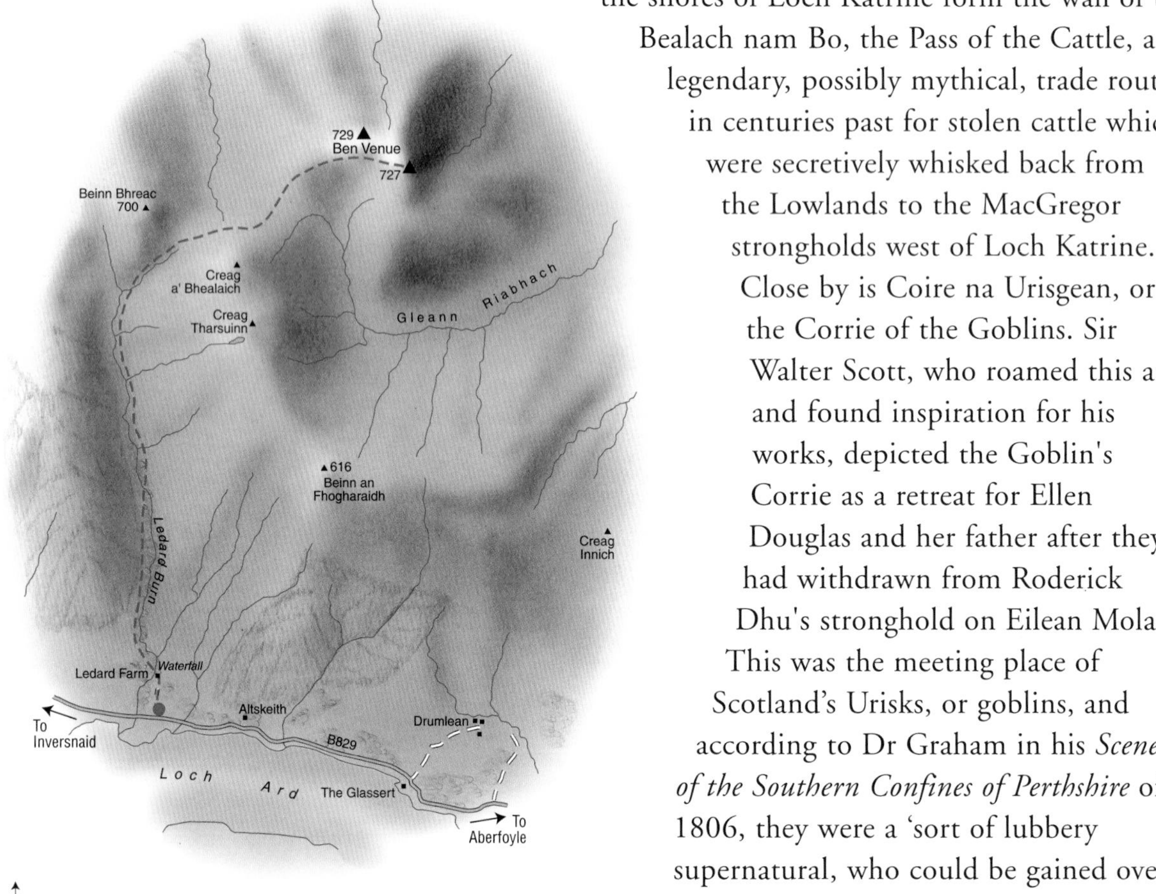

drudgery of a farm. They were supposed to be spread throughout the highlands each in his own wild recess, but the solemn meetings of the order were regularly held in the cave of Benvenew.'

Despite the attractions of Coire na Urisgean, it's best to tackle Ben Venue from the south, rather than tackle the hill head-on up its steep and craggy bluffs from the Loch Katrine side. Start from Ledard Farm on the B829 Aberfoyle to Inversnaid road. From the roadside a footpath points the way – 11km to the Trossachs via the summit of Ben Venue. Take the track which leads past the farm and stop for a moment at a fine pool and waterfall just behind the buildings. Sir Walter Scott stayed hereabouts while working on his notes for *Rob Roy* and *Waverley* and apparently sat here and worked beside the pool when the weather was good.

Cross the footbridge over the Ledard Burn and follow the obvious path northwards. This path is often extremely boggy, but things do become better the higher you climb. The track leads onto the eastern slopes of one of Venue's outliers, Beinn Bhreac, where a wide bealach introduces you to the craggy slopes of Ben Venue itself. Even now, at this comparatively lowly elevation, the first views of the day to the north-west begin to impress. To the west, Loch Katrine stretches out, one of its ancient arms cut off by the strip of land at Stronachlachar. That old arm is now Loch Arklet, running in a transverse line towards the deep trench which holds Loch Lomond. To the north the Crianlarich hills bow their heads to the higher tops of Stob Binnein and Ben More and further east the Ben Lawers range all but dwarfs the neighbouring Tarmachans beyond the tops of Stuc a' Chroin and Beinn Vorlich.

Continue over the high bealach between Beinn Bhreac and Creag a' Bhealaich and along the ridge in a north-east direction towards the summit ridge of Ben Venue. The footpath becomes steeper and weaves through some rocky outcrops to the first of Ben Venue's two summits. Enjoy the view across Loch Katrine to the Loch Lomond hills and the peaks of the Arrochar Alps. Return to the path and follow it as it wends its way through the summit outcrops and shortly after, the summit itself. Ahead of you the view opens up eastwards, along the silvery lengths of Loch Achray and Loch Venachar towards Ben Ledi and the Menteith Hills.

There is a descent route to the north, down the steep heather and rock slopes to Loch Katrine, but I wouldn't particularly recommend it. It's a safer option to return the way you came.

Route Summary

Leave the road and take the track past Ledard Farm. Cross the footbridge over the burn and continue N on the muddy path to a high bealach. Continue over this bealach between Beinn Bhreac and Creag a' Bhealaich and follow the path NE towards the summit. Return the same way.

Map: OS Sheet 57

Access Point: Ledard Farm on the B829 Aberfoyle road

Distance: 13km

Approx Time: 4-6 hours

Grade: Easy/moderate hill walk

Translation: small mountain

Pronunciation: byn ven-noo

Ben Lomond and the Ptarmigan Ridge from the west

Route Summary
A well-signposted footpath climbs through the woods from the car park at Rowardennan. Follow this path onto the S ridge of Ben Lomond and follow the path, and the ridge N to the summit. Descend N, then W to gain the Ptarmigan Ridge. Follow the ridge S to the Tom Fithich burn which is followed to the West Highland Way track. Follow the track S to Rowardennan.

Map: OS Sheet 56

Access Point: Rowardennan Hotel GR360983

Distance: 12km

Approx Time: 5-7 hours

Grade: Easy/moderate hill walk

Translation: beacon hill

Pronunciation: byn low-mond

13 Ben Lomond

Ben Lomond, the most southerly of the Scottish Munros at 974m, is prone to sudden blasts of weather – she raises her beacon on the very edge of the Highland Line, the geological boundary that splits Lowland Scotland from the higher hills of the north.

A day in November 1971 saw Hamish Telfer and I scuttle down to Rowardennan, chased by heavy snow squalls and freezing temperatures. It had been our first experience of white-out, and we didn't relish it at all. The next day the news broke that a party of schoolchildren from Edinburgh were lost in the Cairngorms. Days later they were found; five teenagers and an 18-year-old trainee instructress had died of exposure. A 15-year-old boy and a 20-year-old instructress were found alive, but badly frostbitten and exposed. We weren't that much older, and we had learned an important lesson – to retreat in the face of a storm is no shame.

Lessons learnt? Here I was, over a quarter of a century later, older and presumably wiser, climbing the same hill in wind, rain and scuttling clouds, and enjoying it immensely. Relishing the wind surf in the oaks, birches and larches by the empty puddle-pooled car park at Rowardennan, appreciating the comparative calm as I began to climb through the woods, and anticipating the battle on the forthcoming ridge, the struggle against the raging of the demon wind, the unseen foe who pulls and tugs and harries with undiminished energies. Walks do occasionally become battles, and I can understand where the military mountaineering metaphors came from – to conquer or be conquered, but we rarely do battle with the mountain, more often the battle is with ourselves.

Ben Lomond is a great mass of mica-schist which falls, in the long ridge of Sron Aonaich, to the south. A well-maintained footpath climbs onto this ridge from Rowardennan, past the spring known as the Halfway Well, and then veers to the left to march resolutely northwards over grass and bog, peat and rock. Several years ago this path was 9m wide, a swathe of mud and peat, ever-widening as more and more walkers tried to avoid the morass in the middle. But sterling work by the National Trust for Scotland has turned this into a walker-friendly footpath, and any sense of amenity is balanced by the fact that the hill is gradually healing itself, regenerating and growing to the very edges of the path. In a comparatively short time the wide, ugly scar has been replaced by a narrow, natural-looking footpath which, while still obtrusive, is far preferable to what was there before.

After following the crest of the Sron Aonaich for about 1.5km the path zigzags up the final steeper slopes to reach an 800m long curved ridge from which cliffs fall away to the north-east. The summit cairn and view indicator are at the north-west end of this ridge and in good conditions what a viewpoint this is. To the north the hills of the Arrochar Alps and Crianlarich almost choke off the northern end of Loch Lomond, a jumble of mountains which graphically illustrate the different landscape between the Highlands and the Lowlands, with Ben Lomond marking the boundary.

The hill, not surprisingly, was devoid of people as I breasted the summit ridge. The wind, from the south-west, had harried and pushed me as I made my way uphill and I didn't fancy turning round to face it in the descent. Instead I continued over the summit and down steep slopes to the south-west to the subsidiary top known as the Ptarmigan.

The walk down the Ptarmigan Ridge was a treat. The archipelago of islands in the loch lit up in turn as beams of sunlight burst through the heavy cloud and despite the day's greyness, there was still background colour to appreciate, muted in late-autumn panoply perhaps, but earthtones nevertheless.

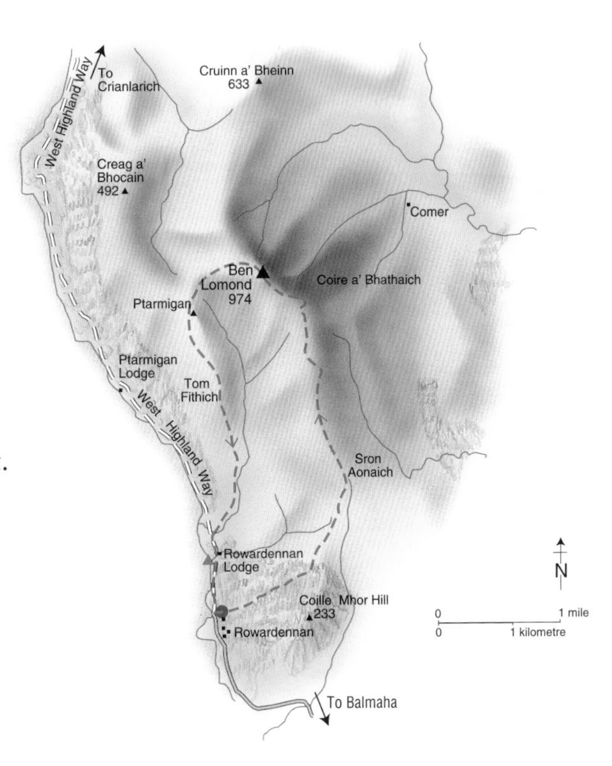

THE WEST HIGHLAND WAY

Running for 152km from Milngavie on the northern fringes of Glasgow to Fort William, the unofficial capital of the Western Highlands, the West Highland Way is Scotland's premier long distance trail.

Opened in 1980, to the protests of many walkers and climbers opposed to the development of long distance footpaths in Scotland, the West Highland Way has proved to be immensely successful, bringing in much needed revenue to small communities along the route. Thousands of walkers stagger into Fort William every year groaning with tales of muddy footpaths, camping in the rain, and the voracious Highland midgie.

But these groans and grimaces hide a deep satisfaction and a sense of achievement. Once the complaints are taken care of the real memories can return: the change in landscape from urban to rural; the sheer beauty of Loch Lomond; the mountains of Crianlarich; the empty splendour of Rannoch Moor; the open jaws of Glen Coe and the magnetic pull of Ben Nevis, towering above the finishing glen. Many of those who walk the West Highland Way will probably never do anything like it again, but the resonances of their days on the trail will stay with them forever.

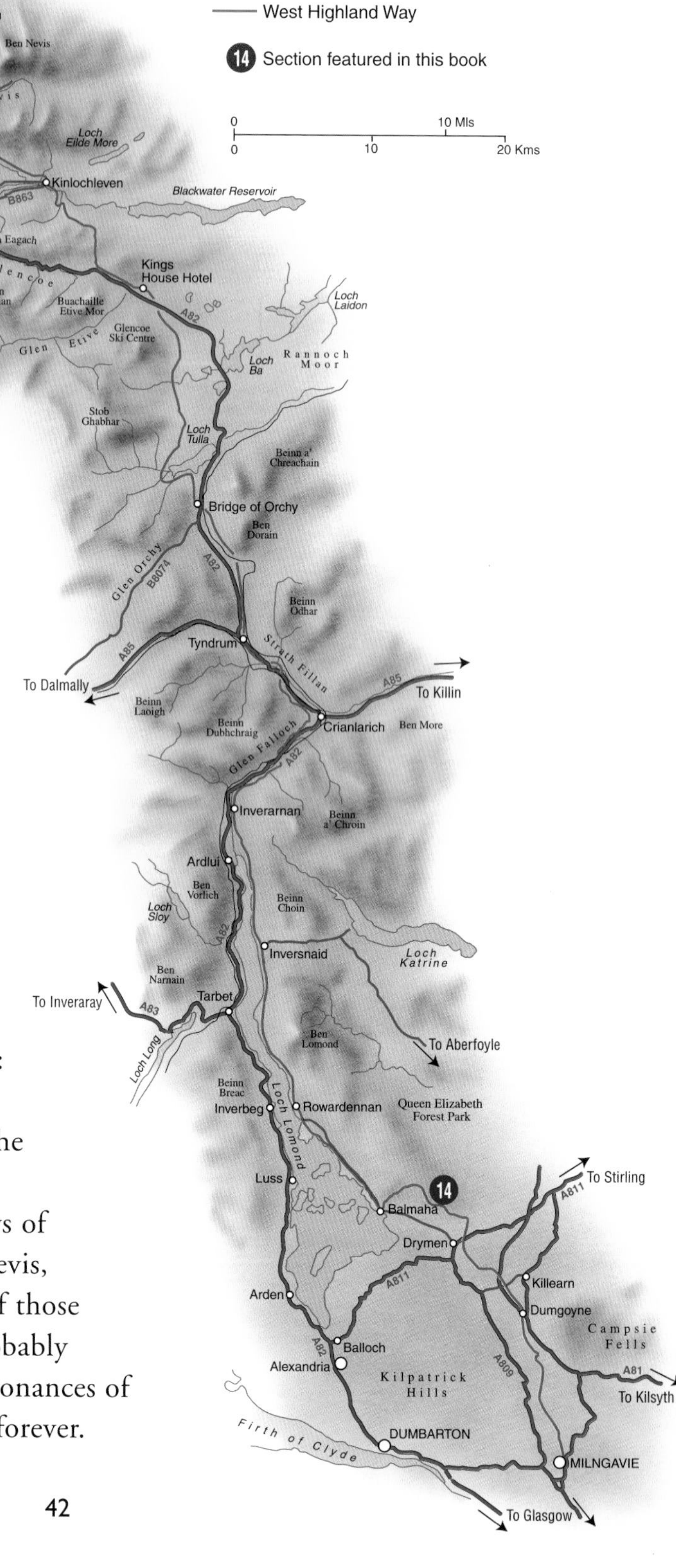

14 Conic Hill – West Highland Way

Despite my own reservations when the idea of the West Highland Way was first mooted (I felt a signposted trail went against the traditional exploratory aspect of hill walking in Scotland and could create an 'access corridor', with landowners preventing walkers from straying from the official line of the route. Thankfully I was wrong), I have to confess that in many ways it has been a huge success, encouraging thousands of foreign backpackers to visit Scotland and tempting even more home-based walkers to sample the delights of a multi-day trip through some wonderful country.

Curiously, the Way not only attracts multi-day backpackers but day trippers too, leaving their car to tramp a few kilometres of the trail before returning by public transport or another car. One of the most popular day sections is the ascent of Conic Hill above Balmaha, a fairly easy and straightforward ascent with extensive views from the summit towards both the Highlands, and the Lowlands, for Conic Hill stands slap-bang on the Highland Boundary Fault. Theoretically at least, all that is north of the line is the Highlands, and all that lies below is the Lowlands, and there is no better place to observe this disparity in landscape form than from Conic Hill.

To the south the Gargunnock and Fintry Hills lead in to the northern escarpment of the Campsies and through the wide gap of Strath Blane you might just glimpse the tower blocks of Glasgow. Further west the Kilpatrick hills dominate before falling away into the Vale of Leven behind which stands the distant chimney of the Inverkip Power Station on the River Clyde. Beyond it, on a clear day, natural forms reassert themselves in the shape of the mountains of Arran.

Route Summary

Leave the road and follow farm and forest tracks through the Garadhban Forest. The West Highland Way is well marked by its acorn symbol. After 2km the route swings W, crosses a minor road and continues climbing to the edge of the forest. Cross the Burn of Mar and climb the E ridge of Conic Hill, noting that the path runs slightly to the N of the hill's summit ridge. Leave the path and climb to the summit. Return to the path and follow it W, down steeply to the forest edge to join a forest walk which ends in the public car park at Balmaha.

Map: OS Sheets 56 and 57

Access Point: A811 road E of Drymen opposite Blarnavaid Farm GR889487

Distance: About 10km

Approx Time: 4-6 hours

Grade: Easy hill walk

Translation: from the Gaelic A' Coinneach, moss or bog

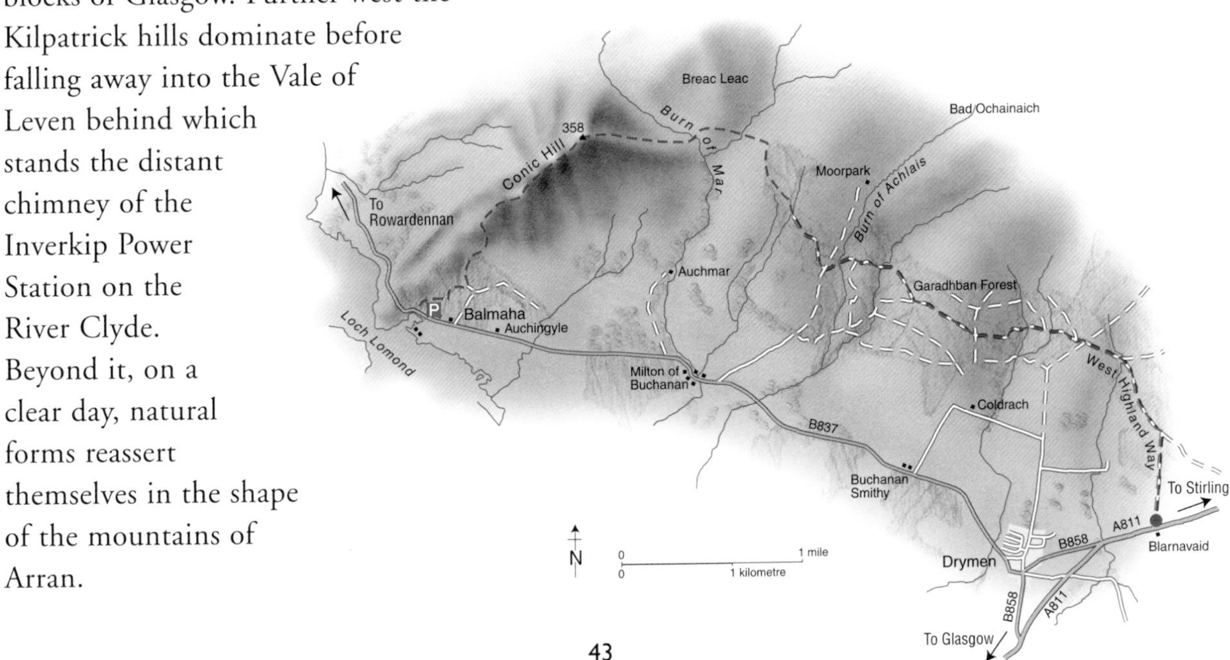

The West Highland Way at Conic Hill and Loch Lomond from the air

Immediately at your feet the island-speckled waters of Loch Lomond remind us why this loch is so revered in song and story. Here lies a stretch of water which unselfishly shares itself between the Highlands and the Lowlands, wide, spreading and generous in its southern reaches, but gradually growing narrower as it reaches northwards before the steel-grey waters are choked off by tumbling hillsides and crags. Ben Lomond rises over everything and beyond it the tumble of mountains goes on and on. Across the loch the Luss hills give a gentle preamble to the wild form of the Arrochar Alps and the surrealistic shape of their jewel, Ben Arthur, or The Cobbler.

Conic Hill itself has been described as a 'fairly steep-sided hogsback ridge', although it does appear to be reasonably conical in shape when viewed from Balmaha. It's more likely that the origin of its name comes from the Gaelic A' Coinneach, which refers to moss or boggy ground, and there's plenty of that around.

The hill can be climbed directly from Balmaha but a long and steep man-made staircase ruins such an ascent. Better, if you can arrange transport back to the start, to try a linear route, following the line of the West Highland Way from the A811 just east of Drymen. Continue through the Garadhban Forest before climbing the eastern ridge of Conic Hill from the headwaters of the Burn of Mar, and then drop down to Balmaha. The steep staircase never seems quite as bad on the descent!

15 The Whangie – The Work of the Devil?

Writing in Glasgow's *Evening Citizen* over a hundred years ago, Hugh MacDonald described The Whangie of Auchineden Hill near Drymen: 'The Whangie is a vast section of the hill that has by some means been wrenched asunder, leaving a lengthened and deepened chasm yawning along the lines of separation.' It's a description that caught the public's attention, for The Whangie became one of the most popular walks in the wider Glasgow area.

Imagine a smooth hillside, at the far end of which, as though by some malevolent force, a section has been pulled away, leaving a long, narrow ravine between it and the original hillside. The edges of both parts form a pinnacled crest. Some would suggest that this natural phenomenon was the work of the devil! The story claims that after hosting a gathering of witches and warlocks in the Kilpatrick Hills, Satan was flying to another meeting and flicked his tail, tearing apart the hillside over which he was flying.

The truth is less sinister but equally dramatic. The geological feature of The Whangie was caused by glacial 'plucking', the action created by extreme temperatures which froze the rock slabs to the glacier. As the glacier began to move, it 'plucked' the hillside, causing a long fracture to form.

Start at the Queen's View car park on the A809 Glasgow to Drymen road. A gap in a wall leads to the obvious path which climbs uphill towards a stand of conifers where a ladder stile crosses a fence. There are two paths here – the upper path runs along the top of the escarpment of Auchineden Hill to the trig point at its western end, while the lower path runs along the foot of the escarpment and offers a bit of protection from the weather if it's a windy day. At the western end of the hill both paths converge, and lead to the trig point at 386m.

Take the path from the summit westwards and drop down to broken ground, looking out for the crags which appear on your right.

Route Summary

Start at the Queen's View car park on the A809 Glasgow to Drymen road. Follow signposts through a gap in the wall to where a path climbs uphill towards conifers. Cross the fence by a ladder stile, and follow the upper path along the escarpment of Auchineden Hill to the trig point at its W end. Go W from the summit and drop down to broken ground, looking out for the crags which begin to appear on your right. Follow the path into The Whangie itself, through the cleft, exiting past a smaller flake at the N end known as The Gendarme. Go past this feature, taking the lowest path and follow it back along the foot of the hill, all the way back to the ladder stile and the downhill slope to the car park.

Map: OS Sheet 64

Access Point: Queen's View car park on the A809 Glasgow to Drymen road

Distance: 5km

Approx Time: 2-4 hours

Grade: Easy hill walk

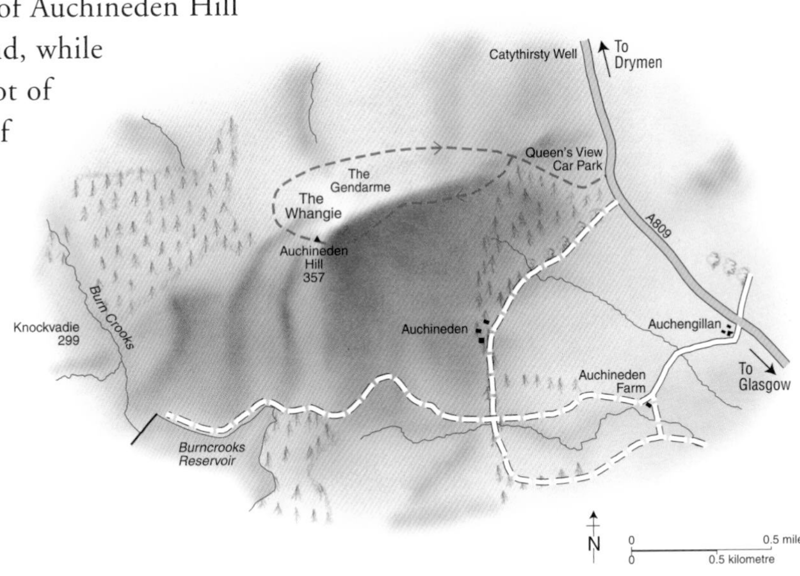

Soon the path seems to go inside the rock face, and in essence that's exactly what it does! Follow it into The Whangie itself, with rock walls rising sheer on either side of you. The cleft is about 100m long and rises on both sides to over 9m. At one point the walls become less than 90cm apart! Follow the path through the cleft, exiting past a smaller flake at the northern end known as The Gendarme. Take the lowest path along the foot of the hill to the ladder stile and the downhill slope to the Queen's View.

16 The Campsie Fells – Glasgow's Hills

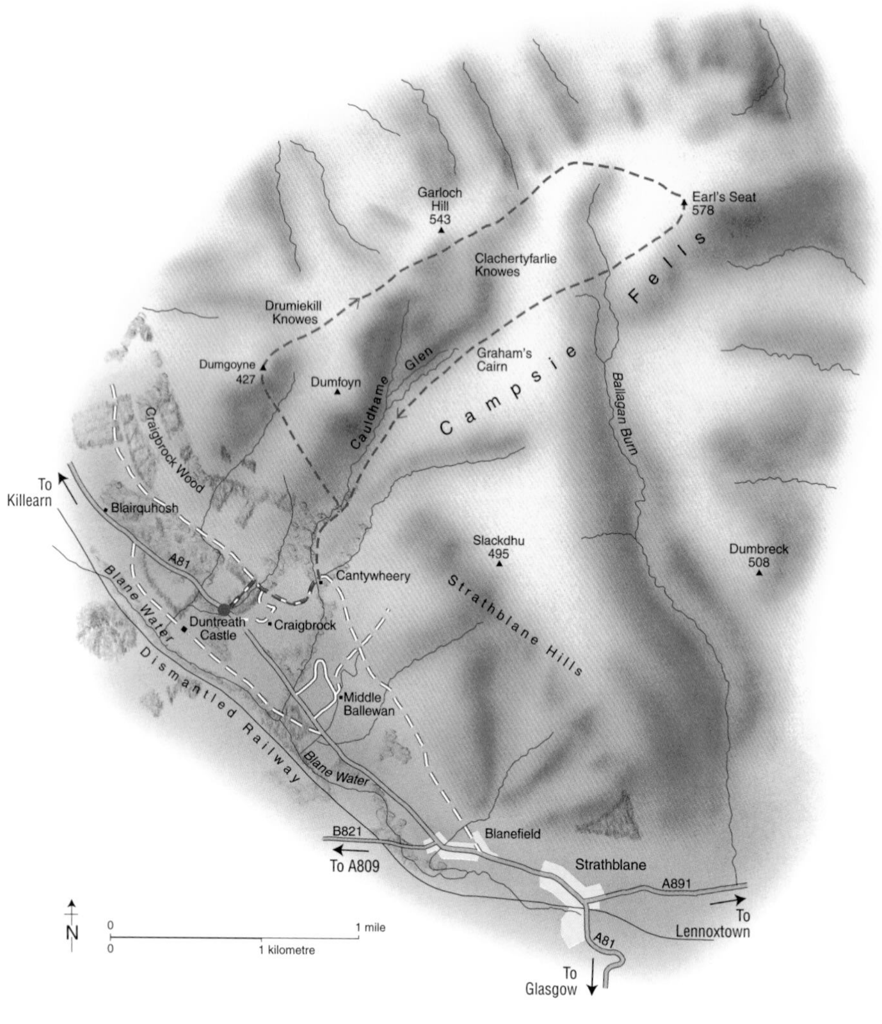

Rising just north of Glasgow, the high moorlands of the Campsie Fells have introduced generations of folk to the delights of hillwalking and mountaineering. Dumgoyne, the Fort of the Arrows, is an ancient volcanic plug at the western end and Earl's Seat, at 578m, is the highest of the Campsie hills. This route takes in both these landmarks to give a fairly easy hill walk, with wide views to the south over the urban skyline of the city and contrasting views to the north towards Ben Lomond and the jumble of hills that mark the Highlands. Leave the A81 Blanefield to Killearn road in Strath Blane about 2.5km west of Blanefield near Craigbrock Farm. Take the private road past the farm and follow it towards Cantywheery cottage. Just before you reach the cottage cross over a bridge, go through

a gate and take a grassy track which runs up the hill towards an obvious black crag which sits clearly above Craigbrock Wood. Pass to the north-west of this crag and find a stream which runs downhill on the left, cross it and then cross a drystone wall and follow rough tracks west-north-west, contouring round the slopes of Dumfoyn. Cross another stream and climb steadily up a sheep track which runs across the southern slopes of Dumgoyne to reach its broad south-west ridge. Follow the easy grass slopes of the ridge which leads to the summit.

From the top, descend north-east to a shallow col and continue over the broad grassy ridge just north of Drumiekill Knowes. Continue north-east along the ridge to the grassy bumps of Clachertyfarlie Knowes. Descend gently, cross some wet and boggy ground and climb the final grassy slopes to the summit of Earl's Seat. This hill is probably named after the Earl of Lennox whose lands once extended on the south side of the Campsie Fells.

Descend south-west across the bogs of Ballagan Burn, climb gentle slopes and cross a fence just before Graham's Cairn. Follow the burn in the Cauldhame Glen on its south side and eventually you will rejoin your uphill route just above Cantywheery Cottage. Follow the private road back to the A81.

Dumgoyne, Campsie Fells and Glengoyne Distillery from The Whangie

Route Summary

Take the private road past the farm and follow it to a bridge just before Cantywheery Cottage. Cross the bridge and follow a track passing NW of an obvious black crag. Pass Dumfoyn and follow sheep tracks to the broad SW ridge of Dumgoyne. Follow the ridge to the summit. Descend NE towards Clachertyfarlie Knowes and then climb Earl's Seat. Descend SW towards the Ballagan Burn, cross Graham's Cairn and follow the Cauldhame Glen burn back to Cantywheery Cottage.

Map: OS Sheet 64

Access Point: A81 near Craigbrock Farm

Distance: 12km

Approx Time: 3-5 hours

Grade: Easy/moderate hill walk

THE BORDERS AND SOUTH-WEST

This area lies between the Glasgow and Edinburgh conurbations in the north and the border with England in the south. It's an area rich in historical association and the hills, whilst not particularly high, should never be underestimated. It's only in the past few years that I've come to appreciate the subtle grandeur of these hills and the secretive splendour of many of the byways. The walking in Galloway is among the most rugged and challenging in Scotland and I would urge readers to seek out the priceless little corners to be found in areas like Ettrick or the long Minchmoor ridge. The Pentlands in particular, so close to the Scottish capital, must be one of the most underrated hill ranges in the country although it offers a wide assortment of low- and high-level walks.

THE WALKS

Hundleshope Heights from the north near Peebles

17 The One and Only Merrick

Route Summary

Descend E along the road from the Bruce's Stone car park. Cross the bridge, ignore the sign for the Buchan Burn, but cross the stile on the left and follow the signpost to Loch Valley and the Gairland Burn. Cross a field on the face of Buchan Hill, to a gate in the wall. Go through the gate and into the hanging valley that contains the Gairland Burn. Follow the path to the outflow from Loch Valley and then to Loch Neldricken, cross a wall by the Murder Hole and follow the W slopes of Ewe Rig to the smaller Loch Arron, before continuing to a small col above Loch Enoch. Climb Redstone Rig to the Merrick's summit.

The knuckle of The Merrick dominates the hills around Loch Trool and this 'branched finger' is the highest in the so-called Range of the Awful Hand. At 814m it's the highest summit in the Galloway Hills. My favourite route to the summit approaches via the four lochs (or the five lochs: the largest island on Loch Enoch has a loch of its own), to the east of the hill and then follows the long east ridge, the Redstone Rig, to the summit.

In Glen Trool, at the start of this walk, the monumental Bruce's Stone celebrates a clash with English forces in 1307 when Robert the Bruce was just beginning his campaign for the Scottish throne. He knew this area well and the broken hillsides and scattered woodland of Glen Trool were ideal for his style of guerrilla warfare.

The route to the granite uplands follows a valley which runs off Glen Trool in a north-east direction. From the Bruce's Stone car park descend eastwards. Cross over the Earl of Galloway's bridge at the bottom, ignore the sign for the Buchan Burn, cross the stile on the left and follow the signpost to Loch Valley and the Gairland Burn. The route gains height quickly as it crosses a field on the face of Buchan Hill, towards a gate in the wall at the top of the field.

Cross over the gate and into a new landscape; gone are the sylvan pleasures of lovely Glen Trool; instead the empty uplands lie ahead, a glaciated wilderness of moor and mountain. The path follows the Gairland

Rig of the Jarkness and Loch Valley above Glen Trool in the Galloway Hills

Burn, rising steadily to the outflow from Loch Valley. From there follow the western shore of the loch on a path which climbs onto a new level, one which contains the waters of Loch Neldricken.

A wet and indistinct path now follows the south-west shores of the loch and crosses a wall by the 'Murder Hole', an area of deep water which is said never to freeze over. The path runs alongside a wall which follows the western slopes of Ewe Rig to the smaller Loch Arron, before continuing up towards a small col overlooking Loch Enoch with its reflections of Mullwharchar rising beyond – a curious name in a land of curious names (try The Wolf Slock, Craigmawhannal and Craigmasheenie). Mullwharchar is apparently derived from the Gaelic, Maol Adhairce, meaning the Hill of the Huntsman's Horn. It is said that the silver sand of Loch Enoch's beaches was once collected for sharpening knives.

Beyond the south-west shores of Loch Enoch, the long line of Redstone Rig rises to The Merrick's summit. Hard work now on this long pull to the summit, from the grey granite of the Enoch basin to the dark flaky shales of the summit slopes, but all the effort is worthwhile with views to Craignaw in the east, the broad ridge of Tarfessock and Shalloch of Minnoch to the north and Mulldonoch and Lamachan Hill to the south.

A grassy descent contours the Neive of the Spit and a short rise leads to the cairn on Benyellary, the eagle's hill. Follow the path steadily downhill beside the Whitehead Burn to the bothy at Culsharg. From here a very muddy path leads southwards, alongside the Buchan Burn, back to the car park in Glen Trool.

Descend by the Neive of the Spit and Benyellary, following the path downhill beside the Whitehead Burn to the bothy at Culsharg. A muddy path follows the Buchan Burn back to the car park in Glen Trool.

Map: OS Sheet 77

Access Point: Bruce's Stone car park, Glen Trool

Distance: About 16km

Approx Time: 8-10 hours

Grade: Strenuous hill walk

Translation: From meurach, the branched finger

Rough Firth, Rough Island and Castle Point from Mote of Mark, Rockcliffe

18 The Solway's Castle Point

Kippford and Rockcliffe are not the best-known of the National Trust for Scotland's properties, but they are quiet, atmospheric places which were once, paradoxically, havens for smugglers. Just over a hundred years ago local people constructed a walkway, the Jubilee Path, to mark the Diamond Jubilee of Queen Victoria in 1897. I walked this Jubilee Path in its centenary year as far as Castle Point, (Castlehill Point on the OS map) an airy, windswept place with distant views across the Solway towards the swell of the Cumbrian Fells and enjoyed the real change from mountains and northern vistas. It's a walk I tend to reserve for November days, when the hills put on their grey shroud, or as a break from interminable motorways on the way north from lecture tours or other business in the deep south.

One of the highlights of the walk is the Mote of Mark, the remains of a Celtic fortress which was used between the fifth and seventh centuries. The site was excavated in 1913 and several finds were made including fragments of French pottery, glass from

Germany and baked clay moulds which could have been used as casts. This archaeological site was gifted to the National Trust for Scotland in 1937 by John and James McLellan in memory of their brother, Col. William McLellan. The walk's further destination, Castle Point, is a fine vantage point with a direction indicator board identifying the surrounding landmarks.

From Dumfries take the A711 through Dalbeattie then the A710 for 5km, turning right for Kippford. From the car park at the north end of Kippford, walk into the village. On reaching the Post Office turn left at the Jubilee Path sign. The road then bears right and soon the tarmac stops – continue now on a good footpath, with views over to the bird sanctuary of Rough Island.

The path rolls along its headland through gorse and broom towards the edge of a forest. A narrow lane runs to the road at the top of Rockliffe. Turn right, follow the road downhill and at the seafront turn left. After a couple of hundred metres a signpost indicates 'The Merse'. Follow this private road and then take the footpath, marked by a sign, that bears off to the right. Cross a footbridge and continue through some more broom and gorse. The path now follows the shore and at one point actually drops down onto the gravelly beach. Passing the last house the path swings round to visit the grave of Joseph Nelson who was drowned in a shipwreck in 1791. Keep following the path, cross a stone stile and follow the path around the perimeter of a field to reach a gate. Go through and tackle the final climb to Castle Point.

The return route is slightly different. Retrace your steps to Rockcliffe, turn left past the car park, cross the road and follow a narrow lane to the area called the Mote of Mark. Cross a meadow, bearing left to cross a footbridge. Straight ahead lies a notice board at the foot of the Mote of Mark. From the top of the Mote descend by the path leading off from the right. Follow this path, crossing others, back to the edge of the forest again. Take the outward road back to the car park.

Route Summary

From the Post Office in Kippford follow the Jubilee Path to Rockcliffe. At the seafront turn left to a sign indicating 'The Merse'. Follow this private road to a signposted footpath. Follow this path, over a footbridge, down to the foreshore, past the grave of Joseph Nelson to Castle Point. Return to Rockcliffe, follow a lane to the Mote of Mark. From the top of the Mote take the path back to the forest and follow the outward route back to Kippford.

Map: OS Sheet 84

Access Point: Car park at N end of Kippford

Distance: About 9km

Approx Time: 2-4 hours

Grade: Easy low-level walk

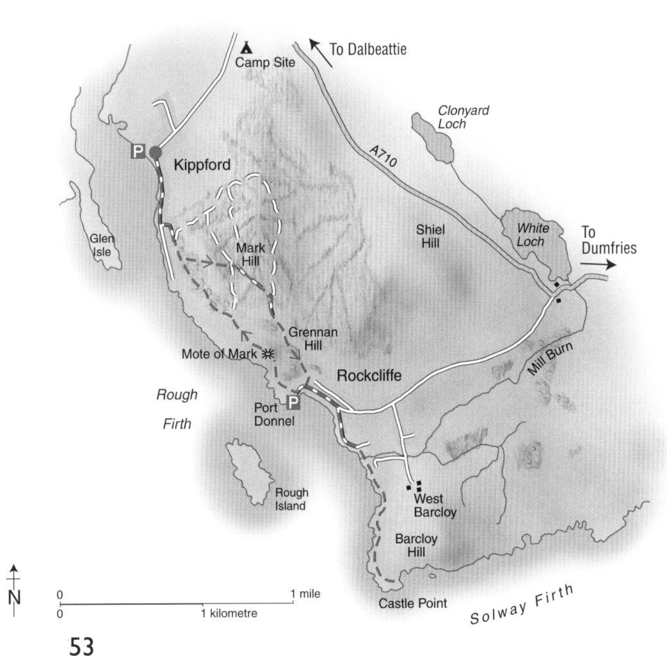

19 Criffel – The Hill of the Sweetheart

Route Summary

From the parking place at Ardwall Farm a gate on the left gives access to a track. After a short distance a signpost on the right points out the route. Follow the track to a gate which leads into the forest and along the Craigrockall Burn. Reach the open moorland above the forest where the upper slopes of Criffel rise on the left and those of the subsidiary top of Knockendoch on the right. Follow the path to the summit. Next take the path NW then N to Knockendoch. Descend SE to meet the Craigrockall Burn where it emerges from the forest. Take the route of ascent back to Ardwall Farm.

Map: OS Sheet 84

Access Point: Ardwall Farm, GR971635

Distance: 6.5km

Approx Time: 3-4 hours

Grade: Easy hill walk

Translation: raven's hill

Dominating the town of Dumfries, Criffel rises 569m above the estuary formed by the Solway and the Nith, and provides a notable northern landmark when seen from the Lakeland Fells in the south. The name of Criffel comes from the Norse kraka-fjell or krakkaval, which means raven's hill, a bird which is considered sacred in Scandinavia. Despite its comparatively low height the ascent of the hill makes a good introduction to the hill-walking game and provides a fairly stiff afternoon's walk. Try and keep it for a clear day, for the views from the summit are extensive – the Lowther, Moffat and Ettrick hills, the Lake District Fells, Isle of Man and the foreshore of the Caerlaverock National Nature Reserve.

I would suggest you both start and finish in the village of New Abbey, renowned for its Sweetheart Abbey, an ancient Cistercian building, one of three in the Galloway area, founded by John Balliol's wife Devorgilla in 1273. Begin near Ardwall Farm, which is reached from the A710 about 3km south of New Abbey. Just before the farm entrance there is a parking place and a large gate on the left gives access to a track. Follow it and after a short distance a signpost on the right points out the route to Criffel's summit. At the far end of this track a gate leads into the forest, and after a short distance follows the bubbling line of the Craigrockall Burn all the way onto the moorland above.

Once clear of the forest, the upper slopes of Criffel rise on the left and those of the subsidiary top of Knockendoch on the right. Follow the obvious path to the summit cairn, Douglas's Cairn, believed to date from the Bronze Age, and trig pillar. From the summit follow the path north-westwards then north to Knockendoch. From there, descend in a south-easterly direction to meet the Craigrockall Burn where it emerges from the forest and then follow your route of ascent back to Ardwall Farm.

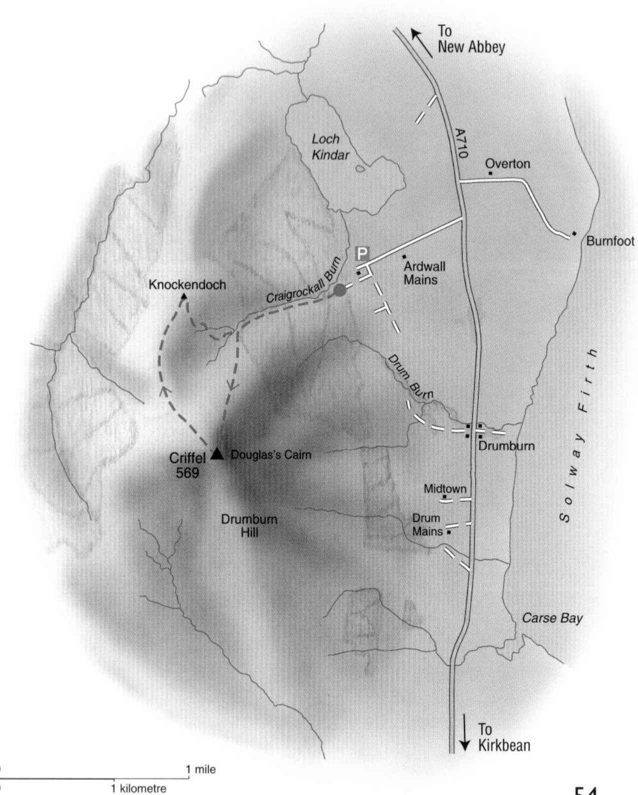

THE SOUTHERN UPLAND WAY

When you stand above the cliff-tops of Portpatrick and gaze westwards across the sea to Ulster, you quickly become aware that, as you look towards the vastness of this other country, with its different cultures, different history, and different ambitions, there is also an entire breadth of another country right behind you, a variety of lands as different from Central Scotland and Highland Scotland as from that ancient province across the waters.

The Southern Upland Way, 340km of it, takes you through the heart of those lands, individual regions, each proud of its own history and contribution to the Scottish nation: across the Rhinns to Loch Ryan, through the tumbled lands of Galloway, the industrial heritage of the Lowthers and Wanlockhead; the hills of historic Ettrick Forest and the Minchmoor; Melrose and the memory of St Cuthbert; the rolling Border hills and their great open skies, and finally, the east coast and the finale at Cockburnspath, where the dawning reality of what you have achieved is heightened by the knowledge that you have crossed a country, from west to east, against the very grain of the land itself.

Unlike the West Highland Way, this long trail isn't really charity-walk terrain. It's a tougher route, crossing the corrugations of a hilly landscape rather than following the valleys and troughs. A long-distance trail, anywhere in the world, is the sum of all the good and bad points. The Southern Upland Way has more highlights than troughs and offers a rich experience for any walker.

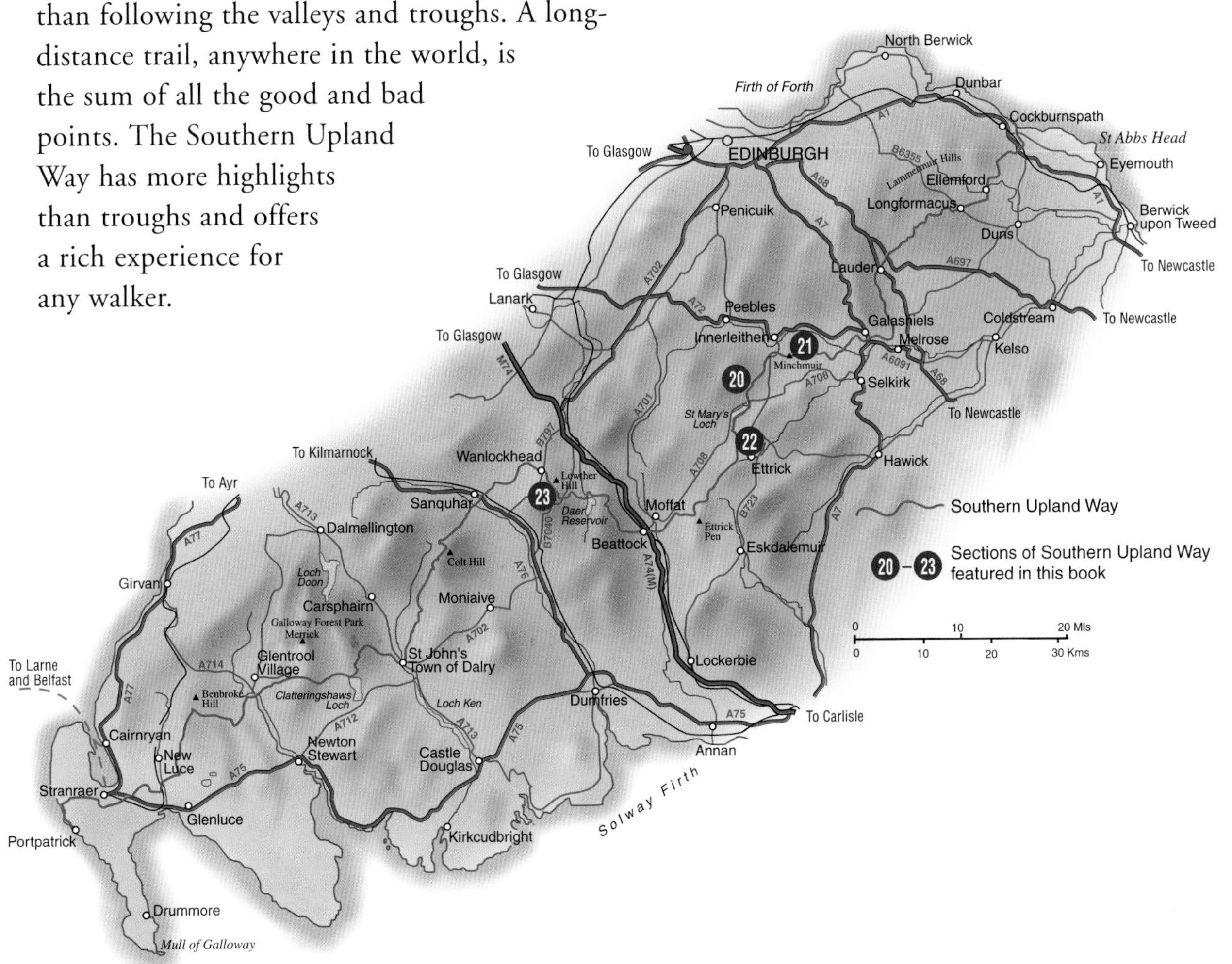

Route Summary

From Tibbie Shiel's Inn follow the track along the S shore of St Mary's Loch. At the N end of the loch cross the bridge and follow the signs across a field to the A708. Cross the road, continue NW through a field by Dryhope Tower. Continue N, skirting the E slopes of South and North Hawkshaw Rigs, to Blackhouse. Follow the track through forestry to reach the lower E slopes of Deuchar Law. Continue N then NE over Blake Muir and Fethan Hill before descending to the B709 at Kirkhouse. Continue by the road NE to Traquair.

Map: OS Sheet 73

Access Point: Tibbie Shiel's Inn, on the A708

Distance: About 20km

Approx Time: 6-8 hours

Grade: Easy hill walk

20 The Southern Upland Way – St Mary's Loch to Traquair

The Southern Upland Way, from Portpatrick to Cockburnspath, was Britain's first coast-to-coast long-distance trail. Although the route has been criticised for the amount of forestry it passes through, many sections of it offer walking on a grand scale. One such is that between St Mary's Loch on the A708 Selkirk to Moffat road over Blake Muir to Traquair. You'll need a couple of cars for this linear route, or some good soul to drop you off and pick you up at the end of the walk.

Tibbie Shiel's Inn is an historic hostelry, beautifully positioned at the southern end of St Mary's Loch. Apparently James Hogg the Ettrick Shepherd used to meet here with Sir Walter Scott, the farmer and the gentleman brought together by their common love of literature. The Southern Upland Way follows the eastern and southern shores of St Mary's Loch, past the sailing club buildings, through the trees and along the shore past Bowerhope Farm, to the far end of the loch. Field paths deviate away from the obvious route to the A708 road, following the Yarrow Water for a short distance before crossing a stile onto the road. Across the road another stile drops you into a field where a path climbs uphill past Dryhope Farm and its ruined towerhouse.

From Dryhope the route angles gently uphill to a col between Ward Law and South Hawkshaw Rig. The path then contours the lower eastern slopes of South Hawkshaw and North Hawkshaw Rigs, working its way up a narrowing valley to where a couple of houses, and another ruined tower, lie in the cusp of the hills.

Just before the buildings, cross the Douglas Burn, probably named after the infamous Border fighting family, which runs down from its lonely headwaters between Blackhouse Heights and Dun Rig. Dun suggests an ancient fort and Blackhouse Heights is associated with the house and ruined tower that you will pass.

The Border family of Douglas were traditionally known as the Black Douglas, not only because of their swarthy appearance, but because of their reputation amongst their enemies. The old castle here is called Blackhouse. An older tower on the site is thought to have been the home of Sir James Douglas, who fought alongside Robert the Bruce during the Wars of Independence in the early fourteenth century, and who carried the Bruce's heart to the

Crusades before burying it in the graveyard of Melrose Abbey, where it lies today. A modern farmhouse has been built immediately adjacent to the ruins, behind which is another house, a dour-looking building which is perhaps more appropriately called Blackhouse!

A long uphill section takes you high beyond the houses and into a forestry plantation, but only for a kilometre or so. The trees are soon left behind and you are greeted by a raw spaciousness and open skies with the hill track rolling on ahead, winding gently up and down over the rounded breasts of Blake Muir, the grassy slopes falling away on either side to deep valleys. The distant Moorfoots and the historic Minch Moor dominate the horizon.

Beyond Blake Muir the well-worn hill path begins to descend gradually, with The Glen valley to your left. To the right the bald pate of Minch Moor peaks beyond its forested slopes, and other hills lead the eye down to the rounded top of Mountbenger Law. At a farm at its foot James Hogg had a pretty unsuccessful time as a farmer. Continue to descend, contouring the eastern slopes of Fethan Hill, then through a gate, and on to a lane that takes you to the B709, which runs north to Traquair.

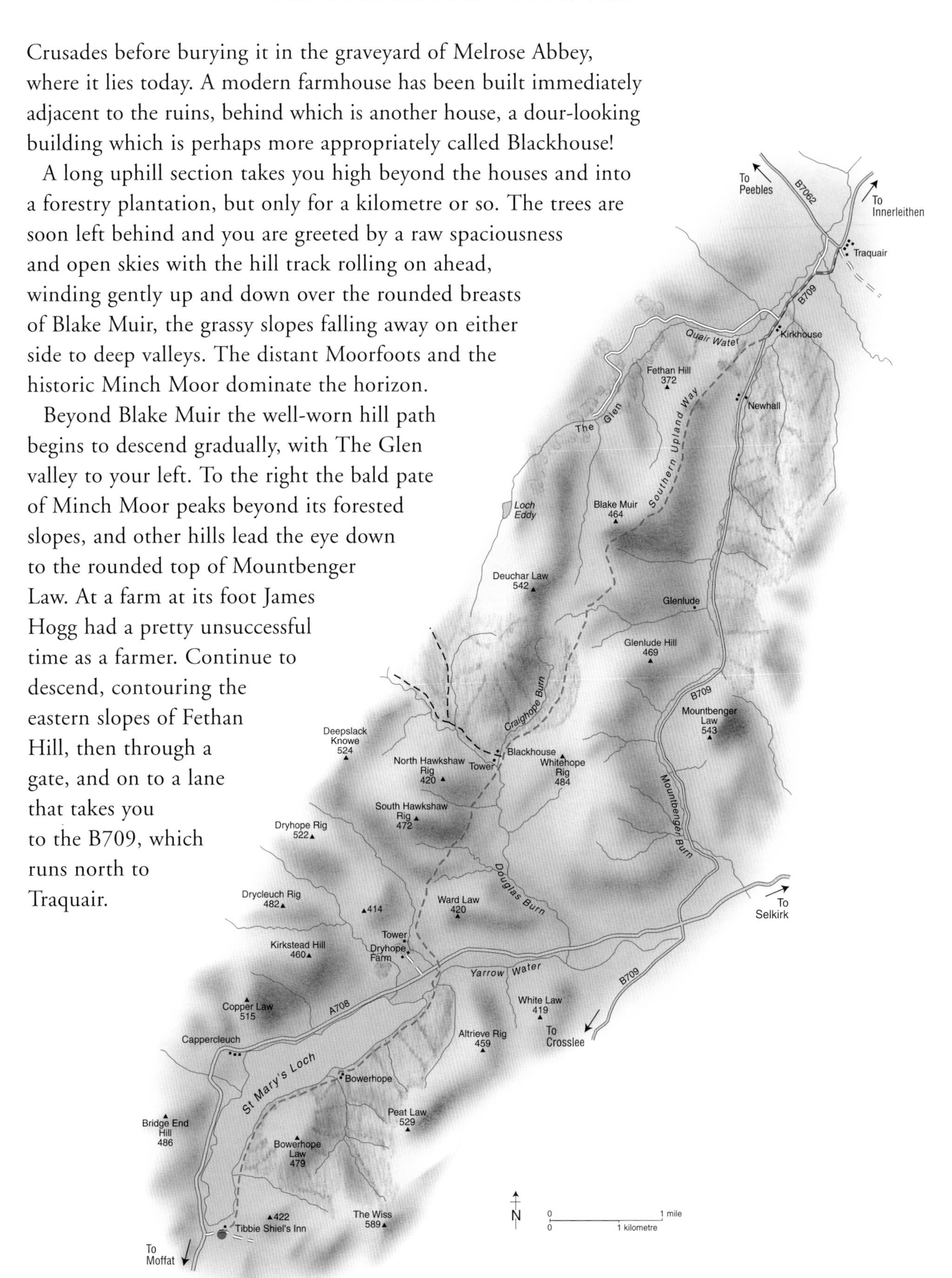

21 Minchmoor and the Three Brethren

Route Summary
From Yarrowford follow the Yarrow Water E towards Selkirk. At the second bridge a sign points to a 'Public Footpath to Galashiels'. Follow this uphill right of a wood. Pass the youth hostel, go through two gates, and follow the track over the col between Foulshiels Hill and its northern outlier. Descend to the Long Philip Burn beyond which the path reaches a gate. Go through the gate, turn left onto the new track and follow it to the Three Brethren. Walk W now to the Broomy Law, and then Brown Knowe. Continue W towards Traquair Forest. At its edge another footpath signposted as the Minchmoor road descends a ridge into some woods above Yarrowford.

Map: OS Sheet 73

Access Point: Yarrowford on the A708 GR413300

Distance: About 16km

Approx Time: 5-7 hours

Grade: Easy hill walk

This walk is not only one of the most popular in the Borders but it also celebrates the opening of Scotland's very first youth hostel, Broadmeadows, in 1931. For the best part of a decade I worked as a warden for SYHA and the original concept was dear to my heart. In these days of ultra-modern 'youth hotels', I'm encouraged that hostels like Broadmeadows still exist for those who like the idea of 'cheap, simple accommodation in wild areas'.

Starting close to the historic Yarrow Water this route climbs steadily and comfortably up to the Three Brethren, returning by the Minchmoor, a road that's been followed by kings, princes, outlaws, drovers, walkers and cyclists since time immemorial.

Yarrowford lies on the A708 just west of Selkirk. There's a small parking area near the telephone box. From there follow the Yarrow Water back towards Selkirk. When you reach the second bridge look for a sign which says, 'Public Footpath to Galashiels', and follow it uphill to the right of a wood. Pass the youth hostel and go through a couple of gates. The track begins to bear right, leaving the woods behind and climbing over the col between Foulshiels Hill and its northern outlier before dropping down to cross the Long Philip Burn. Beyond, it narrows as it reaches a gate in the

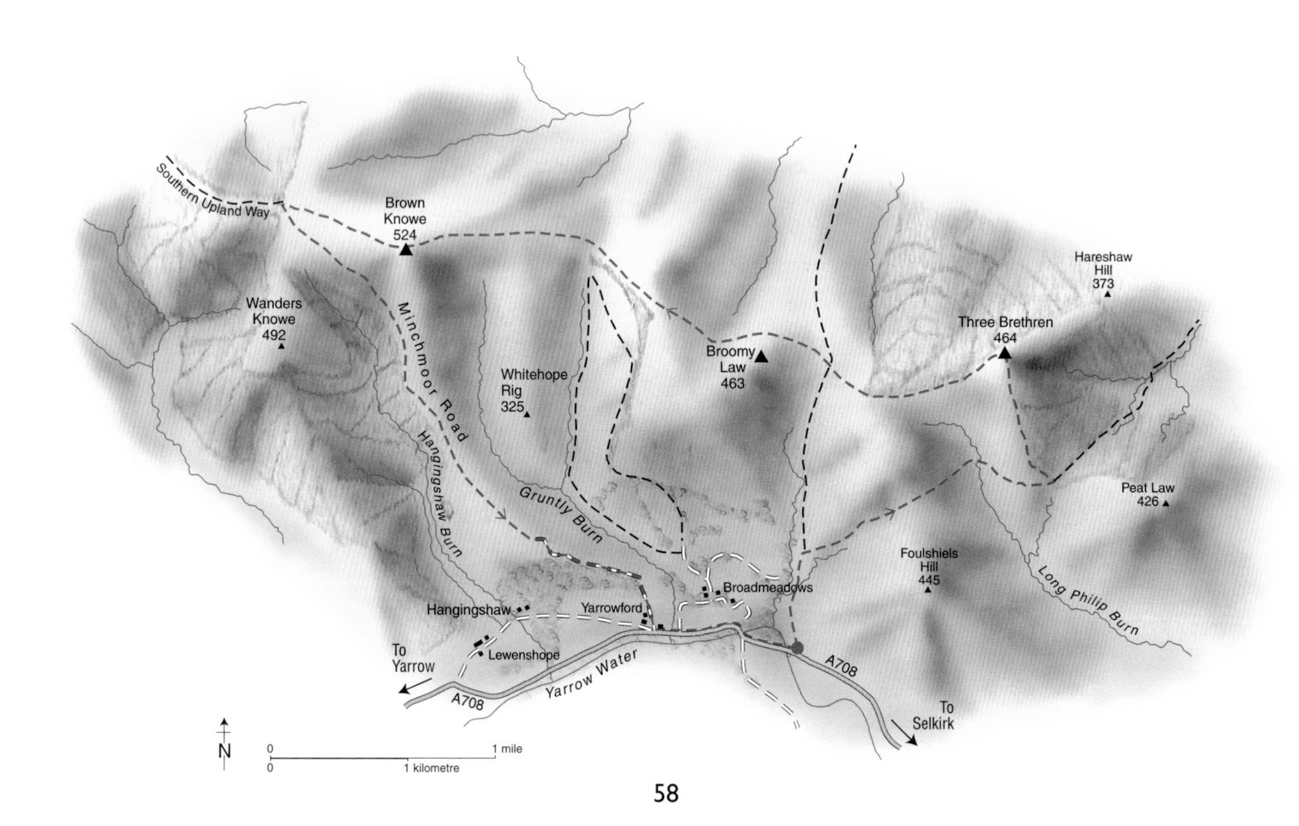

The Southern Upland Way above Broadmeadows

fence, and then another, wider track. Turn left onto this and follow it to the Three Brethren, three tall cairns, one standing within each of the properties of Selkirk Burgh, Yair and Bowhill.

The summit is on the route of Selkirk's Common Riding, an annual event which shows the independent attitude of these Border towns, something that's also illustrated by the partisan support of local rugby. Once, walking out, I met a group of walkers whose size and appearance suggested they might be rugby players. I innocently asked them if they knew the result of the previous day's international between Scotland and Australia. Little did I know Scotland had been thrashed 37 points to 8 and that two of the walkers I had met were Scottish players trying to forget the game!

Head west now along the broad path to the Broomy Law, down into a little wooded glen and then uphill again towards the summit of Brown Knowe, where at 524m a cairn marks the high point of the walk. Continue westwards along the path towards the Traquair Forest but just as you reach its edge you'll see another footpath signposted as the Minchmoor Road.

Edward I came this way to conquer Scotland in 1296 and the Marquis of Montrose crossed the Minchmoor *en route* to Traquair House where he had hoped to find shelter.

The Minchmoor Road drops down the ridge between the Hangingshaw Burn and the Gruntly Burn, past some woods lower down, and then into some more woods above Yarrowford. Keep to the path as it leaves the woods above some houses. Turn right, then left to reach the main road and your waiting vehicle.

Looking north towards Loch of the Lowes from Peniestone Knowe, Ettrick

22 A Taste of Ettrick

I love the Ettrick area. Although the hills are largely swathed in great rectangular shrouds of conifers and the glens have been tamed by modern agriculture there are still strong echoes of former times, those resonances of old which consolidate Ettrick's spirit. This whole area was once an ancient hunting forest, the sporting ground of lords and princes, but it wasn't only wild beasts that were the prey. These were the hills and glens that sheltered the patriot William Wallace when he survived as an outlaw in the late thirteenth century. And the Bruce too. And didn't the Black Douglas, and later, the Marquis of Montrose haunt this same lofty fastness when they too were being hunted like wild animals?

My son Gordon and I had walked up from the little Ettrick Kirk on the route of an ancient right of way between Craig Hill and Ramsey Knowe and at the high point of the path we stopped and gazed across a wild tumble of hills towards the prominent White Coomb, one of the highest hills in the Borders. Blue hills rolled out in every direction as we sat high above the wonderfully named Scabcleuch Burn and watched a short-eared owl patiently search for prey. We walked to the accompaniment of the curlew's call and were startled by snipe and grouse exploding from the heather below our feet. There is a timelessness here, as James Hogg, the Ettrick Shepherd, experienced when he witnessed the apparition of a drove of Highland cattle, accompanied by three drovers.

Route Summary

Leave the Kirk, turn left onto the minor road. At the end of the road follow a footpath on the left, go through a gate. Follow the path and after 100m reach the right of way. This path runs round the hillside to the saddle between Craig Hill and Ramsey Knowe and descends gradually into the Scabcleuch Glen. Cross a stile over a fence and follow the fence to the left to reach the Southern Upland Way. Turn left, cross a stile and follow the path downhill to the road at Scabcleuch. Turn left and follow the road back to Ettrick.

Map: OS Sheet 79

Access Point: Ettrick Kirk

Distance: About 6km

Approx Time: 2-3 hours

Grade: Easy hill walk

'It is quite evident,' he wrote later, 'that we must attribute these appearances to particular states of the atmosphere, and suppose them to be shadows of realities; the airy resemblance of scenes passing in distant parts of the country, and by some singular operation of natural causes thus expressively imaged in the acclivities of the mountains.'

James Hogg (1770-1835) is widely remembered in Scotland as a contemporary of Robert Burns. Like Burns, Hogg came from a working background and it's thought that his rise to prominence as a poet was due to his friendship with Sir Walter Scott. Earlier in the afternoon we had passed Hogg's memorial in Ettrick, where he was born, and searched in the kirkyard for his grave.

Although comparatively short, this little hill jaunt gives a taste of the open splendour of the Ettrick Forest. From Ettrick Kirk turn left onto the minor road and follow it past the prominent white house. At the end of the road follow a footpath to your left beside the Kirk Burn, go through a gate and follow the sign which indicates a right of way. Follow the path steeply up through grass and bracken and after 100m reach another path which is also signposted as a right of way. This path appears to aim directly towards the large cairn on Craig Hill ahead of you but it soon eases off to the right to work its way around the hillside towards the saddle between Craig Hill and Ramsey Knowe. The path isn't very clear hereabouts and the ground tends to be wet, but once over the saddle the path becomes more obvious as it descends gradually into the upper slopes of Scabcleuch Glen. At this point cross a stile over a fence and follow the fence to the left. In about 100m turn left onto the Southern Upland Way, cross a stile and follow the well-worn path downhill beside the Scabcleuch Burn to the road at Scabcleuch. Turn left onto the road and follow it back to Ettrick.

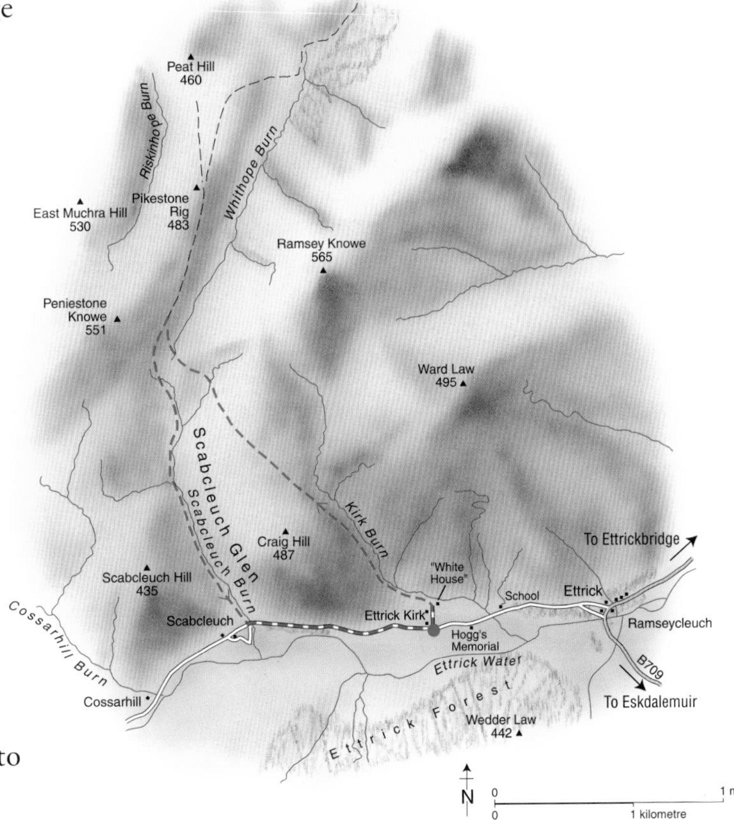

Route Summary
Close to Wanlockhead's visitor centre, signs point out the route of the Southern Upland Way. Follow the route up the slopes of Stake Hill to where it makes a tight curve to the left. Leave the SUW here and follow the path to the Enterkin Pass. From the head of the Pass climb to the summit of East Mount Lowther. Return to the Pass and climb slopes in a NE direction to find the track which climbs to the top of Lowther Hill. From here a road runs NE over a subsidiary top to Green Lowther. Return to Lowther Hill and follow the SUW back to the start

Map: OS Sheet 78

Access Point: Wanlockhead Visitor Centre

Distance: About 12km

Approx Time: 4-5 hours

Grade: Easy hill walk

23 The Lowther Hills

Wanlockhead claims to be the highest village in Scotland, so at 468m above sea level it's only 264m to the summit of Green Lowther at 732m. A hill walk to Green Lowther and its near neighbours East Mount Lowther and Lowther Hill, makes a fine expedition with views which, in clear weather, extend from the Lakeland Fells to the Highlands. Both Lowther Hill and Green Lowther are capped by radar installations, but these don't spoil the walk.

Mines in the Wanlockhead and neighbouring Leadhills area have produced lead, silver and gold, including gold that was used in the making of a crown for James V and his queen. By the eighteenth century a considerable lead mining industry had developed, but commercial mining died out in the 1950s.

From the road above the visitor centre in Wanlockhead follow signposts for the Southern Upland Way. The trail leads out of the village for about 1.5km, up Stake Hill, to join a wider track which soon makes a very tight bend to the left. Leave the Way here and follow the path to the Enterkin Pass. It's said the army of Charles Edward Stuart crossed through here in 1745.

At the head of the Pass climb slopes to the summit of East Mount Lowther. Return to the Pass and climb NE to pick up the track to the summit of Lowther Hill. The actual summit has a fence around it, so walk left to pick up a road on the other side which runs north-east over a rise to the summit of Green Lowther. You can descend by the north-west ridge to the mine workings and the B797 back to Wanlockhead, but it's better to return to Lowther Hill and follow the Way back to the start.

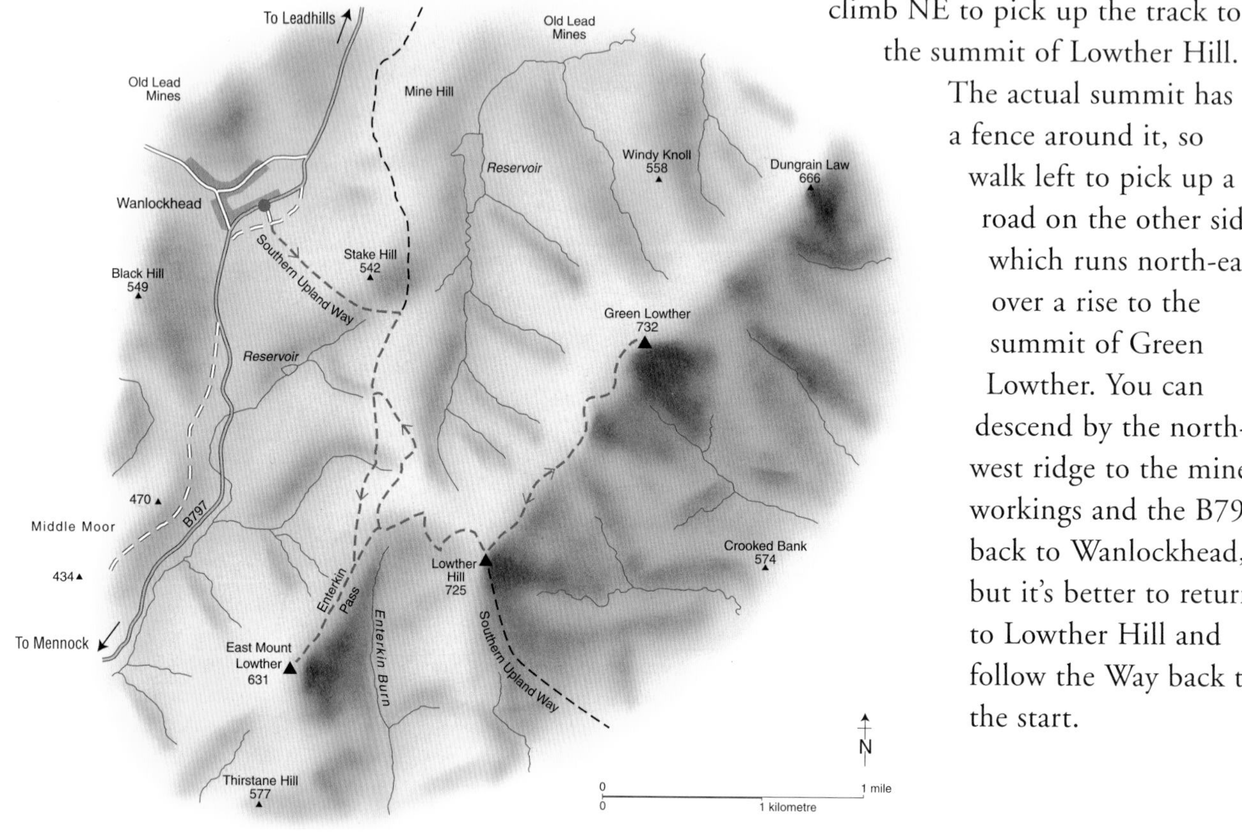

24 Myths and Legends of Hart Fell

Hart Fell and Upper Annandale near Moffat

The Moffat hills look particularly fine in the autumn, burnished in shades of gold and yellow, and this walk takes in one of the Borders' higher tops in an area richly packed with historical myth and legend.

Just above the Auchencat Burn lies the Hartfell Spa, a chalybeate spring contained in its little beehive-shaped shelter. The waters were once believed to have healing properties – try them for yourself, as the climb out of the well's gully is the steepest part of the walk!

Beyond the well you'll cross over the namesake of Edinburgh's best-known landmark, Arthur's Seat, although this one is infinitely wilder than the one in Holyrood Park! The Arthurian legends are strong in the Borders and these hills even have links with Arthur's wise counsellor, Merlin the Magician. The wizard Merlin, it is claimed, once roamed these broad slopes. He was able to transform himself into a hart, a deer often associated with royalty.

More likely the only beasts which truly roamed these areas were cattle. The great hollow of the Devil's Beef Tub was important in former times as a holding place for great herds, when such livestock were the area's most valuable commodity and cattle raids were not infrequent. In 'tubs' like this one, the herd could easily be held and guarded until it was safe to release them.

Start this walk from Ericstane, which is reached by a minor road

Route Summary

Just before the farm at Ericstane a signpost points to Hartfell Spa. Follow the path beside the Auchencat Burn, and climb into a narrowing valley. The path soon leaves the burn to climb to the well itself, and beyond, to reach the ridge. Take a NE bearing over Arthur's Seat to Hart Fell. From the summit trig point head NW, following a line of fences to an obvious left turn. From here continue on a NW line to cross the path on Barncorse Knowe and then left to the top of the Crown of Scotland. Descend to the junction of the Powskein and Whitehope Burns and continue SW to Great Hill with the deep hollow of the Devil's Beef Tub below you. A good path runs downhill above the Beef Tub to Corehead and the road back to Ericstane.

Map: OS Sheet 78

Access Point: Ericstane, GR075107

Distance: 13km

Approx Time: 6-8 hours

Grade: Moderate hill walk

from Moffat. Shortly before you reach the farm at Ericstane a signpost points over the fields to Hartfell Spa. Follow the path beside the Auchencat Burn, and climb steadily into a narrowing valley. After a short distance the path leaves the burn and the sheep-cropped turf to climb to the well itself. Once you've refreshed and revitalized yourself with the water, climb the steep gully above the small beehive-shaped building to reach the ridge above.

Follow the ridge in a north-east direction, over Arthur's Seat to the wide summit of Hart Fell itself. From the trig point head north-west, following a line of fences to an obvious left turn. From here continue on your north-west line to cross the path on Barncorse Knowe and then head left to the top, intriguingly named Crown of Scotland.

From the Crown, drop down to the junction of the Powskein and Whitehope Burns and continue south-west to Great Hill, with the deep hollow of the Devil's Beef Tub below you. A good path runs downhill above the Beef Tub to Corehead and the road back to your waiting car at Ericstane.

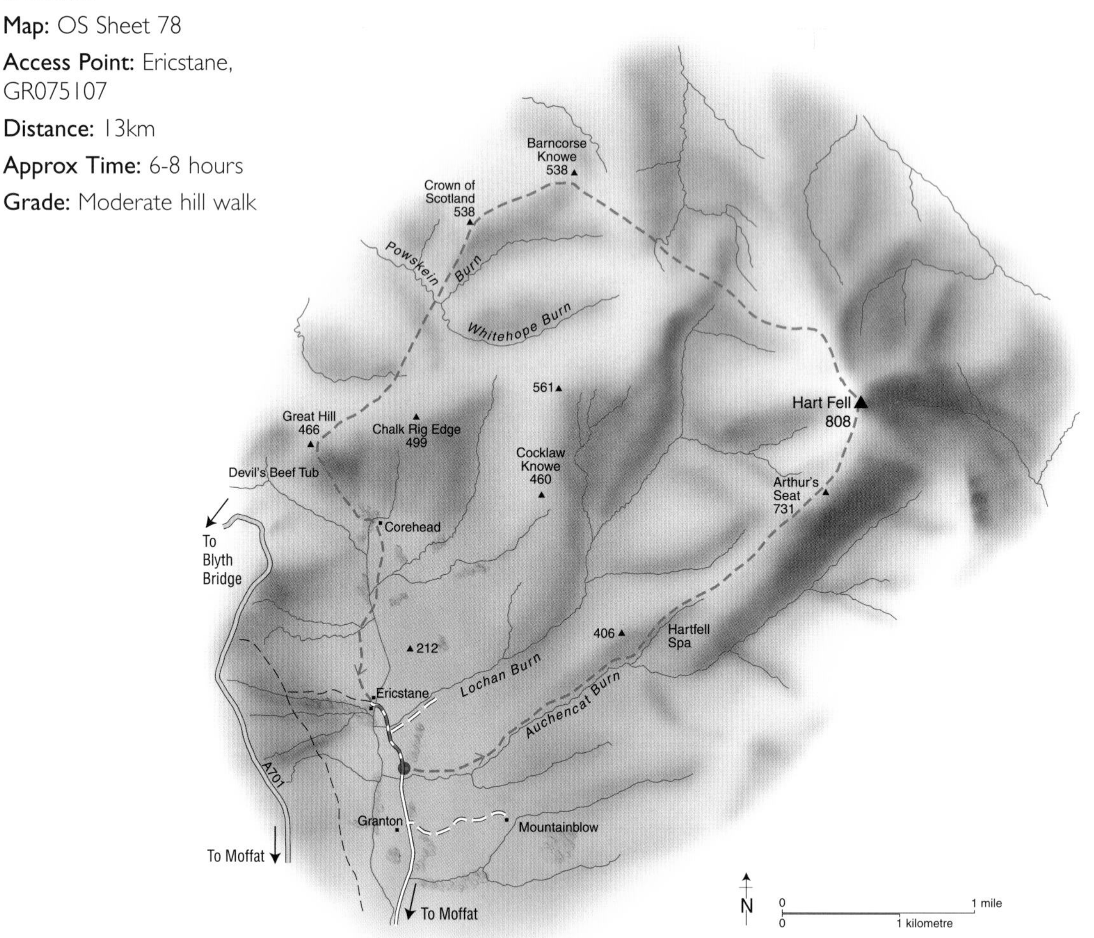

25 White Coomb and the Grey Mare's Tail

The South Tweedsmuir hills, which rise between Moffat Water and the source of the Tweed make up an empty, desolate quarter of rounded hills with boggy skirts. White Coomb at 822m is the highest hill in Dumfriesshire. I once climbed White Coomb along with Hart Fell in the north, but a shorter, and scenically superior route, is to climb it from the top of the impressive Grey Mare's Tail waterfall, before descending into the hill's north-eastern corrie which forms a fine craggy backdrop for Loch Skeen.

The crashing 60m drop of the Grey Mare's Tail waterfall above the A708 Moffat to St Mary's Loch road may not be the highest in Scotland, but it is certainly spectacular and draws car-loads of visitors. The lower part of the footpath has suffered from heavy usage but some sterling work by the National Trust for Scotland has created some secure pathwork. The waterfall, Loch Skeen and White Coomb are all in the Trust's care.

The waterfall itself is formed by the Tail Burn which issues from the moraine-dammed waters of Loch Skeen, an attractive stretch of water that's well set in the craggy north-eastern corrie of White Coomb. In winter the waters of the Grey Mare's Tail often freeze, turning the normally roaring waters into a solid gash of green ice.

The views from the summit of White Coomb are wide ranging, from Criffel in the west to the Eildons in the east and from the Solway Firth to the distant outline of the Lake District Fells. Look out for a colourful display of wild flowers on the steep banks of the Grey Mare's Tail and for wild goats on the hills. Be careful on the path beside the waterfall. Although it is well made it does traverse above steep drops and several accidents have occurred here.

Route Summary

Leave the NTS car park and take the footpath beside the Tail Burn. Follow this path beside the falls to where it begins to level off. Cross the burn well above the falls and walk W over Upper Tarnberry. Follow a wall up Rough Craigs, to where it passes about 100m S of the summit of White Coomb. Descend N for 500m and drop down steep slopes beside the Midlaw Burn to Loch Skeen. Follow the footpath beside the Tail Burn back to the car park below.

Map: OS Sheet 79

Access Point: NTS car park at A708. GR186145

Distance: About 7km

Approx Time: 3-5 hours

Grade: Moderate hill walk

Translation: white corrie

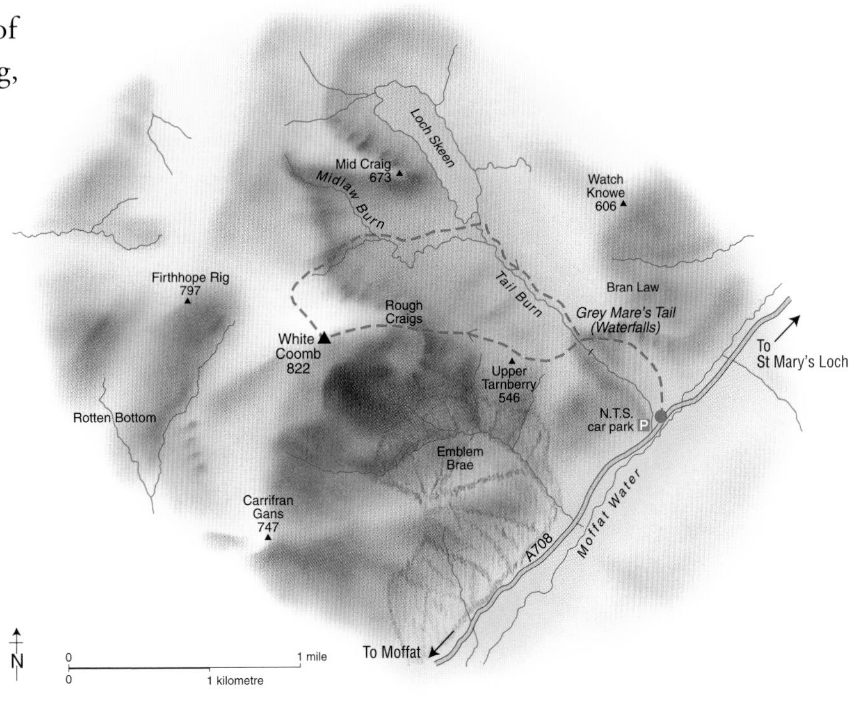

The Eildon Hills from Scott's View near Dryburgh

26 The Eildon Hills – The Hills of Elfland

One of the great landmarks of the Borders, the Eildons lie to the south-east of Melrose and offer a fairly gentle walk to their summits from where the views are extensive. The hills are now part of the gentle St Cuthbert's Way, a long-distance trail between Melrose and Lindisfarne in Northumberland, and since the whole area virtually seeps with history and resonances of the past, I would encourage you to link this walk with a visit to Melrose Abbey, the final resting place of the heart of Robert the Bruce.

Legend claims the Eildons were formed by supernatural powers, when Michael Scott, a wizard, was ordered by the devil to split a single 'Eildon' mountain into three separate hills. The geological explanation is perhaps more prosaic – the hills are the remains of a volcanic lava flow beneath the now eroded sandstone.

Thomas Learmont, known as Thomas the Rhymer, a thirteenth-century bard and seer, apparently lacked the magical powers of Michael Scott. He was spirited away by the queen of the fairies, and it's said he spent seven years in Elfland, an ethereal wonderland set below the Eildon Hills! Less fanciful, but still fascinating is that North Hill was once the site of an ancient city, the home of the Selgovae tribe, said to be an ancient commercial society that was involved in local industry and agriculture and that must have traded widely. Archaeologists suggest there could have been over 300 hut circles here about 2000 years ago. Later, the Romans used the site as a fort and signal station. They called the Eildons 'Trimontium' – the three hills.

A car park is conveniently positioned just opposite Melrose Abbey, and our route to the Eildons takes us back towards the town square. Pass the Mercat Cross and follow the B6359 road south, turning left at the sign which indicates 'Eildon Walk'. Climb some steps and follow the footpath at the top, which runs uphill alongside open fields towards the foot of the hills. From here make your way towards the obvious col between the two main summits, North and Mid Hills. At the col, or saddle, bear right and follow the steepening path to the summit of Mid Hill, 422m, with its prehistoric burial cairn and view indicator. Return the same way to the col and follow the obvious footpath which runs through remains of the Iron-Age hillfort to the summit of Eildon Hill North, 404m, and its ancient Roman signal station.

To return to Melrose by a more circuitous route, descend to the col once again and turn left down a valley. Follow the path until you reach the edge of some woodland. Turn left again along the track which hugs the edge of the plantations. With the steep slopes beginning to ease off, turn left at a path junction, slightly uphill over the eastern ridge of the hill and then downhill again, looking towards the Roman remains at Newstead. The path continues downhill to the edge of the Eildontree Plantation. A short distance beyond, another path bears off to the left around the northern slopes of Eildon Hill North to join the outward path. Turn right and follow the earlier route back into Melrose.

Route Summary

From the Town Square in Melrose follow the B6359 S and turn left at the 'Eildons Walk' sign. Climb the steps and follow the path which runs alongside some fields and eventually reaches the col between North and Mid Hills. Climb to both summits, return to the col and follow the path SE to the edge of a woodland. Turn left, follow the track that hugs the edge of the plantations to a path junction. Go left again and follow this path to the edge of the Eildontree Plantation. Slightly beyond this point another path bears off to the left, all the way back to the outward route from Melrose.

Map: OS Sheet 73

Access Point: Car park opposite Melrose Abbey

Distance: About 10km

Approx Time: 3-4 hours

Grade: Easy hill walk

Translation: Possibly from the Old English eld dun – old fort

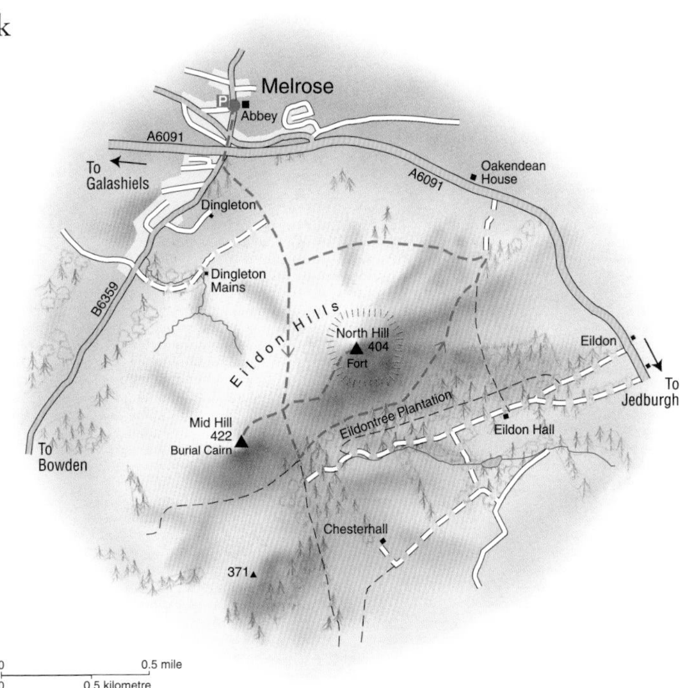

27 The Glensax Horseshoe – Following the Drovers

In the days before sheep became the ubiquitous woolly locusts of the rural Scottish landscape, the rearing of cattle formed the backbone of the Highland economy. Every autumn the small, mainly black, Highland kye were driven south on long-established routes to the famous cattle trysts, or markets. In 1770 the Michaelmas Tryst was established at Falkirk and it's said that as many as 30,000 cattle were sold there in a week. The buyers were predominantly English and the common practice was to then hire some local drovers to take the herds south into England.

Today you can easily trace that great southern drove road – a modern Right of Way between Peebles and Yarrow follows the route, and later it crosses the Minch Moor just south of Traquair. Like many of the drove roads, this one is now enjoyed by walkers and this Glensax Horseshoe links part of the drove road with a tramp over the Hundleshope Heights to form a very fine high-level walking route.

The town of Peebles is our starting point and to reach the beginning of the walk cross the

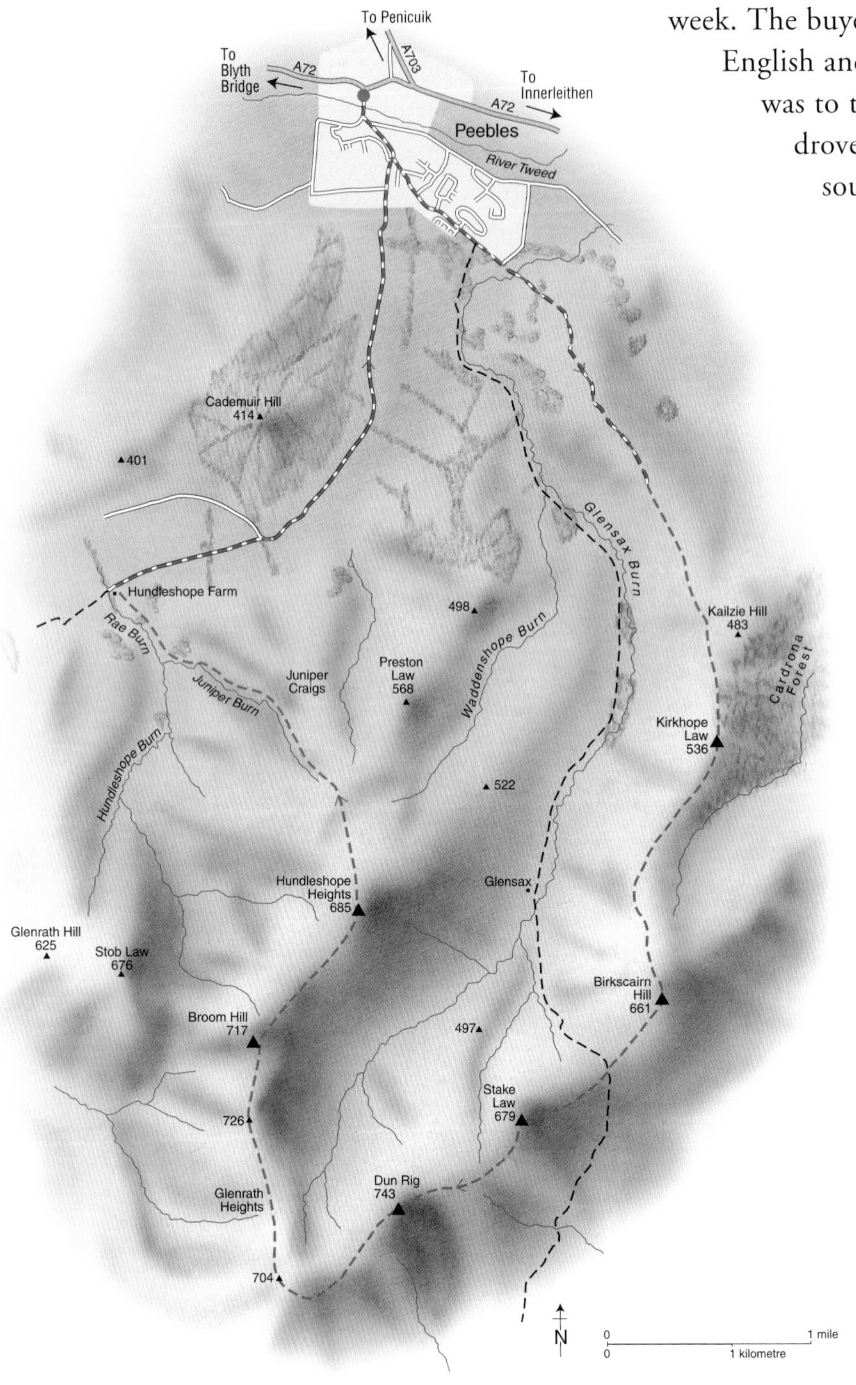

bridge over the River Tweed southwards, turn left and almost immediately right into Springhill Road. A kilometre along the road you can park close to where the tarmac ends. A Scottish Rights of Way Society sign points to a 'Public Footpath by Gipsy Glen to Yarrow,' and an older sign, also pointing out the route to Yarrow, confirms it. Descend into the Gipsy Glen and cross the Yaystoun Burn by a footbridge and then up a steep bank, climbing steadily through trees and a couple of gates out onto the open hillside where the views open out dramatically. The view back over Peebles is fine; 'the comfortable, sonsy and still good-looking matron of the Borderland,' to quote novelist and historian Nigel Tranter.

Higher up, drystone walls mark out the route of the drove road; initially the path stays left of the high ground and follows the contours round to reach a gate and it's from this point, as it heads up towards Kailzie Hill, that you get some inclination of the scale of the drove road itself. The walls which once marked out the route are a good 20m apart, and it's easy to imagine the heaving, sweaty throng of cattle, dogs and men, making their way south towards the Border and their destinations in England.

The route climbs steadily towards the summit of Kailzie Hill, passing the western edge of the extensive Cardrona Forest. The track now follows a wire fence over Kirkhope Law and then up to the summit of Birkscairn Hill. Ordnance Survey maps show the path passing to the west of the summit but on the ground it definitely crosses the summit! Follow the path down from Birkscairn Hill to the col between it and Stake Law and then on to the 743m summit of Dun Rig. This is the high point of the walk and the views are superb with the high ground of Hundleshope Heights to the north-west. Away beyond the valley of the Quair, the forest of Elibank, and the hills of Minch Moor, the unmistakable triple-topped outline of the Eildons is seen on a clear day. To the south, beyond the lower hills and forest of St Mary's Loch, lies the ancient hunting forest of Ettrick.

At this half-way point in the walk it's time to leave the old drove road and descend to the head of Glensax before turning north to return to Peebles. Head west to Glenrath Heights then north over the rolling Broom Hill and Hundleshope Heights. Just beyond the Heights, before the rise to Preston Law, a fence runs north-west along the Juniper and Rae Burns to Hundleshope Farm, where a quiet road runs back to Peebles beside the Cademuir Plantation.

Route Summary

From the end of Springhill Road descend into the Gipsy Glen and cross the burn by a footbridge. Follow the path up through the trees onto the open hillside. Continue to the summit of Kailzie Hill, follow a fence over Kirkhope Law and continue to the summit of Birkscairn Hill. Descend to the col and then climb to the top of Dun Rig. Drop down to the head of Glensax, then bear N over Glenrath Heights, Broom Hill and Hundleshope Heights. Descend to a fence which follows the Juniper and Rae Burn to Hundleshope Farm, where a minor road heads N back to Peebles.

Map: OS Sheet 73

Access Point: Springhill Road, Peebles

Distance: 20km

Approx Time: 7-9 hours

Grade: Moderate hill walk

Scald Law from Carnethy Hill, Pentland Hills

28 Rollercoastering the Pentlands

Stretching for some 24km from the suburbs of Edinburgh to the village of Carnwath in Lanarkshire, the steep-sided hills of the Pentlands dominate the A702 from Fairmilehead to Biggar. Sequestered by the ridge of Turnhouse Hill, Carnethy Hill and Scald Law on one side and Black Hill and Castlelaw Hill on the other, the only real glen of the Pentlands, Glencorse, or the Logan Glen, is a deep L-shaped valley which holds two reservoirs and a number of small houses. A walk across the hills south-east of this glen, followed by a walk through the glen itself, makes a fine day out from Edinburgh.

The ridge between Turnhouse Hill and West Kip comprises the highest tops in the Pentlands and offers extensive views. Some claim you can see Ben Nevis on a clear day but I suspect it would have to be an exceptionally clear day! The views extend as far as the unmistakable outline of the Bass Rock.

Close to the start of the walk is the site of the Battle of Rullion Green where, in 1666, a band of some 900 Covenanters were met by Royalist forces; many were killed, or were captured and either deported or hanged. Even further back, Bronze-Age man built his burial cairns and fortifications in these hills. Another ancient building, the fourteenth-century St Catherine's Chapel, is now, sadly, drowned under the waters of Glencorse Reservoir.

Park at Flotterstone on the A702. Pass the Flotterstone Centre, turn right onto the road and follow it until it begins to bear right. Leave the road here, go through a gate and cross the Glencorse

Burn by the second bridge. Turn right onto a wide footpath and follow it up some moraines and onto the steep slopes of Turnhouse Hill. Climb steadily through a stand of larch and pine before the gradient eases slightly to traverse onto the ridge slightly south-west of Turnhouse Hill. A good, clear path now follows the ridge in a south-west direction over the two White Craig Heads and down to the Lawhead Burn below Carnethy Hill. Cross a fence beside the burn and climb steadily to the old Bronze-Age cairn on the summit of Carnethy Hill. From here a long gradual descent takes you down to the high point of the Old Kirk Road which crosses the ridge from Balerno to Penicuik. Cross another fence and climb steeply up the zigzagging path to the summit of Scald Law, at 579m the highest point in the Pentlands.

Descend again, bearing west, to another col before the short and sharp ascent of East Kip and West Kip. The ascent of these two tops is optional as a good path runs north-west from the col before East Kip, then turns north-east, down steeply into the narrow mouth of Green Cleugh. Turn right, pass the white house called The Howe and gain the tarmac road which runs north-east past Loganlea and Glencorse Reservoirs. Turn sharply right down the Glen and back to Flotterstone.

Route Summary

From the Flotterstone Centre, turn right and follow the road until it bears right. Leave the road, go through a gate and cross the Glencorse Burn by the second bridge. Turn right onto a wide path and follow it onto the slopes of Turnhouse Hill. Climb to the ridge slightly SW of Turnhouse Hill. A path follows SW over Carnethy Hill, Scald Law, East Kip and West Kip. From the col before East Kip a path runs to the NW before turning NE, and down into Green Cleugh. Turn right, pass a house called The Howe and gain the road which runs NE past the reservoirs before turning right down the Glen and back to Flotterstone.

Map: OS Sheet 66

Access Points: Flotterstone car park on the A702

Distance: 13.5km

Approx Time: 4-6 hours

Grade: Moderate hill walk

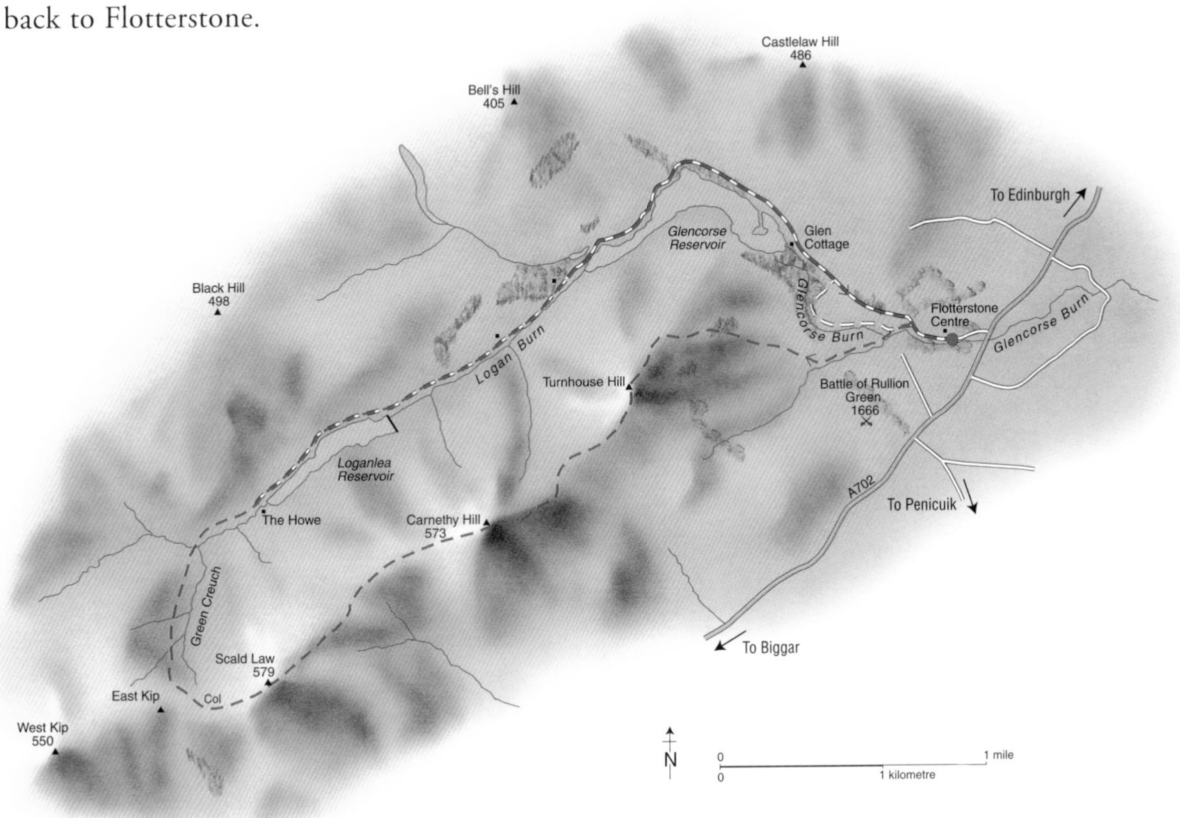

THE EASTERN HIGHLANDS AND COAST

Although the Birnam, Pitlochry and Birks of Aberfeldy walks lie west of the A9, the majority of the routes described in this chapter lie east of the Perth to Inverness road. Other exceptions are Kingussie's Creag Bheag and A' Chailleach in the Monadh Liath, but both these hills are virtually adjacent to the A9.

I've included some of my favourite, less well-known walks in this chapter. The long route over the Minigaig is particularly challenging, while the coastal walk to the remarkable ruins of Findlater Castle is a real treat. Interestingly I've described more walks in this area than any other, probably reflecting the years I've spent living there.

THE WALKS

Cairn Toul from the north, Cairngorms

Crail Harbour, Fife Coast

29 The Fife Coast – Pittenweem to Fife Ness

Route Summary

Leave the car park area by the harbour in Pittenweem, head E for 400m before following a path on the right through a small children's playground. Follow the edge of the adjoining field and halfway across turn right down some steps to the golf course. Continue along the shore past the headland of Billow Ness to Anstruther, entering the town by Shore Street. Turn left into Crichton Street and then Pittenweem Road, following it as far as Elizabeth Place. Turn right onto the Esplanade where a flight of steps, and some stepping stones across a burn, take you to the harbour area. Walk E out of Anstruther towards Cellardyke where a path indicates the coastal path to Crail. Follow the path past Caiplie Farm and Caiplie Caves to Crail. From the town pass Roome Rocks and the caravan park at Sauchope towards the headland at Fife Ness. Return to Crail by the minor road from the golf club. Return to Pittenweem by bus.

It's confession time. Despite my name, which sounds as though it was coined by a tartan-trewd PR executive trying to sell whisky-flavoured shortbread, I don't have an ounce of nationalistic blood in my body. Neither am I particularly patriotic, and although I greatly enjoyed the movie *Braveheart*, as a kind of Scottish western, it left me pretty cold as far as patriotic fervour went.

And while I do happen to be passionate about Scotland's hills, mountains and wild places, I'm also passionate about the hills of the Lake District, the Alps, the Pyrenees, the Himalayas, and other mountain ranges of the world that I've visited. In essence, I've never been disappointed in a range of mountains, but low-lying areas, towns and cities, are a different matter entirely.

Without wishing to narrow my prejudices down to one single place, I have to confess that I've never been terribly enthralled by Fife, so it was with a certain amount of cynicism that I was tempted by both Hamish Brown and Roger Smith, two men whose outdoor opinions I respect, to spend some time walking a 14km stretch of coastline between Pittenweem and Fife Ness, just beyond Crail. It was an eye-opener.

Coastal walking tends to have a pleasure all of its own, and with the constant surge of the sea on one side and the whirling and swooping of gulls overhead, it can be especially atmospheric. One of the delights of this East Neuk walk was the villages we passed through – Pittenweem itself, Anstruther, Cellardyke and Crail, old fishing villages where the reek of sea salt still seems to permeate the

Map: OS Sheet 59
Access Point: The car park by the harbour in Pittenweem
Distance: About 14km
Approx Time: 5-6 hours
Grade: Moderate low-level walk

very stones of the buildings. Fishing and its associated trades have certainly seriously declined in the past century but these places still feel like working harbours.

At one point in the walk I suggested to my companion that the only thing really missing was the sight of a long line of sea cliffs and while he admitted that it was all a bit flat he told me to wait until we reached Caiplie Caves. This isn't a sea cliff, but is a great sandstone bluff, eroded by salt and wind into a series of stacks and arches. The caves here, sometimes known as Carlawchy, were apparently used around 2000 BC. In one of the caves you'll see a drawing of a large animal with spears sticking out of its back. Greek and Latin inscriptions have been found here, indicating use over a long period of time.

One of those associated with the caves is St Adrian – the first bishop of St Andrews. He was apparently murdered in AD 870 by Danish invaders under the command of King Humber. More recently, the self-styled prophet Alexander Penn lived in the caves in the mid seventeenth century. Penn seemed to have been a truly odd character and was later forced out of the caves by local people who exiled him to the Bass Rock where he eventually died.

Throughout this walk I was aware of a real sense of history and I was very taken with the glorious seascapes, particularly from the nose of Fife Ness, at the end of the walk. As we returned down a minor road to Crail I promised myself a return visit to Fife's attractive coastline.

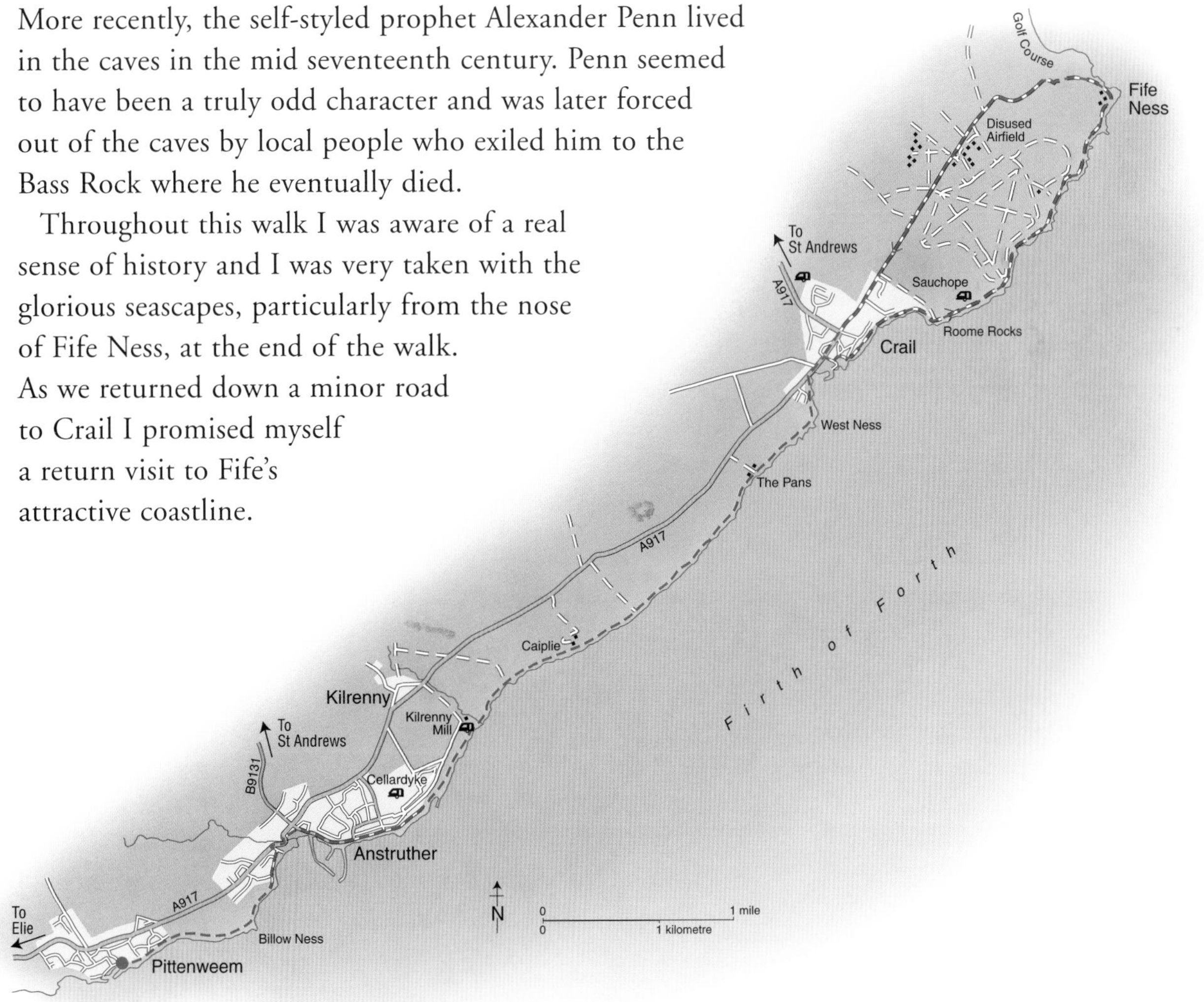

30 Birnam Hill – On the Edge of the Highlands

Route Summary

Opposite the Birnam Hotel walk through the gardens to the lane which leads to Birnam Glen. Follow this, with the Inchewan Burn on your right, below the A9. Immediately below the bridge, a path runs left, uphill to a road where a signpost to Birnam Hill points left. Turn left onto the road, and follow it to where a footpath enters the woods. This path rises round a prominent bend and another narrower path leaves the main one at a marker post. Follow this through woods, below some giant fir trees and on past the remains of the old Birnam Quarry. A signpost marks the way. After 100m another sign keeps you on the right path and past that another takes you uphill to the right.

Straddling the Highlands and Lowlands, Birnam Hill rises 400m above the villages of Dunkeld and Birnam, an area rich in association with Shakespeare's *Macbeth*. The long and easy ascent of the hill, passing Birnam Wood, Rohallion Castle, Duncan's Hill and the Stair Bridge makes an exhilarating afternoon walk with the reward of extensive views in all directions from the summit. This is a circular walk best done in a clockwise direction, otherwise your ascent of Birnam Hill will be long, steep and sustained.

The ornamental garden at the beginning of the walk is in memory of Beatrix Potter, who wrote the popular *Tale of Peter Rabbit* in a house in Birnam. In the garden you'll see the Tiggy-winkles' house, Mr Jeremy Fisher's pond and Peter Rabbit's burrow. The woods on the east-facing slopes of Birnam Hill grow on the site of the ancient Birnam Wood of the witch's prophecy in *Macbeth*. Above the woods is Duncan's Hill, where King Duncan's son Malcolm is supposed to have camped before his historical defeat of Macbeth at Dunsinane. Rohallion Castle is the remains of an old watchtower and Stair Bridge is well worth the short diversion to enjoy the view from its high span, looking down towards Rohallion Lodge and lochs.

Immediately opposite the Birnam Hotel walk through the ornamental gardens to the lane which leads to Birnam Glen. Follow this lane, with the Inchewan Burn on your right, below the A9. Immediately below the railway bridge, a footpath peels off from the lane leftwards, uphill to a tarmac road where a signpost to Birnam Hill points to the left. Turn left onto this road, past a few houses and soon the road becomes a footpath as it enters the woods. After a distance this path begins to rise round a prominent bend. As it rounds the bend another narrower path leaves the main one, at a marker post which is

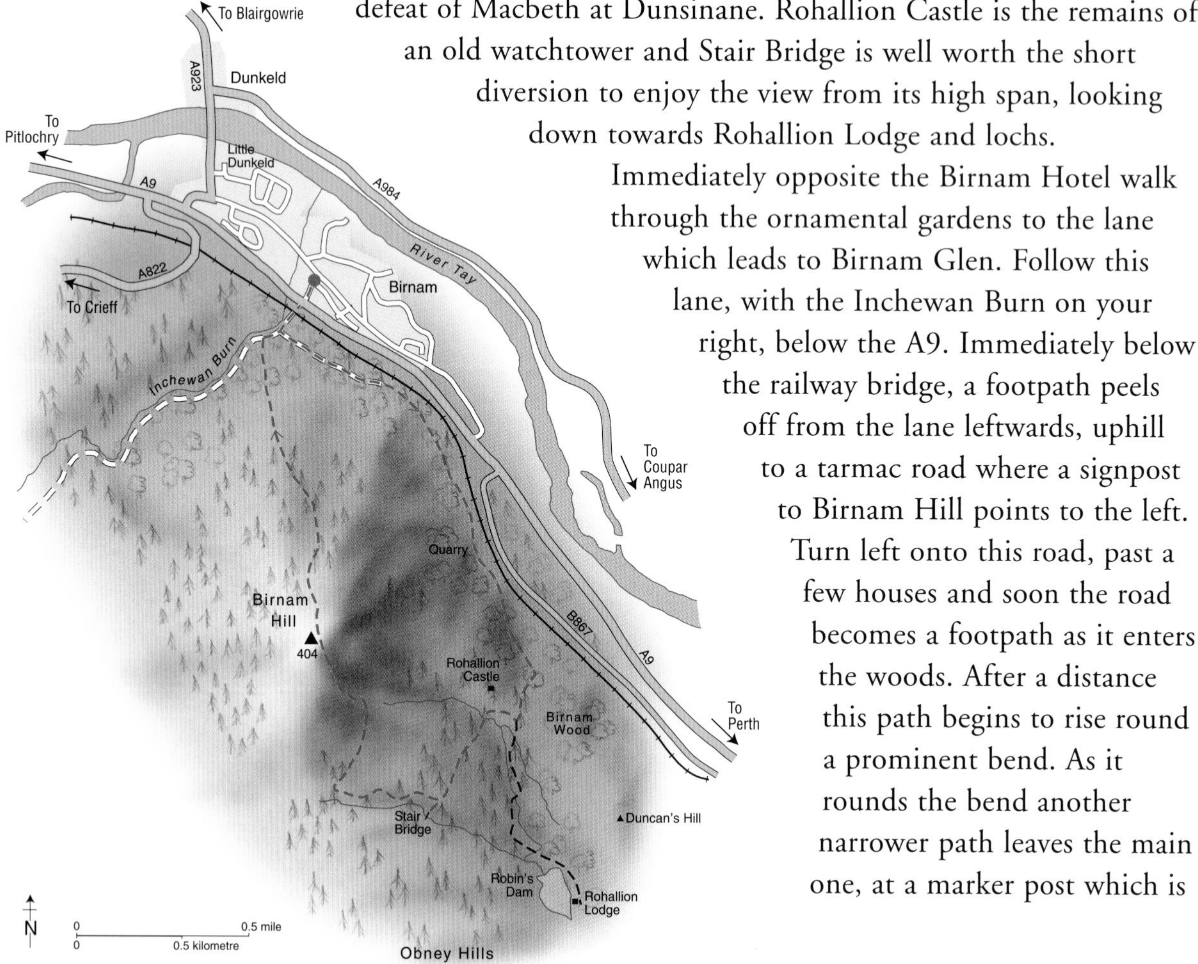

Rohallion Lodge from Stair Bridge, Birnam

ringed in red. Follow this path as it meanders gently through some lovely woodland and below some giant fir trees. After a while the path passes below the remains of the old Birnam Quarry. A signpost marks the way. About 100m further on another sign keeps you on the right path, and just past that yet another sign takes you fairly steeply uphill to the right. Follow this path now all the way uphill, past Rohallion Castle in its bracken hollow, past Birnam Wood and Duncan's Hill to the short diversion to the Stair Bridge.

From the bridge return to the main path and continue uphill to the obvious pass between Birnam Hill on your right and the Obney Hills on your left. From here the path turns sharply right and climbs the hill gently before a series of steep, wooden steps leads to the summit ridge and the large cairn. The view is wonderful, with Schiehallion, the Fairy Hill of the Caledonians, obvious in the north. Further right lies Pitlochry's Ben Vrackie, the giant Beinn a' Ghlo group and the hills of Glenshee. To the south a mosaic of fields and woods is laid before you, with the gentle swell of the Ochils in the far distance. From the summit simply follow the path steeply downhill back to Birnam.

Follow this path, past Rohallion Castle in its bracken hollow, past Birnam Wood and Duncan's Hill to the short diversion to the Stair Bridge. From the bridge return to the main path and continue uphill to the pass between Birnam Hill and the Obney Hills. From here the path turns sharply right and climbs the hill gently before a series of steep, wooden steps lead to the summit ridge and the large cairn. From the summit follow the path back down to Birnam.

Map: OS Sheet 53

Access Point: The Birnam Hotel

Distance: 7km

Approx Time: 2-4 hours

Grade: Easy hill walk

*Moness Burn,
Birks of Aberfeldy*

31 The Birks of Aberfeldy

This may be a short outing and for many a tame excursion, in a land where big hills dominate, but I've always loved the combination of crashing waters and rich, varied woodland.

Whenever I wander hills abroad I always come home to Scotland and feel saddened that so many of our hills' slopes have been overgrazed and that we have been robbed of the rich variety of woodland that should be our natural heritage. A wander through Rothiemurchus, Glen Affric or the Black Wood of Rannoch gives an impression of what could have been. A wander through the Birks of Aberfeldy is a return to older, simpler times.

There are two good times in the year to visit the Birks. In the spring-time, when the rivers are running high and the waterfalls of the Moness Burn pour over the rocky bed in dramatic cascades, or in autumn, when the leaves of the birches are changing from green to burnished gold. These are the woods that inspired Robert Burns to pen his famous tribute, lines that go a long way to reflecting the glory of this wooded, rocky chasm.

The braes ascend like lofty wa's,
the foaming stream deep-roaring fa's,
O'erhung wi' fragrant spreading shaws,
The birks of Aberfeldy.

Robert Burns visited the Den of Moness on 30 August 1787 and the spot where he allegedly wrote his poem is marked on the outward route. As a result of his words, the route along the Moness Falls has been a popular walk for over 200 years. It's now owned and maintained by Perth and Kinross Council.

The Moness Den was planted with deciduous trees in the late eighteenth century, adding variety to the natural pine woodland which had survived on the steep-sided crags and those parts of the gorge inaccessible to browsing animals, but there's a lot more to these woods than just birks, or birch trees. On the lower stretches you'll find beech, rowan, wych elm, hazel and some willow, and higher up the dominant species are oak and the eponymous birch.

From the car park just off the Crieff road in Aberfeldy (well signposted), follow the footpath which leaves the top right-hand corner. Almost immediately, turn left at signposts which indicate Moness Falls and Nature Trail. Cross the footbridge over the burn and begin a long and steady climb up its banks, eventually passing the rocky nook where Burns apparently sat and wrote his poem. Further on, a flight of steps leaves the path on the left, while the footpath continues straight ahead. Follow the steps as they climb higher towards the top of the steep-sided gorge, combining with wooden walkways and bridges to lift you above the very impressive sight of the Falls of Moness, now seen below you.

Cross the bridge above the falls, and keep going left onto a wider footpath which soon takes you to a T-junction with the road that leads to Urlar. Turn right onto this road, follow it for about 100m and go through a gate on the left, to trace a fine grassy track gently downhill towards the derelict farm buildings at Dunskiag. Enjoy the views from this track, up and down the length of Strath Tay from Ben Lawers and Schiehallion in the west to Ben Vrackie and the Grampians in the east. From Dunskiag follow the farm road to where it runs into a tarmac road running into Aberfeldy. Follow this road steeply downhill and turn right at the bottom, back onto the Crieff road and to the Birks car park.

Route Summary

From the car park follow the nature trail all the way to the bridge that crosses above the Moness Falls. Cross the bridge, and bear left until you reach a T-junction. Turn right onto the road, and after 100m go through a gate on the left onto a grassy track. Follow this track past Dunskiag to a farm road, which eventually joins a tarmac road which descends into Aberfeldy.

Map: OS Sheet 52

Access Point: The Birks car park, Crieff Road, Aberfeldy

Distance: About 6.5km

Approx Time: 2-3 hours

Grade: Easy low-level walk

Translation: birches of Aberfeldy

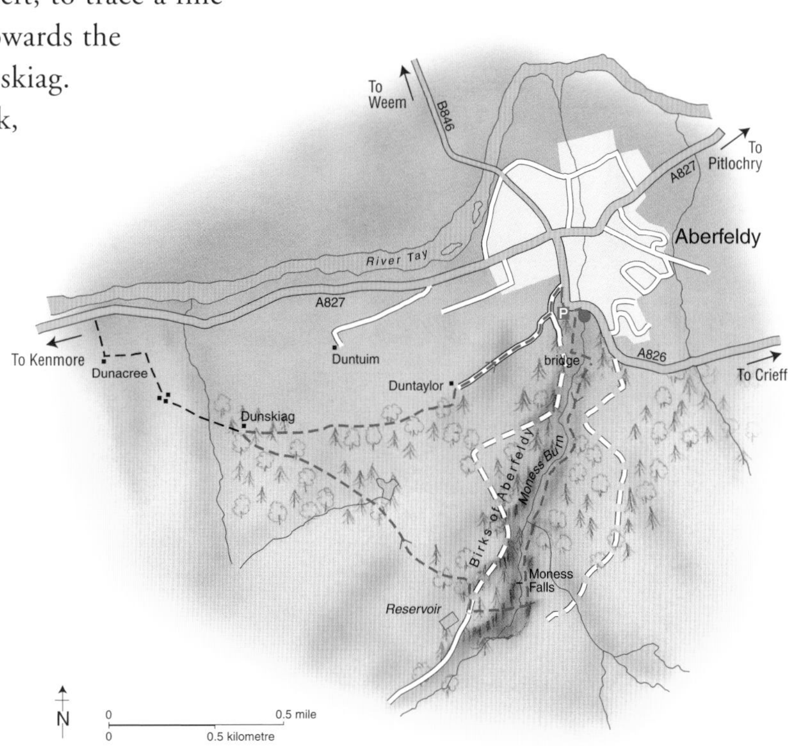

32 Pitlochry's Lochs and Rivers

Route Summary

Leave the car park near the dam and follow the signposted path along the E shore of Loch Faskally. Continue past Faskally House, to the E bank of the River Garry. Continue N to pass under the bridge which carries the B8019 road and in a further 400m cross the river by a footbridge. An optional extension of about 2km each way from here takes you to Killiecrankie.

After crossing the Garry, turn left and walk back under the road bridge, continuing to the confluence of the Garry and the Tummel. Follow the N bank of the Tummel to cross the Coronation Bridge. The route then joins a road to swing away from the loch for a short while, returning to it just past Clunie Power Station.

Water and trees make an irresistible combination, especially when the remnants of autumn's glorious colours are still hanging from the branches. Throw in a dash of history, a good path and the yellows and golds reflected on still waters and you have an ideal walk for a short winter's day, or a day when the high tops are hidden by seasonal mists.

The route begins at a car park near the Faskally dam where there is a visitor centre which explains how hydro-electric power works, and a fish ladder, created to provide safe passage for salmon and trout returning upriver to spawn. Despite its natural appearance,

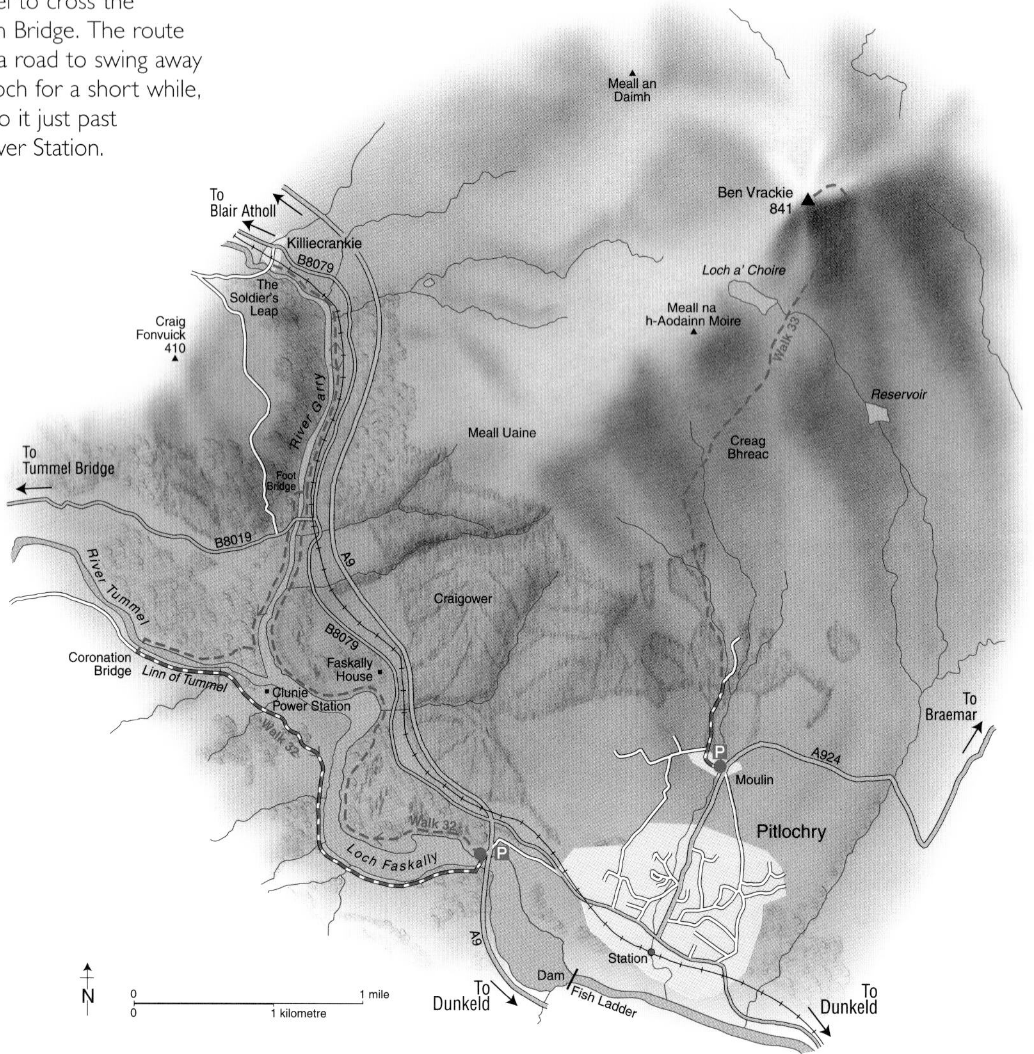

Loch Faskally isn't a natural loch, having been created as part of a huge hydro-electric scheme about 40 years ago. The surrounding area is very well wooded, with fine deciduous plantations which are a joy in autumn and early winter.

Start and finish the walk in Pitlochry, a busy place in summer and all the better for the quieter winter season. Begin at the car park nearest the dam, or alternatively, you could start from the railway station – this is an ideal walk to enjoy between trains.

Follow the signposted path along the east shore of Loch Faskally and continue past the grounds of Faskally House, a mansion which was, until recently, used as an outdoor centre by Strathclyde Region. A couple of hundred metres further on you'll reach the shores of the River Garry, one of two fine rivers feeding Loch Faskally. Pass under the high bridge which carries the B8019 road and in a further 400m cross the river by an attractive footbridge.

The River Garry at Killiecrankie

An optional extension to the walk of about 2km each way takes you to Killiecrankie, where there is a National Trust for Scotland visitor centre. In July 1689 this was the scene of a famous victory for the Jacobite forces under the leadership of John Graham of Claverhouse, known as Bonnie Dundee, who, despite his success, was killed in the battle.

After crossing the Garry, turn left and walk back under the road bridge, continuing to swing right alongside the Tummel, Faskally's other river, and passing the Linn of Tummel, a fine series of waterfalls which crash and thunder over a series of rock steps. This is one of the best sections of the route, a good spot to linger.

Descend here to cross the loch by a footbridge and rejoin the outward route back to Pitlochry.

Map: OS sheets 52 and 53

Access Point: Pitlochry dam car park

Distance: 10km or 14km with the extension to Killiecrankie.

Approx Time: 3-5 hours

Grade: Moderate low-level walk

Further upstream the river is crossed by the Coronation Bridge and the route joins a tarmac road to swing away from the loch for a short while, returning to it just past Clunie Power Station.

Descend here to cross the loch by a footbridge and rejoin the outward route back to Pitlochry. This walk straddles two 1:50000 Ordnance Survey maps, but the path is clear all the way round.

33 Ben Vrackie – Pitlochry's Speckled Hill

Route Summary

From the car park walk through the woodland to a gate (see map on page 80). Go through the gate onto open moorland and follow a path to the col between Creag Bhreac and Meall na h-Aodainn Moire. Cross the col to the dam at the E end of Loch a' Choire and follow the path steeply to the summit ridge. Bear left to the summit. Return the same way.

Map: OS Sheets 43 and 52

Access Point: Car park in Moulin

Distance: About 8km

Approx Time: 3-5 hours

Grade: Easy hill walk

Translation: speckled hill

Pronunciation: byn vraackie

Dominating the Perthshire town of Pitlochry, Ben Vrackie is a little hill of immense character and on a clear day it is one of the finest viewpoints in this part of the world. A view indicator on the summit helps you identify the innumerable hills and mountains that spread out in all directions. The usual starting point for the walk is a car park in the lovely little village of Moulin, about 3km north-east of Pitlochry on the A924 Braemar road.

The name Ben Vrackie is perhaps an acknowledgement of the geological mish-mash of rocks making up the hill. It's a corruption of the Gaelic 'Bhreac', which means speckled, or dappled.

Leave the car park and follow the signposted path through mixed woodland to a gate which gives access to open moorland. Continue on a path which crosses the moor northwards. Beyond the initial wood, a bench has been sited to give walkers a little rest. It's a memorial to Terence Toole, a member of the Royal Australian Air Force, who was killed in a car crash in Australia aged 25. His family came from Perth and had the bench placed on the slopes of Ben Vrackie, a favourite walk of theirs.

Beyond, the path rises to an obvious col between Creag Bhreac and Meall na h-Aodainn Moire. Continue over the shallow col and cross the dam at the eastern end of Loch a' Choire. From here tackle the eroded path which climbs the steep slopes just east of Ben Vrackie's south-west crags. Reach the summit ridge, and bear left for the final few metres to the summit cairn, trig point and direction indicator. This view indicator was built as a memorial to the Leys School in Cambridge, whose pupils were evacuated to Pitlochry during the Second World War. Among the mountains on show are the triple-peaked Beinn a' Ghlo, the unmistakable cone of Schiehallion and a superb view down the great trench of the Tummel and the Tay to Dunkeld and the southern hills beyond. Return to Moulin by the same route.

34 Driesh and Mayar – The Celestial Twins of Angus

The lovely Angus glens of Glen Clova and Glen Doll are heavily coniferised which inevitably means that there is often some confusion over forestry tracks and footpaths. Old traditional routes which lead to the open hillside become covered in trees and new routes, with mundane names given by Forest Enterprise like Waterfalls Walk or Riverside Walk, take snaking routes through the trees using mainly forest roads and drives. Few of them actually lead anywhere.

The most popular hills in this area are Driesh, 947m, and Mayar, 928m, the celestial twins of the Angus glens. The most popular route to the summit of Driesh climbs for a distance up through the Glendoll Forest, following the old Kilbo hill path which runs over the wide bealach between the two hills and down into Glen Isla. My last visit to these hills was on a morning when the mist was well down and my first task was to wade through the signposts and decipher which modern forestry path represented the Kilbo route. I even asked the farmer's wife but she wasn't sure either so I used that age-old technique which works most of the time – I guessed!

I suppose you could call it an educated guess. It had been 20 years since I had been on these hills so memory wasn't a great help, but I could see from the map roughly where the route went. Despite the fact that my old Ordnance Survey map was well out of date I could roughly trace where the route should go, a difficult task when all the trees look very much the same and one track looks like another.

Once across the White Water a forest track runs roughly west for a distance to where a rather rough-looking path climbs steeply through the trees – I couldn't imagine the Forestry Commission building a new path at such an angle, and within an hour, deep in the shadow of dense conifers, an ancient wooden signpost signalled

Route Summary

Walk NW from the car park, cross the bridge over the river and continue W on the forest road to where the Kilbo path turns off to the SW. Follow this old path and eventually leave the forest at a deer fence and follow the track above the Shank of Drumfollow to the high col between Driesh and Mayar. Climb the slopes due E to the summit of Driesh. Return to the col and follow a fence W to Mayar. Descend to the N, drop down into Corrie Fee and find the path which returns to Glen Doll and the YH.

Map: OS Sheet 44

Access Point: Forest Enterprise car park at GR283762

Distance: 14km

Approx Time: 5-7 hours

Grade: Moderate hill walk

Translation: From Gaelic dris meaning bramble or thorn bush; from m' aighear, my delight, or from magh, a plain

Pronunciation: dreesh; may-yer

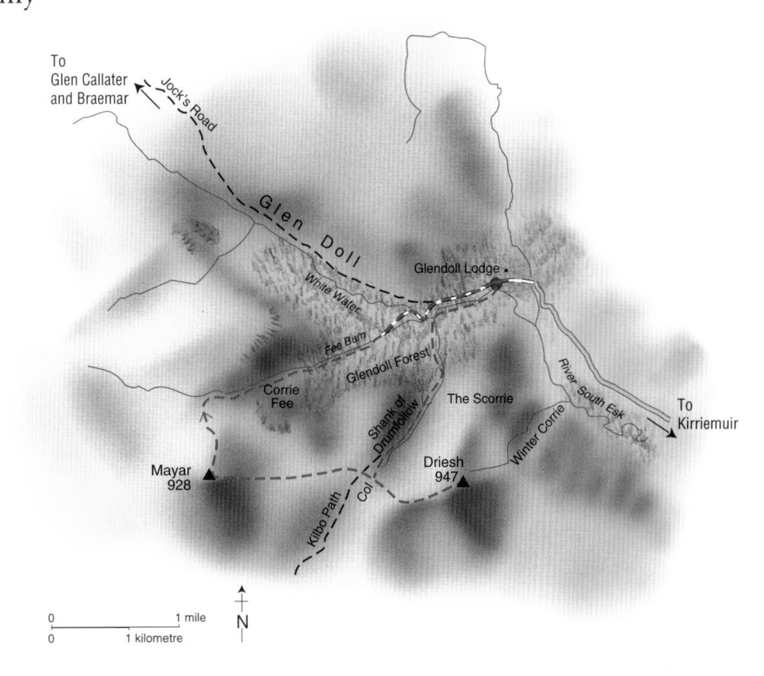

The Scorrie, Glen Doll, and Glen Clova

some success – The Kilbo Path to Glen Isla. I was on my way.

Shortly afterwards the path leaves the forest at a deer fence and rises uphill above the deep Shank of Drumfollow, to the high col between Driesh and Mayar, where Driesh is easily reached in about 1.5km of easy walking. Mayar is reached by returning to the col and following an old fence west over grassy slopes. From the summit, steepening slopes drop away northwards to the head of Corrie Fee where a steep section to the south-east of the burn leads you down past some waterfalls to a footpath, which continues to follow the Fee Burn into the forest. The footpath becomes a forestry road leading all the way back to Glen Doll past the youth hostel.

The next time I visit Driesh and Mayar I'll probably use another route, an alternative ascent, which is steeper but does have the advantage of cutting out a bit of forestry walking. This route climbs The Scorrie, a bold prow which climbs steeply up the west side of Winter Corrie, known locally as Corrie Winter! Cross the White Water by the bridge at Acharn, just east of the youth hostel, follow the forestry fence for a short distance and then climb the obvious steep ridge. At the top of the Scorrie you're well rewarded for your efforts by superb views into the cliffs of Corrie Winter, the redeeming feature of what is otherwise a rather dull hill. From the top of Corrie Winter it's an easy walk to the summit of Driesh.

35 Dark Lochnagar

There are a number of routes to the summit of Lochnagar, and many would suggest the finest approach is from the Invercauld bridge through the Ballochbuie Forest, the oldest stand of Ancient Caledonian pines in Scotland, and The Stuic. Some prefer the route from the north via the estate cottage at Gelder Shiel, while the most popular, and the most eroded, is from the Spittal of Glenmuick at the end of the public road which runs up Glen Muick from Ballater. My own favoured route takes the footpath from Glen Callater via the stalker's path up Carn an t-Sagairt Mor. This is a much longer route, but I think it gives a better sense of the vastness of the great plateaux that run south from Lochnagar towards the Glenshee hills. Lochnagar is seen then as part of a much greater whole, rather than a single isolated hill.

Just south of Braemar, Glen Callater slashes its way into the vast Lochnagar/Glenshee plateau, a high and lonely place, the haunt of red deer, ptarmigan and golden plover. Lower Glen Callater is popular with walkers content with a low-level wander up to Loch Callater, seeking perhaps just a taste of the wildness beyond. For the more adventurous, a bulldozed track runs up onto the Carn an Tuirc plateau from where the splendour of the area is well represented by the view into the depths of Coire Loch Kander.

Route Summary

There is a prominent layby at Auchallater on the A93, 3km S of Braemar. A Scottish Rights of Way Society sign points the direction and a track leads through a gate above the waters of the Callater Burn. Continue on the track as it bends S into the hemmed-in glen and after some distance you'll cross the burn by a bridge, with the slopes of Creag Phadruig rising ahead of you. After 5km, just before the Lodge and the loch, a footpath leaves the track and climbs NE above the loch before bending SE at about 500m. Follow this path as it bends again below Creag an Loch and then around the flanks of Carn an t-Sagairt Mor. Cross the infant waters of the Allt an Dubh-loch before climbing onto the slopes of the White Mounth between The Stuic and Carn a' Choire Bhaidheach. Finally, the path climbs towards Cac Carn Mor of Lochnagar before dipping slightly to the final slopes which lead to the great granite tor of Cac Carn Beag and the summit. Return the same way.

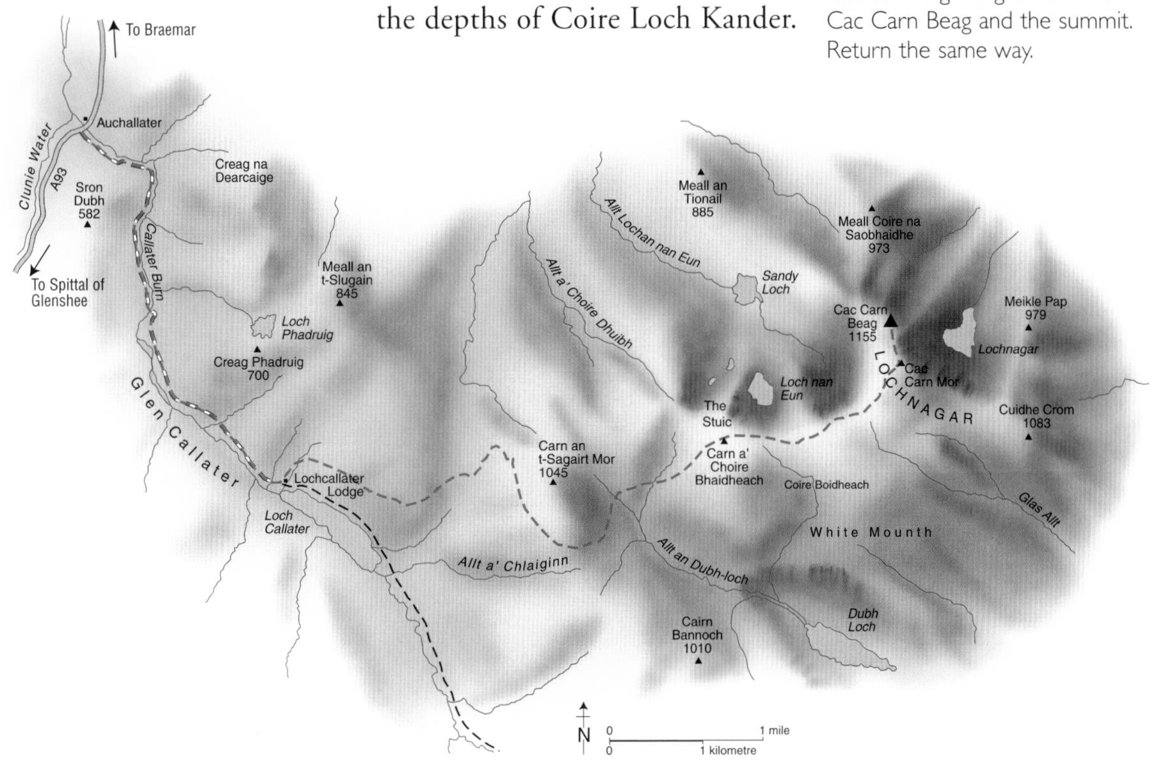

Map: OS Sheets 43 and 44
Access Point: Auchallater on the A93
Distance: 30km
Approx Time: 8-10 hours
Grade: Strenuous hill walk
Translation: named after Lochan na Gaire in the mountain's NE corrie, meaning little loch of the noisy sound
Pronunciation: loch-na-gaar

The name Callater comes from Caladair, which means hard water. The loch itself is just less than 1.5km long and has an average depth of about 3m although it does become deeper in some parts. It is a well-known loch for pike. Glen Callater was at one time known as the 'miracle glen', following the deeds of a local clergyman who was known as Patrick, or Peter, the Priest. Half-way down the glen, on the east side, there is a hill called Craig Phadruig, Patrick's Crag, and behind it Loch Phadruig. To the north-east of Loch Callater lies Carn an t-Sagairt Mor, the big hill of the priest. The story goes that the whole Braemar area was suffering from intensely cold weather. Eventually a holy well near Callater Lodge froze up, leaving the people without any water at all. Peter the Priest was summoned and his prayers were miraculously answered. As he knelt before the holy well the frost began to loosen its grip and a thaw set in. A large stone commemorates the site of Peter's Well, close to Lochcallater Lodge at the north-west end of the loch.

The footpath which leads to Lochnagar leaves the western end of Loch Callater to climb high above the waters before taking a rather circuitous route around the stony flanks of Carn an t-Sagairt Mor. These high Arctic slopes give a wonderful sense of spaciousness, with the ground gradually falling away eastwards into the great trench that holds the Dubh Loch. Crossing the burn of the Allt an Dubh-Loch, the path begins to climb onto the broad plateau of the White Mounth, the highest point of which, Carn a' Choire Bhaidheach, 1110m, lies just a short climb south of the path. It is worthwhile diverting for a short distance to The Stuic, where there is a superb view down into Coire Loch nan Eun.

From the high point of the path, between The Stuic and Carn a' Choire Bhoidheach, this grand high-level promenade drops slightly, skirting the fringes of Coire Loch nan Eun before finally climbing north-east to Cac Carn Mor of Lochnagar and then north to the summit, Cac Carn Beag. Close by is a view indicator, built by the Cairngorm Club in 1924. On a clear day the high ground of Caithness in the north and the Cheviots in the south can be seen.

Before returning, take a look down from the cliffs that fringe the great north-east-facing corrie of Lochnagar. One of the great corries of the Cairngorms, it offers a contrast to the high-level slopes you've been walking and gives meaning to Lord Byron's description of the steep, frowning glories of Dark Lochnagar.

Lochnagar and Creag na Dearcaige from the west

Route Summary
Leave the Bennachie Centre following the Gordon Way waymarked route. Turn left at the bench seat and climb up through the forest staying right at the next crossroads. Leave the forest. On open moorland, continue to the Mither Tap. Descend to the N through a gap in the wall and continue over the moor, over the Rushmill Burn and onto the Maiden's Causeway. Follow this route down to the Aberdeen Turnpike Road, which is then followed S to where the main track turns left. Keep straight on. At the next junction follow the path back to the Centre.

Map: OS Sheet 38

Access Point: The Bennachie Centre near Chapel of Garioch

Distance: 9km

Approx Time: 3-4 hours

Grade: Easy hill walk

36 Bennachie – Aberdeen's Hill

It is, without equal, Aberdeenshire's hill. The name probably comes from Beinn Chioch, or 'the hill of the pap', from the prominent tors which make the summits look like female breasts. Bennachie rises to a height of some 500m, high enough to give it an independence over the lowly hills of this predominantly farming area.

Although I'm not Aberdonian, I did live in the Granite City for a number of years and I visited Bennachie regularly. I would stride out through the forest and onto the heather slopes, making for the Oxen Craig or the great mass of granite and Iron Age fort which crowns the Mither Tap, the summit of the hill.

From the relatively new Bennachie Centre a good path runs up through the forest and onto open moorland, with the Mither Tap prominent on the horizon. This area was once considered 'free land' but in 1859 local landowners decided to divide it up amongst themselves, an act which became known as the Theft of Bennachie.

The views from the summit are extensive, and there is a direction indicator pointing out the prominent landmarks. Descend northwards, through a gap in the ancient wall of the Iron-Age fort and across the moor. Once over the Rushmill Burn the path bears to the right, passing Hosie's Well, before following the course of the Maiden Causeway down to Farquharson Wood. Legend has it that Hosie's Well dates back to 1411 when a local man, taken captive at the Battle of Harlaw, returned to find his sweetheart betrothed to someone else. He died at this spot of a broken heart and the waters of the well are his tears!

Once through the Farquharson Wood turn right onto the old Aberdeen Turnpike Road which once continued to Inverness. Pass behind the Pittodrie House Hotel and continue on the Turnpike Road to where the main track turns left. At this point go straight ahead down a path lined by birches and rowans and at the next junction turn left to return to the Centre.

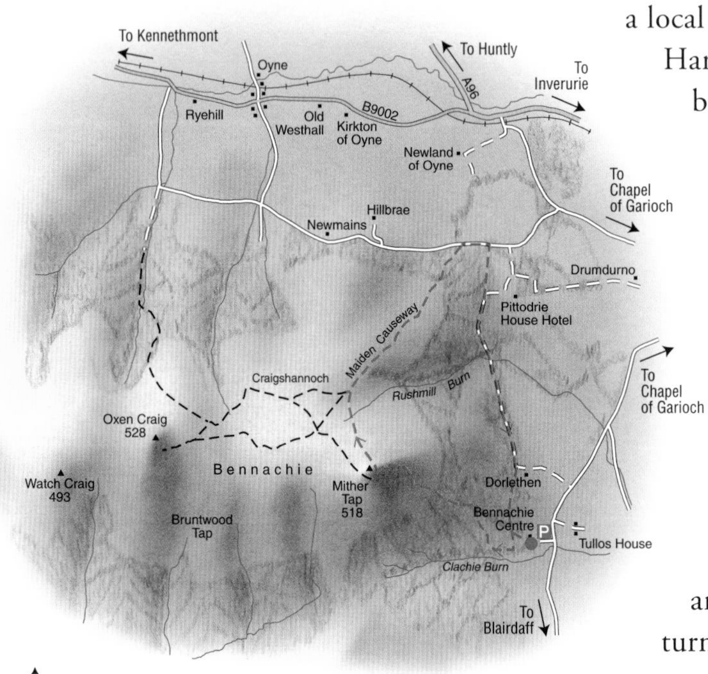

37 A Coastal Walk to Findlater Castle

Route Summary

From the car park E of Cullen harbour follow the road E towards the cliffs. Climb gradually and cross a headland into the next bay before following a grassy track past a bothy. Cross the bay towards Logie Head. Here the path turns a corner into a cove and descends suddenly before climbing steps up to the next headland. Cross the next bay by a track then climb up over some grass to pass through a natural defile in the rocks into Sunnyside Bay. Pass through a bracken-covered area to reach the sandy bay beyond. Follow the path round the bay, note the railway sleeper bridged across a small stream, a point of reference for the return route. Go through a gap in a fence and climb towards the top of the cliffs. Here, the path turns left and crosses a grassy headland to the top of the cove and Findlater Castle. Return to Cullen by the outward route to the railway sleeper bridge. Take the footpath to the left to the top of the cliffs and an old kissing gate.

Findlater Castle, perched dramatically on its sea-pounded cliff, is the destination of this walk, a coastal route which hugs the cliff-line east of the Banffshire village of Cullen. A fine path follows the shore east of Cullen Harbour and skirts a number of golden sandy bays each separated by craggy, rocky headlands. Rafts of eider ducks croon from the rocky coves and overhead seabirds wheel and dive constantly. An ideal summer outing for the whole family.

The ruins of Findlater Castle are well worth a visit, although great care should be taken if you decide to go into any of the remaining vaults. Sloping, sandy floors become very slippery when wet and the windows open out onto big drops to the sea below. The castle's position is a stunning one, clinging to its cliffside perch and it must have been an imposing and impregnable stronghold in its heyday. The castle was built in 1455 by Sir Walter Ogilvie of Auchlevin although the location has been the site of a fortification since the thirteenth century.

Leave the car park immediately east of Cullen Harbour and follow the tarmac road eastwards towards the cliffs. Pass the animal cemetery on your right and continue on a rough path with a rocky foreshore on your left and a gorse-covered hillside on the right. Soon the path climbs gradually and crosses a sharp headland to drop into the next bay before following a grassy track past an old salmon-fishers' bothy. Once across the bay the path hugs the foot of the seabird-infested cliffs as it climbs towards Logie Head. At the headland the path turns a corner into a small secluded cove and descends suddenly before climbing a series of stone steps up to the next headland.

At the bottom of the steps on the other side there is a memorial cairn built by the people of Cullen to Tony

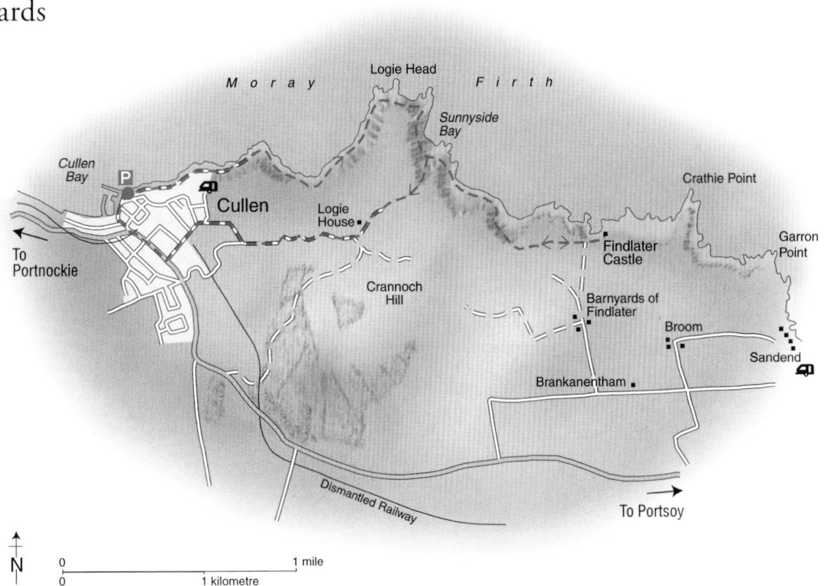

Cullen Bay from Logie Head, North-East Coast

Go through the gate, turn left along the edge of the field to the ruins of Logie House where a metal gate leads you onto a track. Follow this track back into Cullen.

Map: OS Sheet 29

Access Point: Cullen harbour

Distance: About 8km

Approx Time: 3-4 hours

Grade: Easy coastal walk

Hetherington, who re-built them single-handed.

Cross the next bay by a sandy track and at its far end climb up over some grass to pass through a natural defile in the rocks which leads into the broad Sunnyside Bay. At the far side of the bay you can glimpse the gaunt ruins of Findlater Castle. Pass through a large bracken covered area to reach the sandy bay beyond. Follow the path round the bay taking note of a railway sleeper bridged across a small stream. This is a point of reference for the return route. Go through a gap in an old fence and climb up towards the top of the cliffs. Here, the path turns left and crosses a grassy headland to the top of the cove which provides the setting for Findlater Castle. An interpretative sign gives the history of the ruins and a narrow footpath runs down to the castle.

To return to Cullen follow the outward route as far as the railway sleeper bridge at the far end of Sunnyside Bay. Here, a footpath bears left and climbs to the top of the cliffs to an old kissing gate. Go through the gate, turn left and follow the edge of the field to the ruins of Logie House where a metal gate leads you onto a track. Follow this track, past the caravan site, and back into Cullen.

38 Ben Rinnes – The Whisky Hill

Rising boldly above the Laich of Moray, Ben Rinnes climbs to a height of 840m and offers a magnificent viewpoint across the Moray Firth to the mountains of Ross, Sutherland and Caithness. A track, then a footpath runs all the way to the quaintly named summit, the Scurran of Lochterlandoch, and offers a glorious afternoon's walk, the comparative ease of which is out of all proportion to the mountain's height.

The name of the hill comes from the Gaelic Beinn Rinneis, which possibly means headland hill. It's a well-formed hill with a grand conical shape, its slopes easing themselves gradually down to the waters of the River Spey on its north side and considerably more steeply on its southern side. Lying just a few kilometres south-west of Dufftown, Ben Rinnes lies in the heart of whisky country and from its summit you can spot more distilleries than from any other mountain in the country, names which stir the blood of any whisky connoisseur – Balvenie, Glenfarclas, Glenlivet, the Morlach, Knockando, Glenfiddich, Cardhu and many other small distilleries, the life blood of the whole area. As you enjoy a draught of cool water from a hill burn high on Ben Rinnes and see the smoke from the distilleries at the foot of the hills, it's easy to consider Ben Rinnes as providing the very essence of this uisge bheatha, the water of life. It's a nice thought. Here and there on Ben Rinnes you'll come across areas where peat digging, to fire the distilleries, has removed large patches from the hillside.

It's a straightforward walk to the summit. Take the B909 south-west from Dufftown to Glen Rinnes for about 5km to its junction with the road to Milltown of Edinvillie. This road rises to squeeze through the narrow Glack Harness between Ben Rinnes and Meikle Conval and close to the top of the hill you'll see a sign indicating the path to Ben Rinnes beside a layby. Park here, being careful not to obstruct

Route Summary

Leave the parking space and follow the zigzagging bulldozed track which climbs steadily up and over Round Hill. The track continues to Roy's Hill where it changes into a clear footpath which climbs steadily to the broad summit slopes. The summit trig point is situated on top of the prominent granite tor. If you can arrange transport, a complete traverse of Ben Rinnes is possible, continuing W from the summit down the lengh of the Lynderiach Burn to Bridge of Avon. Alternatively, descend in a SW direction to the Hill of Knockashalg before dropping down SE to Wester Clashmarloch in Glen Rinnes and a road walk back to Glack Harness.

Map: OS Sheet 28

Access Point: Car park near the Glack Harness on the Milltown of Edinvillie road

Distance: About 9.5km

Approx Time: 3-5 hours

Grade: Easy hill walk

Translation: headland hill

Pronunciation: byn rin-ess

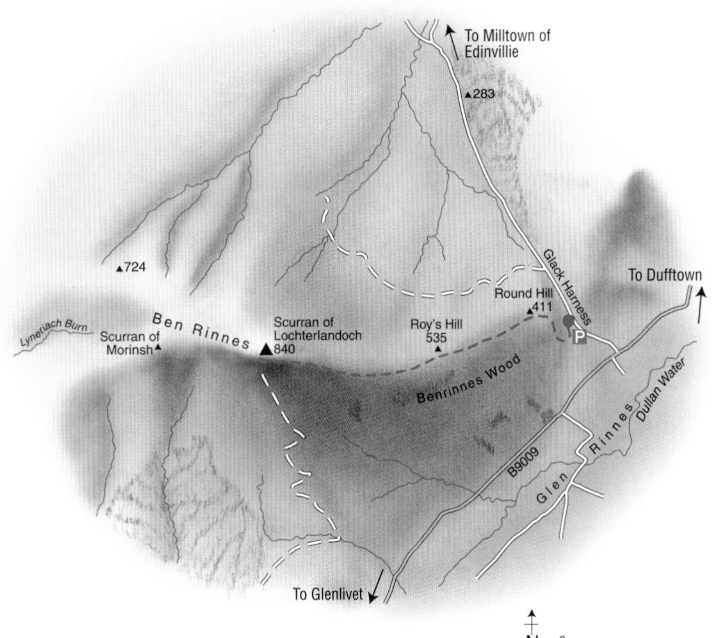

Glen Rinnes from Ben Rinnes with Lochnagar in the distance

the gate, and follow the zigzagging bulldozed track which climbs steadily up and over Round Hill. Beyond this wet and boggy plateau the track continues to Roy's Hill where it dissolves into a clear footpath which, in turn, climbs steadily through wide areas of wet peat before climbing up over a stony surface to the broad summit slopes. The summit trig point is situated on top of the prominent granite tor. If you can arrange transport, a complete traverse of Ben Rinnes is well worthwhile, continuing west from the summit down the length of the Lynderiach Burn to Bridge of Avon. Alternatively, descend in a south-west direction to the Hill of Knockashalg before dropping down south-eastwards to Wester Clashmarloch in Glen Rinnes and a quiet road walk back to Glack Harness.

39 The Abernethy Forest

The Abernethy Forest is a remnant of the old Caledonian pine forest and is believed to be the largest tract of natural pine forest in Britain. It is a superb place for wildlife and is now owned by the Royal Society for the Protection of Birds who have done a sterling job in removing the many kilometres of deer fencing that once littered this whole area. Arguing that many species of birds crash into these fences by mistake, with a high death toll, they have tackled the problem of deer browsing the young pine trees by simply culling the deer, a logical and sensible solution which seems beyond many privately owned estates, who seem to encourage deer numbers, despite the damage they do to trees, shrubs and vegetation.

In spring and summer the heather moorland beyond the forest is alive with the sounds of skylarks, meadow-pipits, wheatears and whinchats. The lochans of the moor are good places to see dunlin, redshank and snipe, while the pine forest itself gives the opportunity to spot crested tits, crossbills and possibly capercaille. This combination of high moorland and pine forest is enhanced even further by its backdrop of high mountains, a corner of the Cairngorms which is probably at its best in the autumn when the sounds of rutting deer echo across the empty lands.

Only a few kilometres from Aviemore, just off the Cairngorm ski road, is Glenmore Lodge, the National Mountaineering Centre. It is open to the public, and its bar makes a welcome place for refreshment after this long walk. Just beyond the Lodge is a public car parking area and from here an excellent track leads onto the Abernethy moors and forest all the way to the RSPB-owned Forest Lodge, and back again via Ryvoan Bothy.

Leave the parking area and follow the wide forestry track for about 400m to where it crosses a stream. Continue on the main path past An Lochan Uaine, noted for its translucent green colour. Legend claims this is where the fairy folk of Glenmore wash their clothes. About 800m beyond the lochan, the path divides.

Take the right fork and continue on this path to the old bothy known as Bynack Stables. Cross the river, the Nethy, by the footbridge, and continue uphill for about 400m. A faint track now merges from the left. This is the old public right of way from Forest Lodge bridge. Follow the path, initially downhill and over fairly open heather moorland. Cross two burns and enter the pine forest. The track continues downhill and eventually joins the river. After 6.5km it reaches the bridge at Forest Lodge.

Cross the bridge and turn left. (The track to the right goes to the village of Nethy Bridge). Pass the cottage and outbuildings of Forest Lodge to where the motor road bears right. At this point a rough road continues uphill through the trees. Follow the track uphill, skirting the eastern edge of Cairn Rynettin and onto more open moorland. After about 1.5km Ryvoan Bothy comes into sight. From the bothy the track drops downhill to return to Glenmore Lodge past Lochan Uaine, the outward route.

Route Summary

Park at the end of the tarmac road just past Glenmore Lodge and follow the forestry track into the forest, past Lochan Uaine to a junction in the paths (see map on p95). Turn right and follow this track to Bynack Stables. Cross the footbridge over the Nethy and climb uphill on a muddy track for 400m to where a very faint and wet track merges in from the left. Follow this track, downhill and over two burns to enter the pine forest. Continue on this track downhill to join the river. After 6.5km cross a bridge and turn left to Forest Lodge where a motor road bears right. Follow a rough road uphill through the trees, past Cairn Rynettin and Ryvoan Bothy to meet the outward track of earlier.

Map: OS Sheet 36

Access Point: Glenmore Lodge

Distance: About 18km

Approx Time: 6-7 hours

Grade: Long low-level walk

Meall a' Bhuachaille and the Abernethy Forest from the north-east

40 Meall a' Bhuachaille – The Hill of the Shepherd

Route Summary

Leave the car parking area just beyond Glenmore Lodge and follow the broad track which runs through the forestry plantation. After 400m cross a bridge over a stream and continue below the S slopes of Meall a' Bhuachaille. Pass An Lochan Uaine with the gable end of Ryvoan Bothy etched on the far horizon. From the bothy climb the obvious footpath to the summit from where another good path runs down to the bealach between Meall a' Buachaille and Creagan Gorm. Turn left here and drop down into the Queen's Forest. Follow the forest track to the road at Glenmore.

It's a fact that you often get a better viewpoint from a small hill than from a larger one. Several miles from Aviemore, Glenmore's Meall a' Bhuachaille, the Hill of the Shepherd, isn't exactly diminutive, but compared to its near neighbours, the high tops of the Cairngorms, it's a dumpy wee thing.

Anywhere else Meall a' Bhuachaille's comparatively lowly elevation of 810m would be fairly significant, but although dwarfed by the Cairngorms, this rounded hill is magnificently positioned right up at the very head of Glenmore, forming one of the boundary walls of the beautiful Pass of Ryvoan. From its summit you can gaze down the full length of Glenmore into the heart of Badenoch, and all the way to the Laggan hills and beyond.

The walk begins and ends at Glenmore Lodge, the National Mountaineering Centre, and continues through the Pass of Ryvoan past An Lochan Uaine, the Green Lochan, so named because local legend has it that the fairy folk once washed their clothes in its waters! It certainly is a magical spot with the translucent green waters reflecting the grey scree of Creag nan Gall, the Hill of the Stranger, behind.

This Pass is the beginning of the old Rathad nam Meirlach, the

Caterans' Road, which ran from here to the glens of Lochaber. The western clans followed its quiet byways on cattle-raiding forays to and from the fertile lands of Morayshire, avoiding all the large centres of population in Badenoch.

From Ryvoan Bothy, a good footpath runs up through the heather to the summit of Meall a' Bhuachaille. It's a fairly hefty pull up to the summit cairn but well worth it for the view. Gaze down on the broad, ochre-coloured moors of Abernethy Forest and the broad sweep up to the sharply defined top of Bynack Mor and along Strathnethy to the high saddle which overlooks Loch Avon, that most secretive of Scottish lochs. Closer at hand is the enormous bulk of Cairngorm itself, and the scalloped hollows of its northern corries.

From the summit a broad, and often very muddy, path runs down to the bealach between Meall a' Buachaille and Creagan Gorm. Turn left here and drop down into the Queen's Forest for a pleasant walk back through the woods to Glenmore.

Map: OS Sheet 36
Access Point: Glenmore Lodge
Distance: 8km
Approx Time: 3-4 hours
Grade: Easy hill walk
Translation: hill of the shepherd
Pronunciation: myowl a vooachil

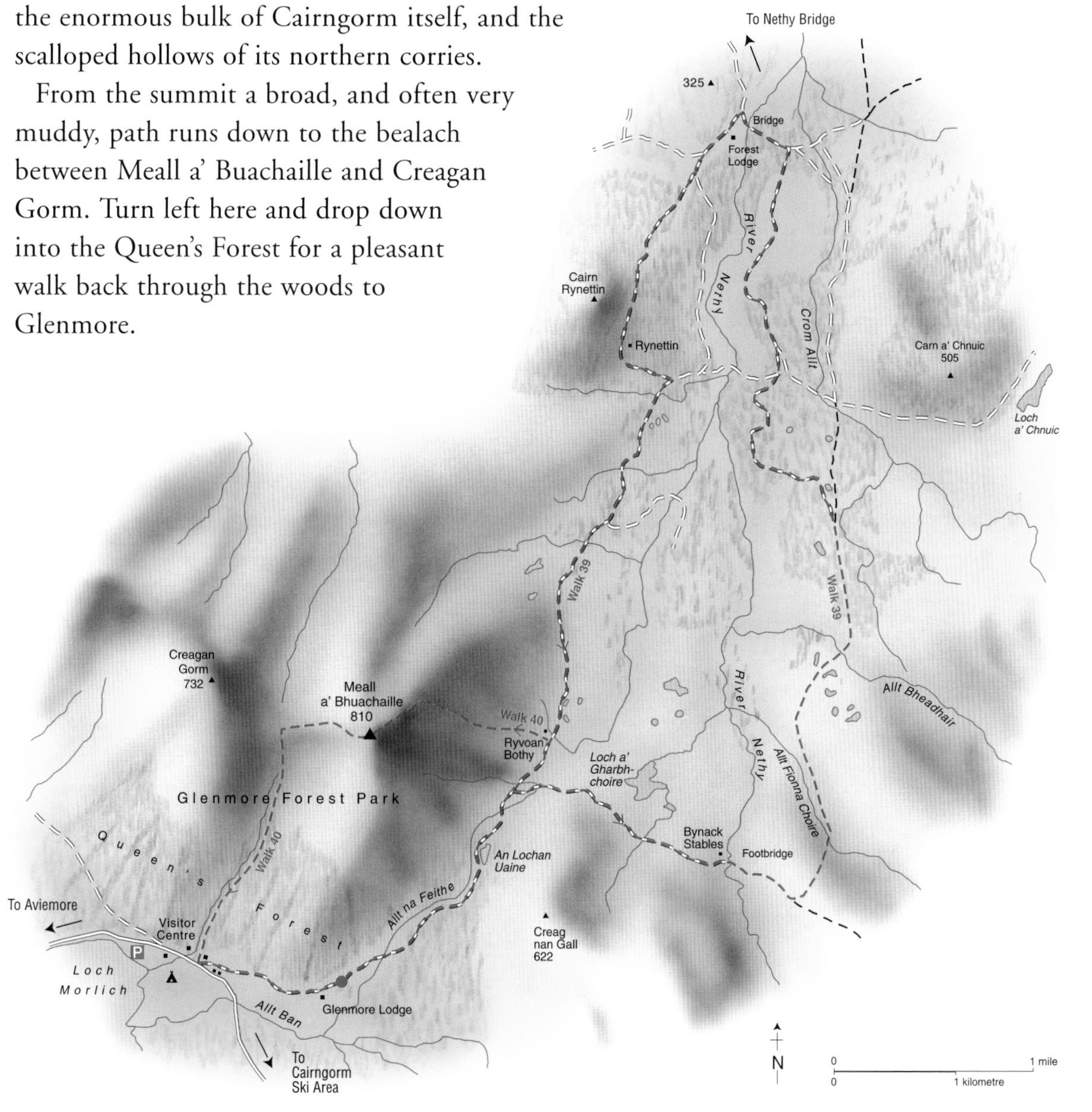

Route Summary

From the car park at the north end of Loch an Eilein, take the path to the visitor centre. Turn left just before the building and follow the loch-side trail around the loch.

Map: OS Sheet 36

Access Point: Loch an Eilein car park

Distance: About 5km

Approx Time: 2-3 hours

Grade: Moderate low-level walk

41 Around Loch an Eilein

Loch an Eilein, with its island castle, is one of the best-known and most loved beauty spots in the Highlands, and is arguably the most picturesque loch in Scotland. With its backdrop of heather-clad mountains, ancient pine forest and craggy skyline, it lies like a jewel amid the splendours of Rothiemurchus Forest, a priceless natural asset of ancient woodland which once offered a home to the likes of bears, wolves, lynx and great elk. Today, you can take a fine walk around its shores and enjoy the sounds and sights of less fearsome inhabitants – crossbills, crested tits, siskin, woodpeckers and buzzards.

Loch an Eilein's chief claim to fame is a castle which is built just off the north-western shore. This ancient keep dates from the fourteenth century and was once a stronghold of the powerful Norman family of Comyns, the Lords of Badenoch. It is also thought by some that the castle was once used by the infamous Wolf of Badenoch, Alexander Stewart, the bastard son of Robert II of Scotland, as a minor fortification mid-way between the grander Comyn strongholds of Ruthven and Lochindorb. Stewart gained his reputation, and his nickname, after burning down Elgin Cathedral, whose abbot had criticised him for having an affair. For his troubles, he was excommunicated from the Roman Catholic Church, until he eventually agreed to pay a penance, crawling on his knees through the town of Stirling, begging forgiveness.

Today the castle is a ruin, overgrown with ivy and birch scrub. It faces the north-western shore of the loch with a blank wall which contains one open door. There is a causeway out to the island, but this can only be seen in periods of severe drought, when the water level of the loch drops substantially. The ruins once gave a home to a pair of ospreys who built an eyrie on its walls, but constant harassment by egg collectors chased them away.

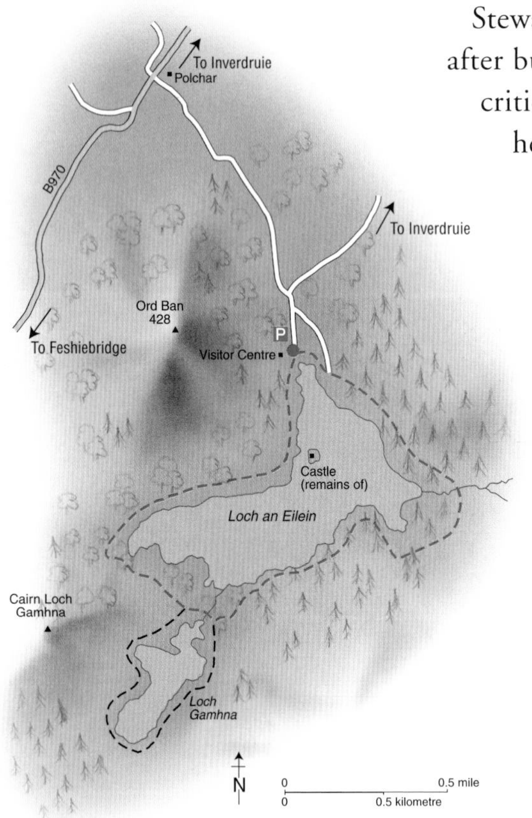

Loch an Eilein, Rothiemurchus

Much of the area around the loch is a remnant of the Ancient Forest of Caledon, the great pine forest which once covered much of the Highlands. But man soon realised that these vast forested areas not only gave shelter to wild beasts, but to vagabonds and outlaws too. Wood was also needed for building and charcoal smelting, and there appeared to be an infinite supply. The pines were felled and floated down the River Spey from Inverdruie. Many of those beasts which made their home in the forest soon became extinct, and the red deer, once a forest dweller, took to the hills.

The name of Rothiemurchus is thought by many to mean the plain of the forest, but a more likely origin comes from the Gaelic Rata-Mhurchuis, the Fort of Murchus. The identity of Murchus, like the Scottish bears, wolves and beavers, is lost in the mists of time.

There is a car park at the north end of Loch an Eilein, which offers easy access to a nature trail which encircles the loch for 5km, and an informative leaflet from the Rothiemurchus Estate Ranger Service in Inverdruie gives advice on a plethora of other good walks in the area.

Braeriach across Rothiemurchus from the north

Route Summary

Leave the car park, cross the road and follow the footpath over the Allt Mor bridge. Continue on this path to the Chalamain Gap, go through the gap and descend to the Lairig Ghru. Climb the hillside opposite by way of the obvious footpath and reach the Sron na Lairige ridge which is then followed S to the edge of Coire Ruadh. Here the ridge swings to the right to meet the E ridge of Braeriach. Follow this ridge to the edge of Coire Bhrochain and then follow the corrie lip to the summit. Follow the rim of An Garbh Choire over Sgor an Lochain Uaine to Cairn Toul.

42 Braeriach's High-Level Classic

In the 1997 revisions of *Munro's Tables*, Sgor an Lochain Uaine was graced with Munro status. This is a hill that will rarely be climbed on its own – its position, high above the magnificent glacially scoured bowl that holds its eponymous lochan, is on the course of the finest high-level hill walk in the country, from Glenmore to Braeriach via the Chalamain Gap, around the rim of the An Garbh Choire, to Cairn Toul and back over the summit of the Lairig Ghru. Sgor an Lochain Uaine lies about a kilometre west-north-west of Cairn Toul and its new elevation to Munro status will be a sickener to all those who have formed a wee path on its southern flanks to bypass its peak. The modicum of energy saved then will be used up later, with interest. It's a great excuse for another day out though!

Braeriach is, of course, the Brindled Upland, and it's an airy place, essentially the joint apex of five corries. Stand by the summit cairn on a clear day and gaze down the long, empty stretch of Glen Dee, past the bulk of Ben Macdui and the long arm of Carn a'

Mhaim on one side and the angular outline of Cairn Toul on the other, and you'll be overwhelmed by a sensation of space and distance, an emotion that wills you to fly. Launch yourself instead around the rim of this enormous corrie that fills the space at your feet, An Garbh Choire, the big, rough corrie – a simple enough name and yet one which manages to evoke all the wildness, barrenness and wilderness of this corrie.

Follow the rim, with gentle boulder-covered slopes easing off to your right, in contrast to the great cliffs of red granite thrust up out of the rough corrie below you. Pinnacles, buttresses, spires and snow wreaths circle these upper tiers until late in summer. You cross the infant Dee here – this great inanimate mound of rock and gravel, scree and moss, its unlikely birthplace here on the roof of Scotland. Some 800m later its voice changes, a forced maturity, as it crashes and surges over the lip of the corrie, to begin its long meandering course to the North Sea at Aberdeen.

With the bouldery swells of Einich Cairn and Carn na Criche suggesting some mild security on your right, stay close to the rim where you enjoy the wildness of the great chasm on your other side. Drop gradually to a col before Sgor an Lochain Uaine, then climb the easy slopes of the new Munro. I hope all the Munro stompers are gracious enough to credit this hill with its proper name, the peak of the little

Descend the N ridge of Cairn Toul to the mouth of An Garbh Choire, cross the moorland in a NE direction to the Lairig Ghru path which is then followed to the Chalamain Gap path. Follow this path back to the start.

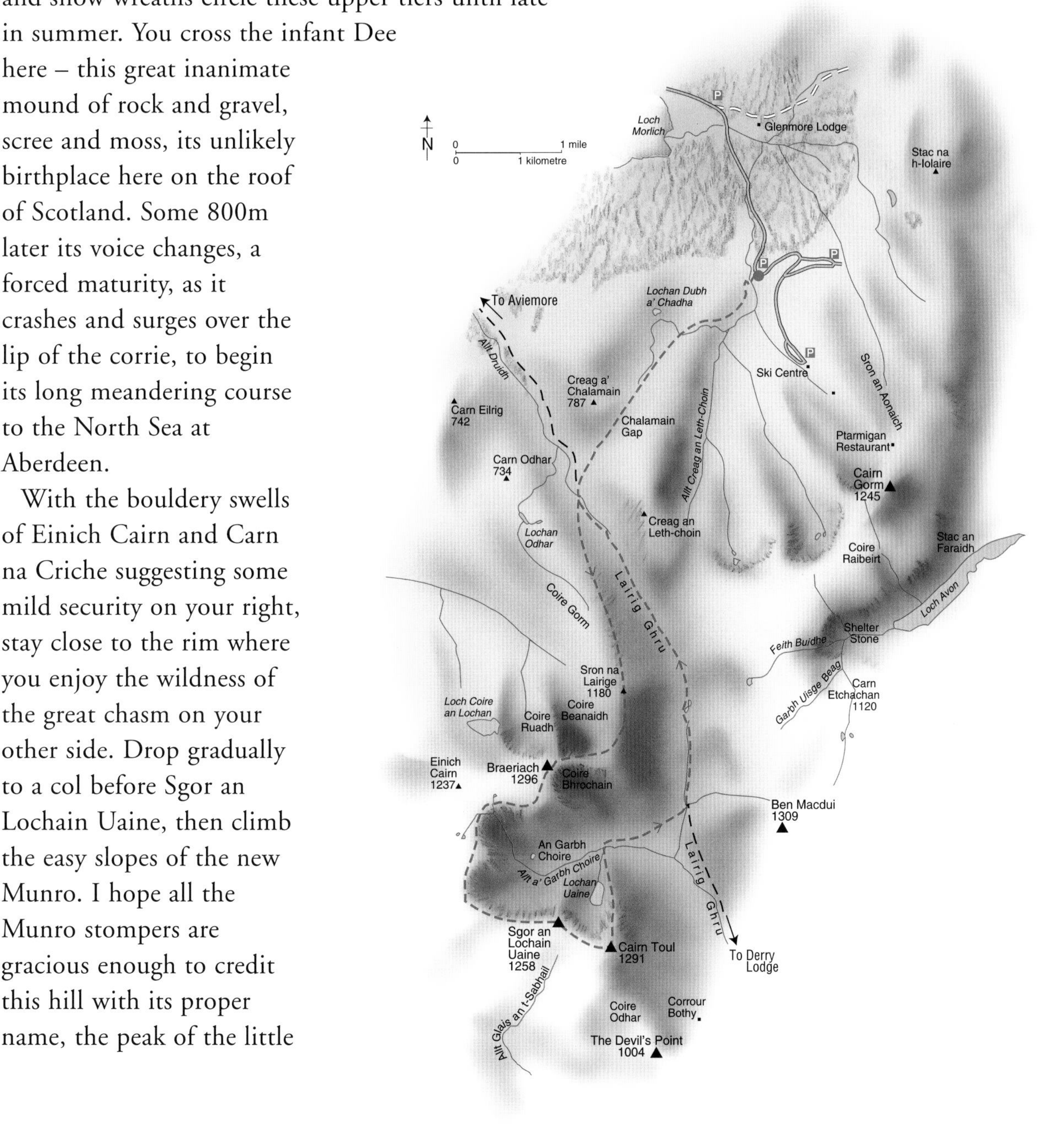

Map: OS Sheet 36
Access Point: Car park in Coire Cas of Cairngorm
Distance: 21km
Approx Time: 8-10 hours
Grade: Moderate hill walk
Translation: brindled upland
Pronunciation: brae-reeach

green loch, and learn to pronounce it properly – try skoor an lochyn oo-anya. Far too many people refer to this shapely hill as the Angel's Peak.

According to Peter Drummond's informative *Scottish Hill and Mountain Names* (Scottish Mountaineering Trust) the name Angel's Peak was devised by a Victorian gentleman, a Mr Copland, as a genteel counterweight to the nearby Devil's Point. The daft thing is that the Devil's Point is only a loose translation of the Gaelic Bod an Deamhain (try pot-in-john), which literally means the 'penis of the devil'. I can't be convinced that contemporary climbers and hill bashers are too sensitive to revert back to the Gaelic name. It's time the Ordnance Survey was firmly told that English translations are simply not good enough for Scottish hills.

Beyond Sgor an Lochain Uaine it's Cairn Toul, the hill of the barn, and a rocky scramble from the summit down into the lochan-side depths of the corrie it shares with Sgor an Lochain Uaine. A steeper descent drops you into the mouth of An Garbh Choire and a long walk, over the summit of the Lairig Ghru and through the Chalamain Gap, takes you back towards Glenmore. It is the finest high-level walk in Britain, and now with three Munros to its credit instead of two.

43 Ben Macdui from the South

Route Summary

Take the private road from Linn of Dee to Derry Lodge. Cross the Derry Burn by the bridge W of Derry Lodge. Follow the track to the Luibeg Burn, turn right and follow the burn to its confluence with the Allt Carn a' Mhaim. Cross the Luibeg Burn and climb the Sron Riach ridge to the cliff top above Coire Sputan Dearg. Head due W to the summit of Ben Macdui before returning to the corrie edge. Follow the path in a NE direction to the outflow of Loch Etchachan, descend the length of Choire Etchachan to Glen Derry, then walk S down the length of Glen Derry to Derry Lodge.

In reminding myself that this book is about favourite walks, not favourite mountains (the two don't always equate) I realise that I could probably describe up to half-a-dozen routes which all culminate on the Arctic dome of Ben MacDui, at 1309m, Britain's second-highest mountain. With its glaciated corries and passes, high remote lochans, bare tundra slopes, and steep precipices, this isn't so much a testimony to the mountain itself as an affirmation of the grandeur and wonder of the central Cairngorms which it dominates.

And yet, even as I write the words, I'm aware that Ben Macdui doesn't so much dominate its surroundings, as merge with them into a single entity. Its summit is the high point of this incredible area we refer to as the central Cairngorms, which has the greatest area of land over 900m and over 1200m in Britain. The great stretch of upland tundra we refer to as the Cairngorm Plateau would be far better described as the Macdui Plateau. But there again, we fall into semantics – how much better it would have been if we had stuck with the old name for this whole range, the Monadh Ruadh, the red rounded hills, rather than name them after Cairngorm, which is after all only one of Macdui's outliers. (I always think of Carn a' Mhaim, Derry Cairngorm, Beinn Mheadhoin, Cairn Gorm and Creag an Leth-choin as Macdui's tops, rather than mountains in their own right.) Maybe we should have called them the Macdui Mountains?

Map: OS Sheets 36 and 43
Access Point: Linn of Dee
Distance: 30km
Approx Time: 8-10 hours
Grade: Moderate hill walk
Translation: hill of the black pig
Pronunciation: byn macdooee

If asked to choose a walk which illustrated all the finest features of the Cairngorms then I would have little hesitation in recommending this big horseshoe walk, a tour of the central massif of the Cairngorms, which heads north from Linn of Dee near Braemar, visits the pine-scented and deer-haunted Glen Luibeg, climbs the long Sron Riach shoulder of Macdui to its spacious summit, touches the edge of the crags and cliffs of Coire Sputan Dearg and visits the spectacular Arctic setting of Loch Etchachan, before heading off down the length of lovely Glen Derry. Aye, it's a big walk, about 30km with about 1500m of climbing, but that distance can be effectively reduced by using a mountain bike to carry you up the 6.5 bulldozed kilometres from Linn of Dee to Derry Lodge.

A track continues west from Derry Lodge, across the bridge over the Derry Burn, then around the lower slopes of Coire Craobh an Oir of Derry Cairngorm as far as the Luibeg Bridge. A well-used footpath runs north on the east bank of the Luibeg Burn. Already, the rounded dome of Ben Macdui is clear, high and almost aloof, but cut sharply and dramatically on its eastern

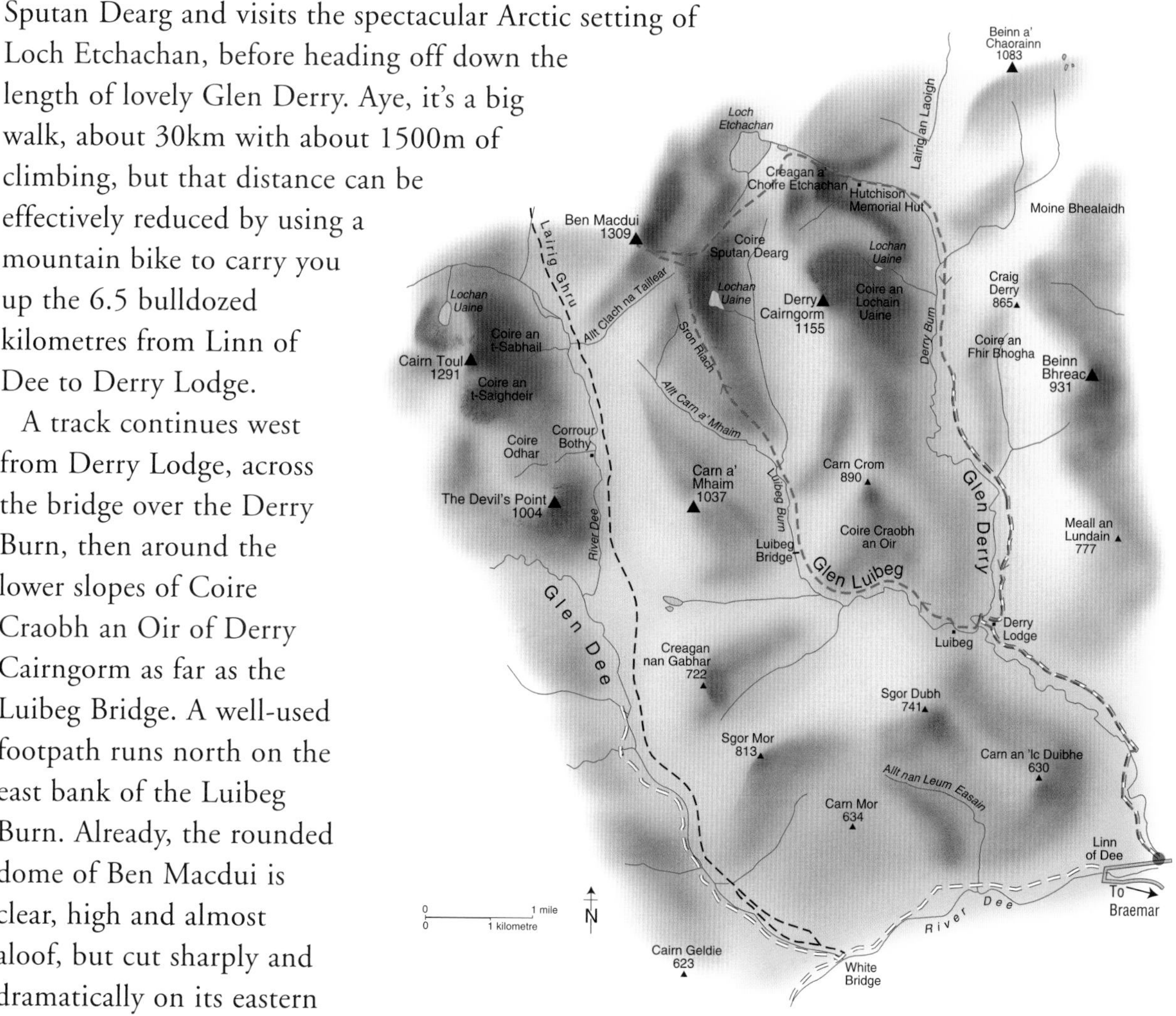

Derry Cairngorm and Loch Etchachan across Loch Avon from the north

edge by the cliff-girt cirque of Coire Sputan Dearg which cradles one of the Cairngorms' four Lochan Uaines (green lochans).

Just after an obvious fork in the burn (Allt Carn a' Mhaim joins from the left), cross the stream and climb the long nose of Sron Riach, the brindled nose, all the way to its conical peak. Follow the rim of the cliff now, with deep views down to Lochan Uaine, but before dropping down into Coire Etchachan turn sharply left and climb the long boulder-covered slopes westwards, past the ruins of the Sapper's Bothy (for many years the armed forces delighted in building stone shelters and huts all over these slopes).

From the summit cairn the views, on a clear day, are superb. Close by lies a view indicator which suggests you can see the Lammermuirs south of Edinburgh and, in the opposite direction, Morven in Caithness. To continue return due east to where a gravelly footpath descends from the Coire Sputan Dearg cliff rim to Loch Etchachan, held firm in the Arctic clench of its eponymous corrie. From its outflow a wide and eroded path drops sharply into lower Coire Etchachan, and down into Glen Derry from where the Lairig an Laoigh path carries you gently back to Derry Lodge.

44 The Corries of Beinn a' Bhuird and Ben Avon

My friend David Craig, a professor of creative writing and a good hillman, suggested that corries always look as if they should cradle cultures. 'The lower lip of the corrie makes a threshold and as I cross it, it rises up behind me and peace encloses me. I've come home.'

David is an Aberdonian, and the dark corries of Beinn a' Bhuird beckon him with all sorts of cultural promise, not least a rock climb called 'Squareface' in the Garbh Choire, a route first climbed by Tom Patey in the 1950s, a secluded jewel of a climb that attracts David as much for its spectacular setting as the simple aesthetics of the line. This is the cradled landscape of David's north-east roots – craggy, granitic and distinctive, a landscape that welcomes him like a prodigal son.

It could be suggested that Beinn a' Bhuird has a split personality. Its western slopes fall away gently onto the boggy plain of the Moine Bhealaidh between Beinn a' Chaorainn and Beinn Bhreac while its eastern side is torn by a string of deep corries. Coire nan Clach, the corrie of stones, falls away sharply from the North Top and is a wild place, almost separated by a great curtain of projecting granite. Immediately to the south is Coire an Dubh Lochan with its archetypal hanging valley lochan and south of that the next pearl on the string is the corrie of the pap, Coire na Ciche, taking its name from A' Chioch, the tor-like rock that gazes down the rough granite buttresses into the dizzy depths below.

These corries can be seen to best advantage from a route that climbs up Gleann an t-Slugain, easily reached from Invercauld, a few kilometres east of Braemar. A dual ascent of both Beinn a' Bhuird and neighbouring Ben Avon offers one of the Cairngorms' classic hikes, a huge hill-day in terms of both distance and character that can be subdued slightly by the use of a mountain bike as far as Slugain Lodge.

Beyond the ruins of the Lodge a footpath sweeps round and into the wide jaws of Glen Quoich and climbs to the head of the glen, past the huge erratic known as the Clach a' Chleirich, the Stone of the Clergyman. Doubtless this is the same cleric commemorated by the Cnap a' Chleirich, the prominent ridge that falls down between Coire nan Clach and the steep glen that falls down The Sneck, (from the Gaelic snaig, or notch), the narrow saddle between our

Route Summary

Take the private road to Glen Quoich. Pass the ruins of Slugain Lodge and continue to the end of the path beyond Clach a' Chleirich. Climb NNE to The Sneck, then continue E to gain the plateau and summit tor of Ben Avon. Return to The Sneck, cross it and continue ESE to the N top of Beinn a' Bhuird. Return to Glen Quoich by the S top and Carn Fiaclach.

Map: OS Sheets 36 and 44

Access Point: Invercauld Bridge

Distance: 40km

Approx Time: 10-12 hours

Grade: Strenuous hill walk

Translation: hill of the fair-haired one; hill of the table

Pronunciation: byn a voord; byn aan

two hills. From here, with the dramatic corrie of Slochd Mor falling away steeply to the north, climb eastwards up the gravelly slopes onto Ben Avon's plateau. The summit tor, Leabaidh an Daimh Bhuidhe, 1171m, lies about 1.5km to the north-east.

Ben Avon isn't as clearly defined as Beinn a' Bhuird. This is a big, complex mass of muscle-bound shoulders which bulge out in every direction, throwing up a central plateau which is pimpled by tor-studded tops. On one of them, a huge outcrop called the Clach Bhan is potmarked by a number of holes, depressions and recesses, the result of rock weathering. There is a fanciful tradition that suggests that these holes have been gouged out of this Stone of Women to create seats in which women once sat to ensure they would have an easy labour.

David Craig, couthy Aberdonian as he may be, is less cynical than me. In his book *Landmarks*, he writes, 'Until I saw the number of these holes and their nearness to each other, the old rite had seemed a bit improbable. It was perfectly natural. The women were not a few beleaguered waifs, they were together. In many of the holes they could have sat holding hands. The female bonding of their condition and of the walk and climb together would have been clinched as they snuggled into these cups that look made for the purpose.'

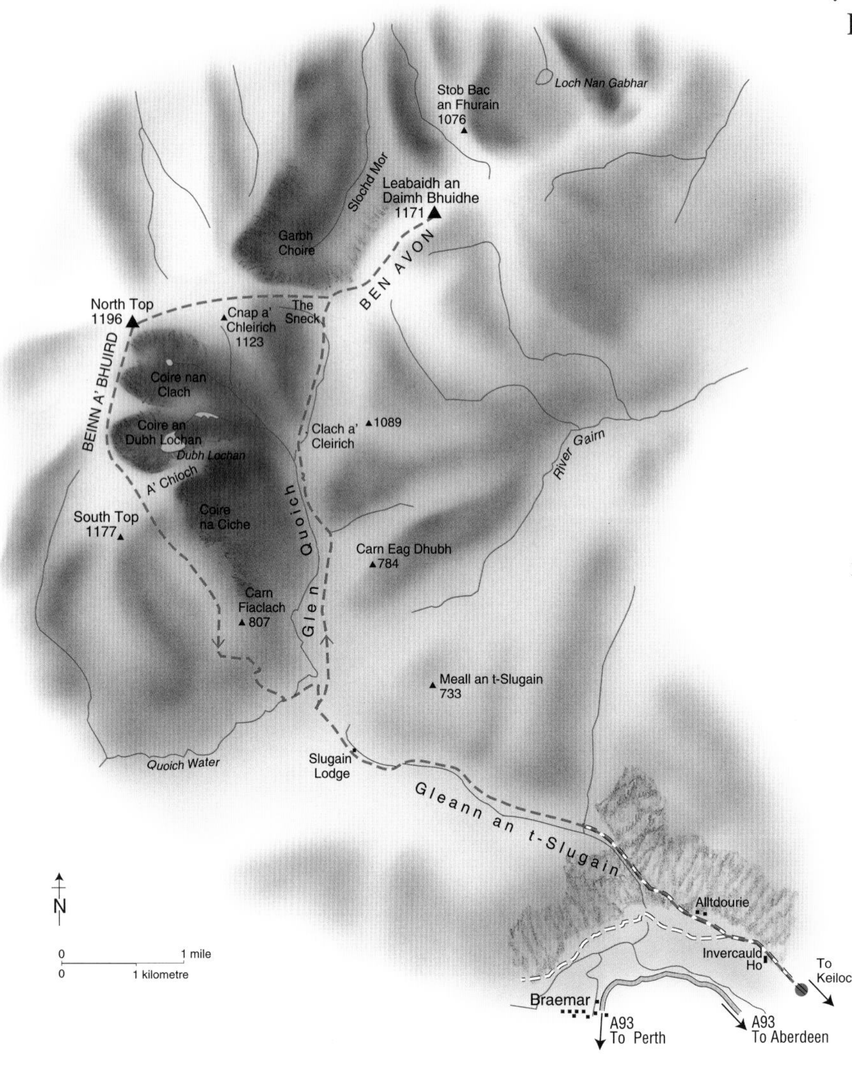

Taken from the river which scours its northern flanks, Celtic scholars believe the name Avon to be a

Beinn a' Bhuird and Glen Quoich

derivative of Ath-fhionn, the bright or fair-haired one. Local legend claims that the wife of Fionn MacCumhail, or Fingal, slipped when crossing the river and was swept to her death.

Returning to the Sneck, great corries fall away on either side, a superb position with rock buttresses soaring up to the green slopes of Cnap a' Chleirich to the south-west. From where The Sneck abuts onto the vast Beinn a' Bhuird plateau, continue in an east-south-east direction to the North Top. This is the summit of Beinn a' Bhuird, and it is distinctly uninteresting, a plain, a prairie: flat and featureless. It lies some 1197m above sea level, but more often than not clouds drench these high parts and visibility is limited to a few rock-strewn metres. A good descent continues southwards to the South Top, skirting the lip of Coire an Dubh Lochain, and then south-east to Carn Fiaclach where a stalker's path leads down into Glen Quoich just to the north of Slugain Lodge.

You can also start from Mar Lodge, about 7km west of Braemar, and follow the track up Glen Quoich, then follow the Quoich water to where this route joins the main descent route beyond the ruins of Slugain Lodge.

The Lairig Ghru from the air – looking south from above Lurcher's Crag

45 The Lairig Ghru

Two major Cairngorm passes have been used as through-routes since time immemorial: the Lairig Ghru from Aviemore in the north to Braemar in the south, and the Lairig an Laoigh which connects Abernethy in the north with Braemar. Both routes once resounded to the movement of cattle: Lairig an Laoigh is the Pass of Stirks, or calves, and it is said that the older beasts were driven over the tougher, less forgiving terrain of the Lairig Ghru.

Caterans, thieves and robbers knew both routes intimately, and armies marched over them too, but history has chosen to commemorate the vagabonds and thieves by such place names as Allt Preas nam Meirleach – the stream of the thieves' bush, or Cnapan nam Meirleach, the small knoll of the thieves. A pair of drunken tailors are remembered in the Lairig Ghru: the Clach nan Taillear is the name of the rock where they tried to shelter from a storm one New Year's Eve, after trying to negotiate the Lairig after a night of merrymaking in Abernethy and Inverdruie, and I can never walk through the Lairig without recalling an old friend of mine, Jim Collie of Tullochgrue, who would annually wheel his old bicycle over the pass to visit a friend at Inverey near Braemar, and to attend the Royal Braemar Gathering. Jim, who was fond of an occasional dram of whisky, kept his own supply in a secret place near Corrour. Every year he would be fortified on his cycle excursion with a nip, and enjoy another one on the way back home to Aviemore next day.

The Lairig Ghru rises to a height of 833m and isn't to be taken lightly. The pass can become blocked by deep, drifting snow, even in June, and the narrow Lairig often acts as a wind funnel, even when it is comparatively calm on Speyside and Deeside. A north-to-south crossing is best; the climb up into the great V-shaped pass through the ancient Caledonian pine forest of Rothiemurchus is one of the great walks in Scotland.

The forest trail which leaves the B970 Aviemore to Glenmore road at Coylumbridge thrusts you into the forest without preamble. Scots pines line the pathside and birches grow in extravagant excess, juniper bushes cover the floor and a rich, luxuriant undergrowth of heather, blaeberry and mosses give an impression of timelessness. Follow the signposted path that breaks off at 917100 to the left of the main forest trail and leads to the Cairngorm Club footbridge, just below the confluence of the Allt Druidh from Lairig Ghru and the Am Beanaidh from Gleann Einich.

Beyond the bridge the grassy clearing was once cultivated as the croft of Allt Dhru, and shortly after, at a junction of four paths, the route to the Lairig turns sharply right and climbs high above the Allt Druidh, through a forest of short and stocky Caledonian pines. I love these trees, they represent the spirit of Rothiemurchus, the spirit of the Caledonian pine forest – stunted relics, perhaps, but still portraying an indomitable spirit, facing the fiercest of the elements with a worldly bravado. As you eventually leave the trees take a look back behind you. Like a green ocean, the tree tops flow northwards to lap gently on the foothills of the Monadh liath mountains on the other side of Strathspey.

Pass along peaty moorland now for a couple of kilometres, a once boggy route which has been improved considerably by footpath reconstruction work. Just before you reach a large, dumpy moraine, which once housed the Sinclair Memorial Hut, a path appears on your left, dropping down from the Chalamain Gap above.

Scree slopes and crags now hem in the pass: Creag an Leth-choin on the left and Sron na Lairige on the right. The path snakes its way up the narrow trough to the summit of the pass at 835m.

Route Summary

From Coylumbridge follow the path that leaves the road just before the campsite and follow it past Lairig Ghru Cottage. At the first junction turn left and continue on this path all the way to the Cairngorm Club footbridge. Cross the bridge and continue over a grassy area to re-enter the forest by the river. At the next path junction turn right and climb up through the forest. Continue on this path all the way over the pass and shortly after the aluminium bridge that crosses the River Dee near Corrour the path bears left to curve round below Sron Carn a' Mhaim, crosses the Luibeg Burn by a footbridge and runs down Glen Luibeg to Derry Lodge. Follow the wide track down Glen Lui to the Linn of Dee.

Map: OS Sheets 36 and 43

Access Point: Coylumbridge

Finish: Linn of Dee

Distance: 30km

Approx Time: 10-14 hours

Grade: Long hill walk

Translation: Pass of Druie

Slightly beyond, the Allt na Criche, or the March Burn, crashes down the steep hillside, only to vanish below the boulder fields. It re-appears further down the pass as a series of lochans, known nowadays as the Pools of Dee. The old name was Lochan Dubh na Lairige, or black tarn of the Lairig.

Descending now, the narrow confines of the pass begin to widen out again and one of Scotland's finest corries displays itself on the right. This is An Garbh Coire, the big rough corrie, a great wild scooped-out hollow which bites hungrily into three Munros; Braeriach, Sgor an Lochain Uaine and Cairn Toul. It is one of the great features of the Cairngorms and I would rank it among the top three corries in Scotland, along with Coire Mhic Fhearchair of Beinn Eighe and Toll an Lochan of An Teallach.

The path soon reaches easier ground as it drops into Glen Dee where it follows a level course all the way to Corrour.

Beyond the Allt Clach nan Taillear, a collection of oddly ribbed stones on the east side of the path are called Clach nan Taillear, a memorial to the two tailors who once tried to shelter here.

Further south a footbridge crosses the River Dee over to Corrour Bothy below the Devil's Point.

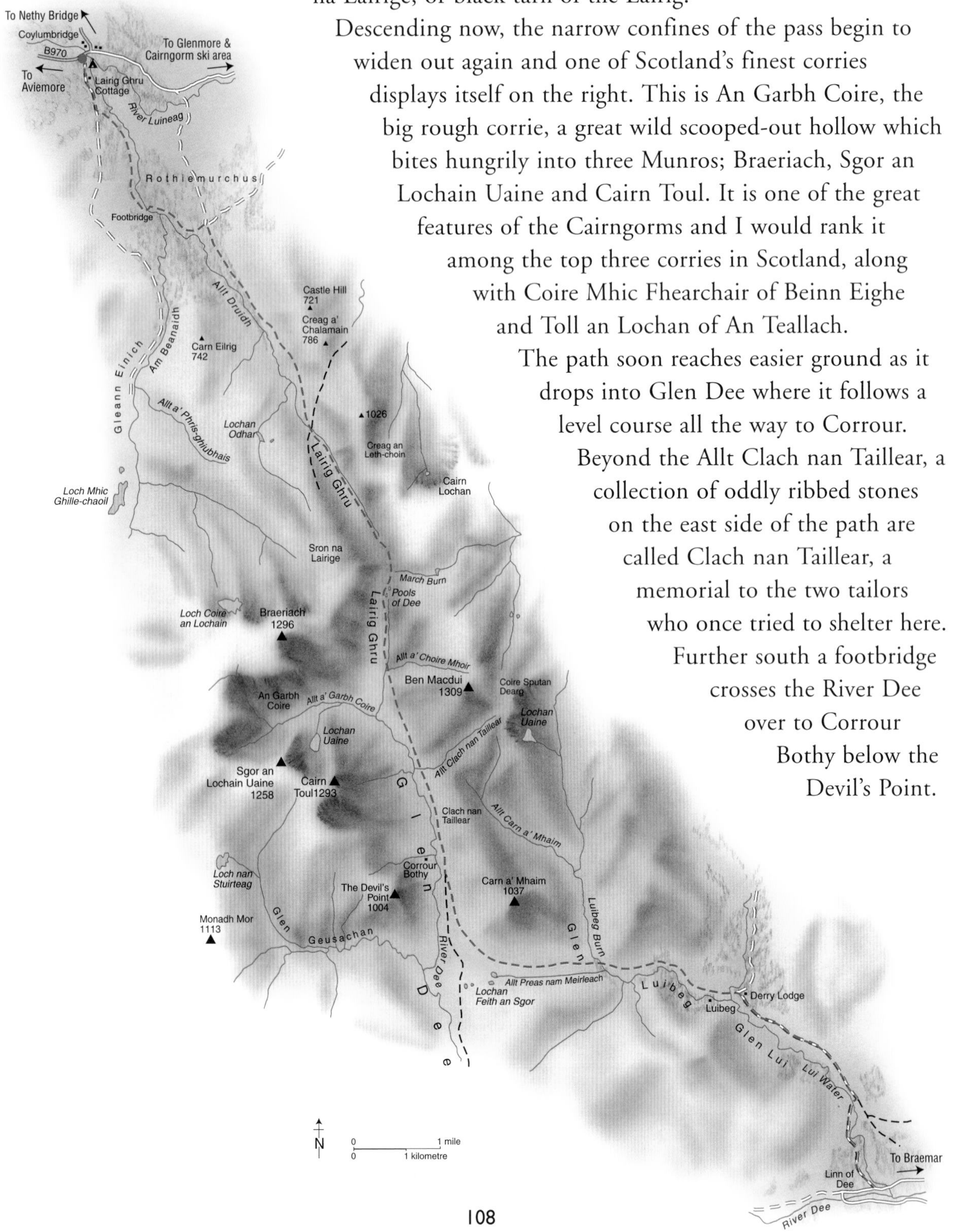

The Lairig Ghru from above the Pools of Dee looking north-west

Some would suggest that such man-made structures should have no place in a wild area like the Cairngorms; the views are very fine, however; above on the east side, the slabby rock faces of Carn a' Mhaim lead north to the screes of Beinn Macdui. South, the views of the Devil's Point and the opening of wild Glen Geusachan, its green floor hemmed in by rocky hillsides, look especially impressive.

Just past Corrour the Lairig track divides at a signpost. The right branch goes down the east side of the narrowing Glen Dee to the White Bridge and the Linn of Dee, but the more scenic left branch climbs gently round the foot of Sron Carn a' Mhaim, passes the peaty tarn of Lochan Feith an Sgor and then gradually drops into Glen Luibeg where a fine view north highlights the cliffs of Coire Sputan Dearg on Beinn Macdui.

A bridge crosses the Luibeg Burn 400m upstream and the first copse of trees below here is Preas nam Meirleach or the Copse of the Robbers. After the burn the path crosses the Sands of Lui, a stretch of gravel washed down by floods of last century, and wanders through the winding Glen Luibeg with its scattering of pines to the old keeper's house at Luibeg, and then the disused Derry Lodge. A bulldozed track then runs down the length of Glen Lui to a gate at the Linn of Dee, a series of dramatic gorges in the River Dee, and the finish to one of Scotland's truly great walks.

Looking towards Loch Insh, Strathspey, from Kingussie's Creag Bheag

46 Kingussie's Creag Bheag

For well over 20 years I've lived close to the Badenoch town of Kingussie, which once had a reputation as a good place for those with chest complaints – the fresh air was apparently spiced with the heady scent of pine from nearby woods. Indeed the name Kingussie is derived from the Gaelic for 'the head of the pinewood.'

This little hill walk is one that I reserve for those days when I have to clear my head, or when I need a quick fix of distant views and fresh pine-scented air as an antidote to stuffy offices and the eyeball-glazing effects of computer screens. It shouldn't be too difficult for even chesty walkers and offers a fine exhilarating stroll to the summit of the small hill which overlooks Kingussie – Creag Bheag, the little crag.

Kingussie is the ancient capital of Badenoch and is the old kirktown of the castle of Ruthven. There was a settlement here as far back as AD 565, when a chapel dedicated to St Columba of Iona was established. The present village didn't really come together until the late eighteenth century when the Duke of Gordon placed an advert in the *Aberdeen Journal* encouraging tradesmen, manufacturers and shopkeepers to settle there, and for a while it became the centre of a weaving and spinning industry. The Highland Folk Museum in the village is well worth a visit.

Creag Bheag is a fine little summit which offers views up and down the length of Badenoch, taking in the Monadh Liath, the Cairngorms, the Glen Feshie hills, the Gaick hills and the

Route Summary

Leave the golf club car park and bear left through the caravans for about 100m to a stile over the fence into the birchwoods. Across the fence, follow the left boundary of the golf course, pass the first hole and go on through the woods. At the end of the wire fence turn left and follow the path to a stile which crosses a deer fence. Cross the fence and continue uphill. After a short distance the path deviates right, through a hole in the wall and continues on the opposite side, climbing gradually. Pass below a Scots pine with steep, rocky walls bounding the right-hand side of the path. As you leave this crag behind keep to the wall and head towards some prominent Scots pines. Follow the wall below more pines to where another wall bears in from the right. Follow this wall uphill, past a prominent nobule of rock to an exposed area of heath. Cross the open area and meet another path mountains of distant Lochaber. There are some good little crags on its southern slopes which offer some short rock climbs. In high summer the midgies are awful.

The best route is from the car park near Kingussie golf club. Bear left through the caravans for about 100m to a stile over the fence into the birchwoods. Over the fence, follow the left boundary of the golf course, past the first hole and on through the woods. At the end of the obvious wire fence turn left and follow the path to a ladder stile which crosses a deer fence. Cross the fence and continue uphill on the path with pines on your left and juniper and birch on your right. After a short distance the path deviates slightly to the right through a hole in the dry stone wall and continues on the opposite side, climbing gradually with a steep crag on the right. Pass below the branches of a fine old Scots pine with steep, rocky walls bounding the right-hand side of the path.

As you leave this crag another path bears right towards some obvious crags which are popular with local climbers, but keep to the broken wall and make your way towards some prominent Scots pines in the distance. Enjoy the views across the village of Kingussie towards the distant Cairngorms. Follow the wall below more pine trees to where another wall bears in from the right. Follow this uphill through the heather, past a prominent lump of rock to a more open area of heath. Once across this you'll meet another path coming up from the left. Turn right onto this and follow it to the summit where you can enjoy views up and down the length of Strathspey.

Return to the last path junction and continue past your original route, descending gradually south to the forest where the path swings right and drops downhill to a gate in the fence. This leads past the house called Creag Beag and into Kingussie's West Terrace. Follow this to Ardvonie Road, turn left and go round into Middle Terrace then first left into Gynack Road. Follow this road back to your starting point.

coming up from the left. Turn right onto this path and follow it to the summit.
Return to the last path junction and continue past the earlier route, descending S to the forest where the path suddenly swings right and drops downhill to a gate in the fence. This leads past the house called Creag Beag and into Kingussie's West Terrace. Follow this road to its junction with Ardvonie Road, turn left and follow this road round into Middle Terrace then first left again into Gynack Road. Follow this road back to your starting point.

Map: OS Sheet 35

Access Point: Kingussie Golf Club car park

Distance: 6km

Approx Time: 2 hours

Grade: Easy hill walk

Translation: small crag

Pronunciation: crayk bek

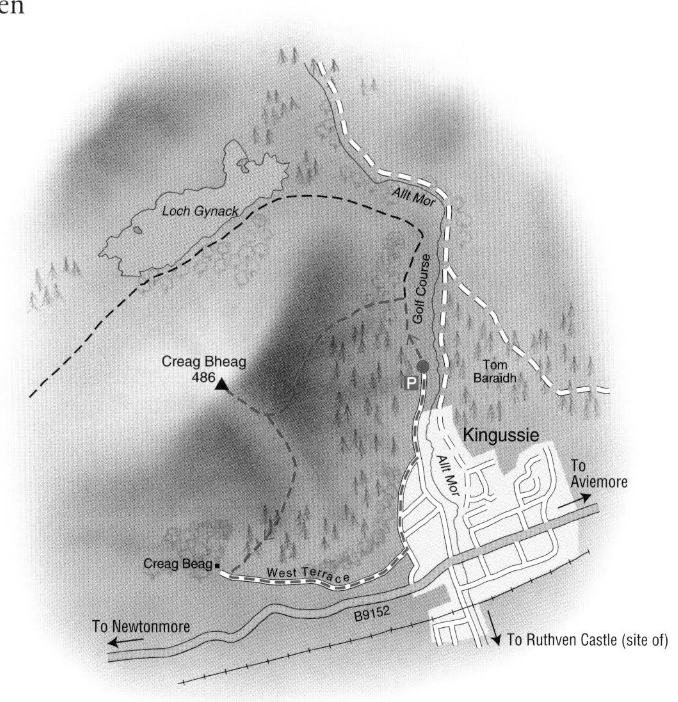

47 General Wade's Badenoch Road

Route Summary

From Newtonmore follow the road to Ralia, past the visitor centre and follow the tarmac road to Etteridge. Cross the A9, pass a house on your left, climb uphill and turn left past more buildings onto General Wade's old road. Follow the road past Phones, Luibleathann and Milehouse of Nuidhe to the A9 near Ruthven. Cross the road, climb a stile over a fence onto an old section of tarmac road which is then followed below an underpass to Ruthven. Follow the B970 to Kingussie, then the old A9 back to Newtonmore.

Map: OS Sheet 35

Access Point: Newtonmore's Main Street

Distance: About 24km but there is very little uphill involved and the route is straightforward. It can be shortened by some 5km by taking the bulldozed track from the A9 about 1.5km south of Ralia to Phones and picking up General Wade's road from there.

Approx Time: 6-8 hours

Grade: Long low-level walk

This section of military road was travelled by Thomas Pennant during his tour of 1774, who described it as: 'a very fine road formed by the soldiery lent by the Government, who have sixpence a day from the country besides their pay.'

Today it forms a fine low-level walk along a section of an eighteenth-century military road built by General George Wade and his squads of soldier navvies to enforce the subjugation of the Highlands. This section is part of General Wade's longest military road, from Dunkeld to Inverness, and runs from Etteridge on the A9 just south of Newtonmore to Ruthven near Kingussie. It is possible to walk the old road between these two points by using two cars, but many will prefer to make a long round walk of it, although this does involve a fair bit of walking beside quite busy roads. Having said that, the section I've described from Newtonmore to Ralia is very quiet and the ongoing route from Ralia to Etteridge, though tarmacked, is not used by cars, although it is in fairly close proximity to the busy A9 trunk road. The 5km section between Kingussie and Newtonmore follows a footpath beside the road.

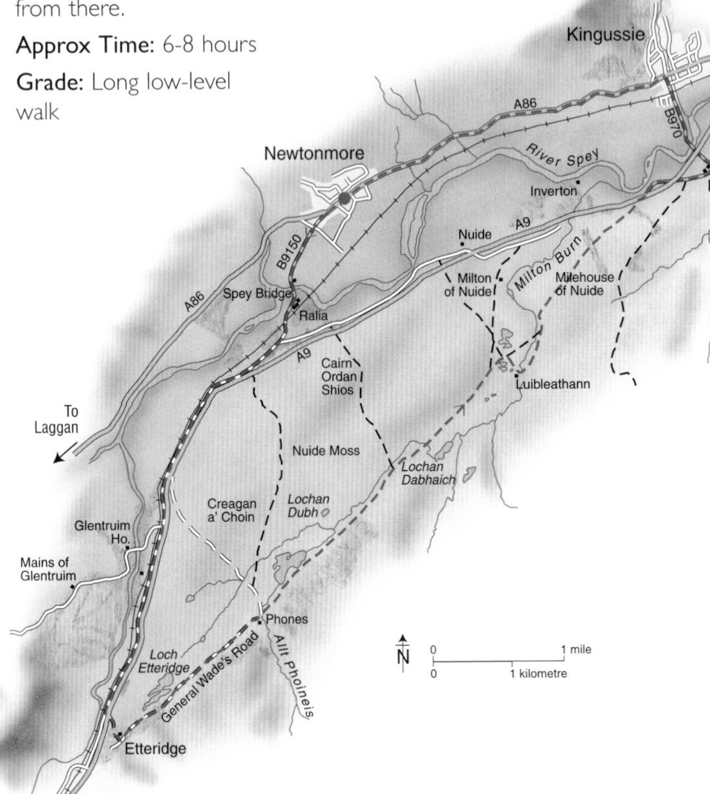

From Newtonmore's main street head south-west out of the village. Newtonmore is a corruption of the English translation of Baile Ur an-Sleibh, the new town of the moor.

Pass the shinty field and clubhouse, and cross the bridge over the River Spey towards Ralia. Avoid the main A9 trunk road by following the old A9 road, now part of a cycleway between Perth and Inverness, past the tourist centre at Ralia, over the Glen Truim road and almost as far as the Crubenmore Bridge, some

General Wade's Military Road midway between Etteridge and Ruthven, Badenoch

8km from Newtonmore. Before you reach the bridge look out for a minor road and house on the opposite (east) side of the A9. Take great care crossing the A9 and follow the minor road past Etteridge and onto the route of General Wade's road. Follow the path north-eastwards past Loch Etteridge to Phones, Lochan Dabhaich, Luibleathann and Milehouse of Nuide to the A9 about 1.6km short of Ruthven. At this point you'll have to cross the busy trunk road again to a stile on the north side where a tarmac road runs above the River Spey before going through an underpass below the A9 to Ruthven Farmhouse. The remains of Ruthven Barracks lie on a knoll which reputedly housed a castle belonging to Alexander Stewart, the Wolf of Badenoch. A succession of castles have been built on the site, the last one captured by General David Leslie from the Marquis of Huntly in 1647. After that the site was used by various garrisons of soldiers and Ruthven Barracks itself was burnt down in 1746 in the aftermath of Culloden. From there the B970 is followed over the Spey Bridge to Kingussie (comes from the Gaelic Cinn a' Ghiuthsaich, head of the pine wood).

There is a reasonably good footpath which runs along the south side of the old A9 road between Kingussie and Newtonmore, but before you leave Kingussie it's well worth visiting The Highland Folk Museum of Am Fasgadh. A new folk park, part of Am Fasgadh, can be seen on your left as you reach the outskirts of Newtonmore.

Blair Castle from the south looking towards Glen Banvie

48 The Minigaig – Blair Atholl to Kingussie

Until General Wade built his road over Drumochter Pass between Atholl and Badenoch, the main route through the high Grampians was by way of an upland bridleway called the Minigaig. The route runs across a great wedge of high, broken land which lies between the Pass of Drumochter in the west, and the line of Glen Tilt, Glen Geldie and Glen Feshie in the east.

The Minigaig starts in Blair Atholl and runs a 50km course to Kingussie in Badenoch, and replaced the older, and longer, Comyn's Road some time before the seventeenth century. The route's high point reaches an elevation of 837m between the headwaters of the Bruar and the Tromie, a stark, remote place of high undulating moorland and wide open skies, deer infested, and haunted by ptarmigan and eagle. Anyone who is thrilled by remote and stark landscapes cannot fail to be touched by the character of the Minigaig; a series of ridge over ridge, horizon over horizon, rolling moors and shadow-stained glens, clear-cut land and glistening water, serenaded by the melancholy song of the golden plover. It's a great hike for the long daylight hours of summer, but I suspect most walkers would want to break it into two, with a bivvy out somewhere on the atmospheric high ground of the pass itself.

Blair Castle is the historic starting point, and Diana's Grove marks the way, a dark wood of largely exotic conifers. The track runs to Old Blair, where another track strikes off in a north-west direction beside the Banvie Burn, climbing gently through dense woods of birch, larch and pine. Keep in sight of the chuckling burn which passes through a series of cascades, pools and deep-set ravines, all darkly shaded in bottle green. After a short time, the hump-backed Rumbling Bridge is passed, but not crossed, as both the Minigaig and Comyn's Road march forward as one, through a gate into the Whim Plantation to another gate at the end of the woods. The old routes split here. Comyn's Road runs onwards, while the Minigaig drops down to the burns where it crosses the Quarry Bridge onto the West Hand Road.

The track begins to incline gently as it pulls away from Glen Banvie up the glen of the Allt na Moine Baine. Soon the road crosses the burn and skirts around the long open slopes of Carn Dearg Beag to drop into the shallow valley of the Allt an t-Seapail, the stream of the chapel. Just after the old trackside stone which marks the old 3-mile milestone there is a fine ancient circular well by the name of Fuaran Bhadenoch, another indication of this road's antiquity and its ultimate destination.

It's also about here that the line of the original Minigaig leaves the West Hand Road for a short distance to meander across the eastern slopes of Meall Dubh. Pass another large cairn, the Carn Mhic Shimidh, this one a memorial to a battle between the Murrays of Atholl and a raiding party of Frasers led by Simon Lovat. The cairn marks the spot where Lovat was slain. Not far from the cairn the old path meets up with the West Hand Road again for its final stretch to the bothy beside the Allt Sheicheachan. The burn outside the bothy is easily forded and the path is fairly indistinct as it makes its way into Glen Bruar.

At the beginning of the nineteenth century, Glen Bruar was described as follows: 'About eight miles north of Blair Atholl, you descend into a glen which is wild and desolate. The heather being old is rather of a brown than a purple colour, but there is some relief of greensward near the lodge and more in various patches near the winding source of the Bruar. At the right of the entrance

Route Summary

From Blair Castle follow the Banvie Burn through the Whim Plantation (see map on p116). Cross the Banvie by the Quarry Bridge and follow the West Hand Road as far as the bothy beside the Allt Sheicheachan. Ford the burn by the bothy and cross the slopes of Druim Dubh into Glen Bruar. Go N, pass Bruar Lodge, and ascend the slopes of Uchd a' Chlarsair. Cross the high ground to the W of Leathad an Taobhain for about 5km and eventually descend into Coire Bhran. Follow the Allt Bhran in a NW direction to Glen Tromie. About 1.6km beyond Bhran Cottage cross the Tromie by a bridge, ascend the nose of Sron na Gaoithe and continue on paths to Beinn Bhiudhe. Descend N to Ruthven and the road to Kingussie.

Maps: OS Sheets 43, 42 and 35

Access Point: Blair Atholl, GR866663

Finish: Kingussie, GR755005

Distance: 50km

Approx Time: 2 days. 1 night out.

Grade: Strenuous 2-day hill walk

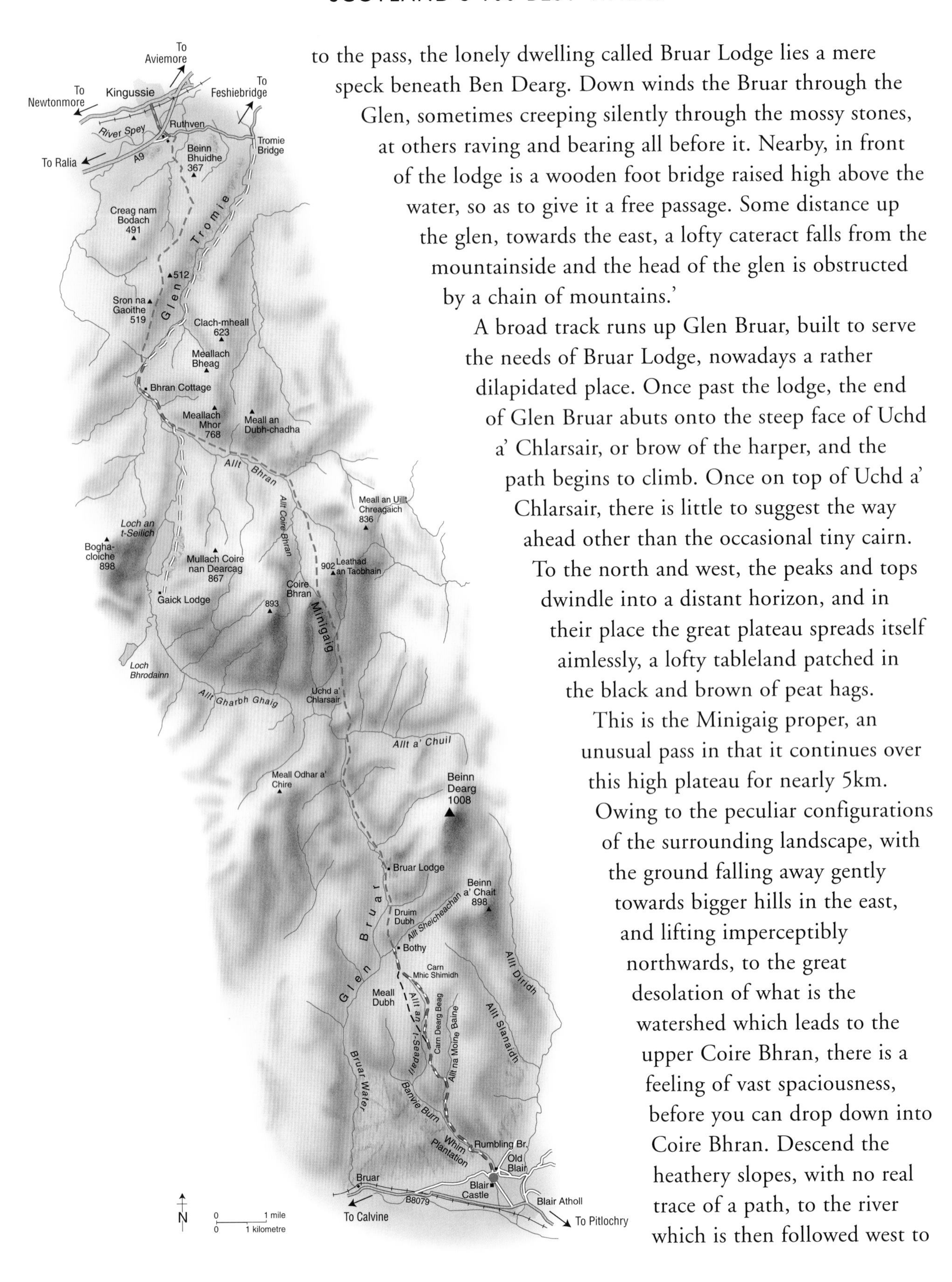

to the pass, the lonely dwelling called Bruar Lodge lies a mere speck beneath Ben Dearg. Down winds the Bruar through the Glen, sometimes creeping silently through the mossy stones, at others raving and bearing all before it. Nearby, in front of the lodge is a wooden foot bridge raised high above the water, so as to give it a free passage. Some distance up the glen, towards the east, a lofty cateract falls from the mountainside and the head of the glen is obstructed by a chain of mountains.'

A broad track runs up Glen Bruar, built to serve the needs of Bruar Lodge, nowadays a rather dilapidated place. Once past the lodge, the end of Glen Bruar abuts onto the steep face of Uchd a' Chlarsair, or brow of the harper, and the path begins to climb. Once on top of Uchd a' Chlarsair, there is little to suggest the way ahead other than the occasional tiny cairn. To the north and west, the peaks and tops dwindle into a distant horizon, and in their place the great plateau spreads itself aimlessly, a lofty tableland patched in the black and brown of peat hags.

This is the Minigaig proper, an unusual pass in that it continues over this high plateau for nearly 5km.

Owing to the peculiar configurations of the surrounding landscape, with the ground falling away gently towards bigger hills in the east, and lifting imperceptibly northwards, to the great desolation of what is the watershed which leads to the upper Coire Bhran, there is a feeling of vast spaciousness, before you can drop down into Coire Bhran. Descend the heathery slopes, with no real trace of a path, to the river which is then followed west to

Glen Tromie from Sron na Gaoithe

join up with a bulldozed track, leading to the tarmac road, which runs up the length of Glen Tromie to Gaick Lodge.

An old Gaelic bard once described Glen Tromie as 'Gleann Tromaidh nan Siantan' – the glen of the stormy blasts, and in the depths of winter, that description just about sums it up. Things are better at other times of the year, with birch, alder and juniper decorating the river banks. After the starkness of the higher reaches of the Minigaig, the green tranquillity of Glen Tromie is welcome.

About 1.5km past the old Bhran Cottage, nowadays used as a storage hut by the estate, a narrow bridge carries you across the river before beginning the long ascent of Sron na Gaoithe, the Nose of the Winds. It's a gentle climb over the Sron, and as you pass the crest of the ridge the views open up northwards in vast scale. The twin villages of Newtonmore and Kingussie nestle under the great swell of the Monadh Liath, and here and there a tell-tale splash of river shows where the Spey meanders through its wide flood-plains. The track can easily be seen from here, picking its way over the heather slopes towards the small crest of Beinn Bhuidhe.

It's an easy descent from here down to Ruthven, and the gaunt outline of Ruthven Barracks perched atop their prehistoric mound. General Wade constructed the building for his dragoons on the same hill which Comyn had used in the thirteenth century, and which Finn MacCumhail, or Fingal, had allegedly used away back in the very mists of time. Wade's building had a short life span though, some 25 years, before being burnt down in 1746 on the orders of Charles Edward Stuart, on the run from Culloden.

It's only 2.5km or so to Kingussie now, by the minor road which runs below the relatively new construction of the A9 – the latest, and the least attractive, of all the roads through the eastern Grampians.

49 A' Chailleach, Monadh Liath

Route Summary

From the end of the tarmac road up Glen Banchor, follow a bulldozed track N up the glen of the Allt a' Chaorainn. At the end of the track drop down a steep bank to the left to a footbridge over the river. Follow the river N to its confluence with another burn from the left. Follow this burn until it is narrow enough to cross, pass the Red Bothy and find a crude footpath which climbs in a NNE direction all the way to the summit. Return the same way.

Map: OS Sheet 35

Access Point: End of public road in Glen Banchor, GR693998

Distance: 10km

Approx Time: 4-6 hours

Grade: Moderate hill walk

Translation: the old woman

Pronunciation: a kaalyach

I'm probably the only person in the country who would put A' Chailleach in his favourite top 100 hills, but I have good reasons for doing so. I was taken to task a while ago in a book review which complained that I had dismissed Ben Chonzie in Perthshire as uninspiring and a rather mediocre destination for a hillwalk. The writer went on to say she lived close to the hill, indeed it was her local hill, and for that reason she would wish to defend it.

I can understand that sort of reaction. My local Monadh Liath have suffered a bad press over the years at the hands of a number of otherwise distinguished writers who have dared suggest that the swelling breasts of Carn Dearg, Geal Charn and A' Chailleach were no more than an upland peat-bog. 'Unrelentingly tedious', claimed one author who, at his age, should know that there is no such thing as a dull hill; only people are dull and if we happen to have a rather uneventful day on one of the many comparatively unexciting hills that exist in Scotland, then that experience tends to colour our thinking into a shade of blotchy grey.

Maybe I have to go back to Ben Chonzie, get to know it better, explore it more and learn its secrets, for that's how I've come to know the Monadh Liath and how I've learned to respect this range of rounded, bald hills, how I've come to enjoy its open aspect as atmospheric and rich in sensual pleasure.

Like my critic from Ben Chonzie I too go on the defensive when my home hills are criticised. Can't these people open their eyes and see that while the summits may be rounded and as bald as me, they nevertheless rise above a clutch of side glens which divert from the main glen, Glen Banchor? Indeed the whole area is rather like the back of a hand, with several long fingers running southwards from a great central plateau. There is a wide open aspect, a spaciousness, and that personal glow which comes from knowing that you live within the rustle of the hills' skirts.

A' Chailleach is the high point of the first of those fingers, while Carn Dearg is several fingers up the glen. Carn Sgulain is the high point of the plateau from which these fingers run. A' Chailleach, my favourite (because she's closest to home?) offers her best profile from the footpath which runs north from the car park that folk tend to call Shepherd's Bridge. Her north-east-facing corrie, which is her finest feature, is hardly spectacular but when snow swathes the steep, rocky flanks of her north-east buttress she casts aside her aged sobriquet (A' Chailleach means the Old Woman) and turns into a ravishing beauty, with a smile that would melt the very snows of her delicate brow.

The usual route of ascent is from the end of the footpath which runs north from the Shepherd's Bridge car park, which is at the end of the public road in Glen Banchor. Long heather-clad slopes roll down from A' Chailleach's summit ridge in a southerly direction and from the crossing of the Allt a' Chaorainn (drop down the slopes to your left at the end of the bulldozed track and you'll find a footbridge), it's a long relentless pull up these slopes to the summit. Things improve as you climb higher – once over a series of peat hags the going becomes easier over stony ground. In winter, on skis, the hill makes a starting point for a tour of all the Monadh Liath tops, a magnificent day out in good conditions, and I've watched swallows cleave the still air of a summer's evening as I've lain on the upper slopes, drunk with the pleasure of the place. Familiarity doesn't breed contempt but contentment, so perhaps I'm just going to have to spend more time on Ben Chonzie, and learn something of its own, personal character.

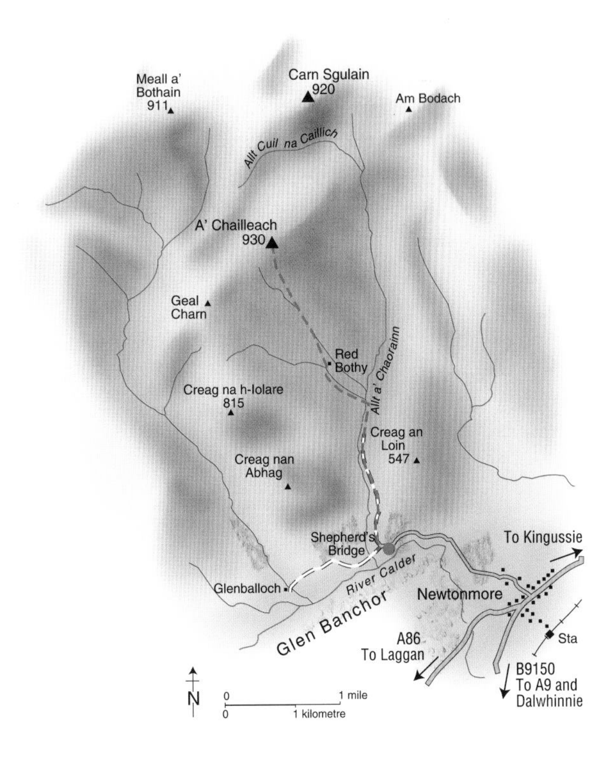

THE CENTRAL HIGHLANDS

This area is bordered by the waters of Loch Linnhe in the west, the Great Glen in the north, the A9 in the east and stretches of the Rannoch Moor in the south.

The hills of Glencoe, the Mamores and Ben Nevis are well known and justifiably popular and hills like Creag Meagaidh, Ben Alder and the Buachaille Etive Mor are amongst my own personal favourites. In total contrast the Rannoch Moor is one of the flattest areas in Scotland, but in terms of wilderness its quality is the equal of any Scottish mountain.

THE WALKS

50	Creag Meagaidh – A Hope for the Future	16km
51	Beinn a' Chlachair – Single Malt Quality	20km
52	The Big Bastion of Ben Alder	50km
53	The Moor of Rannoch	28km
54	Stob Ghabhar and Stob a' Choire Odhair	20km
55	Buachaille Etive Mor – The Great Herdsman	13km
56	Bidean nam Bian – Howffs and Hills	10km
57	The Aonach Eagach	6.5km
58	The Ring of Steall	15km
59	Glen Nevis' Gorge and Meadows	6km
60	Ben Nevis and Carn Mor Dearg	20km
61	The Easains – Stob a' Choire Mheadhoin and Stob Coire Easain	15km

Ben Nevis and Glen Nevis from An Gearanach, Mamores

50 Creag Meagaidh – A Hope for the Future

Route Summary

From Aberarder Farm take the path which runs all the way up Coire Ardair to Lochan a' Choire. Climb steep grassy slopes to the NW then up steep talus to The Window. At the far end of the bealach turn left and climb the zigzag path onto the plateau bearing right towards Meg's Cairn, then along a narrowing ridge to the summit. Return E to the corrie edge and follow the ridge SE and NE over Puist Coire Ardair and Sron a' Ghoire. Descend open slopes beside the Allt Bealach a' Ghoire to the Allt Coire Ardair, cross it and return by the outward path to Aberarder.

Map: OS Sheet 34

Access Point: Aberarder Farm on the A86 GR479875

Distance: 16km

Approx Time: 7-9 hours

Grade: Strenuous hill walk

Translation: bogland rock

Pronunciation: crayk mechie

'Leave the interpretive centre at Aberalder Farm and at the back of the building go through a gate into the forest. Take the winding trail that climbs the hillside through a tunnel of birch, alder and rowan. After some distance, reach a clearing where you'll glimpse the high, vegetated cliffs of Coire Ardair. Continue through the green tunnel on a rich undergrowth of heather and blaeberry, splashed with the colours of Alpine flowers, before reaching the edge of the wood at Lochan a' Choire where you might just catch sight of the huge native red deer.'

In a couple of hundred years time that might be the route description for the popular walk up the length of Coire Ardair at the foot of Creag Meagaidh, that great 1128m whaleback that lies mid-way between Fort William and Aviemore. The visionary plan of Scottish Natural Heritage, now 10 years into practice, is already showing signs of extraordinary success.

A decade ago SNH did the unthinkable – they dramatically reduced the number of red deer in the estate by capturing and selling them to deer farms. What's more they got rid of the sheep, which have done more damage to the Highland landscape than any number of booted feet. The results have been dramatic. Wander up Coire Ardair and you'll walk through a sea of young trees that have been given an opportunity to grow without having their heads bitten off. I won't be around when that forest matures, but I hope my grandchildren know the Creag Meagaidh story as they sit and enjoy the bird song in the golden glades. It's a wonderfully encouraging start to a mountain walk – so often we wander up slopes that sadly illustrate the ravages of man and beast, but here there is the scent of hope, promise and luxuriant new life.

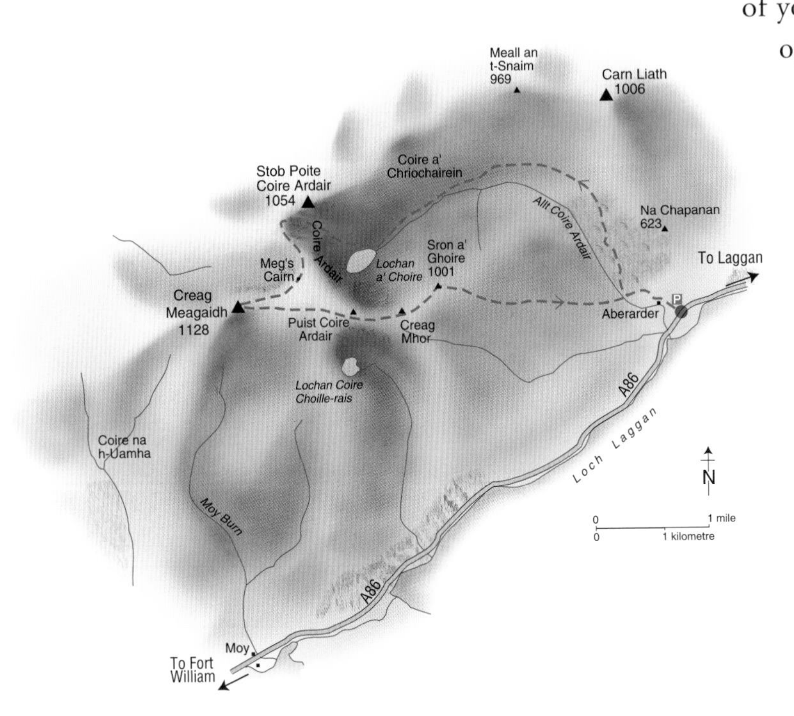

It will be an amazing experience to wander out of a deciduous

Coill a' Choire, Sron a' Ghoire and Stob Poite Coire Ardair, Creag Meagaidh

woodland onto the shores of Lochan a' Choire, lying deep below its huge array of vegetated cliffs. Laid out for more than 1.6km and in places reaching higher than 450m above the dark waters, the cliffs are breached only by a high bealach, commonly known as The Window, a glaciated gap in the curtain which offers access from the corrie floor to the high plateau summit slopes.

It's a steep climb to this gap – up a twisting moraine, then a scramble on loose talus up this corner of the corrie. The climbing eases off through the bealach. The western views (you can even see Ladhar Beinn in Knoydart on a clear day) beyond Glen Roy offer a few moments of respite before a long curving climb to Meg's Cairn, an unexplained mound of earth covered in stones. Now it is just a final climb to the panoramic summit.

Straddling the historic Druim Alban, the spine of Scotland, you can clearly identify the watershed, with the River Roy draining to the west, and Spey Loch (just hidden by an intervening ridge), source of the infant Spey running to the North Sea. Great hills surround you – from the Cairngorms to Ben Nevis – one of the best views in the country. It's always sad to leave this prairie-like plateau, a dotterel-haunted place of sedges and moss that runs out to great beetling shoulders. A well-defined ridge runs south-east then east over Puist Coire Ardair and Creag Mhor, where open slopes can be followed to Aberarder, back to the beginnings of a forest and a real hope for the future of our Scottish landscape.

Lochan na h-Earba and Binnein Shuas, Badenoch

51 Beinn a' Chlachair – Single Malt Quality

Ever since a prominent member of the old Scottish National Ski Council told me that Beinn a' Chlachair was on their hit-list of future ski developments I've felt a protective concern for the hill. I must say this comment was made a number of years ago when ski-ing as an industry was much more optimistic than it is now, so it is unlikely that the bowl-shaped Coire Mor Chlachair will ever resonate to the well-oiled ring of chairlift machinery.

The attractions of such a hill for skiing are understandable. Beinn a' Chlachair lies close to the A86 Laggan to Fort William road and an access track of sorts runs south from the main road to the end of Lochan na h-Earba. The north-facing slopes tend to hold snow well and the big corrie I've already mentioned turns white at the first wintry forecast. I've skied there myself, plodding up the hill track to the Bealach Leamhain, then climbing up the long whaleback of the hill's north-east ridge to the summit cone which sits precariously above steep crags. Then comes the finale – long runs down the hill's north-west and northern slopes, 2km which drop over 700m. The SMC's *Ski Mountaineering in Scotland* also recommends the north-east corrie which is often snow-filled.

Hamish Brown refers to this hill and its two neighbours, Geal Charn and Creag Pitridh as the Malt Hills. I suppose Beinn a' Chlachair does sound like some obscure single malt whisky and I know from several ascents of this hill that it can offer a similar shock. One day stays fixed in my memory. Snow threatened but never fulfilled its promise. A blustery wind intermittently poked holes in the low cloud to expose a ragged blue sky but, like the snow, the sun didn't fulfil its promise either. We intended climbing Beinn a' Chlachair and its two western neighbours, Geal Charn and Creag Pitridh. At 24km this would be a long day given the conditions, but our itinerary was loose. If we didn't climb all three hills it didn't matter, which was just as well, because we didn't!

The long walk-in up the length of the Allt Coire Pitridh was uneventful. Snow flurries chased us on and the sporadic bursts of sunshine lit up the hillsides with a bright intensity of colour which was almost dazzling. We stopped and sheltered behind a boulder high on the summit of the Bealach Leamhain, looking down at the wind flurries on the Loch a' Bhealaich Leamhain below us. A short climb onto Chlachair's long ridge, a wander along to the summit, and we could drop back to the bealach and climb Geal Charn and Creag Pitridh. It seemed so simple, but we hadn't accounted for the strength of the wind.

A steep and snowy climb took us onto the north-east ridge where the gale lay in wait for us. As soon as we breasted the rocky crest the first charge hit us like a battering ram. Breathless and almost blinded we managed to struggle on, exhilarated during the brief respites when the wind dropped, and battered when it attacked again. At one point we adopted what seemed like logical tactics, dropping down on the southern side of the ridge and climbing diagonally, hopefully in the lee of the wind. But not this wind. By the time we reached the ice-girt summit we felt as if we had just gone 10 rounds with Lennox Lewis.

The descent back to the bealach was no less eventful. Every time we had to cross an icy section of ground the wind crept up behind us and hit us hard, blowing us across the ice. By the time we reached lower ground the snow had come on. Unable to speak, we looked at each other, pointed downhill and nodded. Geal Charn and Creag Pitridh could wait for another day.

Route Summary

Follow the track to the head of Lochan na h-Earba and take the stalker's path which follows the Allt Coire Pitridh (see map on page 127). Climb to the bealach above Loch a' Bhealaich Leamhain and climb the steep slopes to the S to gain Beinn a' Chlachair's NE ridge. Follow this broad ridge to the summit. Descend by your outward route or by the hill's N ridge back to Lochan na h-Earba.

Map: OS Sheet 42

Access Point: Luiblea, GR432830

Distance: 20km

Approx Time: 7-9 hours

Grade: Moderate hill walk

Translation: stonemason's hill

Pronunciation: byn a klaachar

52 The Big Bastion of Ben Alder

Route Summary

From Kinloch Laggan cross the bridge over the Pattack and follow the track past some houses and into the forest. Cross a stile by a gate and follow the path by the river all the way to Loch Pattack. At the end of the loch turn right onto a footpath, cross a suspension bridge over the river and follow the footpath to Culra. Just before the bothy cross the river again by another footbridge to gain the south bank. Follow this path now into the corrie which cradles Loch a' Bhealaich Bheithe, pass the loch and continue to the Bealach Breabag. From the col turn right, climb steep slopes to the wide plateau of Ben Alder. Stay close to the cliff edge until you reach Lochain a' Garbh Choire. The summit lies beyond. Descend NW by Meall an t-Slugain to reach the Bealach Dubh track which is then followed to Culra and the inward route.

Map: OS Sheet 42

Access Point: A86 at Kinloch Laggan, GR555898

Distance: About 50km

Approx Time: 2 days

Grade: Strenuous hill walk

Translation: hill of the rock water

Pronunciation: byn awlder

The view of Ben Alder down the length of Loch Ericht from the A9 is often a stirring one. Much of the time the same view is dull and grey, as if the waters of the loch merge with the very edge of the world, but when the sun shines on the snow-fringed tops of Ben Alder and the air is clear, it is as though the hill was only a couple of kilometres away. But it isn't.

Ben Alder is a remote hill, a big bastion of a hill that demands a long walk-in, and I reckon it's all the better for that – it turns an ordinary hill-walk into an expedition and gives the mountain an air of isolation, of seriousness. A friend of mine was badly frostbitten during a winter weekend a few years ago and two others severely underestimated the remoteness of the hill and had to be helicoptered out. You don't mess with Ben Alder.

The hill's north-eastern extremities can be reached by mountain bike, a long haul along the seemingly endless kilometres of bulldozed track past the opulent Ben Alder Lodge to Culra. A far better option, if you have the time, is to walk in from the north, from Kinloch Laggan, up the length of the River Pattack. Make a two-day trip of it, camping, or staying at a bothy.

The Pattack is a grand river of intense character. Bubbling, swirling, crashing under a canopy of pines are waterfalls, just north of the Linn of Pattack, and probably the most impressive in the area, a powerful aquatic display of thundering waters crowned by an almost permanent rainbow. Throughout its length are other, smaller falls, and tiny coves and bays that just beckon you for a swim. A good track follows its meandering course through stands of proud old pines until higher up, closer to Loch Pattack, the countryside widens to give good views of Ben Alder, Geal Charn, Beinn a' Chlachair and the Matterhorn-like shape of the Lancet Edge of Aonach Beag.

A short distance from Culra, a stream runs down from the high corrie that holds Loch a' Bhealaich Bheithe, and joins up with the Allt a' Chaoil-reidhe, which pours down from the Bealach Dubh between Ben Alder and the Lancet Edge. Beyond the loch, a path crosses the craggy Bealach Breabag, with another sneaking off westwards to reach the prominent ridge which skirts the rim of the impressive Garbh Choire. After 800m or so, a high-level lochan, the Lochan a' Garbh Choire reflects the scudding clouds, and indicates the point to leave the corrie edge and cross the huge, flat plateau, to the summit cairn and trig point at 1148m.

In misty weather accurate navigation is essential. Ben Alder is a vast, high plateau containing about 160 hectares of ground above the 1000m contour. Cairngorm-like, it is surrounded by fine corries, particularly those which show their sculptured faces to the east.

My usual descent route from the summit heads north-west via Meall an t-Slugain and down to the Bealach Dubh where an

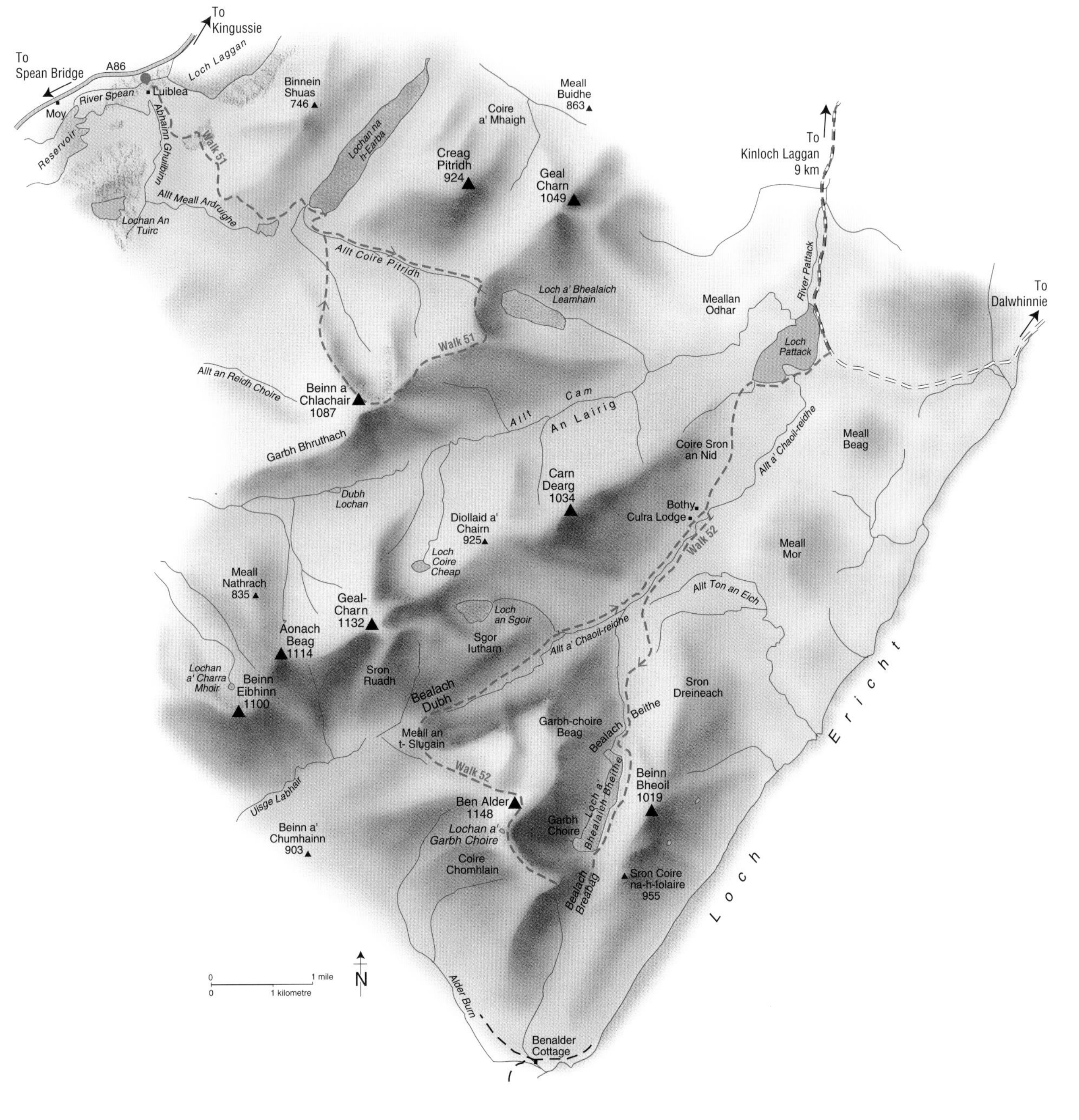

excellent footpath runs back to Culra. There has been some exceptional footpath work carried out on the track, and the bothy book at Culra contains many compliments to whoever has sweated so hard. Ben Alder Estate is one with a long reputation of kindness and hospitality to walkers. It is certainly much appreciated.

53 The Moor of Rannoch

Consider the ambitious nature of an agricultural project started in 1763 by one Ensign James Small, the government factor to the then forfeited estate of Struan Robertson. With the assistance of a number of soldiers-cum-navvies, he dug a row of five trenches on a remote plot of land on the Rannoch Moor. Small's intention, apparently, was to 'drain and sweeten the soil'. Not surprisingly, nothing came of the project.

The Soldiers' Trenches, as they came to be known, fall into insignificance when compared with the building of the West Highland Railway line, which runs along the south-eastern margin of the moor, before turning north to cross extremely boggy ground to Rannoch Station. This project taxed the great engineers of the day – eventually the track was laid on a bed of floating brushwood, a fact that probably escapes most travellers today as they wake up to a Rannoch dawn on the night sleeper from Euston.

I suspect it didn't take long for The Soldiers' Trenches to fill with sphagnum moss and bog water, and just as the remaining green corrugations (which can be seen today about 5km south of

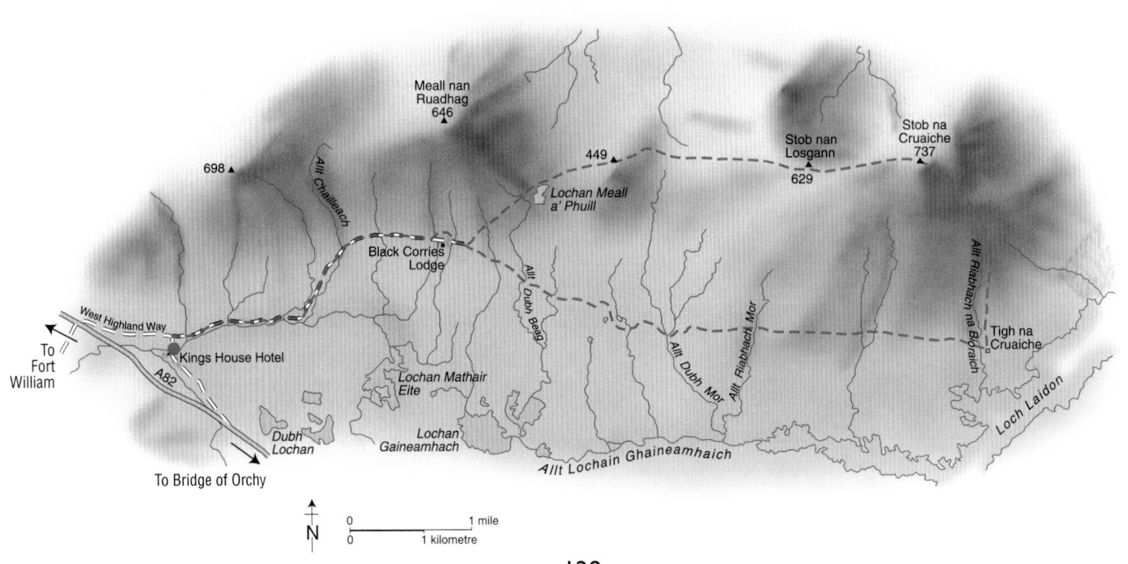

Rannoch Station) are a testament to man's enterprise, so the railway line reminds us that, despite the unqualified success of the railway, man's audacity in attempting to tame this Moor of Rannoch, is second only to his comparative inability to subjugate this huge region of knolls, rocks, spattered pools and blanket bog.

Certainly the A82 road crosses the western reaches of the Moor, but between that line and the railway is an enormous tract of land that must be the nearest thing we have to genuine wilderness in Britain. A surrealist wilderness, for in this land of the mountain and the flood, the Moor of Rannoch represents a flat, tussocky wilderness so level that you can walk in a straight line for 16km between the 290 and 300m contours.

In shape it is a great inverted triangle with its points being Loch Tulla, Kings House Hotel and Loch Rannoch. Its northern boundary is Stob na Cruaiche and the high ground south of the Blackwater Reservoir, and to the west it is bounded by the great wall of mountain that makes up the eastern fringe of the Blackmount Deer Forest. The south-eastern boundary is another huge escarpment, the Wall of Rannoch, made up of Beinn an Dothaidh, Beinn Achaladair and Beinn a' Chreachain and the lower hills which run north-eastwards to Loch Rannoch. In all the Moor of Rannoch covers an area of about 155 sq km.

I've crossed the Moor several times and have always been thrilled by its lonely emptiness. In 1792 The Revd John Lettice, later chaplain to the Duke of Hamilton, wrote of the Moor: 'An immense vacuity, with nothing in it to contemplate, unless numberless mis-shapen blocks of stone rising hideously above the surface of the earth, would be said to contradict the inanity of our prospects'. Lettice's sentiments convey his enmity with such a landscape. I find it immensely appealing, an empty quarter where the spirit can soar in unfettered abandon. I find it moving and I find it humbling.

Here's a taster, a fairly substantial taster that gives a full flavour of the place. From the Kings House Hotel on the Moor's north-west corner follow the track eastwards and north-eastwards past Black Corries Lodge. Between 3 and 5km past the Lodge the path fizzles out and although the OS map suggests there is a footpath, I've never found it. Nevertheless the going isn't too hard and for all the Moor's reputation for being a huge quaking bog, it is reasonably dry underfoot. Continue on a rough easterly bearing to the old

Route Summary

Follow the track E of Kings House Hotel, past Black Corries Lodge to a point which is at about GR333549. Continue roughly E to the ruin of Tigh na Cruaiche, then follow the Allt Riabhach na Bioraich uphill in a N direction. Continue to the summit of Stob na Cruaiche, and follow the ridge W to Stob nan Losgann. Then continue to point 449m where a path can be picked up which leads back to Black Corries Lodge and the Kings House Hotel.

Map: OS Sheet 41

Access Point: Kings House Hotel, A82

Distance: 28km

Approx Time: 8-10 hours

Grade: Moderate hill walk

ruin of Tigh na Cruaiche, high above the northern shores of Loch Laidon. From there, climb northwards beside the Allt Riabhach na Bioraich, steeply at first then flattening out before a final steeper slope leads to the superb viewpoint of Stob na Cruaiche. Here, high above the saucer-like moor, you can get a real sensation of being hemmed in by great mountains on three sides. Only to the east is there any sense of space, astonishing when you consider you're in the midst of 155 sq km of flatness.

With the Blackmount and Etive hills beckoning, head west along a rocky ridge to Stob nan Losgann and then onto a broad and featureless subsidiary which has a track running across it. Follow the track past Lochan Meall a' Phuill to Black Corries Lodge and the outward trail to Kings House. It is a big day of some 28km, but it will make you a Rannoch convert. Can a moor share the same attributes as our highest mountains? The Moor of Rannoch can.

54 Stob Ghabhar and Stob a' Choire Odhair

Route Summary

Follow the track along the N bank of the Linne nam Beathach from Forest Lodge. Leave the track at the small iron hut and head N on a footpath beside the Allt Toaig. At GR252446 the path crosses another burn and W of it a broad ridge rises to Beinn Toaig and the summit of Stob a' Choire Odhair. Descend W to a wide bealach and continue W uphill before turning SW up steep slopes to reach the Aonach Eagach. Follow this ridge to where it meets the broad SE ridge of Stob Ghabhar which is then climbed to the summit. Descend by the SE ridge back to the Allt Toaig and the earlier ascent route.

In the SMC *Guide to the Central Highlands*, author Peter Hodgkiss describes Stob Ghabhar, the hill of the goat, in glowing terms: 'For complexity of form and for the splendour of its corries and glens, this hill has few equals in the Central Highlands.'

Stob Ghabhar on foot, Stob Ghabhar by ski or with all the paraphernalia of the snow and ice climber is always challenging. Hidden away, high on the hill's glacier-scarred eastern corrie, lies the extravagantly named Upper Couloir, a target for many strong SMC parties in the latter years of the nineteenth century, before it eventually succumbed to the united efforts of A E Maylard, Professor and Mrs Adamson, and a Miss Weiss in 1897.

My own ascent of the Couloir, a steep inset gully which cleaves the upper buttress of the eastern corrie, was undramatic but memorable for all that, one of a number of different hued strands which weave a fond tapestry of Stob Ghabhar recollections in all the seasons of the year.

One recollection is of a New Year's ascent a few years ago. As we drove over the Rannoch Moor a rising sun shone off a great bank of cloud which in turn reflected the pink rays onto the hills in front of us. It was odd to see the sunrise and the pink tints of an Alpenglow at the same time, and in the same direction. Everywhere was frozen – the ground was iron hard, great swathes of solid ice covered the tracks and the waterfalls, hundreds of them on every hill from the previous day's rain, were frozen solid, stopped in their downward flow by the intense cold.

We took the westwards track from Forest Lodge near Loch Tulla, intent on Stob a' Choire Odhair and Stob Ghabhar. Several years ago I skied around these two Munros with Steve Spalding from Pitlochry. I recalled a wonderful little arête at the top of Stob Ghabhar's east ridge, a thin spine of rock with big drops on either side. On that day it was protected by a double cornice, and I remember tip-toeing very tentatively across it, skis lashed onto my pack, very aware that a misplaced footing could have serious consequences. How I longed for the comfort of a rope that day.

Stob a' Choire Odhair is an easy enough walk, making full use of a wonderful old stalker's path to gain height quickly, but as we traversed the glacier-scarred hollow to Stob Ghabhar we realised the truth behind the statement which claims there is no such thing as winter hillwalking in Scotland – it is mountaineering. We were reminded of this as we climbed towards the start of the Aonach Eagach ridge, cramponing up a steep slope in hard snow conditions. We were out of the sun, it was intensely cold and there was a very real air of gravitas about the place. As if to compensate for our discomfort, the little Aonach Eagach ridge, which I mentioned earlier, was easy. It wasn't corniced at all and we crossed it just behind an eight-year-old lad, roped together with his father.

It was only a short pull now to the summit where the sun had brought out the hordes. There were 19 of us sitting enjoying the sun and that, I'm afraid, was just too many for me. We made our escape down great sheets of snow, enjoying the downward rush as we glissaded into the evening sun.

Map: OS Sheet 50

Access Point: Forest Lodge, GR271423

Distance: 20km

Approx Time: 6-8 hours

Grade: Moderate hill walk

Translation: peak of the goat; peak of the dun-coloured corrie

Pronunciation: stop gower; stopa kora ooer

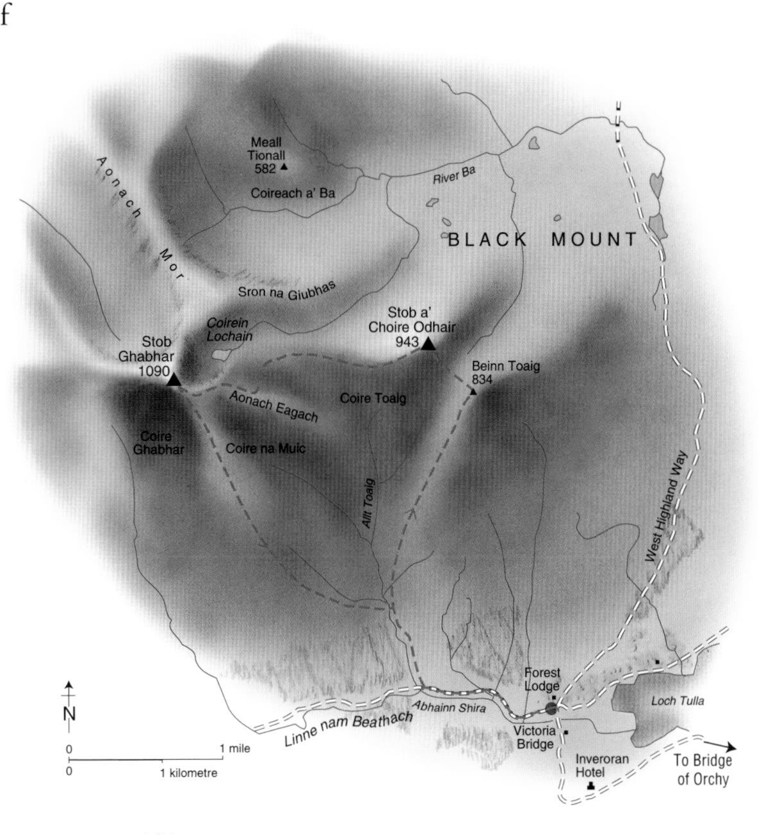

55 Buachaille Etive Mor – The Great Herdsman

Rising in a squat pyramid from the acute angle made by Glen Coe and Glen Etive, this Great Herdsman of Etive dominates its surroundings like no other mountain in Scotland. Its main ridge flanks Glen Etive for 6.5 wild kilometres and its main peak, Stob Dearg, 1021m, is the epitome of mountain grandeur.

Rhyolite walls rise from the flat moorland bedrock, splintered and riven by great gullies which partition well-known features: Crowberry Tower, the Rannoch Wall, Slime Wall, Curved Ridge, the North-East Buttress, names which bring a quickening of the spirit to anyone with a passion for this magnificent lump of rock.

My own passion for the hill evolves from years of rock climbing, in both summer and winter; loitering around its flanks, taking from its solid presence something of its spirit; evoking from it some sense of belonging, a relationship that helped shape my own nascent mountaineering desires into something much more lasting and worthwhile.

While generally recognised as a climber's mountain, the Buachaille has much to commend it to hillwalkers, and the traverse of its 6.5-km long ridge now puts two Munros in the bag, Stob Dearg, 1021m, and Stob na Broige, 956m, one conveniently at either end of the ridge. While some walkers will be happy to tackle the airy and sinuous Curved Ridge, which as the name suggests 'curves' a route up the Rannoch face of the mountain, others will happily head round the corner to Lagangarbh, where the more open aspect of Coire na Tulaich, directly behind the Scottish Mountaineering Club hut, offers a less horrific prospect.

A track crosses the River Coupall by a footbridge and makes its way steeply up into the bowels of the corrie where it continues to climb rocky slopes and terraces before taking on the steep slopes above in a series of zigzags. This can be a difficult section in winter conditions and a few years ago some walkers were avalanched on this very spot. Whatever you do, try and avoid the obvious narrowing gully at the top of the corrie. Instead, scramble up the steep ground beside the gully to top out on the broad ridge above.

Ahead now lie the peaks of the Blackmount Deer Forest, and to your left the rocky scree covered ridge which leads to the Stob Dearg summit. As you approach the top the ridge begins to narrow in a rather satisfying way and after one or two false summits you'll

Route Summary

Cross the bridge over the River Coupall and pass the Lagangarbh climbers' hut. Take the right fork in the path into Coire na Tulaich following the west bank of the burn. Climb up the corrie to its head where screes mark the ascent to a flat bealach. Turn E and cross red and pink boulders and scree trending E then NE along a ridge which narrows appreciably towards the summit. Return to the flat bealach and traverse the ridge to Stob na Broige, returning to Altnafeadh by the Lairig Gartain Pass to the NNW.

Map: OS Sheet 41

Access Point: Altnafeadh, GR221563

Distance: 13km

Approx Time: 6-8 hours

Grade: Moderate hill walk

Translation: big herdsman of Etive

Pronunciation: booachil etiv moar

Buachaille Etive Mor and the River Coupall, Glencoe

reach the large cairn which appears to sit on the very edge of nothing, with the great boggy mattress of the Rannoch Moor spread out before you like a map.

From Stob Dearg a superb high-level promenade runs in a rough south-west direction, linking together three other tops, each of which is worthy of Munro status. Just over 1.6km away, Stob na Doire's conical north-east face looks particularly impressive, and beyond it the ridge twists its way over stony ground on the gradual rise to Stob Coire Altruim.

The Buachaille's other Munro, Stob na Broige, is easily reached over a series of undulations and gives extensive views down the length of Glen Etive towards Ben Starav. To return to your starting point you're best to head back over Stob Coire Altruim to the bealach between it and Stob na Doire. From here slopes lead in a north-north-west direction into the Lairig Gartain where a footpath returns to Altnafeadh.

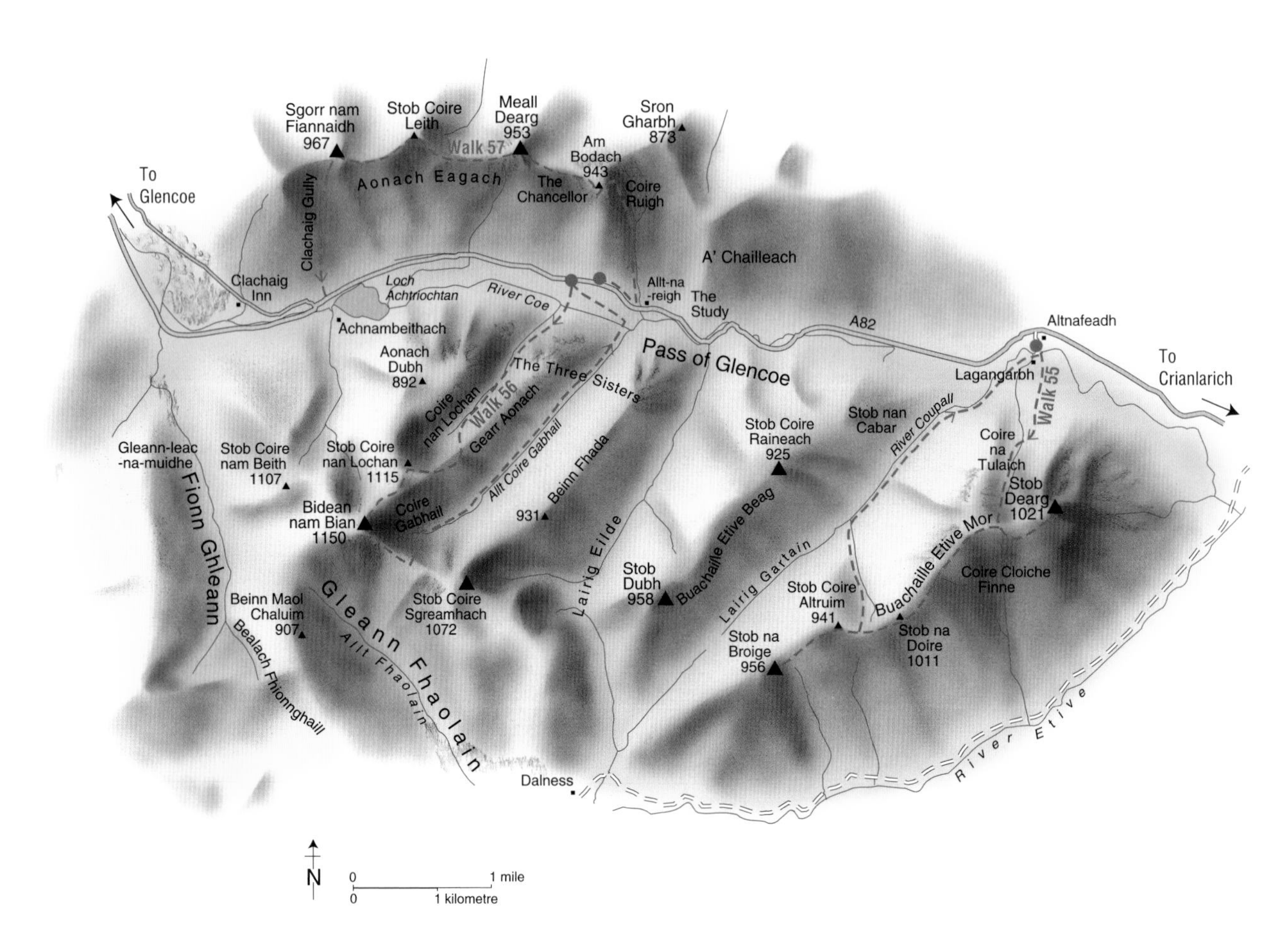

56 Bidean nam Bian – Howffs and Hills

I'm not a great lover of bothies, which attract walkers like flies to dung, but I am a staunch advocate of howffs. Bothies evoke images of man on the landscape, but howffs feel as though they are integral to the mountain – only partially shaped by man's hand, but sharing the soul of the hill. What exactly is a howff, I hear you say? Well it's a simple shelter, created from the stone of the mountain, usually built in a niche below an overhanging crag, or in a crack between great rocks; or in a hidden crevice.

The best howffs are rarely obvious – because the builder wasn't creating a public shelter, but a private bower to escape to. And the best howffs of all are old, cloaked in their own mystery.

There's a fine one on the route up to Bidean nam Bian. The floor is packed hard and firm below its rock-overhang roof, the protective dry stone wall has been built with loving attention and there is a density in the structure which cries out its impunity to the elements. Across the corrie, beyond the roar of the burn, a rockwall rears up steeply, vertically. I know that crag well, almost as intimately as I know any portion of stone in this rocky land for it was there I learned to climb. Over three decades ago, spotty faced and skinny, nervous and unassured, shown the ropes, literally, by cockily confident gangrels. I learned much from them but more importantly, in climb after climb, I learned to love this place, its crag and its burn, and its little howff.

I rarely pass by this way without diverting to it, just to sit within its damp walls and enjoy a cup of coffee while I slide into a dwam of nostalgia. It was from here that I first climbed Bidean, on a dank wet day that made the porphyr too slippery for climbing. We went for a pad instead, up the length of the corrie, past the lochans and over boulder scree to reach the foot of Stob Coire nan Lochan's east ridge, just where it levels out to become Gear Aonach. A rocky scramble took us to the summit from where a southerly ridge sweeps down into a fine bow-shaped col. Little did I see that day of the great crags of Dinner Time Buttress and Church Door Buttress as we made our way steeply up the other side to the rocky summit of Bidean nam Bian. I recall a great exhilaration when told I was standing on the highest hill in Argyll, that ancient county of the mountain and the flood.

Bidean retires rather shyly behind its outliers, but it's actually

Route Summary

From the layby on the A82 drop down to the River Coe and cross it by the footbridge (see map on page 134). Follow the path up into Coire an Lochan as far as the lochans in the upper corrie. Beyond the lochans bear left to gain the E ridge of Stob Coire nan Lochan. Scramble to the summit then descend S and SSW to a bealach before climbing steeply to the summit of Bidean nam Bian. Follow the ridge SE to the top of Coire Gabhail, descend into the corrie by way of the steep path and scree slopes and follow the path the length of the corrie to another footbridge over the River Coe. From the bridge a path returns to the lay-by.

Map: OS Sheet 41

Access Point: A82, GR168569

Distance: 10km

Approx Time: 5-7 hours

Grade: Moderate hill walk

Translation: peak of the mountains

Pronunciation: beetyan nam beeoan

Stob Coire nam Beith, Bidean nam Bian from Stob Coire nan Lochan, Glencoe

more of a mountain massif than a single top. Essentially this Peak of the Mountains couldn't have a better name, for its summit is the culmination of four great ridges which give way to no fewer than nine separate summits and cradle three deep and distinctive corries. It even has a secondary Munro these days; Stob Coire Sgreamhach was promoted to Munro status in the 1997 revisions. A number of alternative routes ascend Bidean nam Bian but my usual route is this one, by Coire nan Lochan and its eponymous peak.

The linking of Stob Coire Beith offers a good descent route to Achnambeithach at the western end of Loch Achtriochtan, but there's a whole ridge waiting your attentions to the south-west, a glorious ridge with wonderful views down the length of Etive to the fabled lands of Deirdre, a ridge which skirts the head of Coire Gabhail before climbing the boulders and screes of the new Munro, Stob Coire Sgreamhach. A descent can be attempted down the 3-km length of Beinn Fhada, but it's awkward and difficult in snowy conditions. An escape from the Fhada ridge can be made by dropping down steep slopes into Coire Gabhail, but you have to backtrack quite a distance to avoid a deep chasm that lines the upper corrie floor. Better to return down the north-west ridge of Stob Coire Sgreamhach towards Bidean and drop down the steep headwall of Coire Gabhail, then down scree slopes to where the corrie begins to open out. A footpath then offers easier going down through the great jumble of boulders that fill the woodlands at its mouth, then down to the footbridge over the River Coe.

But the real bonus of this descent route is another little howff, this time well hidden in the confusion of giant boulders and trees. Most regular visitors to the Glen Coe hills will know the location of my first howff, but I'm keeping this other one secret; a lovely hidden spot where I can go, drink the last of my coffee and prepare myself to descend into that other world to which I also belong.

57 The Aonach Eagach

It can be a daunting sight. A switchbacked fin of rock, steep-sided and exposed with a number of pinnacles which look as though they could well bar any progress. And to make matters worse you have to negotiate the most awkward move before you even set foot on the ridge proper. It's a situation that has deterred many, but it's good to get it into perspective. In snow and ice the traverse of the Aonach Eagach is a winter mountaineering expedition, a fantastic outing for those who are experienced in such things. In summer it's no more than an exhilarating walk, and in terms of seriousness this Notched Ridge of Glen Coe doesn't even begin to compare with the Cuillin of Skye, or the Corrag Bhuidhe ridge of An Teallach. Even the A' Chir ridge on Arran is harder.

The big put-off to many walkers is that the Aonach Eagach is officially graded as a Grade 1 rock climb, but all that means is that here and there you're going to have to use your hands – but the actual scrambling sections are more exhilarating than serious. I've never met a hillwalker who hasn't been thrilled by it.

Almost 4km in length and boasting two Munros, the ridge itself is the crest of the steep, scree- and gully-riven wall that forms the northern barrier of Glen Coe and it's recommended that once you take the first tentative steps off the summit of Am Bodach at its eastern end, you stick with the ridge until the end. A descent from anywhere in-between poses more difficulties than the ridge itself, and navigation along the crest couldn't be easier.

A car park to the west of the house at Allt-na-reigh is the usual starting point. A signpost points the way up behind the house, where a well-used footpath climbs up into Coire Ruigh. Higher up a junction of paths offers a choice of route; go left for a more direct approach to Am Bodach via its rocky south-east ridge, or go

Route Summary

Take the path behind the house of Allt-na-reigh up the slopes of Am Bodach (see map on page 134). Follow the edge of the crags to the left of Am Bodach's cairn in a WNW direction. A descent starts the ridge traverse proper. Follow the ridge to Meall Dearg then follow a line of fence posts along the crest and traverse the Crazy Pinnacles. More fence posts accompany you to Stob Coire Leith, before the ridge levels out towards Sgorr nam Fiannaidh. Descend due S of this summit, picking a route with care through rocky outcrops. The alternative descent is 800m further W of the summit and follows a very eroded path on the W side of Clachaig Gully. (NB This path has a lot of loose stones and rock on it and there is a danger of knocking scree into the Gully where climbers could well be put in danger.)

Map: OS Sheet 41

Access Point: Allt-na-reigh, GR 176566

Distance: 6.5km

Approx Time: 3-5 hours

Grade: Moderate hill walk/scramble

Translation: notched ridge

Pronunciation: oenoch egoch

The Aonach Eagach Ridge from Meall Mor, Glencoe

right to continue up Coire Ruigh, following a stream which takes you close to the main Am Bodach/Sron Garbh ridge just north-east of Am Bodach's summit. Make your way up grassy slopes onto the broad ridge and climb the remaining slopes to the summit, and your first breathtaking view of the sinuous, rocky ridge before you.

The descent from Am Bodach to the ridge proper is considered to be the crux of the route! In effect what we have is a 20m drop-off, which looks much worse than it actually is. Face inwards, and look for the well polished holds – they're definitely there, and in a few moments you'll be down on the crest of the ridge, striding purposefully along the fairly easy gradient to a top beyond which lie the slopes to the first Munro, Meall Dearg, 953m.

The next section, between Meall Dearg and Stob Coire Leith, is best. A number of 'gendarmes', the Crazy Pinnacles, appear to bar progress and while the path and the crampon marks of generations of climbers make route-finding relatively straightforward there may be one or two sections which raise your pulse rate. But the scrambling is easy, the situation is exhilarating and once the two final pinnacles are surmounted (they offer the most exposed scrambles on the route), there is always a mild sense of disappointment. The rest of the ridge, into a dip immediately

Bidean nam Bian and Loch Achtriochtan from the summit of Am Bodach, Glencoe

before Stob Coire Leith and then an easy walk on a broad ridge to the second of the Munros, Sgorr nam Fiannaidh, 967m, is always an anti-climax. I was once so exhilarated by the ridge that I reached the end, turned round immediately, and followed it all over again in the opposite direction. I don't think my appetite for the Aonach Eagach could ever be completely sated.

From the summit of Sgorr nam Fiannaidh there are several descent options. Some will prefer to continue in a north-west direction to include Sgorr na Ciche, the Pap of Glencoe, in their traverse. Experienced walkers may continue west for about 500m before leaving the ridge and picking up the diabolical footpath that drops down to the Clachaig Inn beside the deep slit of the Clachaig Gully. This is a steep, scree-scabbed, knee-wrenching descent and isn't generally recommended, although I have to confess it's the route I usually take – the quickest descent to the pub! Probably the safest route is to continue west for a couple of hundred metres or so, then turn south-eastwards into the corrie of the Altan t-Sidhein and weave a route through the outcrops and boulders all the way down to the road near Loch Achtriochtan. Great care should be taken on any of the suggested descent routes. These slopes are steep.

58 The Ring of Steall

Route Summary

From the car park at Polldubh follow the Nevis gorge footpath to the triple hawser bridge at Steall. Cross the bridge and follow the footpath below the waterfall and into Coire Chadha Chaoruinn where the path rises in a series of zigzags to the summit of An Gearanach, then 500m further on, An Garbhanach. Follow the obvious ridge now to Stob Coire a' Chairn, Am Bodach and Sgorr an Iubhair. Head N now, across the Devil's Ridge to Sgurr a' Mhaim and descend back to Glen Nevis by the NW ridge above Coire Sgorach.

The 15-km Mamores Ridge has long been considered one of the great Scottish hillwalks, with Glen Nevis separating it from the Grey Corries in the north, and long slopes running down to Kinlochleven in the south, all well served by a network of old stalkers' paths. A traverse of the ridge, from Sgurr Eilde Mor in the east to Mullach nan Coirean in the west, is a demanding day along a high switchbacked route, with an interesting deviation to take in the dramatically named Devil's Ridge between Sgorr an Iubhair and Sgurr a' Mhaim. Despite its name the Devil's Ridge is far from demonic, although in winter it certainly demands respect.

A shorter, but no less dramatic route takes in four of the Mamores Munros – An Gearanach, 982m, Stob Choire a' Chairn, 981m, Am Bodach, 1032m, and Sgurr a' Mhaim, 1099m. Commonly known as the Ring of Steall, these hills form a high mountain wall around Choire a' Mhaim at the head of the Steall flats, birthplace of the Grey Mare's Tail of the Steall Waterfall. The Ring of Steall boasts four other tops over 914m, including the recently demoted Munro of Sgorr an Iubhair, to give a route of 15km and over 1200m of climbing. Views extend across Ben Nevis, the Aonachs, the Grey Corries and Loch Linnhe to the hills of Ardgour and Morvern.

The Ring of Steall is an outing I've never tired of, in summer or winter, and the walk-in before the actual climbing is paticularly fine.

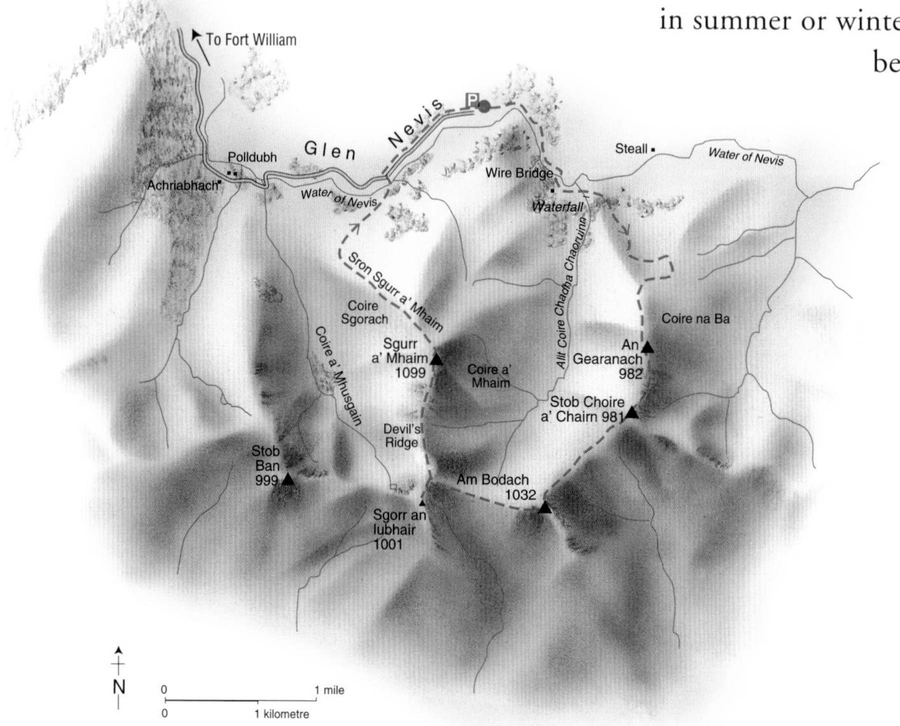

From the car park at Polldubh a track weaves through the trees above the Himalayan-like Nevis Gorge, a place which WH Murray once described as the 'best half mile in Scotland'. Suddenly the path is squeezed out into a flat, green meadowland through which the Water of

Am Bodach from Stob Coire a' Chairn, Mamores

Map: OS Sheet 41
Access Points: Polldubh car park in Glen Nevis
Distance: 15km
Approx Time: 6-8 hours
Grade: Moderate hill walk

Steall flows quietly, as though unaware of what fate, and the Nevis Gorge, has in store for it. Below the 100m Grey Mare's Tail, by the old cottage of Steall, a triple hawser bridge offers a route across the river to where a footpath runs east past the hut, below the waterfall and a tree-clad buttress into Coire Chadha Chaoruinn.

Cross the Allt Coire Chadha Chaoruinn where another path leads to some long zigzags and takes you onto the north-west spur of An Gearanach, which roughly translates as 'the complainer' – perhaps because it was unmarked on the old OS map! A short ridge runs south to An Garbhanach. Here another ridge continues south west for a short distance before rising to the summit of Stob Coire a' Chairn. Big drops fall off to the south into Coire na Ba which eventually leads down to the heights of Kinlochmore and Kinlochleven.

The worst over, you can start to really enjoy yourself now, with a long ridge undulating towards Am Bodach, before swinging west and north-west to reach the peak of the yew, Sgorr an Iubhair.

North of here, the Devil's Ridge reaches its high point at Stob Choire a' Mhail before narrowing again in its link with the stony slopes of Sgurr a' Mhaim. At the narrowest section, a footpath

Glen Nevis Gorge and An Gearanach, Mamores

drops down on the east side avoiding major difficulties before taking a scrambly route back onto the ridge. From here the slopes open on to the wide quartz-covered slopes of Sgurr a' Mhaim before descending a curving ridge above Coire Sgorach. A final steep descent down the nose, the Sron Sgurr a' Mhaim, takes you back into Glen Nevis about 2km west of the car park at Polldubh.

59 Glen Nevis' Gorge and Meadows

It has been described as 'the greatest half mile in Scotland' and WH Murray, that doyen of Scottish mountaineering writers, once suggested it is a 'gorge scene of Himalayan character'. From the public car park at the end of the road in Glen Nevis, a footpath runs through the oaks, rowans, birches and pines high above the tumultuous and tortured waters of the Nevis Gorge, before reaching the comparative sanity of flat meadowland below the long silver streak of the Steall Waterfall.

The Himalayan comparison is accurate, as the narrow, rocky footpath traces its way through the woods high above the churning waters of the River Nevis as it hurries down from the Steall meadows above to the comparatively flat lower Glen Nevis. In the course of this short journey the raging waters have gouged pots and cauldrons out of the river bed, and the steep walls of the gorge have been hollowed and smoothed into great chambers. And all the while the rock walls echo to the sound of this aquatic thunder.

As you climb higher into the gorge, the footpath and river come closer together to squeeze their way through the narrow gap at the top, and suddenly, without warning, the whole scene changes.

Instead of the raging waters, the river takes on a stately air as it meanders across the meadowflats of Steall. Ahead of you, like a white slash against the cliffs of Sgurr a' Mhaim, is the 110m Steall Waterfall. At the foot of the waterfall is a tiny whitewashed cottage, now a mountaineering club hut, which can only be reached by a three-tier wire bridge across the river.

This is one of the most popular walks in Scotland, and justifiably so. Start at the car park at the end of the public road in Glen Nevis. Follow the signpost which points the way of the 'Public Footpath to Corrour, and Rannoch'. Follow this path into the trees, ignoring the diversion to the right which you pass shortly after the start. The path climbs higher and crosses a couple of streams, and soon you get your first view up towards the Steall Waterfall. As the path continues to climb, it becomes rockier and you'll encounter several easy scrambly sections. After 20 minutes or so, just as the path and the river come closer together, a squeeze through some rocks takes you into upper Glen Nevis, a flat area of meadows. Continue following the path towards the wire bridge which crosses the river to Steall Cottage. This path actually runs all the way to Corrour Station, and ultimately to Dalwhinnie, but you don't have to go that far! It's probably worth carrying on for 800m or so to the old ruins at Steall before retracing your steps back past the wire bridge to the entrance to the gorge.

Here, to the right of the gorge footpath, another path picks its way through a gap in an old wall. Beyond the wall the path becomes quite distinct as it zigzags its way above the gorge with superb views up to Sgurr a' Mhaim, and down Glen Nevis to the sweeping ridges of Mullach nan Corean. Follow the zigzags up to a plateau crowned by a substantial cairn, and then follow it as it descends through the pines, oaks and rowans back to the lower path, a few hundred metres short of the car park.

Route Summary

Leave the car park at the end of the public road in Glen Nevis and follow the signposted footpath all the way to the Steall meadows. Follow the path towards the wire bridge which crosses the river to Steall Cottage. Continue to the old ruins at Steall before retracing your steps back past the wire bridge to the entrance to the gorge. To the right of the footpath, another path goes through a gap in a wall. Beyond the wall it zigzags its way high above the gorge to a grassy plateau and a cairn. Leave the cairn and follow the path as it descends through the trees to the lower path, a few hundred metres short of the car park.

Map: OS Sheet 41

Access Point: Polldubh car park in upper Glen Nevis

Distance: 6km

Approx Time: 2-4 hours

Grade: Easy low-level walk

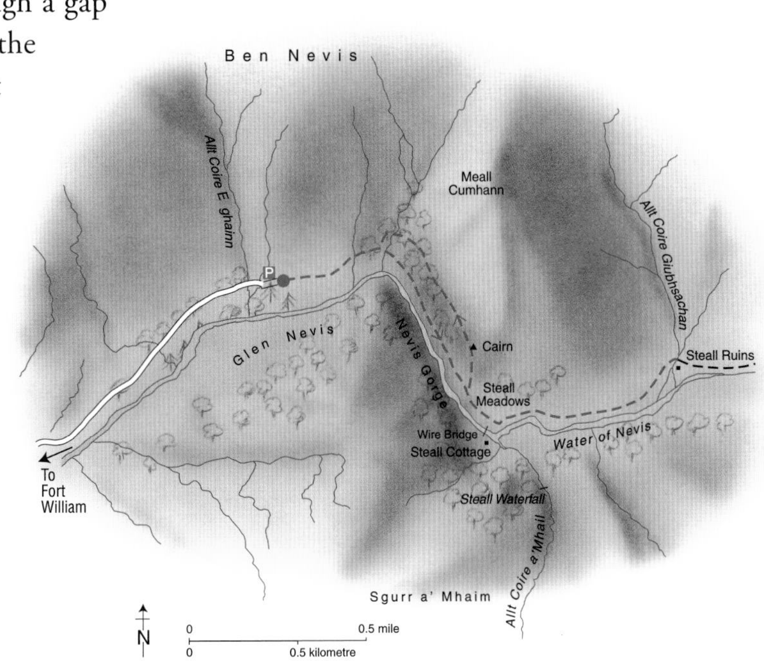

Route Summary

Take the tourist route from Achintee in Glen Nevis to Lochan Meall an t-Suidhe. Pass the lochan below Carn Dearg and descend to the valley of the Allt a' Mhuillin. Cross the river near GR154739 and climb E up steep slopes to gain the Carn Beag Dearg ridge. Follow it SSE to Carn Mor Dearg, cross the arête to the E ridge of Ben Nevis and climb to the summit. Descend by the tourist track.

Map: OS Sheet 41

Access Point: Achintee in Glen Nevis

Distance: 20km

Approx Time: 7-9 hours

Grade: Strenuous hill walk

Translation: possibly terrible or venomous or heavenly; big red hill

Pronunciation: byn nevis; kaarn more jerrack

60 Ben Nevis and Carn Mor Dearg

Hamish Brown once described Britain's highest mountain as a harlot, a mountain of 'loveless loveliness'. I think I know what he was alluding to, for the Ben solicits the unwary and the inexperienced, offering a benign façade which veils its true heart, a heart which is as cold as stone.

I love Ben Nevis, and yet I hate it. I'm drawn to it, and yet it frightens me. Its curves and corries, cliffs and gullies are familiar to me, yet I'm a stranger in its grasp. Of all Scotland's mountains only the brooding Liathach in Torridon has the same effect on my spirit; unwelcoming and aloof and not a little scary. I'm not sure why this should be, but I think mountains have characters, even if that assumed disposition is only a summation of our own perceptions, experiences and prejudices, and I'm afraid my own perception of Ben Nevis is of a cold-hearted temptress.

For many, Ben Nevis represents a simple challenge – to climb to the highest summit in the land. At 1344m above sea level that's not a challenge that is easily met, or rewarded. It involves a long and tiresome toil up a rough track to a summit which on most days is shrouded in cloud. In summer you have to share your experience with hundreds of others, and in winter the conditions are generally arctic. More people die on Ben Nevis in winter than on any other mountain in Scotland.

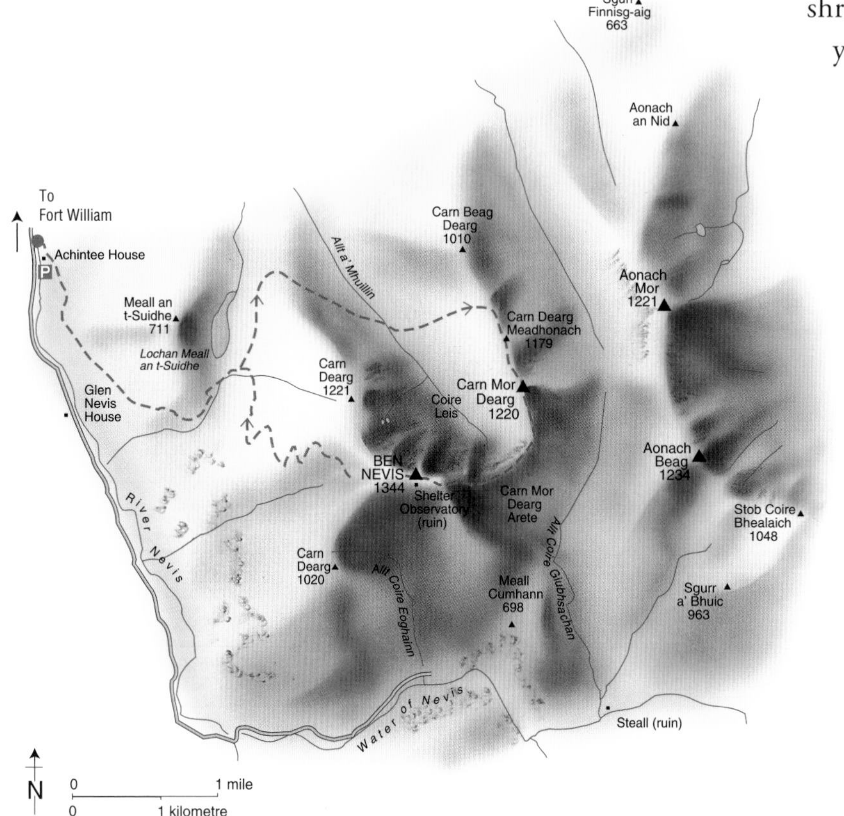

The origin of the name Nevis is rather obscure, but the general belief is that it means 'terrible', from the old Irish Gaelic word neamhaise, or the Highland Gaelic word nimhaise, meaning 'no beauty'. Others believe the word comes from

Ben Nevis and Carn Mor Dearg from Aonach Mor

neamh which could be 'heaven'. Either interpretation seems apt, but one thing is certain. On a good day the ascent of Ben Nevis, via the glen of the Allt a' Mhuillin and neighbouring Carn Mor Dearg, is one of the finest high-level walks in the Highlands, an ascent which intimately introduces walkers to another aspect of this mountain we enigmatically refer to as, simply, the Ben.

Begin your ascent from Achintee in Glen Nevis and follow the so-called tourist route (don't be tempted by such descriptions as 'tourist tracks' – that particular route was never designed for tourists), as far as the Half-Way lochan below Meall an t-Suidhe. Keep heading north, down into the glen of the Allt a' Mhuillin, across the river and up the heather and granite slopes of Carn Beag Dearg. From here, a superb high-level promenade carries you over Carn Dearg Meadhonach to Carn Mor Dearg, 1220m and from this elevated traverse the true splendour of Ben Nevis becomes apparent.

Across the depths of Coire Leis it looks as though some malevolent force has taken a scalpel through the Ben's dome-like profile, revealing innards of frowning crags, buttresses and towers, the true heart of the mountain. Great scree fans give way to narrow tortured gullies that invite mountaineers into their clammy depths, stone-chutes that even in summer are often choked with dirty, stone-flecked snow and ice. Generations of climbers have pioneered long and difficult routes on the rock and when the mountain changes its face, chameleon-like, with the advent of winter snows, the climbers return with axes and crampons to test themselves on the white frozen shroud, where the cold throbs through your body like toothache.

This naked display of the north-east face of Ben Nevis is, in anyone's terms, a magnificent sight, and renews enthusiasm for the summit. A slender tendon of rock joins Carn Mor Dearg to Ben Nevis, a high arête that forms a graceful, sensual curve of rock – what is essentially the south-west wall of Coire Leis. This Carn Mor Dearg arête is a rocky tightrope, broader than it first appears, and a narrow path skirts along its eastern edge. Marginally exposed, enough to raise the heart-beat, there are nevertheless few difficulties and in no time you find yourself trudging up the rocky slopes above Coire Leis to the summit of Ben Nevis.

An orange Nissen hut, ruins of the old meteorological station, myriad cairns and litter greet you at the top. It's not my favourite summit. Unsightly cairns cross the narrow plateau leading you downwards to interminable zigzags, paths of loose scree, and eventually, Glen Nevis. The great paradox of Ben Nevis.

61 The Easains – Stob a' Choire Mheadhoin and Stob Coire Easain

61 Route Summary

From the parking place at Fersit take a rough SW line to gain the ridge. Climb two small rises and continue SSW to Stob a' Choire Mheadhoin. Descend SW down rocky slopes to the bealach and climb a rock-strewn ridge SSW to Stob Coire Easain. Descend the NW ridge to the open moorland of Coire Laire. Follow the river until you reach a bulldozed track. Follow the track through the forest and from the far side of the forest turn left, and descend to the old British Aluminium Company railway track which can be followed back to Fersit.

These elegant hills are generally known as the Easains, but Hamish Brown once nicknamed them This Yin and That Yin, and the names seem to have stuck. I like the Ying and Yang element, and you can prolong the oriental metaphor just a tad by suggesting that, like Siamese twins, they are joined at the hip by a high bealach which makes them a delightful pair to combine into a single walk.

Bordering the edges of one of Scotland's true wilderness areas, the vast acres of the Rannoch Moor, the situation of these hills gives them an air of remoteness and wildness, their apparent isolation from neighbouring hills accentuated by the waters of Loch Treig which bite deep into the moor at their feet, like a long fiord. Extra dramatic effect is given by the huge wall of Stob Coire Sgriodain on the other side of the loch. Views of the Grey Corries and Mamores are superb.

Map: OS Sheet 41

Access Point: Fersit, GR350782. Tulloch Station is on the Glasgow/Fort William Railway

Distance: 15km

Approx Time: 5-7 hours

Grade: Moderate hill walk

Translation: peak of the middle corrie; peak of the corrie of the little waterfall

Pronunciation: stop kora vane; stop kora esan

The minor road from the Laggan/Spean Bridge road at Tulloch to Fersit passes the old house where Rudolf Hess was held captive during the war. I wonder what he thought of these hills and whether he ever remembered them during his long years of imprisonment in Spandau. Near the head of Loch Treig there's a parking area close to where the Fersit road turns off. From this point take to the slopes of Creag Fhiaclach following a rough south-westerly line onto the ridge. Further south the east-facing slopes of the ridge become quite steep and broken so it's best to reach the crest of the ridge as soon as you can.

Once on the ridge you're faced with a 4-km walk to Stob a' Choire Mheadhoin, 1105m, but with ever-widening views to the south-west you find yourself drawn along irresistibly, over a couple of steeper steps in the ridge towards the stony summit slopes of Mheadhoin. From the flat summit table, stop to admire Stob Coire Easain, 1115m, rising sharply above the slabs of Coire Easain Beag, steep slopes leading to a fine, sharp peak – all that a mountain should be!

From Stob a' Choire Mheadoin descend south-west down rocky slopes to the bealach. Ascend a rocky ridge west-south-west to reach Stob Coire Easain's eastern ridge. The climb to the summit is steep and in winter conditions can hold great ice sheets. From the summit cairn follow the steep north-west ridge which drops down to the moors of Coire Laire. Follow the Allt Laire until you reach another bulldozed track. This leads through a forest plantation and down easy slopes to the old British Aluminium Company railway track, which returns to your starting point.

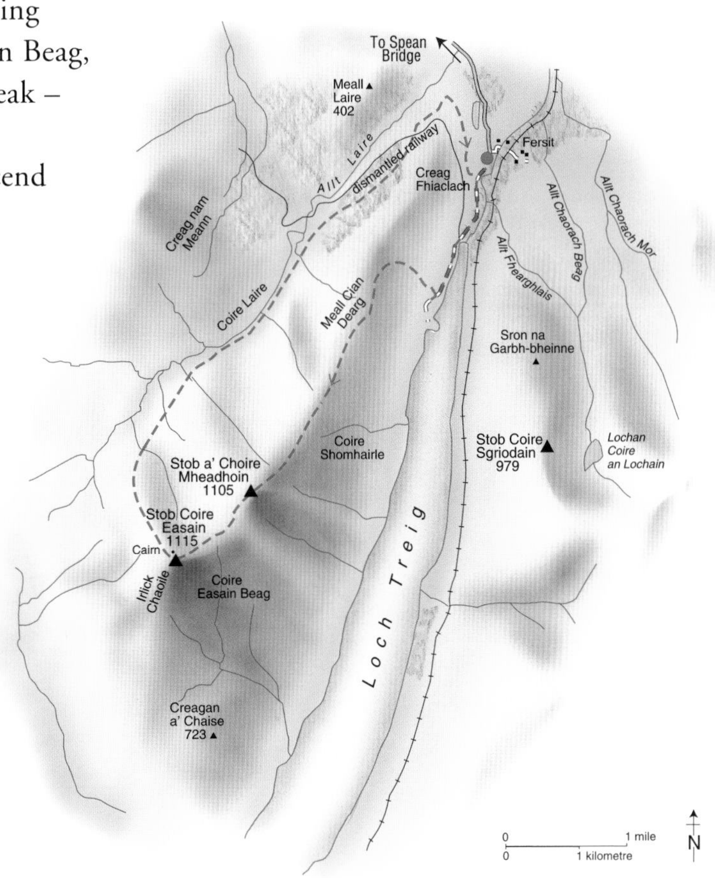

THE WESTERN HIGHLANDS

The Western Highlands includes those areas west of Loch Linnhe and the Great Glen. Its northern boundary is the A890, Lochcarron to Achnasheen road.

The main feature of this area is the preponderance of great sea lochs, biting deeply into a landscape where the mountains rise to over 914m from sea level. Inland lochs, like Loch Shiel and Loch Quoich similarly mirror high mountains. While the hills of Knoydart, once reckoned to be the last remaining wilderness in Britain, are becoming more and more popular, the Corbetts of Rois-Bheinn, Glenfinnan and Garbh Bheinn of Ardgour are relatively unfrequented.

THE WALKS

62	Garbh Bheinn of Ardgour	13km
63	The Hills of the Rois-Bheinn Peninsula	16km
64	The Glenfinnan Corbetts	12km
65	Streap	14km
66	Sgurr na Ciche	21km
67	Knoydart's Ladhar Bheinn	35km
68	Beinn Sgritheall	10km
69	The Saddle/An Diollaid	16km
70	Gleouraich and Spidean Mialach	12km
71	Sgurr nan Ceathreamhnan	22km

Sgurr nan Ceathreamhnan from above Allt a' Chomlain to the south

62 Garbh Bheinn of Ardgour

I've never been lucky with Ardgour weather, but one visit in particular is firmly fixed in my memory, for despite shocking conditions, my expectations of the mountain were met in every way. The rain was sweeping down Ardgour's Glen an Iubhair in sheets, spouting off the hillsides in a thousand new waterfalls.

This is a long and rugged glen at the best of times and the huge, rocky hill that rose steeply on my left is well named the Rough Hill. Garbh Bheinn, at 885m, falls just short of the 3000ft (914m) mark, but is well guarded by steep slabs, ridges and buttresses of crystalline gneiss. Roughness, coarseness, and ruggedness dominates – Garbh Bheinn of Ardgour, on a wild day, is the very epitome of such asperity.

I'd lost count of how many times I had gazed across at Ardgour from Ballachulish where Garbh Bheinn's sharp outline always suggested mountain promise, that same promise which exists within the ragged form of Arran's Sleeping Warrior when viewed from the Ayrshire coast. But Arran is an island, sequestered from the mainland by the waters of the Firth of Clyde, and although Ardgour is very much part of mainland Scotland, it too lies across a neck of water suggesting a romanticism, and isolation, that it doesn't truly deserve. But the mystery prevails, the mountain still draws the eye and you have to go to it. Despite the numerous occasions I had gazed at it dancing on the sea in the heat of the sun, clear for all the world to enjoy, my visits inevitably clashed with bad

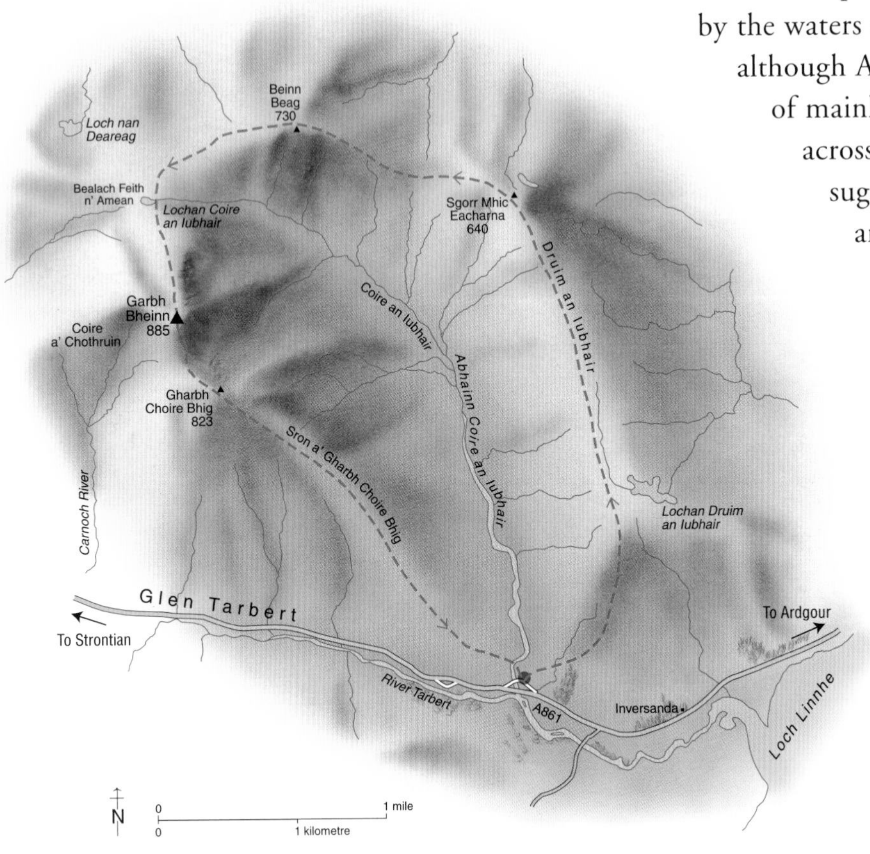

weather. Garbh Bheinn of Ardgour is still, however, high on my list of favourite places, a rough diamond in an area of shimmering pearls.

The normal route up Sron a' Gharbh Choire Bhig is fairly straightforward, a long climb up a rocky ridge, all the way to the top of the Sron, which offers imposing views of Garbh Bheinn's south face, a veritable sea of broken gneiss. On the left of the Sron is Coire a' Chothruin, the source of the Carnoch River which flows into Loch Sunart at the west end of Glen Tarbert. From Sron a' Gharbh Choire's summit, a rough descent north-west drops you down to a rocky bealach from where a steeper, slabbier ridge climbs directly to the west ridge of Garbh Bheinn. Once you reach this ridge the summit cairn is only a few metres east, perched on the very edge of its south face, a superb eyrie from which to gaze across Loch Linnhe at the mountains of Glen Coe and Lochaber. A steep and awkward descent can be made to the Bealach Feith n' Amean in the north and back down Coire an Iubhair to the road, but most folk return to the bealach below the west ridge and descend in a rough north-east direction into Coire an Iubhair, where a path traces its way down between the crags and boulders.

A longer route, with superb views of Garbh Bheinn's rocky north-east face, is offered by the ridge to the right of Coire an Iubhair, Druim an Iubhair. This long, broad ridge sweeps round the side of the glen in a great curve, climbs over the knobbly summits of Sgor Mhic Eacharna and Beinn Beag, before dipping steeply down to the Bealach Feith n' Amean. From here, some precise navigation, and a steep, awkward climb leads to Garbh Bheinn's narrow summit. If you're fit, and a fairly competent scrambler, this is a route with wonderful rewards, especially if, unlike me, you get some good weather.

Starting up the broad grassy ridge to the east of Coire an Iubhair I knew that if the weather didn't improve I would probably never make Garbh Bheinn. The Druim an Iubhair starts steeply up a fairly short craggy hillside and soon levels out onto a broad hummocky ridge dotted with silver pools. Behind me squalls were setting up whirlpools across Loch Linnhe and the hills of Appin merged into the cloudy sky.

It didn't take long for me to realise that my enemy wasn't the rain but the wind. I dropped down east into the lee but could see the wind gusting snow showers across the ridge ahead of me. Even in

Route Summary

From the car park beside the bridge, head NE to climb the S slopes of the Druim an Iubhair. Continue N along the broad ridge, ascend Sgorr Mhic Eacharna before descending in a ENE direction to reach a high bealach. Climb the steep E slopes of Beinn Bheag, pass the summit and descend steeply to Lochan Coire an Iubhair. From here climb steep grassy slopes then rocky slopes to gain the N ridge of Garbh Bheinn. Pass above the steep buttresses to the summit then descend the Sron a' Gharbh Choire Bhig back to your starting point.

Map: OS Sheets 40 and 49

Access Point: Bridge over the Abhainn Coire an Iubhair, A861

Distance: 13km

Approx Time: 6-8 hours

Grade: Strenuous hill walk

Translation: rough hill

Pronunciation: gaaravin

Garbh Bheinn, Ardgour from the east across Loch Linnhe

the lee it was a struggle to stay upright. The waterlogged ground beneath my feet was covered in slushy snow and I realised I wasn't going to make it much further.

But even on such a day good fortune can smile, and during one short lull in the weather I managed to creep up the back of Sgor Mhic Eacharna. Miraculously I wasn't sent scurrying back down by the gale but managed to brace myself between some rocks, from where I took a number of photographs of Garbh Bheinn, glorious in full frontal rocky splendour. What a marvellous mountain this is. Its eastern face is so full of character, bounded by rocky features – the Great Ridge on the left climbing up to the summit in a sweep of gneiss with Great Gully to its right. The Pinnacle Ridge and north-east buttress are other principal bastions.

Sheltered a little now, I managed to make reasonable progress over Beinn Bheag from where I slithered down a steep, slushy ridge to Lochan Coire an Iubhair in the Bealach Feith n' Amean. The ascent of Garbh Beinn's northern flanks looks fearsome but fortunately for me a great snow ramp bypassed most of the difficulties. It was, however, very steep and I clutched my ice axe with white knuckles. From the summit, the descent and short climb to Sron a' Gharbh Choire Bhig was straightforward, but it was a tired McNeish who toiled down the final ridge back to the car and a pint of beer in Ardgour.

63 The Hills of the Rois-Bheinn Peninsula

The rough and rocky hills of the Moidart peninsula, just south of the Fort William to Mallaig road, are small in height but enormous in character. I walked these hills as a birthday treat several years ago and the night before I camped on the shore of Loch Ailort and enjoyed one of the most stunning western sunsets I've ever seen. The dying sun set over the Cuillin of Rum in a burst of yellows and reds and within moments the waters of the sea-loch itself were running blood-red. It was a good omen for my birthday walk.

Druim Fiaclach, Sgurr na Ba Glaise, Rois-Bheinn and An Stac (the latter three are Corbetts) form a lovely horseshoe ridge around Coire a' Bhuiridh, the yellow corrie, just south of Lochailort in the north-west corner of Moidart.

A farm track runs in an east-north-east direction from Inverailort and crosses a burn, which issues from a low col between the hillock of Tom Odhar and the north-east ridge of Seann Chruach. You should follow the footpath through the col and onto the open moorland beyond where the Allt a' Bhuiridh chuckles down from the corrie above.

Cross to the east bank of the river and climb the western slopes of Beinn Coire nan Gall, heading towards the col between it and Druim Fiaclach. From the col, climb to the summit of Fiaclach by its steep north ridge. Druim Fiaclach is made up of two long and narrow ridges. The best route lies along the south-western one where you

Route Summary

Take a farm track ENE from Inverailort, then a footpath through the col between Tom Odhar and the NE ridge of Seann Chruach. Cross to the E bank of the Allt a' Bhuiridh, climb the W slopes of Beinn Coire nan Gall to the col, and climb the steep N ridge of Druim Fiaclach. Follow the SW ridge to a small col, continue S over another bump to a high lochan. Go WSW, over another top then onto the summit of Sgurr na Ba Glaise. Descend to the Bealach an Fhiona. Follow a wall to the E top and trig point of Rois-Bheinn. Return to the bealach, descend rocky slopes to the N and ascend slopes to the summit of An Stac. Descend N, then NNE to Seann Chruach, then down its NE ridge to the woods above the Tom Odhar col. Return by the path to Inverailort.

Map: OS Sheet 40

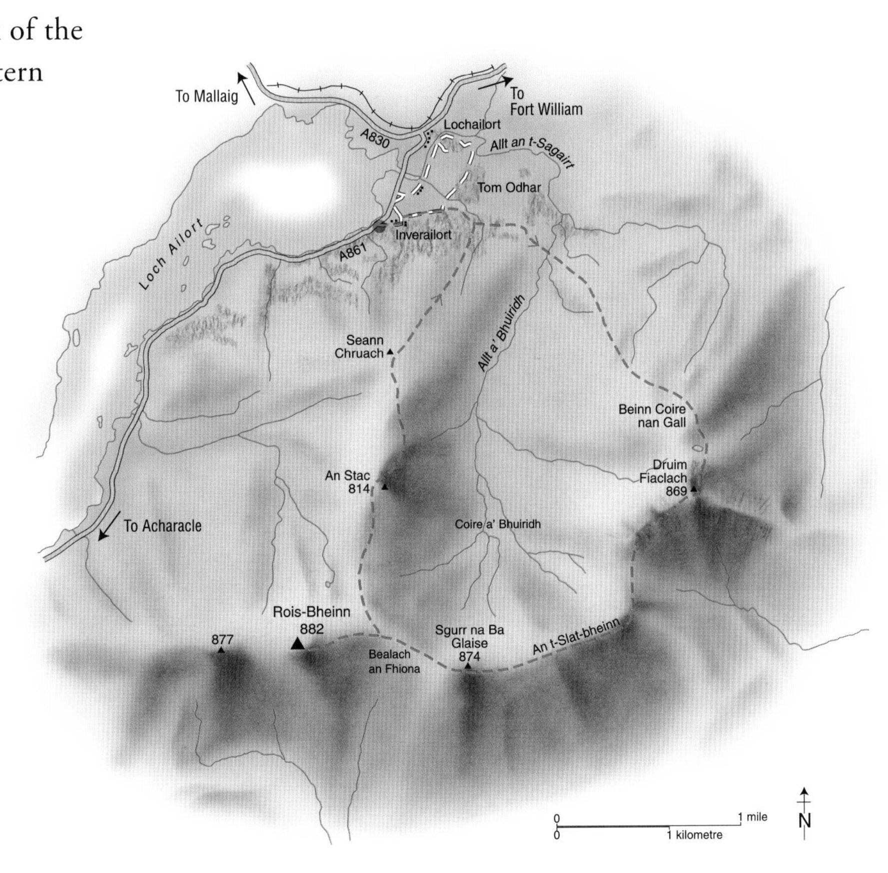

Rum, Eigg, The Sound of Arisaig, Ardnish and Loch Ailort from Rois-Bheinn

Access Point: Inverailort
Distance: 16km
Approx Time: 6-8 hours
Grade: Strenuous hill walk

can enjoy the airy spaciousness, with far-flung views in every direction, and where you can gaze down into the depths of its great wide open southern corrie.

From here the route rollercoasters up and down, along broad, then narrow sections of ridge. Ahead lie the big climbs, first up onto Sgurr na Ba Glaise, 874m, the Peak of the Grey Cow, an unusual name and the highest hill of the day, Rois-Bheinn itself, 882m.

From Sgurr na Ba Glaise, descend the steep slopes which lead down to a wide col, the Bealach an Fhiona. From here an ancient dry stone wall follows the steep and very rocky slopes of Rois-Bheinn to its eastern summit and trig point. The views are fantastic looking out westwards along Loch Ailort to the open sea where the isles of Eigg and Rum dance on glistening waters, and beyond to the Tir-nan-Og of the ancient Celts.

By the time you return to the Bealach an Fhiona you will be more than aware of the great lump called An Stac, 814m, which effectively blocks your homeward route. Its ascent involves more steep and rocky slopes, the steepest yet, and the longest too – a good pull of over 300m at the end of what has been a fairly strenuous day.

From the summit descend northwards, then north-north-east down rocky slopes to Seann Cruach, then descend its north-east ridge to the woods above the Tom Odhar col. Drop down through the woods to the col and make your way back to Inverailort.

64 The Glenfinnan Corbetts

The rocky bluffs and rugged landscape of northern Moidart has one big attribute above all others. There are no Munros here. That means there are no real footpaths, no erosion, no lines of cairns and no roadside car parks. There are however, 10 very fine Corbetts and considering these lower hills begin more or less at sea-level, you can get a day out worthy of any bigger hills.

The memorial to the Raising of the Standard at Glenfinnan is a well-known spot, with Loch Shiel lapping hills on either side. On the western shore rise two Corbetts, Beinn Odhar Bheag, 882m and Beinn Mhic Cedidh, 783m, which, along with Beinn Odhar Mhor, offers a very fine horseshoe round. Curiously, the small dun-coloured hill, Beinn Odhar Bheag, is higher than its neighbour, the big dun-coloured hill, Beinn Odhar Mhor, but less bulky.

Beinn Mhic Cedidh is the first top, a short walk alongside the West Highland railway, a climb up onto the hill's north ridge by way of an easy gully and a leisurely ramble up a rocky, narrowing ridge. There are superb views westwards towards the Rois-Bheinn hills and beyond towards Eigg, Rum and Skye.

A tiny collection of rocks point the way to the next hill, Beinn Odhar Bheag, linked by a broad ridge and high bealach. Try to catch a glimpse of the fiord-like Loch Shiel below. And what a reward it is, steel-grey, narrow and stretched out from its head at Glenfinnan in a south-west direction, cutting its way through these rugged mountains. Across its trench Sgurr Ghiubhsachain, Sgorr Craobh a' Chaorainn and Druim Tarsuinn rise from a tableland of bluffs and hollows.

A high-level ridge connects Beinn Odhar Bheag to Beinn Odhar Mhor before a long ridge leads back towards Loch Eilt, and your starting point.

Route Summary

Cross the Allt Lon a' Mhuidhe and follow the railway line W to the bridge over the Allt a' Choire Bhuidhe. Cross to its W bank and climb to the foot of the N ridge of Beinn Mhic Cedidh. Follow the ridge to the summit, descend E to the Bealach a' Choire Bhuidhe and ascend the NW ridge of Beinn Odhar Bheag. From the summit follow the N ridge to Beinn Odhar Mhor. Descend NW to Allt a' Choire Bhuidhe. Cross the railway and return to the start.

Map: OS Sheet 40

Access Point: E end of Loch Eilt

Distance: 12km

Approx Time: 5-7 hours

Grade: Moderate hill walk

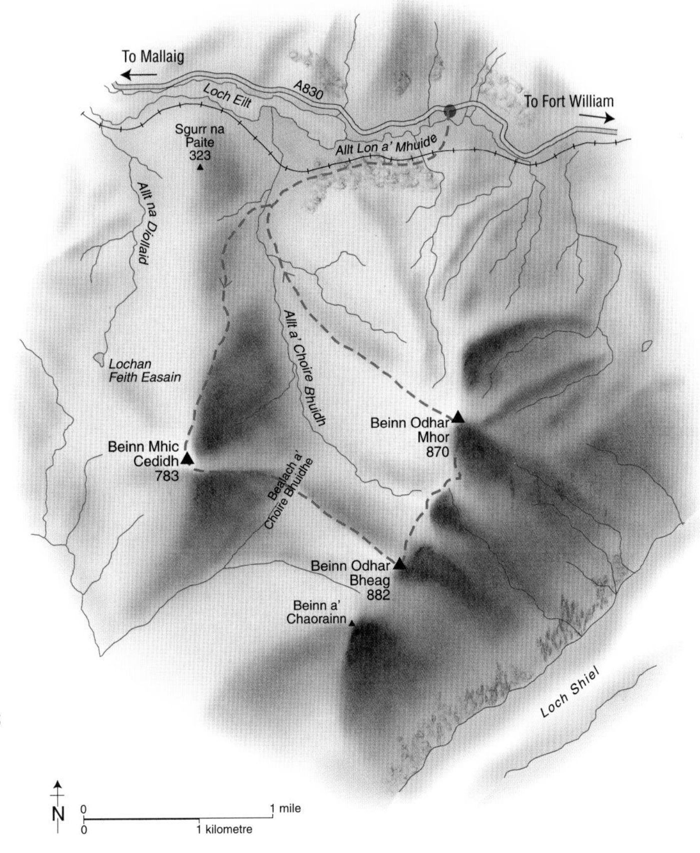

65 Streap

Route Summary

Follow the forest track up Gleann Dubh Lighe on the W side of the burn. At the end of the track a short diversion heads through a short break in the trees to a fence and gate. Cross over and head in a NW direction to reach a col between Beinn an Tuim and Stob Coire nan Cearc. From the col climb the SW slopes of Stob Coire nan Cearc and follow the undulating ridge to the high bealach below Streap. Ascend Streap by the knife-edge ridge which leads to the summit. Descend in a SE direction and climb a short distance to Streap Comhlaidh. From here descend the S ridge to gain the forest track which runs S past the bothy, to gain the outward forest track of earlier.

Map: OS Sheet 40

Access Point: A830, GR931744

Distance: 14km

Approx Time: 6-8 hours

Grade: Moderate hill walk

Translation: climbing hill

Pronunciation: strehp

It's a curious name for a mountain. Streap, a verbal noun which suggests the act of climbing. The 'climbing hill' would be a fair translation, and an even better description, as it's the culmination of a long ridge which climbs steadily to separate Glen Finnan from Gleann Dubh Lighe, a long ridge which narrows and sharpens to a knife edge just below it's rounded summit.

A bunch of us attempted to climb Streap just before Christmas one year but gale-force winds dampened our enthusiasm. We baled out before we reached the narrow ridge; down the steep slopes of the Bealach Coire an Tuim to Corryhully Bothy and a walk back down Glen Finnan. I went back on Christmas Eve, on a damp day of low mist and drizzle which promised to improve as the day went on, and it did.

A forest track works its way through the conifer plantations of lower Gleann Dubh Lighe, near the western end of Loch Eil. The crashing, cascading stream made a cheery companion as the track climbed steadily through the low mists, shroud-like and eerie. It was good to escape the trees eventually. The forest track terminated in a wide clearing, and I crossed a fence onto the open hillside. Now came the hard work of the day.

Old tracings of footpath, now overgrown and rutted, make a rising traverse around the lower eastern slopes of Beinn an Tuim into Coire an Tuim. From the prominent bealach at its head rocky slopes rise steeply northwards to a broad, craggy ridge which leads to a deep-cut col, the Bealach Coire nan Cearc. From the damp confines of this high pass, more rocky slopes climb steeply, this time to the summit of Stob Coire nan Cearc, a shapely top of rocky bluffs through which a faint path traces its way northwards, over an intermediate knoll to the col south-west of Streap.

It was about here that the low clouds, which had hidden everything from sight all morning, began to break and thin out. Across the depths of Coire nan Cearc to my right, black crooked fingers of rock pointed to the heights of Streap Comhlaidh and its steep southern slopes. In the half-light these gnarled fingers looked malevolent, the crooked fingers of doom, adding to my apprehension of the ridge ahead. I knew it was narrow, and I knew it was steep and I was all too well aware that a slip or a stumble could have nasty consequences. Solo hillwalking undoubtedly heightens the senses, but it also switches on the safety valve which subconsciously makes you take more care than normal.

From the col the ridge climbed and then levelled out, a tight arête of mossy grass, before steepening into the final ascent of the mountain. A gravelly path links some easy scrambling sections before opening out onto the summit slopes. By now the cloud had cleared and I was aware of the spaciousness of the views, down to the head of Loch Arkaig, west to the Knoydart hills, and east to the snow-capped bulk of Ben Nevis.

A steep descent from the summit links to a high-level ridge which connects Streap to its easterly neighbour Streap Comhlaidh. An immensely long ridge creeps north down to the headwaters of Loch Arkaig while another ridge leads south to a subsidiary top, before long open slopes sweep down to the boggy headwaters of the Dubh Lighe. An old track passes some ruins, then the Dubh Lighe bothy, before entering the forest again and connecting with the track of the morning. It made a grand Christmas Eve.

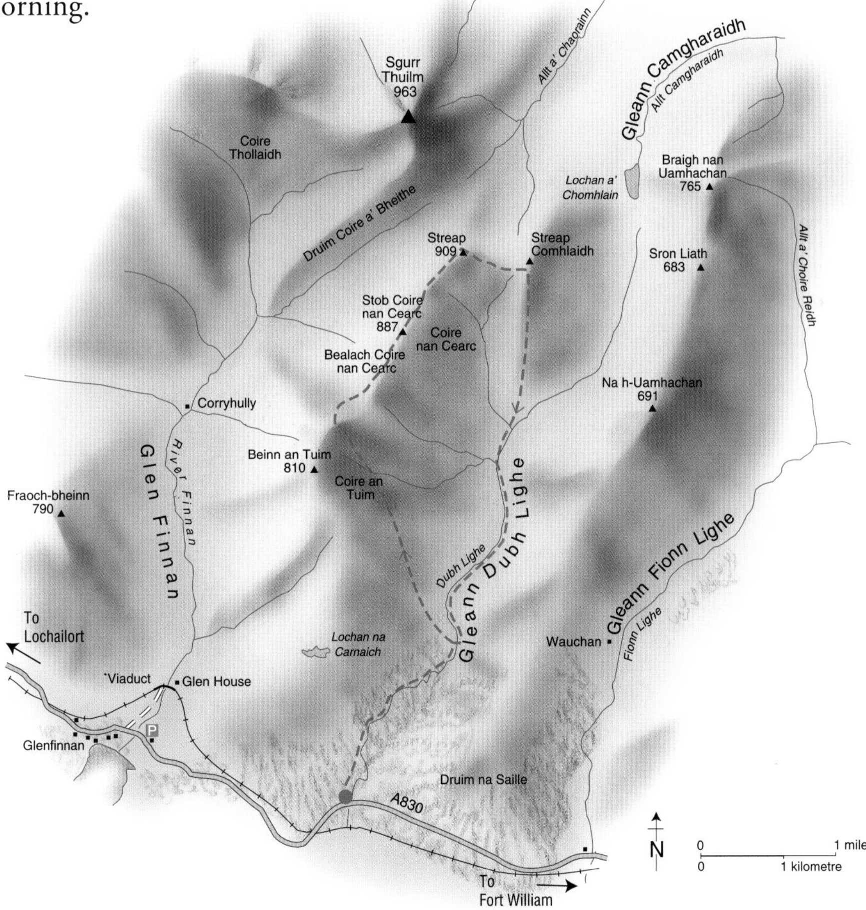

66 Sgurr na Ciche

Knoydart is a peninsula. I sometimes have to remind myself of that fact because the area has all the characteristics of an island, and Knoydart's inhabitants tend to have an island mentality. You just have to visit Inverie's pier when the Mallaig ferry comes in to understand what I mean.

While Knoydart's perimeters are bounded mostly by water the neck of land that does bind it to the mainland has much the same effect in isolating it from the hinterland. The Rough Bounds of Knoydart form a mountainous barrier, crossed only by a couple of footpaths and Sgurr na Ciche, at 1040m, is the highest point in the Rough Bounds.

It's a particularly dominating mountain, a steep-sided 'pap', similar to the Pap of Glencoe but bigger, and certainly recognisable from many distant points. The most obvious route of ascent is up the Druim a' Ghoirtein, the long ridge which rises in one steepening swoop all the way from the head of Loch Nevis to the summit, but you have to get to the head of the loch first. On one memorable occasion I was taken up Loch Nevis by my friends the Robinsons of Doune, who dropped me off and picked me up later, but on every other occasion I've

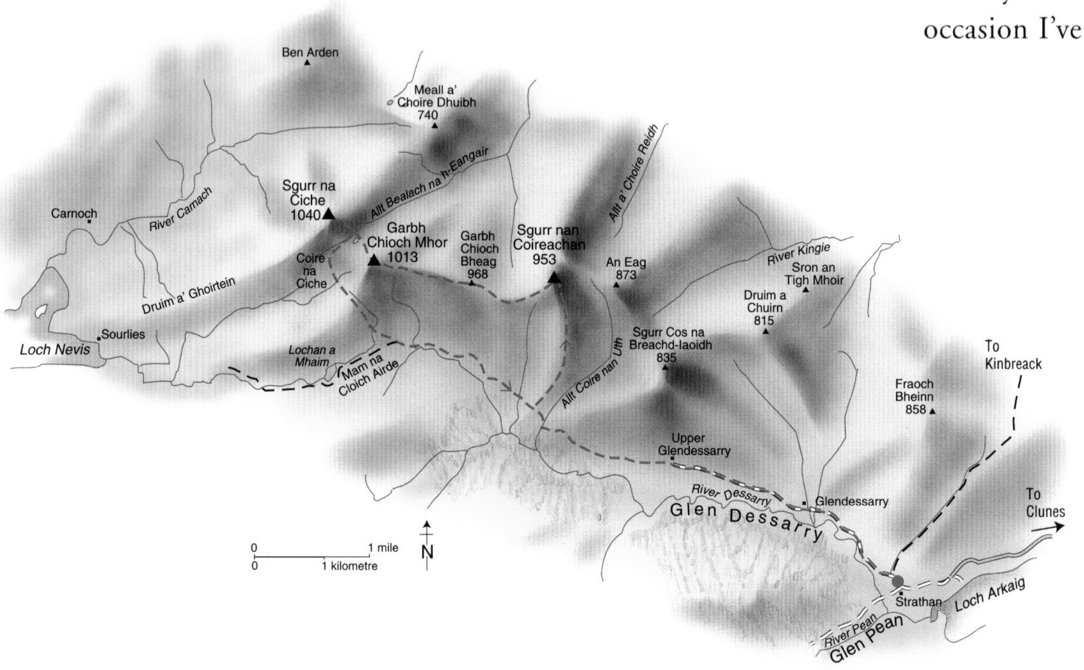

climbed Sgurr na Ciche, I've come from the east, linking it with Sgurr nan Coireachan, 953m and Garbh Chioch Mhor, 1013m, a sensible alternative since the three mountains are linked by a long rocky ridge, the traverse of which makes a highly enjoyable triple-Munro day.

A single-track road runs along the north shore of Loch Arkaig and stops near Strathan, where there is some car parking space at the end of the road. A bulldozed track runs north into Glen Dessarry and is ideal for a mountain bike. Go past Glen Dessarry house and continue as far as Upper Glendessarry where you will have to dump the bike – you can chain it to the fence. Beyond Upper Glendessarry a footpath continues above the forestry and soon crosses the Allt Coire nan Uth beyond which the steep south ridge of Sgurr nan Coireachan can be followed to the summit. It's a fairly rough and rocky route, but that's a characteristic of these hills as you quickly discover.

From the summit follow the steep footpath which weaves its way down to the Bealach nan Gall, a broad rock-festooned pass, before climbing steeply again to the 'rough breasts'. On the crest of the rocky ridge now follow the line of an old stone wall over these Garbh Chiochs, past Garbh Chioch Bheag, with the craggy slopes of Coire nan Gall dropping away to the north, and onto the narrowing ridge of Garbh Chioch Mhor. Beyond the summit the wall continues westwards, then north westwards down into the col of the Feadan na Ciche, the whistle, or chanter of the breast! When the wind blows through this narrow gap you might just hear the ghostly music.

From the bealach, another rough and rocky place, the path to Sgurr nan Ciche weaves a rather intricate course up through the crags but in most conditions you can follow it quite clearly. When the hill is snow covered it's a different story but you can then often follow shelves and runnells in the snow to link up an ascending course to the narrow summit and its trig point. The view is sensational, down the length of Loch Nevis and out to Rum and Eigg with the other hills of the uncompromisingly Rough Bounds to the north. Meall Bhuide and Luinne Bheinn are close at hand and the distant summit ridge of Ladhar Bheinn, the jewel of Knoydart.

Take care in the descent back into the Feadan gap, the rock slabs are often slippery and in mist navigation can be tricky. From the

Route Summary

Take the track to Glen Dessarry, then follow the path past the house of Upper Glendessarry to reach the Allt Coire nan Uth. Just beyond the burn climb steep slopes to the summit of Sgurr nan Coireachan. Descend in a WSW direction to the Bealach nan Gall and continue W up rocky slopes to the ridge which leads to Garbh Chioch Bheag and then Garbh Chioch Mhor. Beyond the summit the ridge narrows considerably on the descent to Feadan na Ciche. From the pass take the obvious grassy ramp which leads to a succession of ledges which lead through the rocky screes and blocks to the summit rib. From the summit return to the Feadan Gap. From here descend SW down the course of the Allt Coire na Ciche, steep in places, to a grassy terrace from which easy slopes drop down to the Mam na Cloich Airde Pass. Follow the path back to Glen Dessarry and Strathan.

Map: OS Sheets 33 and 40

Access Point: Strathan

Distance: 21km

Approx Time: 6-8 hours

Grade: Strenuous hill walk

Translation: peak of the breast

Pronunciation: skoor na keesh

Sgurr na Ciche from Druim a' Ghoirtein to the south-west

bowels of the gap head down the narrow gully towards Coire na Ciche and where the gully opens out below Garbh Chioch Mhor, skirt its south-west slopes to descend steep grassy slopes down to the pass at the head of Glen Dessarry. From there a well-used footpath takes you back to Upper Glendessarry, then back to Strathan.

67 Knoydart's Ladhar Bheinn

The peninsula of Knoydart was cleared in the mid nineteenth century when, in April 1853, factor James Grant and his henchmen, under orders from Josephine Macdonell of Glengarry began tearing off the thatched roofs, pushing over the walls and killing the livestock of the cottars who lived around the shores of Loch Hourn and Loch Nevis. The Macdonells of Glengarry had run up huge debts and the Knoydart folk were forced to take up an offer of paid transport to the New World so the family could sell the land. Sixteen families refused to go and took to the hills like hunted deer. A whole string of settlements were cleared and their

Ladhar Bheinn and Stob a' Choire Odhair from the east

names run together like a litany, a grim memorial of the awful events of the time – Skiary, Runival, Barrisdale, Inverdorchaill, Inverguseran, Airor, Doune, Sandaig and Inverie. One journalist, Donald Ross, wrote at the time, 'the voice of man was gone from Knoydart.'

The people were taken aboard the trading ship the *Sillary*, bound for Australia, or so they thought. When the ship reached the mouth of Loch Hourn the captain decided Australia was too far so he took his human cargo to Canada instead, innocent folk displaced from their homeland with absolutely no control over their future.

The flockmasters soon took over with their black-faced sheep, and when that became uneconomical the whole peninsula was given over to deer stalking.

It's so easy to be pessimistic about the future of a place like Knoydart, to dwell in the sadness of the past and lose sight of the future, but as you take the shoreside footpath from Kinlochhourn to Barrisdale you can't escape the ghosts and whispers of the past. Pass the low-walled remains of Skiary and they're there. Drop

Route Summary

Follow the loch-side path from Kinlochhourn to Barrisdale. A bridge crosses the river above Barrisdale to a path which in turn crosses the saltings to meet a stalkers' path below Creag Bheithe. Follow this path up zigzags, round the nose of Creag Bheithe and through some woodland into Coire Dhorrcail. Cross the Allt Coire Dhorrcail and climb grassy slopes W to the ridge of Druim a' Choire Odhair. Follow this narrowing ridge to the crest of Stob a' Choire Odhair, then on to the summit ridge of Ladhar Bheinn. A cairn at this point is often mistaken for the summit, but the true summit lies a short distance W. To complicate matters further an OS trig point lies at the W end of the ridge. Follow the lip of the corries SE to the bealach SW of Stob a' Chearcaill. From here descend grassy slopes in a SE direction to the Mam Barrisdale, where a track runs N to Barrisdale itself.

Map: OS Sheet 33

Access Point: Barrisdale

Distance: 35km (From Kinlochhourn)

Approx Time: 2 days

Grade: Moderate hill walk

Translation: hoof or claw hill

Pronunciation: laarven

down from the high pass to the little sanctuary of Runival and they're there. Pass the roofless church at Barrisdale Bay and visit the tidal burial-isle of Eilean Choinnich and they're there. Climb up into Coire Dhorrcail of Ladhar Bheinn and search for the remains of shielings and they're there again. Only the high tops of the mountains offer redemption from the past and Ladhar Bheinn is, by far, the finest.

This, the most westerly Munro on the mainland, can be climbed from several directions; from Folach in Gleann na Guiserein, south-west of the mountain, by Coire a' Phuill from the Mam Barrisdale, or by the magnificent Coire Dhorrcail from Barrisdale. The latter route is by far the finest.

It's a good 10km hike from Kinlochhourn to Barrisdale and while some walkers are happy to walk in, climb Ladhar Bheinn and walk out in a single day I think that's pushing it a bit. Far better to make a weekend of it, enjoy the loch-side path to Barrisdale – I reckon it's one of the finest low-level walks in the country, and tackle Ladhar Bheinn from there. Many walkers underestimate this hill and are often shocked by its complexities of ridge and corries, and its sheer size. Give it some respect.

From Barrisdale a wooden bridge crosses the river and a boggy track runs off to the right. Follow it across the salt flats to where a zigzag stalker's path climbs on to the lower reaches of Creag Bheithe. Then follow the path south-west through the trees in the lower reaches of Coire Dhorrcail, a magnificent bowl which is enclosed by the subsidiary peaks of Stob a' Chearcaill on the east and Stob a' Choire Odhair on the west. These form a horseshoe of ridges and peaks which enclose the corrie to form a high cirque of riven cliffs and buttresses. This side of Ladhar Bheinn is owned and cared for by the John Muir Trust, who are attempting to regenerate the native Caledonian pine woods on the lower slopes of the corrie.

The Druim a' Choire Odhair forms the north-west boundary of Coire Dhorrcail and can be reached by a fairly stiff climb up grassy slopes from the corrie floor. The ridge itself rises gently in a series of rocky protuberances, each eyrie outlook confirming upward progress above the sea level of Loch Hourn away below. This fiord-like sea loch bites deeply landward in a long sinuous curve. It's been suggested the name Hourn comes from the Norwegian word which means 'bow-shaped', but I prefer the old Celtic interpretation of 'Hell-like'. Beinn Sgritheall dominates the skyline to the north and it doesn't take long before the jagged peaks of the Cuillin of Skye compete for your attention.

As the Druim a' Choire Odhair gains height it begins to narrow appreciably, ultimately to its own top, Stob a' Choire Odhair. From here a scythe-shaped col links to the summit ridge, with a fairly steep but easy scramble up the final few feet. The summit, 1020m, is on the west-north-west ridge just a short distance from the junction.

Ladhar Bheinn is not only a magnificent mountain, but a complex one, rising above a series of corries which bite into its steep north-eastern slopes. A good descent to the Mam Barrisdale follows the line of these corries, down to the Bealach Coire Dhorrcail, round the head of another steep corrie before the junction with the long Aonach Sgoilte ridge, and then down to another bealach before Stob a' Chearcaill, and the long, wet, slippery slopes which lead down eastwards to the Mam Barrisdale. From here a good track takes you back to Barrisdale and the loch-side path to Kinlochhourn.

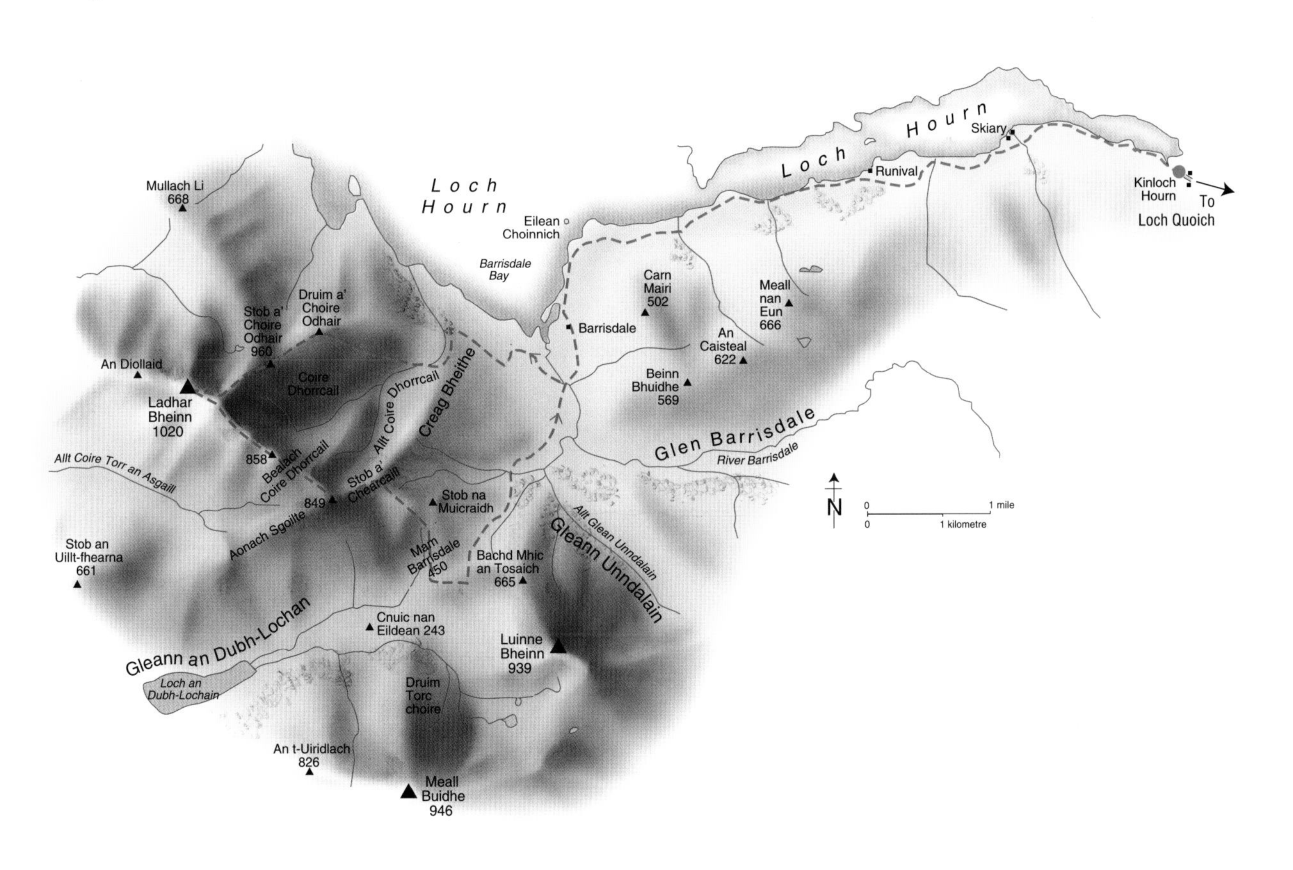

Route Summary
Follow the old hill track N up through some scattered woods and head for an obvious break in the escarpment above. Beyond the crags turn NE and cross some moorland to reach the W ridge of Beinn Sgritheall. Climb the ridge all the way to the summit. Continue E along the summit ridge to where it narrows. Descend to the Bealach Arnasdail where a stream is followed down to Arnisdale and the Loch Hourn road.

Map: OS Sheet 33

Access Point: Opposite Eilean Rarsaidh on the Glenelg/Arnisdale road GR815120

Distance: 10km

Approx Time: 5-7 hours

Grade: Moderate hill walk

Translation: hill of screes

Pronunciation: byn skreehal

68 Beinn Sgritheall

For me it'll always be Gavin Maxwell's hill, the mountain that rises from that ring of bright water as a memorial to what he achieved as a writer and a naturalist. Beinn Sgritheall, 974m, dominates the rough quarter between Loch Hourn and Glen Shiel and its rocky skirts dip into the waters that lap Camusfearna, the Bay of the Alders, the name that Maxwell gave to Sandaig, his home for several years.

Since Maxwell's death there have been a number of calls for some sort of permanent memorial to him. Some would like to see Sandaig re-built. At the end of his wonderful book, *Raven Seek Thy Brother*, Maxwell wrote: 'Tonight at the last sentence of a dream I stand in thought before the Camusfearna door. Someone someday perhaps may build again upon that site, but there is much that cannot ever be rebuilt.' But that doesn't stop people trying.

Eilean Bhan, the lighthouse island, may become the Maxwell memorial. The Born Free Foundation, run by actress Virginia McKenna, has apparently taken on the island with the idea of preserving the buildings where Maxwell worked before his death. I think we make too much of memorials. To anyone to whom Maxwell means anything, Camusfearna and Beinn Sgritheall stand as a natural monument to his achievements.

The south face of the mountain, the face that frowns across the waters of Loch Hourn to Knoydart, is scree-girt and very steep, rising almost 1000m in only 1.6km. Despite that, the easiest routes are on that side of the hill. Access to the hill is easiest here and you can avoid the worst of the screes.

Just above the Arnisdale road, at a point opposite Eilean Rarsaidh, there is a wooded hillside called Coille Mhialairigh. There's evidence above the woods of the benign nature of this south-facing part of the hill. A

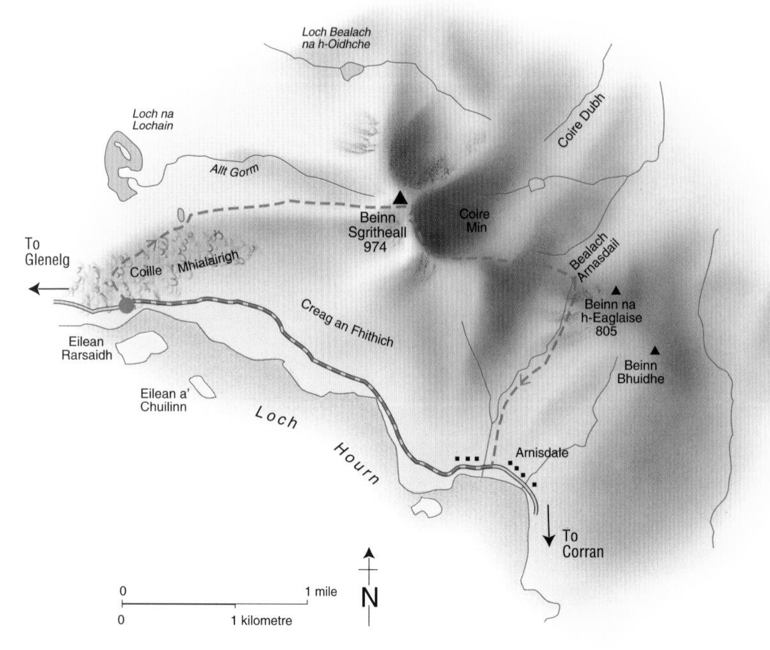

Beinn Sgritheall and Loch Hourn from Rubha Camas na Cailinn

faint path leads to an old shieling on the hillside, a soft sanctuary that gazes up the length of fiord-like Loch Hourn to where it becomes choked by tumbling mountain slopes. Across the waters, the most westerly Munro on the Scottish mainland rises, like Sgritheall, from the very water's edge. Ladhar Bheinn offers the best of company on a cloud free ascent of Beinn Sgritheall. The narrow path continues north-west, across a rough escarpment onto the west ridge of the mountain near a tiny lochan, another good place to stop and reflect. From there the ridge rises in rocky, bouldered steps, becoming increasingly steep as the summit comes into sight – and what a prominent summit it is. Dominating the whole of the Glenelg peninsula, the watery views offer the finest malt blend of seascape and mountain – Loch Hourn in all its far-reaching glory, and over the Sound of Sleat to Rum and Eigg.

Sgritheall is often likened to a tent, with a long sagging ridge-pole. The traverse of this ridge is an exhilarating prospect. Initially narrow and exposed with a touch of scrambling, it smooths out into a magnificent high-level promenade all the way to the eastern top. A long, steep descent takes you down to the Bealach Arnasdail, and down to the loch-side village. As you descend from the summit you'll be left in no doubt how this hill of screes got its name!

69 The Saddle/An Diollaid

Route Summary

From the roadside SE of the quarry at Achnangart a path runs W to a bealach between Biod an Fhithich and Meall an Odhar. From here go S then SW to the foot of the Forcan Ridge. Climb the ridge to Sgurr na Forcan then continue W down steep rocks and traverse a narrow ridge to the E top of The Saddle and then the summit. Drop down to the Bealach Coire Mhalagain and then climb to the NW top of Sgurr na Sgine. Follow the ridge SE to the summit. Descend by Faochag and its NE ridge.

Map: OS Sheet 33

Access Point: Achnangart, GR968142

Distance: 16km

Approx Time: 6-8 hours

Grade: Moderate hill walk/scramble

Translation: the saddle; peak of the knife

Pronunciation: an dee-alat

Glen Shiel is popular with hillwalkers, but its popularity is because there are no fewer than 20 Munros accessible from the A87 running down its length. With nine Munros to the south, seven accessible in one day-long expedition, and 11 on the north side, the area is tailor-made for the car-borne hill basher.

It is perhaps a negative testimony to the Munro-bagging game that the South Glen Shiel ridge is popular simply because you can bag seven 3000ft (914m) summits in one outing. It is neither the finest hill outing in Scotland, nor the most exhilarating ridge in the Highlands, and you're faced with a long road walk at the end. The Munro-bagger also ignores the finest features of these hills, the wonderful corries that are carved out of the northern slopes.

While, for most, seven ticks in the book make up for the loss, I would trade all seven mountains, plus the 11 Munros on the other side, for one wonderful hill, the epitome of all that's good in the West Highland mountains. I suspect The Saddle, 1010m, is upheld by most as the finest mountain in the area, and its long eastern Forcan Ridge is a narrow and exhilarating scramble in its own right. Climbed with the neighbouring Munro, Sgurr na Sgine, 946m, and its top, Faochag, this outing is the best in the area.

Seen from the steep slopes of Faochag the Forcan Ridge appears like a humped stegosaurus back – a narrow spine created by rough plates of rock, culminating in its very own top, Sgurr na Forcan, before dipping slightly and rising again to the east top of The Saddle, the most disappointing aspect of the hill – not the top but the name. Why do we have to anglicise these wonderful names? I'm going to start a campaign to call this by its Gaelic name, An Diollaid (try: an dee-alat). A similar oddity has occurred in the Lake District where the lovely Cumbrian name Blencathra has been given the unimaginative sobriquet of Saddleback. Ugh!

The approach to the foot of the Forcan Ridge follows a beautifully crafted stalkers' path which leaves Glen Shiel just south-east of the hideous quarry at Achnangart and eases you up for more than 450m to a grassy bealach (another saddle, or col if you prefer the Welsh!) between Biod an Fhithich and Meallan Odhar. Head south over Meallan Odhar and then continue south-west across another grassy bealach to reach the foot of the rocky staircase that soon narrows into the Forcan Ridge.

Try and stick with the crest of the ridge, in the knowledge that if it all becomes too exposed and airy you can easily drop down to the right where a path weaves its way up and through the lesser difficulties. The continuation to The Saddle from the top of the Forcan Ridge, Sgurr na Forcan, is narrow and steep in places and involves one particularly steep down-climbing section. The holds are there if you look for them and again, if things get too hairy you can avoid the awkward step by an easier route on the south side.

Don't argue too much about which of the two Saddle summits is higher. They're about 100m apart and apparently the same height. Oddly, the one which you're looking at always seems the higher! Descents can be made down the north ridge over Sgurr na Creige, or west and then north round Coire Uaine, but most will want to add Sgurr na Sgine to their tally and this Munro, and its outlier, Faochag (The Whelk) are about 1.6km south-east of the summit.

Sgurr na Sgine can be easily climbed from the Bealach Coire Mhalagain, up onto the north ridge which is then followed round the head of Coire Toiteil to the summit. Descend north and then round the corrie rim to Faochag whose steep uniform north-east ridge can be followed back to the A87.

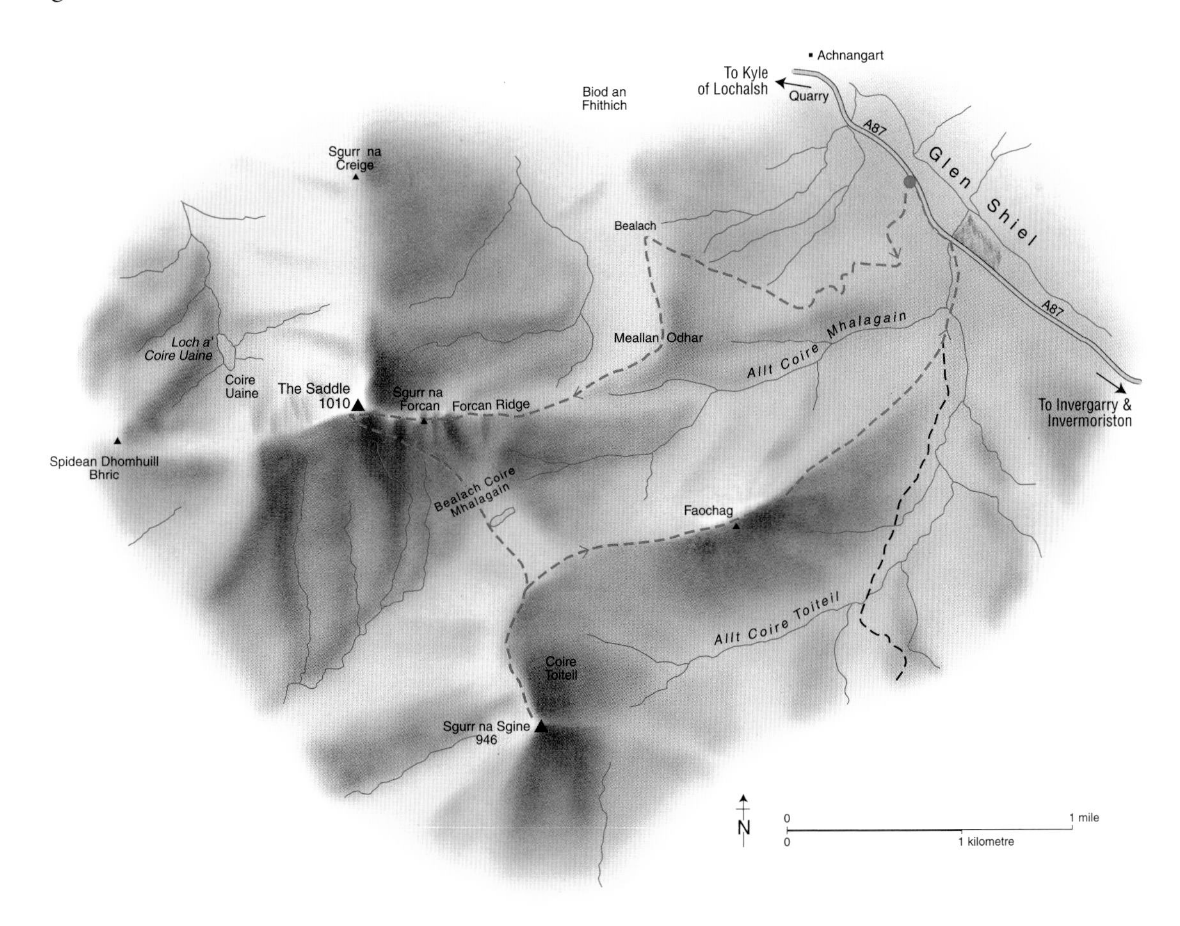

70 Gleouraich and Spidean Mialach

Route Summary

A cairn on the W side of the Allt Coire Peitireach indicates the start of a stalker's path. The path moves on to a grassy spur at the foot of Gleouraich's S ridge and then zigzags uphill to the summit slopes. From here a walker's path traces its way to the summit crest. A wide stony ridge continues E, drops and then rises to Craig Coire na Fiar Bhealaich. Another stalker's path zigzags down to the Fiar Bhealach. A climb brings you to the summit of Spidean Mialach. Descend easy slopes SW past Loch Fearna and down Coire Mheil to the roadside.

Map: OS Sheet 33

Access Point: Loch Quoich, GR029030

Distance: 12km

Approx Time: 4-6 hours

Grade: Moderate hill walk

Translation: uproar or noise; peak of wild animals

Pronunciation: glaw-reech; speetyan mee-a-lach

Gleouraich and Spidean Mialach are real tongue-twisters. As mountains go they're straightforward enough to climb, just hard to pronounce. Try Glaw-reech and Speetyan Mee-a-lach.

Difficult as they may be to pronounce, Gleouraich and Spidean Mialach are well worth a visit. They lie to the north of Loch Quoich just beyond Glengarry and they must be among the most accessible of all the hills in the Western Highlands. This makes them an ideal outing for a short winter's day, as I discovered one fine January day a few years ago. A road runs alongside the loch which laps at the hill's feet, and superb stalker's paths carry you quickly and easily on to the summits.

A small cairn on the west side of the Allt Coire Peitireach, close to the road, indicates the beginning of what soon turns out to be one of those magnificent footpaths of old. It seems to lift you like an elevator from the lower slopes to the summit in no time at all. This path zigzags its way efficiently across a grassy spur and then works its way uphill and along the steep edge of Gleouraich's south-west ridge. What a spot this is.

With an arm of Loch Quoich hundreds of metres below my feet, the view along the length of the main part of the loch was majestic, with the rest of Knoydart's big hills, Sgurr na Ciche, Luinne Bheinn, Meall Buidhe and Ben Aden, all clearly visible. With the stalker's path now only a slight indentation in the snow I continued to the top of the ridge, then sharply upwards to the summit, the hill of uproar, at 1035m above sea level.

There was certainly little uproar today, it was still, quiet and very peaceful.

With some warmth offered by the winter sun it was a great excuse to sit by the cairn and simply fester for half an hour, drinking both my coffee and the views

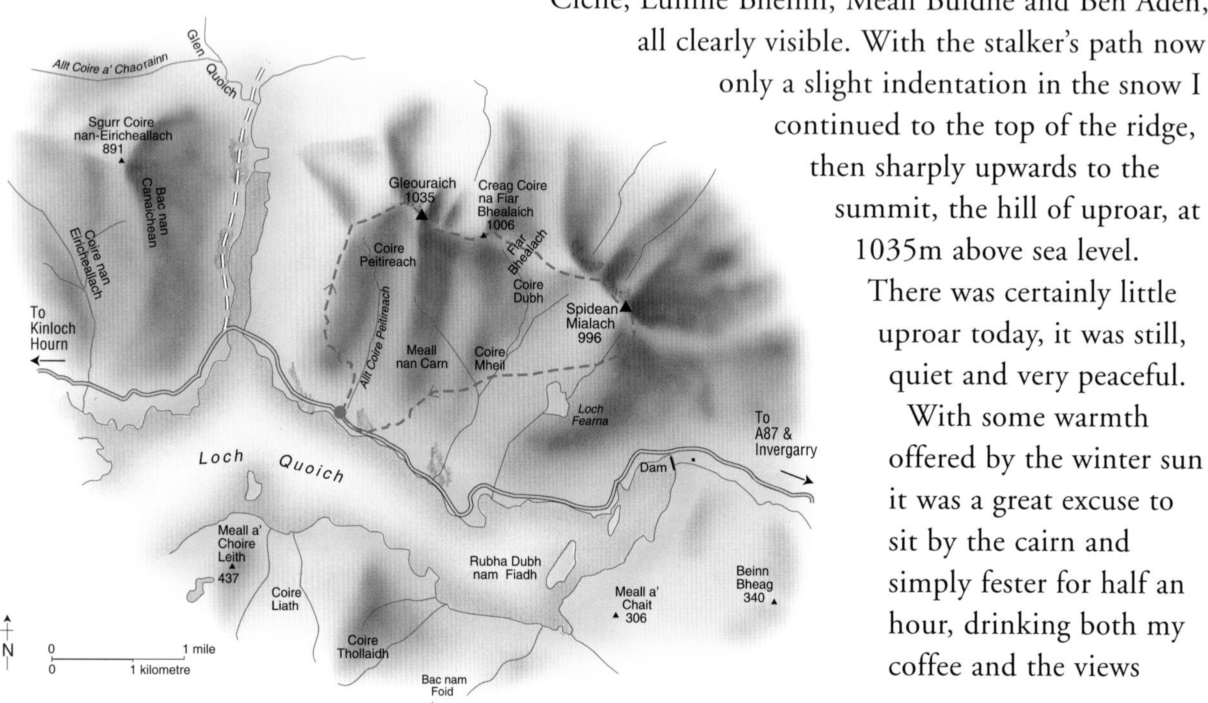

Gleouraich and Spidean Mialach from the north-west

around me. To the south Ben Nevis stood out defiantly against the blue sky, its white shroud bright and shining. Creag Meagaidh, or at least the backside of Creag Meagaidh, was equally plastered with early snow and to the north the hills of the South Glen Shiel ridge and the mountains of Affric were clear and spotlessly white.

From the summit the ridge flows on eastwards. It drops and then rises again to ascend an intermediate top, Creag Coire na Fiar Bhealaich, beyond which a steep drop to another excellent stalker's path takes you to the Fiar Bhealach. From this pass you climb onto another subsidiary top from which a broad ridge sweeps round the top of the corries to the cairn on Spidean Mialach, the peak of wild animals, at 996m.

It was still early as I dropped down the slopes back to the road. The sun was sinking into the jumble of peaks that is Knoydart, casting long shadows from the west and turning the hills to silhouettes. It was great to linger and enjoy the views, and the bitter-sweet sensation of not wanting to leave the high places, conflicting with the desire for a drink and a hot bath, which inevitably won.

Sgurr nan Ceathreamhnan from the east

71 Route Summary

Start from Alltbeithe, reached either from the Loch Beinn a' Mheadhoin roadhead in Glen Affric (16km) or An Caorrann Mor near Cluanie. From Alltbeithe a path climbs beside the Allt na Faing and leads directly to the ridge just W of An Socach. Climb easy slopes to the summit. Return to the ridge and follow it W again, over Stob Coire nan Dearcag to the E top of Ceathreamhnan. Continue over rocky ground to the summit. Descend to Alltbeithe by the S ridge of the west top.

Map: OS Sheet 25

Access Point: Alltbeithe, GR080202

71 Sgurr nan Ceathreamhnan

The road west beyond the Crask of Aigus follows the River Beauly, a winding and stately river fed by the drainage of three great inland glens, Affric, Cannich and Strathfarrar. The Caledonian pines of upper Glen Affric are particularly splendid, with the waters of Loch Beinn a' Mheadhoin and Loch Affric reflecting the high hills which loom on either side of the glen. The SMC guide to the Northwest Highlands claims Glen Affric is the finest glen in Scotland. A remote youth hostel, Alltbeithe, offers access to the finest of the hills, Sgurr nan Ceathreamhnan.

This is a magnificent mountain, the hub of a plethora of tight ridges which link with other high tops. At least four sinewy ridges radiate from the summit that forms the apex of five huge corries. The longest of these runs north to the head of Loch Mullardoch and in the middle of that ridge is Mullach na Dheiragain. Although given separate Munro status, it is, in fact, merely an outlier of Ceathreamhnan.

As Scottish hills go, Sgurr nan Ceathreamhnan is fairly remote and all approaches to it tend to be long unless you book in at Alltbeithe Youth Hostel at its foot. A well-known hill walker has proclaimed in print that this is the mountain top where he wants his ashes scattered. If nothing else, it will give his mates a long day out!

Distance: 22km
Approx Time: 7-9 hours
Grade: Strenuous hill walk
Translation: peak of the quarters
Pronunciation: skoor nan keroanan

A convenient route from the south runs through to Alltbeithe via the An Caorann Mor from Cluanie Inn on the Kyle road. The footpath is boggy in its upper reaches and lower down in Glen Affric. An alternative route runs alongside Loch Affric, beginning at the car park at the east end. Follow the path south of the loch, running east. Turn right onto the footpath at Athnamulloch and continue right along the River Affric to Alltbeithe. From the hostel another path follows the line of the Allt na Faing into the high reaches of Coire na Cloiche and then onto the high bealach just west of An Socach. Unnamed on the OS maps, this hill is dwarfed by higher, more rugged neighbours, the great bulk of Mam Sodhail to the east and the soaring lines of Ceathreamhnan in the west.

An Socach's western ridge begins to narrow as it crosses Stob Coire nan Dearcag, then climbs high above Coire nan Dearcag, with glimpses of its high-level lochan, before crossing Ceathreamhnan's east summit to top out on the rocky perch that is the culmination point of all Ceathreamhnan's ridges. Munro-baggers will undoubtedly want to add Mullach na Dheiragain to their tally. Lying about 4.5km along the north-east ridge of Ceathreamhnan, there is some justification in climbing it on its own from the north, from Glen Elchaig to the head of Loch Mullardoch. From there grassy slopes give easy access to the rockier north-west ridge and the summit cone.

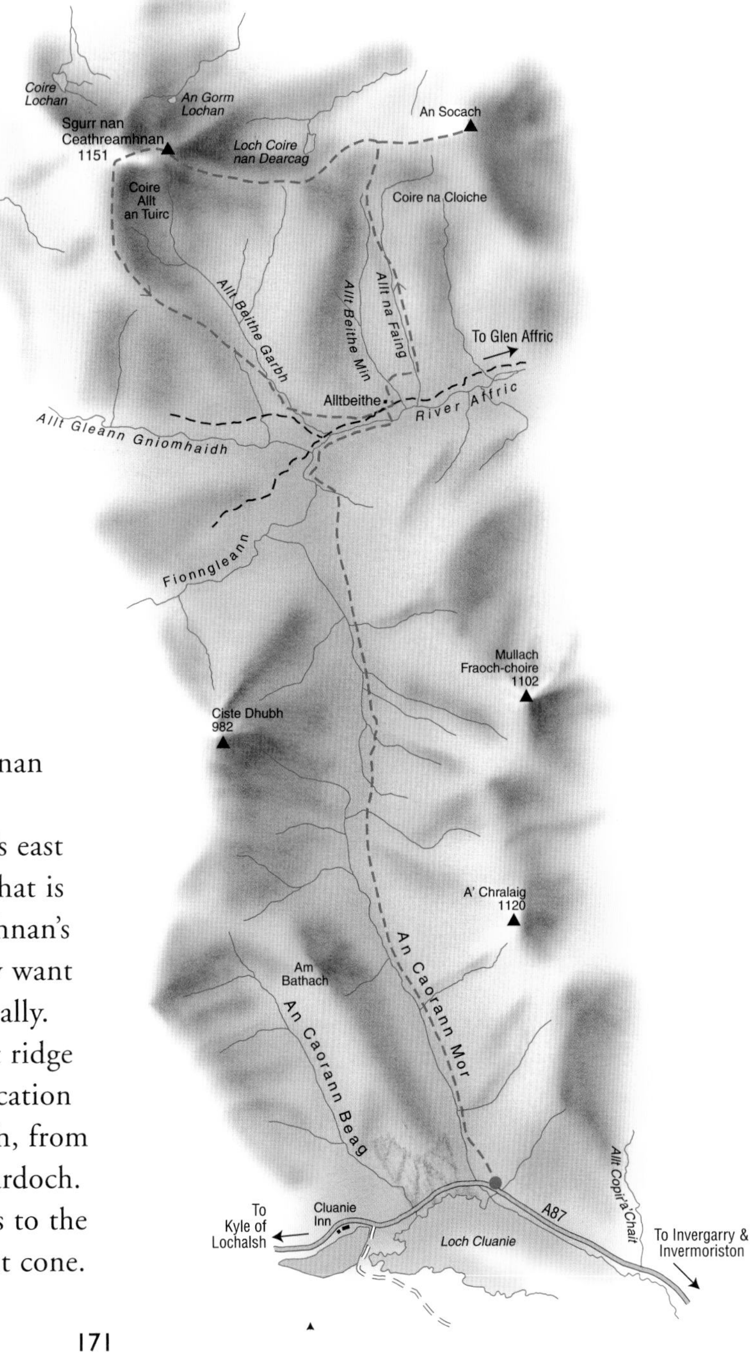

The Northern Highlands

This area covers all the Scottish mainland north and west of the A890 Lochcarron to Achnasheen road.

For most regular Scottish hill walking aficionados, this area, particularly those remote hectares north of Ullapool, is what walking in Scotland is all about. The likes of Torridon and the Letterewe wilderness have no equal, anywhere, while remote Seana Braigh is one of the most isolated Munros we have. But it's the individuality of peaks like Coigach, Stac Pollaidh, Suilven and Foinaven that give this northern area its real character, while low-level walks like the one around Rhubha Mor, and the classic to Sandwood Bay, offer that delicious blend of mountain and sea that makes this area one of the finest in Europe for wild walking.

The Walks

Suilven, Sutherland, from the north-west

72 The Coire Lair Horseshoe

The Coulin forest's Coire Lair, north-west of Achnashellach, is dominated by three splendid hills: Beinn Liath Mhor, the Big Grey Mountain at 925m, Sgorr Ruadh, the Red Peak at 960m, and Fuar Tholl, the Cold Hollow at 907m. A traverse of these three tops around the skyline of the corrie is, as the SMC guide to the Munros understates, a rewarding walk. It is one of the classic horseshoe routes in Scotland, taking in two fine Munros and certainly one of the most impressive Corbetts, the crag-girt Fuar Tholl.

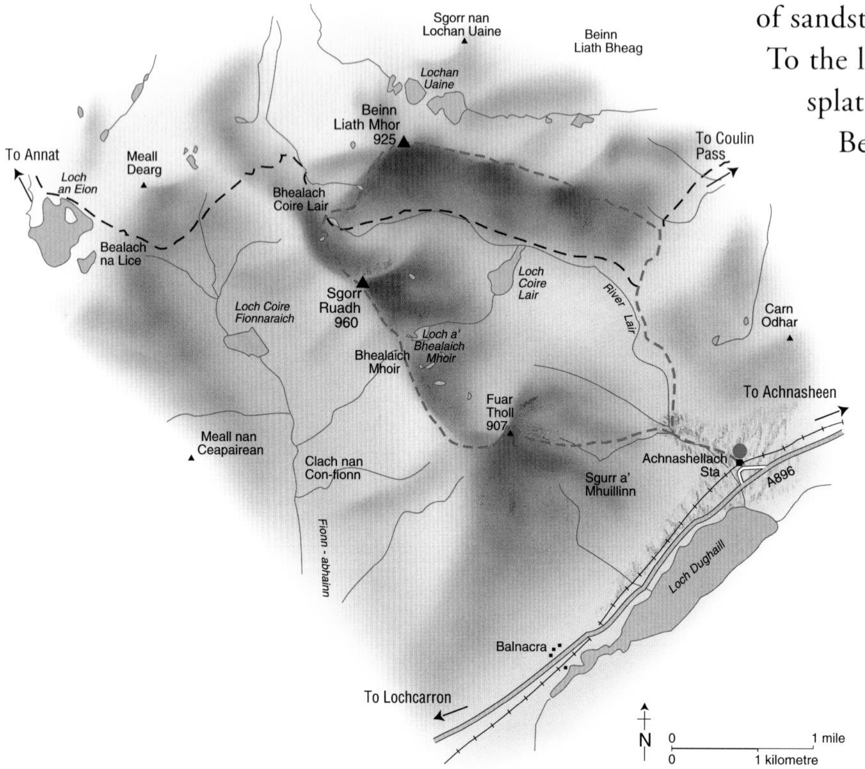

A forest track runs from Achnashellach Station on the A890 and as you approach the tumultuous River Lair, look out for a footpath bearing off to the left, to follow the east bank of the river through a veritable jungle of rhododendron bushes and trees. I've never known this footpath to be anything other than running with water, but consolation comes from the sheer power of the waterfalls in the adjacent river course. All too soon, the thunder of the river is left behind, as the now stony path bears right and breaks free of the woods to begin climbing pine-dotted slopes into Coire Lair itself. A large cairn, situated on a huge plinth of sandstone, marks a junction. To the left a path crosses lochan-splattered moors to the Bealach Mhoir. Straight ahead another path climbs the long slopes of the corrie. Follow this path for a short distance before turning right at the next junction. This new path runs in a north-east direction to skirt the south-east slopes of Beinn Liath Mhor on its way to join the Coulin Pass. At its high point, take to the heather and boulder slopes of Beinn Liath Mor's south-east top, the hardest section of the route. From this top, marked on the OS map as point 876m, a shining white quartzite ridge leads to a shallow bealach before climbing to a subsidiary sandstone summit.

Another undulating ridge of quartzite scree and moss leads to the summit, where the view of the leviathan Torridon tops is superb. Take care on this summit, though, because you're likely to concentrate too much on the northwards view, rather than on where you're putting your feet, and a tumble on the sharp quartzite blocks hereabouts could have nasty consequences. Additionally, great care is required on the descent to the Bealach Coire Lair, navigating through and around some steep red sandstone crags and an awkward cliff-girt knoll which is best avoided on its left.

From the lochan, which seems to fill the narrow bealach, a path climbs up over grassy slopes to a small lochan on the north-west ridge of the day's second peak, Sgorr Ruadh. From there it's a straightforward, if steep, scramble on a scree-covered footpath all the way to the summit.

The next hill, beyond the Bealach Mhoir, is Fuar Tholl, the smallest of the three but the finest. Fuar Tholl is living proof that Munro-bagging is a nonsense, albeit a delectable one! Many walkers come to Coire Lair and climb the two Munros, leaving the best hill in the area for another time, probably post-Munro completion.

Fuar Tholl radiates three spurs, to the north, the south and to the south-east, and it's on these spurs that the great rock features of the mountain are prominent. Between the north and the south-east spurs lies the Mainreachan Buttress, a magnificent mass of terraced sandstone which seems suspended above a tiny lochan below the north face of the mountain. The rock climbing here offers some of the best sandstone routes anywhere in the country.

Fuar Tholl is best climbed by taking its northern slopes head-on, crossing the top of the Mainreachan Buttress to reach the summit. From here an interesting line of descent follows the rim of the south-east corrie, a ridge which is tight and rather airy near the top. Soon you can scramble down to the lochan in the corrie and then down the slopes back to the River Lair. If the river is low you can easily cross to the opposite bank to the outward path back to Achnashellach. If, however, the river is high you're best staying on the south bank all the way down to the railway line.

Route Summary

From Achnashellach Station follow the path through the forest into Coire Lair. At the path junction follow the NE path for a short distance to its highest point, before taking to the steep heather-covered slopes of Beinn Liath Mhor. Climb to its E top and follow the ridge in a WNW direction to the summit. Descend to the Bealach Coire Lair and from there climb S onto the NW ridge of Sgorr Ruadh. Follow the steepening ridge to the summit. Descend to the Bealach Mhoir and climb the N slopes of Fuar Tholl to its summit. Descend by the narrow SE ridge then E to the River Lair and the railway.

Map: OS Sheet 25

Access Point: Achnashellach Station

Distance: 16km

Approx Time: 6-8 hours

Grading: Strenuous hill walk

Beinn Damh, Sgurr na Bana Mhoraire and Loch Damh across Upper Loch Torridon

Route Summary

100m W of the bridge over the Allt Coire Roill a stalker's path runs through woodland beside the river's gorge. Follow this path until it divides. Go right in a SW direction to the Toll Ban corrie. Climb to the col between Sgurr na Bana Mhoraire and Beinn Damh. Continue SE to the first of the false summits which is bypassed on the right. Cross a boulder-strewn dip to the next summit from where a narrowing ridge leads to the true summit. Most people will be happy to descend the way they came, but a steep alternative descent is possible via the hill's NE ridge, down to the Drochaid Coire Roill. Most of the difficulties on the ridge can be bypassed on the right.

73 Beinn Damh

While the triple magnets of Beinn Alligin, Liathach and Beinn Eighe draw the mass of hillwalkers to their steep flanks, little Beinn Damh, the most westerly of the mountains which flank the south shore of Upper Loch Torridon, offers comparative solitude, despite the fact that it shares many of the attributes of its higher neighbours. Steep flanks, beautifully scooped corries and craggy shoulders give this 903m Corbett a genuine Torridonian character and, given its position between the other hills of the Beinn Damh and Coulin deer forest and of course, the Torridonian triptych of Alligin, Liathach and Eighe, there is some justification in claiming it is a better viewpoint than any of its more illustrious neighbours.

There is room to park several cars on the A896 Shieldaig to Annat road just above the Loch Torridon Hotel near the bridge over the Allt Coire Roill. Walk back up the road towards Shieldaig for about 70m, and go through a wicker gate on the left, where you'll find a stalker's path which climbs uphill through the forest of pines and rhododendrons. After about 800m the rhododendrons fade out and the trees become smaller. Exposed pine roots create a slippery hazard as they poke through the skin of the earth, and as you near the upper limit of the trees take care because your attention will undoubtedly be taken by the sight of a 25m waterfall: the Allt Coire Roill takes a dramatic plunge over a sandstone cliff into the chasm below.

Map: OS Sheet 24
Access Point: A896 near the Loch Torridon Hotel
Distance: 12km
Approx Time: 5-7 hours
Grade: Moderate hill walk
Translation: hill of the stag
Pronunciation: byn dav

As you emerge above the tree line the footpath divides. The left branch follows the Allt Coire Roill towards the Drochaid Coire Roill, and the right fork climbs into the Toll Ban, the White Corrie. Take this latter route and follow the path as it climbs steeply up the slopes of the corrie towards the broad col which separates Beinn Damh from Sgurr na Bana Mhoraire. It's well worth walking south-west across this broad saddle to gaze down the very steep westerly scree slopes into Loch Damh below, and an even better view can be enjoyed by making the short diversion to the summit of Sgurr na Bana Mhoraire.

This saddle top is pretty featureless moorland and the path becomes indistinct as you head south-east towards the first of two subsidiary tops, which are easily bypassed on its west side. Great quartzite boulders fill the dip between the two subsidiary tops and from the second one, a narrow ridge makes its airy way to the main summit, where the cairn sits on the very edge of the steep Coir' an Laoigh. The views are wonderful, as one would expect from a mountain sited with the Torridon giants on one side and the tops of the Coulin deer forest on the other.

The north-east ridge, the Stuc Toll nam Biast, offers a steep and intimidating line of descent to the pass of the Drochaid Coire Roill, where the left fork of the ascent route runs across. This route makes a better alternative ascent route – it is always easier scrambling uphill than down. If you do decide to descend this way, bear in mind that most of the difficulties can be avoided on the right. Most folk will be more than happy descending the way they came.

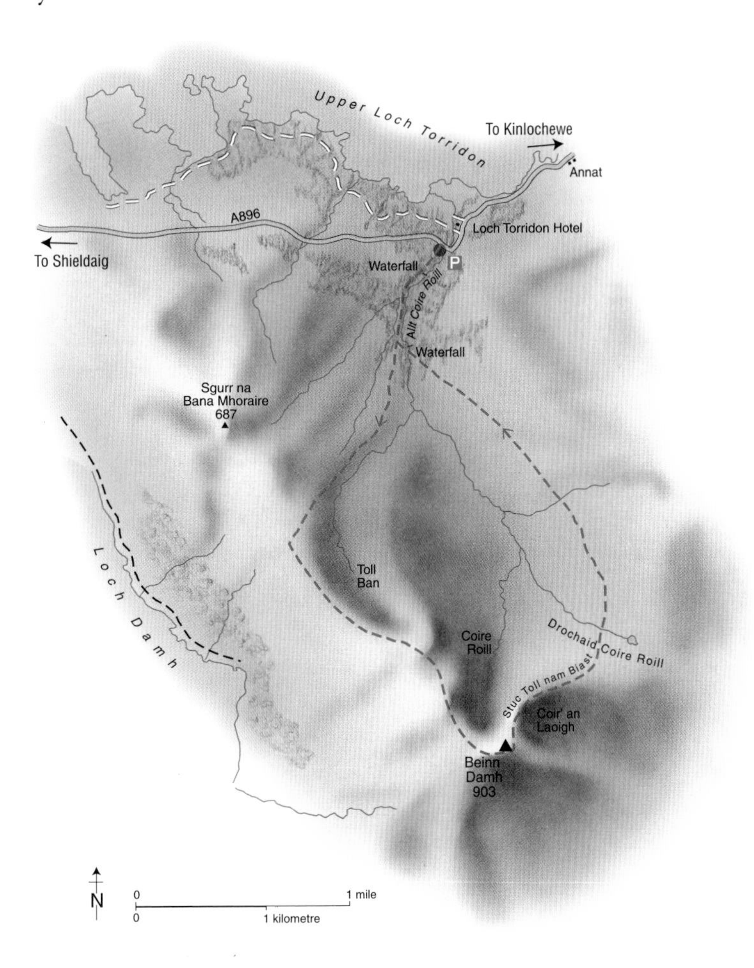

Route Summary

Follow the path which crosses the moorland towards Coir' nan Laoigh of Tom na Gruagaich. Climb to the head of the corrie and ascend Tom na Gruagaich. Descend N down a rocky ridge to a col beyond where the ridge becomes broader. Climb NNE over a knoll, drop a little height to a bealach and then climb NE to Sgurr Mhor, the summit of Beinn Alligin. From here descend steeply ENE then east down a narrow ridge to a col. Follow the well-marked path over the Horns of Alligin, using hands as well as feet in places. From the third 'Horn' continue the descent SE to the moorland and the track in Coire Mhic Nobuil is joined.

Map: OS Sheets 19 and 24

Access Point: Coire Mhic Nobuil bridge car park

Distance: 10km

Approx Time: 4-6 hours

Grade: Moderate hill walk

Translation: jewelled hill

Pronunciation: byn alligin

74 Beinn Alligin – The Jewel of Torridon

It's when you see Beinn Alligin from the southern shore of Loch Torridon that you realise how graceful this mountain is. The rounded bastion of Tom na Gruagaich, the natural cleft of the Eag Dubh and the gentle descent to the Na Rathanan, the Horns of Alligin all aspire to the mountain's nickname of the 'Jewelled One'. While Alligin's neighbours, Liathach and Beinn Eighe take your breath away by their sheer size and apparent machismo, Beinn Alligin wears a gentler robe, but she is still a big hill rising to a high point of 922m. With a gently curving ridge crossing four distinct tops the traverse of the whole mountain, including the three towers of the Horns, makes a superb expedition, but one that still demands the utmost respect.

A small, leafy car park on the south side of the Torridon-Diabeg road lies beside a bridge over the tumbling waters of the Abhainn Coire Mhic Nobuil. On the opposite side of the road a footpath climbs up through chaffinch-loud pinewoods and into Coire Mhic Nobuil but to the left of the road bridge another path begins – a waymarked route which runs north-north-west across rough lower slopes and higher sandstone slabs and bluffs to the steepening nose of Na Fasreidhnean. Easy scrambling takes you onto the south ridge of Alligin's newest Munro, Tom na Gruagaich, at 922m.

As you breast the summit beside the OS pillar the abruptness of

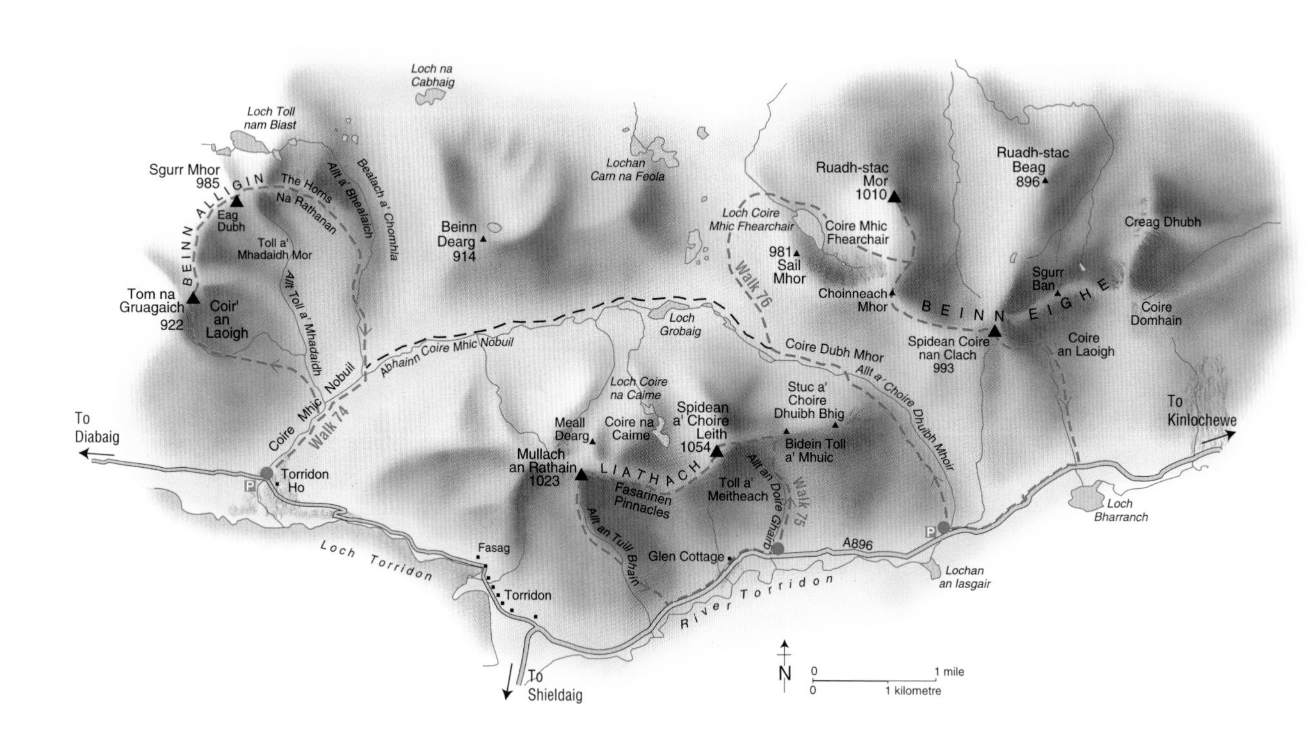

Loch Torridon and Applecross Forest with the Isle of Skye beyond from Tom na Gruagaich, Beinn Alligin

the view takes your breath away. Westwards lies the long finger of Skye's Trotternish Ridge and beyond it, the hills of Harris and the low-lying profile of Lewis. In front of you the Horns of Alligin give way to Beinn Dearg, which in turn gives way to the multi-peaked Beinn Eighe. Beyond that, Slioch and the hills of the Great Wilderness roll on in a confused and manic jumble.

Care is required on the steep and loose descent from Tom na Gruagaich, round the rim of Toll a' Mhadaidh Mor, over a slight bump to where a steepish climb leads you to the main summit, Sgurr Mhor, 986m, just beyond the great gash of Eag Dubh na h-Eigheachd. The rubble of this natural rockfall fans out in the corrie away below your feet, testimony to the fact that the forces of nature are still powerful and potentially destructive.

From the summit you can easily re-trace your route back to the start, but a complete traverse of a hill is always a more satisfactory conclusion to any walk. Fairly steep slopes drop down to a col at 757m from where the first of the three Horns of Alligin can be climbed directly, with an exposed scramble. A footpath avoids the difficulties on the right above steep grassy slopes but the Horns themselves pose little technical difficulty, just good exposed scrambling on clean sandstone holds. From the third, and last Horn, continue the descent in a south-east direction to the moorland below where a stalker's path can be picked up and followed back to the Coire Mhic Nobuil footpath.

Liathach, Torridon from the west

75 Liathach – The Grey One

Scientists tell us the mountains of Torridon were raised as a vast plateau some 30 million years ago and carved into their present shape. The rock of the original chain, now exposed as quartzite caps, is reckoned to be 600 million years old. The sandstone below them, and the platforms of gneiss on which they stand are thought to be in the region of 2600 million years old. Is it any wonder these mountains of Torridon exude an air of primeval dominance?

Could this be one of the reasons so many of us enjoy being amongst mountains? The only constant in our modern world is change, and yet here, sitting on a block of 600-million-year-old quartzite, there is a sensation of permanence which is at odds with man's transitory nature; a comforting sensation which transcends our own fleeting time-span. To be at one with the mountain is to accept its prehistoric age and respect it, to try, despite all our limitations, to understand it, to know it. It took me a long time to know Liathach. Its presence unsettled me, and I knew I couldn't feel right about it until I'd climbed it.

Liathach, the Grey One, has two Munro tops, Spidean a' Choire

Leith, 1055m, and Mullach an Rathain, 1023m and the course of its 8km ridge crosses six lesser tops. The southern flank of the mountain looks steep and impregnable, but there are breaches in its defences – they're just not too obvious.

The usual ascent route starts just east of Glen Cottage in Glen Torridon and climbs up to the steep upper slopes of Toll a' Meitheach, a shallow corrie high on the hill's sandstone flanks.

The footpath follows the Allt an Doire Ghairbh over rocky steps, heather and steep grass and leads over a break in a rock band which seems to cross the face of the mountain. It's a steep scramble into the upper reaches of the corrie where a scree gully gives access to the ridge just west of Bidein Toll a' Mhuic.

Enjoy the views eastwards towards Beinn Eighe, then turn and follow the twisting ridge towards the triangular-shaped face of Spidean a' Choire Leith, the first of the Munro summits. Despite the rock and loose scree the ridge poses little difficulty.

Spidean a' Choire Leith is Liathach's highest point and the views are extensive, all the way from Ben Hope in the north to Ben Nevis in the south. Chances are you won't even notice the views for your eyes will be set on the spectacular outline of the ridge that lies ahead. It is extremely narrow and much of its length is broken and shattered into a series of spires, the Fasarinen Pinnacles, the ancient sentinels of Liathach.

These shattered quartzite gendarmes fall away dramatically into Coire na Caime on the north side, one of a number of north-facing corries which make up the other face of Liathach, a more broken and less austere aspect which is hidden from the tourist in Glen Torridon. A traverse across the summits of the Fasarinen Pinnacles is a wonderfully airy and exposed scramble and those with some experience of rock climbing will seek out the holds willingly. Everyone else will be happy to follow an exposed but well-used footpath which contours the southern side of the pinnacles. This path leads to the second Munro of the hill, Mullach an Rathain, the aptly named 'hill of the row of pinnacles'.

A wide, grassy ridge leads to the summit and the OS pillar. To the north a short, stony arête runs out to the highest of the pinnacles and the lower peak of Meall Dearg overlooks Coire na Caime. A long ridge runs westwards down to the subsidiary top of Sgorr a' Chadail, with fabulous views across Loch Torridon, but the descent route goes westwards and south of the summit cairn, a

Route Summary

Just E of Glen Cottage climb steeply up the craggy hillside into the Toll a' Meitheach (see map on page 178). Higher up the corrie continue NE over steep ground to the col on the main ridge. Follow the ridge NW then west over two tops to the cone of Spidean a' Choire Leith. Descend SW to a level grassy section. Continue over, or around the pinnacles of Am Fasarinen. An exposed path avoids the difficulties on the S side. Beyond the pinnacles it's an easy stroll to Mullach an Rathain. From the summit the descent back to Glen Torridon is via the SW ridge, although a slightly quicker descent to Glen Torridon is via the corrie of the Allt an Tuill Bhain.

Map: OS Sheet 25

Access Point: A896, 800m east of Glen Cottage

Distance: 12km

Approx Time: 6-8 hours

Grade: Strenuous hill walk

Translation: grey one

Pronunciation: leeahach

narrow ridge dropping towards a broadening slope of broken, scree filled gullies and worn terraces and down towards the road alongside the Allt an Tuill Bhain. It's then only a short walk back to the car beyond Glen Cottage in Glen Torridon, which gives an opportunity to reflect on your new-found understanding of the Grey One. Somehow the steep sandstone flanks appear less forbidding now.

76 Beinn Eighe – A Mountain Range in Miniature

Route Summary

Leave the car park and follow the broad track which leads up Coire Dubh Mhor (see map on page 178). At GR934594 take another path which runs N round the prow of Sail Mor and traverses the hillside before climbing up into Coire Mhic Fhearchair. Cross the outflow of the loch and follow the E side of the loch before climbing screes and rough slopes SE to reach the ridge which leads to the summit, Ruadh-stac Mor. Return to the top of the access gully and walk in a SW direction towards the E end of Choinneach Mor. Now follow the main ridge SE over another col before the climb to Spidean Coire nan Clach. Return along the ridge for a short distance to a prominent SSE spur which offers access into Coire an Laoigh and a footpath which returns you to the A896 E of your starting point.

Map: OS Sheets I9 and 25

Access Point: Car park on A896 Glen Torridon road

Distance: I6km

Approx Time: 6-8 hours

Grade: Strenuous hill walk

Translation: file hill

Pronunciation: byn ay

For many walkers Torridon symbolises all that is fine in wild mountain country. It's an evocative name, conjuring up an image of leviathan hills with long lines of mural precipice, rounded and terraced bastions topped by sharp-pinnacled ridges, and summits capped by grey Cambrian quartzite. There's an enduring quality to the hills, no doubt due to their hoary antiquity, and while all are rugged, all are varied in aspect. Beinn Alligin is elegant, shapely, bejewelled. Liathach is a monster and breathtakingly huge, while Beinn Eighe isn't so much a single hill as a small range of hills, complex and idiosyncratic.

Beinn Eighe is separated from Liathach by the narrow pass of Coire Dubh Mhor. It has no less than seven high peaks, including Ruadh-stac Mor and Spidean Coire nan Clach. A series of massive north-facing corries culminate in what is arguably one of the most impressive amphitheatres in Scotland, Coire Mhic Fhearchair (I would only put An Teallach's Toll an Lochan ahead of it in terms of grandeur) whose lochan reflects the tiers of the spectacular Triple Buttress. This is an awesome structure of quartzite cliffs rising from their sandstone plinth to fill the inner recess of the corrie.

A hillwalk over all seven peaks makes a long and serious expedition but a straightforward and scenic route traverses two Munros and visits the splendour of Coire Mhic Fhearchair *en route*. The starting point is the National Trust car park by the A896 in Glen Torridon just west of the Allt a' Choire Dhuibh Mhoir. The footpath has been repaired in recent years and offers a fast highway through Coire Dubh Mhor, past the vertical eastern ramparts of Liathach. An alternative, longer walk in could begin at the Coire Mhic Nobuil car park, following the track along Abhainn Coire Mhic Nobuil to Coire Dubh Mhor.

Beinn Eighe and Coulin Lodge across Loch Coulin

Beyond the obvious watershed, a small lochan, another path peels off to the north around the skirts of Beinn Eighe's Sail Mor. Soon the path begins to climb past some fine sparkling waterfalls, up a final, steeper rise and into the grand hall of Torridon's mountain king, Coire Mhic Fhearchair.

The route to the summit of Ruadh-stac Mor is now fairly straightforward. A sketchy footpath follows the north-eastern shore of the lochan and climbs through a jumble of rocks to reach a prominent gully in the south-east recess of the corrie. Badly eroded and filled with scree it offers an energetic scramble onto the eastern enclosing arm of Coire Mhic Fhearchair which runs out northwards to Ruadh-stac Mor, 1010m, climbing gently over white quartzite screes to the summit.

Return along the ridge you've just climbed to the top of the access gully from the corrie below. Climb now in a south-west direction towards the eastern end of the dome of Choinneach Mhor from where the main Beinn Eighe ridge runs south-east over another rough col before climbing a steeper, narrower rocky ridge past the OS trig point at 972m, to the second Munro, Spidean Coire nan Clach, 993m. The best descent route is to return west to a prominent south-south-east spur from where you can drop down steeply into Coire an Laoigh, where a stalker's path can be easily followed to the A896 in Glen Torridon. A short walk back on the road returns you to the car park from where you started.

Route Summary

Leave the car park and follow the path which runs along the N bank of the river. Cross the Abhainn an Fhasaigh by a footbridge and turn right onto a path which runs up Gleann Bianasdail. Take the well worn path which climbs N towards Slioch's SE corrie. Gain the SE ridge and climb to the trig point summit. From here follow the ridge which leads to the north top. Follow the E ridge to Sgurr an Tuill Bhain and descend S to meet your outward route.

77 Slioch

Slioch, the Spear, points the way to one of the finest mountain landscapes of Scotland. From the summit of this rocky fortress you stand on the very edge of an area that's become known to hillwalkers as the Great Wilderness, a watery land of loch and crag, cradled between the great arms of Loch Maree and Little Loch Broom. This is backpacker country with rich rewards like A' Mhaighdean, Ruadh-stac Mor, Beinn Mor Dearg and the finest of them all, An Teallach. But Slioch holds her 981m head high in such company – a mountain of steep rocky crags which presents an almost impregnable air as you view it from the road which winds its way along the south shore of Loch Maree.

With great buttresses rising steeply on three sides of the hill, Slioch's great corrie, the Coire Tuill Bhain, hollows out its eastern flanks and offers a break in its fortress-like defences. In winter conditions you can understand why the locals call this the White Hollow. And it's this big corrie that gives access to Slioch's two summit ridges, which offer views south across the dramatic Torridon landscape, up the length of Loch Maree and across Lochan Fada, towards the jumbled landscape of the Great Wilderness.

While Slioch is separated from her northern neighbours by Lochan Fada, she dips her toes in Loch Maree, the largest loch north of the Great Glen. Covering 28 square km, it's now thought that Loch Maree was once a great sea-loch, part of Loch Ewe. That would explain the size of the flood plain at its Incheril head and why Kinlochewe is so named. St Maelrubha, who travelled from Iona and evangelised the Isle of Skye, visited Eilean Maruighe, one of the loch's islands, in the seventh century and enshrined it as a place of pilgrimage. Eventually the name of the island was corrupted to Maree, and the whole loch took on the same name.

A footpath runs west from the new car park at Incheril and eventually follows

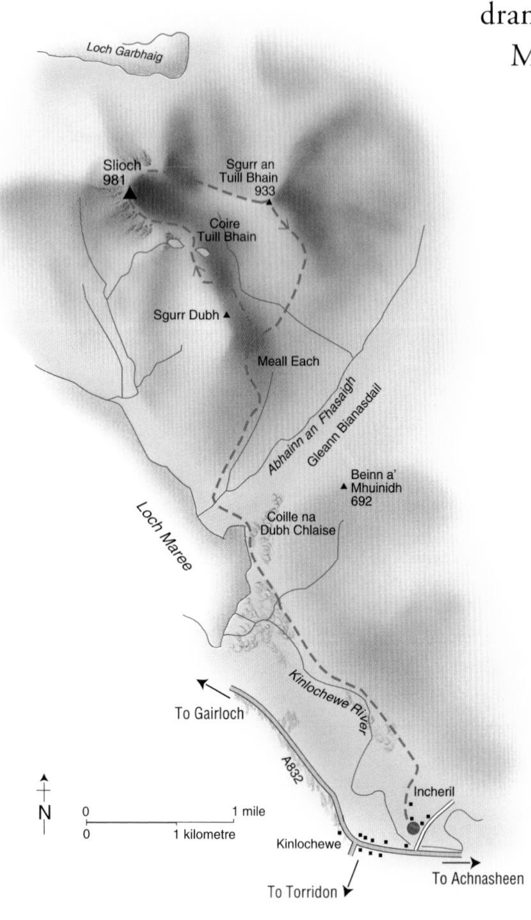

Slioch and Loch Garbhaig from the north-west

Map: OS Sheet 19
Access Point: Incheril, Kinlochewe
Distance: 20km
Approx Time: 6-8 hours
Grade: Moderate hill walk
Translation: from Gaelic sleagh, a spear
Pronunciation: slee-och

the riverbank to what is now the head of Loch Maree. A footbridge crosses the Abhainn an Fhasaigh, and you have to leave the main path here, following a narrower, yet more eroded route which takes a north-north-east line up Gleann Bianasdail. The path climbs steadily and conditions underfoot improve the closer you come to the open mouth of Coire Tuill Bhain below Meall Each. You can now see your route to the summit. A curving ridge forms the corrie wall ahead of you. A path breaches it just south of the main rise to the summit at a little col which saucers a pair of matching lochans. Above the lochans the path weaves its way steeply through crags and outcrops before easing off as you approach the trig point. The trig point is given the same height as the cairn immediately to the north, but the second one is the better viewpoint.

Rather than descend the way you came, follow the east ridge towards Sgurr an Tuill Bhain. This narrows with superb views down to Lochan Fada below you. Continue to the summit and drop down its steep southern slopes back into the corrie, from where you can follow the earlier path back to Gleann Bianasdail and Loch Maree.

78 A' Mhaigdean – The Fisherfield Round

Route Summary

From the Dundonnell road take the track up Gleann Chaorachain to Shenavall. Walk SE beside the Abhainn Strath na Sealga to Achneigie, cross the stream and ascend the steep slopes of Beinn a' Chlaidheimh to the SW. From the summit follow the continuing ridge over Sgurr Ban, Mullach Coire Mhic Fhearchair, Beinn Tarsuinn, A' Mhaighdean and Ruadh Stac Mor. Return to the A' Mhaighdean bealach and follow the stalker's path down past the Fuar Loch Mor to the main Dundonnell to Poolewe track. Return to Shenavall and your starting point.

Map: OS Sheet 19

Access Point: A832 road at Corrie Hallie

Distance: 40km

Approx Time: 10-14 hours

Grade: Strenuous hill walk

Translation: the maiden

Pronunciation: ah-vatyin

Strath na Sealga, the valley of hunting, is a delightful place, cradling the meandering Abhainn Strath na Sealga. Spotted orchids, bog asphodel, lousewort and milkwort add fringes of colour to the valley floor, made fragrant by the aromatic scent of the plentiful bog myrtle.

To the south lies a jumble of mountains that is generally referred to as wilderness; an emotive term, used loosely to evoke wildness and emptiness. But Milton once defined wilderness as 'a place of abundance', a definition which American philosopher and poet Gary Snyder suggests catches the condition of energy and richness that is found in wild systems, '...all the incredible fecundity of small animals and plants, feeding the web. But from another side, wilderness has implied chaos, eros, the unknown, realms of taboo, the habitat of both the ecstatic and demonic. In both senses it is a place of archetypal power, teaching and challenge.'

The high-level promenade from the bothy at Shenavall around Beinn a' Chlaidheimh, Sgurr Ban, Mullach Coire Mhic Fhearchair, Beinn Tarsuinn, A' Mhaighdean (said to be the most inaccessible Munro in Scotland), and Ruadh Stac Mor is indeed a challenge, a round route of 30km with over 2200m of ascent. And that's not counting the 7km walk in from Dundonnell to Shenavall!

Beinn a' Chlaidheimh lies due south of Shenavall Bothy. The northern slopes of the hills are steep so it is probably best to walk south-east by the Abhainn Strath na Sealga to Achneigie, cross the river and then start climbing the hill by its north-east slopes.

As you climb higher the heather gives way to alpine grasses and great fields of quartzite. The summit ridge of Beinn a' Chladheimh, which sits spot on the Munro Plimsoll line is tight and narrow, a good ridge over three separate tops. From the summit the view shows wilderness in all directions. Below, Loch a' Bhrisidh is set in its craggy cirque before a dazzling white slope of quartzite stretches up to the summit of Sgurr Ban, appropriately translated as the White Peak! I recall gazing across the gulf of Gleann na Muice to the west, where the craggy gneiss outcropped slopes of Ruadh Stac Mor and A' Mhaighdean rose into a turmoil of cloud, defending their reputation as Scotland's remotest Munros.

Sgurr Ban, 989m, although splendidly quartz capped, can be ascended on grass for much of the 400m climb from the bealach. It has a plateau-like summit, but immediately south, Mullach Coire Mhic Fhearchair presents a contrasting image. Its steep, bouldery slopes, seamed with long scree gullies and protruding crags run upwards to a narrow top. Loose scree forms much of the ascent but the top is worth the effort with a large cairn 1019m above sea level, the highest summit of the round. The western face of the hill is of pink sandstone, split by long gullies. The summit cone, like Sgurr Ban, is of Cambrian quartzite. The main feature of Mullach is a ridge of gneiss which extends south-east into the head of Gleann an Nid, terminating in a series of spiring pinnacles.

Between Mullach and the next Munro, Beinn Tarsuinn, is a little bump top, Meall Garbh. Lying at the corner of a curving ridge it can be avoided by the good path which runs along the foot of its north-facing slopes. A boggy bealach leads to the grassy slopes of Tarsuinn, 937m, a mountain which forms the red sandstone tiered headwall of Gleann na Muice and a curving ridge cradling a lochan in its clench. From this point there is little evidence of man – not a track, not a road, not a blemish. Wilderness in any sense.

A short drop from the narrow sandstone summit takes you onto a flat-topped table, then a series of pinnacles, which call for some careful scrambling. Steep scree slopes drop down to a peat-hagged bealach. Long easy angled slopes come next, leading to one of the finest mountain summits in the country. Hamish Brown once told me that the view from A' Mhaighdean was the finest in Scotland. A jagged outline, which must be the Cuillin, peeps over Beinn Eighe and across the sea. The ridge of Trotternish seems to stretch into the hills of Harris. Remote lochs lie below: Gorm Loch Mor, the Dubh Loch and the Fionn Loch stretch out towards Loch Ewe and the sea.

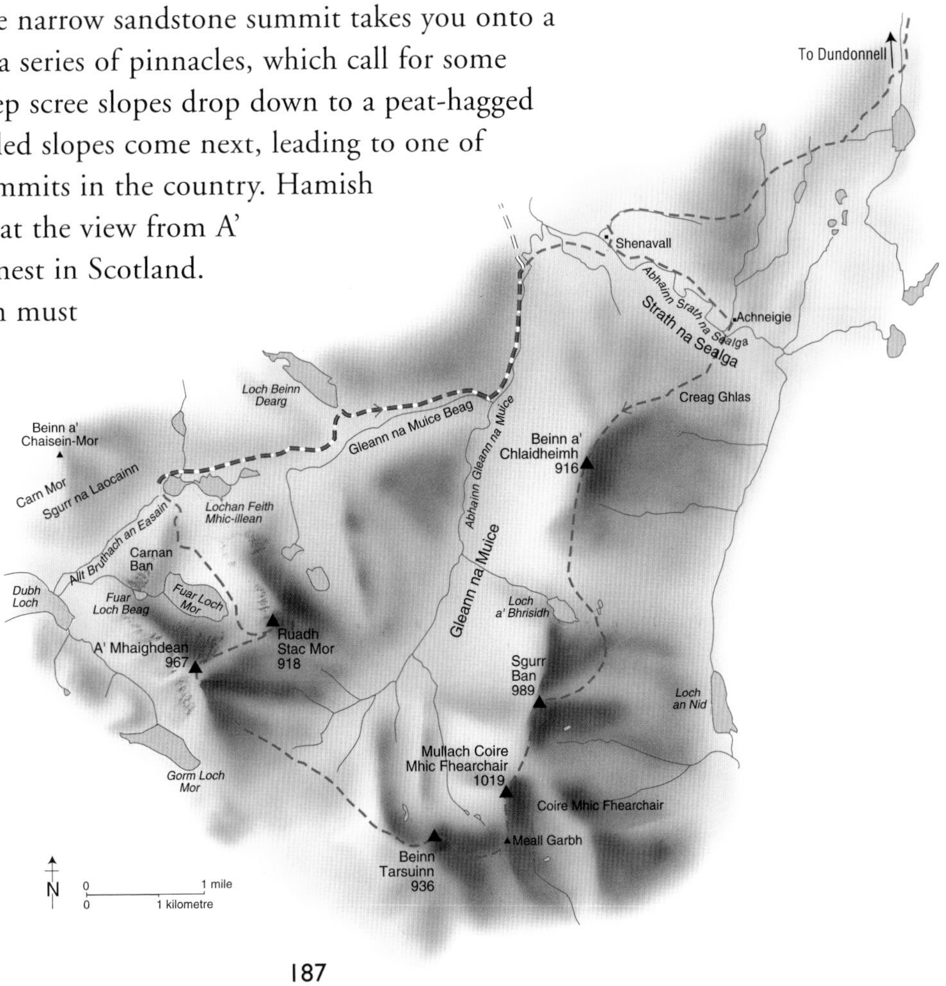

To Dundonnell
Shenavall
Abhainn Srath na Sealga
Strath na Sealga
Achneigie
Creag Ghlas
Loch Beinn Dearg
Beinn a' Chaisein-Mor
Carn Mor
Sgurr na Laocainn
Gleann na Muice Beag
Abhainn Gleann na Muice
Beinn a' Chlaidheimh
916
Lochan Feith Mhic-illean
Allt Bruthach an Easain
Carnan Ban
Fuar Loch Mor
Gleann na Muice
Dubh Loch
Fuar Loch Beag
Loch a' Bhrisidh
Ruadh Stac Mor
918
A' Mhaighdean
967
Sgurr Ban
989
Loch an Nid
Mullach Coire Mhic Fhearchair
1019
Gorm Loch Mor
Coire Mhic Fhearchair
Meall Garbh
Beinn Tarsuinn
936
N
0 1 mile
0 1 kilometre

On the other side of the Fionn Loch great crags rise skywards; Beinn Airigh Charr and the Carnmore Crags.

From the bealach north of A' Mhaighdean steep broken slopes lead to the summit of Ruadh Stac Mor, 918m. Back at the bealach, a stalker's path runs downhill below the base of Ruadh Stac Mor, past the brooding Fuar Loch Mor and over the high moorland to the main Dundonnell to Poolewe track beside Lochan Feith Mhic'-illean. Follow this north down Gleann na Muce Beag, back to Strath na Sealga and the Shenavall path back to Dundonnell.

79 An Teallach

Route Summary

Leave the A832 road and follow the track through Gleann Chaorachain and across the Allt Chaorachain. Continue on the path across rocky slabs and heather towards Shenavall but before you begin the descent bear right and climb Sail Liath. From the summit follow the ridge of An Teallach to the Corrag Bhuidhe Buttresses (which can be avoided on the left). Scramble over the pinnacles to Lord Berkeley's Seat, descend and climb to the summit of Sgurr Fiona. Continue NNE to Bidein a' Ghlas Thuill.

Map: OS Sheet 19

Access Point: A832 Corrie Hallie

Distance: 22km

Approx Time: 10-12 hours

Grade: Strenuous hill walk

Translation: the forge

Pronunciation: an tyalach

Like great billows of smoke the cloud fumed from the corrie – somewhere down below us in the depths of Toll an Lochain there could well have been a roaring fire tended by some ancient semi-mythological forgeman. As the cloud poured over the corrie lip, momentarily hiding the rotten teeth of the mountain's broken skyline, we pondered on the meaning of An Teallach.

The Forge is as good a translation as any. My companion, John Mackenzie, enthused about the redness of the ancient sandstone, glowing like the coals of a roaring furnace. I preferred the smoking cloud analogy, particularly since everywhere else the mountain tops were clear – only An Teallach, the Forge, kept its cloud cap.

This mountain dominates the Strathnasheallag Forest, with 10 tops above 3000ft (914m). Its wonderfully serrated rocky crest reaches a high point on Bidein a' Ghlas Thuill, 1062m, and another of its peaks, Sgurr Fiona, 1060m, is also a Munro. But the real attraction of An Teallach is its 4km ridge around the mountain's eastern corrie, Toll an Lochain. For much of its length this is a sinuous, sharp edge which offers the walker an exhilarating scramble – better, if shorter, than the Aonach Eagach.

John and I had been enjoying a long walk through the Letterewe and Fisherfield Forests for a television programme – our finale was An Teallach, arguably Scotland's finest mountain. And argue we did. Lord John, Earl of Cromartie and Chief of Clan Mackenzie eulogised on the character of the mountain. I borrowed a quote and called it a 'rotting, peeling carcase of a mountain, hideously disgustful' and yet, at the same time, quite magnificent.

It is rotten – the sandstone is crumbling and the spires and pinnacles are tottering. Even the wonderful Corrag Buidhe buttresses to which we escaped from the eroded footpath, have crumbling holds which makes a simple scrambling excursion a serious one. I almost left a BBC cameraman with a sore head – the block which seconds earlier had been my foothold just missed him. And yet, it's easy to sweep aside these discrepancies and behold the mountain for what it is – one of the most loved in Scotland.

It's a hill of Tolkienesque character, made even more so as we climbed the steep and awkward corners of Corrag Buidhe in the swirling mists. The first steep slab is a delight. We climbed rounded sandstone 'woolpacks', piled high on top of each other, for a good 10 or 15m. A level stretch of scree leads to the crux, a steep shallow chimney, well marked by crampon scratches. An abseil sling at the top suggests the regular use of a rope, particularly sensible in winter conditions. A tip-toe along a narrow crest was made more exquisite by the company of Brocken Spectres, the sun casting our elongated shadows on the mist below us, before the climb up onto Lord Berkeley's Seat. It took seven seconds for a stone dropped from the summit block to reach the screes below.

Who was Lord Berkeley? According to Peter Drummond's excellent *Scottish Hill and Mountain Names*, the good Lord was a gentleman who, for a bet, sat with his feet hanging over the edge. John Mackenzie seemed even better informed, he told me Lord Berkeley was a nineteenth-century empirical physicist!

Like Lord John's politics, Lord Berkeley's Seat leans slightly to the left, and one day it will no doubt tumble into the depths of Toll an Lochain below. For now, it's the last crazy pinnacle before Sgurr Fiona, the Peak of the Wine.

The best view of An Teallach is probably that from the old 'Destitution Road' between Braemore Junction and Dundonnell.

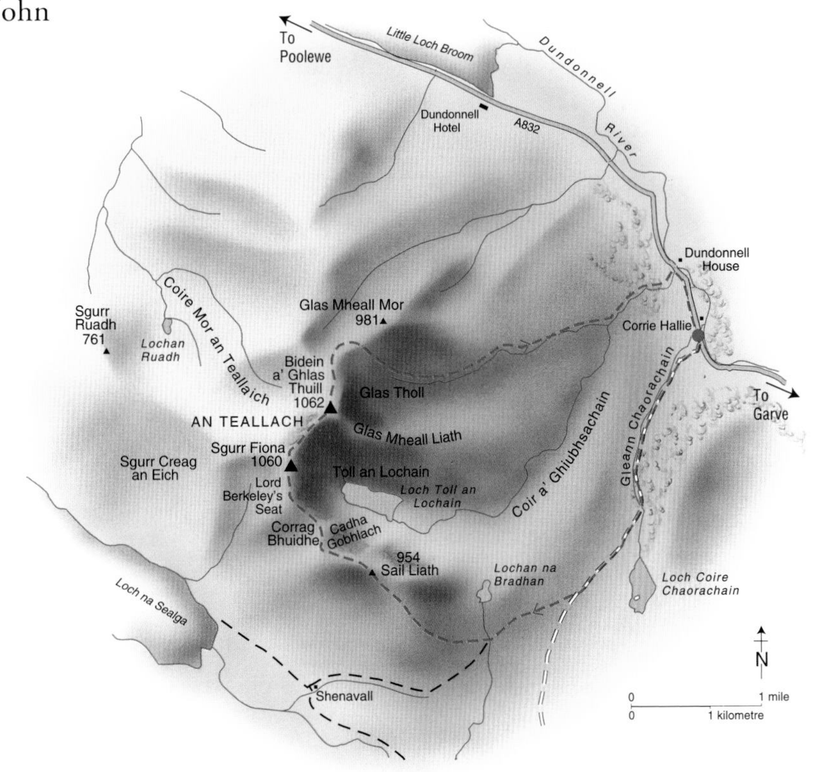

Sgurr Fiona and Sail Liath, An Teallach from the east

Three ridges, Glas Mheall Mor, Glas Mheall Liath and Sail Liath form two corries, Glas Tholl and Toll an Lochain. The main summit, Bidein a' Ghlas Thuill, lies at the apex of the middle ridge and the main ridge, while Sgurr Fiona forms a bend on the main ridge as it curves round southwards and becomes a narrow, serrated arête which ends on Sail Liath.

The mountain is best climbed from the A832 at the foot of Corrie Hallie. A track runs south-west through the trees of Gleann Chaorachain, crosses the Allt Gleann Chaorachain and climbs west over rocky slabs to the foot of the Sail Liath ridge. A rounded afterthought to the main ridge, Sail Liath's summit is dome shaped, and an eroded footpath leads down sharply to a high bealach from which the first of the ridge's summits is climbed.

Most walkers avoid the Corrag Bhuidhe buttresses. Eroded paths skirt the buttresses and Lord Berkeley's Seat before climbing Sgurr Fiona. The route steepens again after Fiona as you descend north-north-east over some pretty rocky ground to the wide, slabby col, and a long pull onto the highest summit, Bidein a' Ghlas Thuill. The normal descent route continues north from the summit to the obvious col and then drops down steep slopes eastwards into Coire a' Ghlas Thuill. Follow the north side of the stream to the Garbh Allt waterfalls from where a good path takes you back to the A832.

80 Seana Bhraigh

While A' Mhaighdean in Letterewe is generally regarded as Scotland's remotest Munro, Seana Bhraigh isn't far behind. Lording it over the vast empty quarter between Inverlael and Strath Mulzie, Seana Bhraigh, 927m, lies to the north of the Beinn Dearg group and demands a serious trek to reach its summit. But it's worth the effort for the wonderful view across the void of the Luchd Choire to Seana Bhraigh's eastern top, Creag an Duine. It's a scene of vast spaciousness and on a good day you'll be rewarded with the whole of the Northern Highlands stretched out around you.

Seana Bhraigh can be climbed fairly comfortably along with its somewhat distant neighbour, Eididh nan Clach Geala, to make a fabulous outing which makes maximum use of some good stalker's paths. Walk up through the forest from Inverlael on the Ullapool road to reach Gleann na Sguaib where a rocky path climbs high onto the Beinn Dearg/Cona Mheall col. Before you reach the col, just beside the Eas Fionn waterfall, a small cairn by the side of the track marks the beginning of an excellent stalker's path which climbs the hillside to Lochan a' Chnapaich. This is a lovely spot, a small mountain lochan that seems to reflect the richness of the natural artistry around it – the broad sweep of the heavens, the white clouds and the dark, rocky backdrop of the crags. A great place to sit and do a bit of reflecting yourself.

A short backtrack from the lochan allows you to climb northwards onto the broad spur which emanates from Eididh nan Clach Geala. Follow it past a small lochan tucked away in the heathery folds, and continue to the quartz summit.

From this vantage point, broad grassy slopes lead north-east past the head of Coire an Lochain Sgeirich, where a footpath runs up from the Druim na Saobhaidhe above Glen na Sguaib – a good alternative descent route. More lochans dimple the

Route Summary

Follow the track up through the forest to Glen na Sguaib and continue up the glen to the Eas Fionn waterfall. At this point a stalker's path climbs the slopes to the NE to reach Lochan a' Chnapaich. Ascend Eididh nan Clach Geala by its SW spur. From the summit head NE to skirt the top of Coire an Lochain Sgeirich and continue to the top of Cadha Dearg. Skirt the head of the corrie and climb NW to the summit of Seana Bhraigh. Return to the top of Coire an Lochain Sgeirich and follow the footpath back to the forestry track at the foot of Glen na Sguaib via the Druim na Saobhaidhe.

Map: OS Sheet 20

Access Point: Inverlael on A835

Distance: 25km

Approx Time: 8-10 hours

Grade: Strenuous hill walk

Translation: old upper part

Pronunciation: shena vry

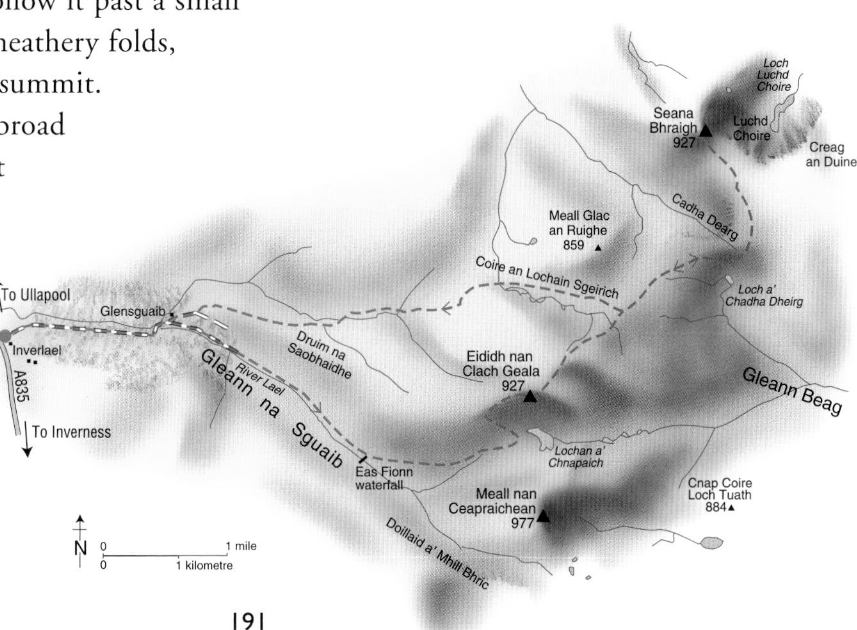

Seana Bhraigh from the air with the mountains of Inverpolly and North-West Sutherland in the distance

surface of this grassy plateau, what Craig Caldwell called 'a wilderness of lochans' in his book *Climb Every Mountain*. The navigation can be awkward here in misty conditions, but a rough path does erratically weave around the lochans towards the rim of the impressive Cadha Dearg, the Red Pass. I once sat here for a good 30 minutes watching a golden eagle as it quartered the air space in search of food, at ease in this wild, atmospheric corrie, with great crags forming its eastern and northern extremities. I recall I had to drag myself away with some reluctance, but the summit was close and the walk around the great rim is no hardship. It's then up long, grassy slopes, skirting a bump that can knock your navigation out in cloudy weather, and up final stony slopes to the summit – a breathtaking point with a windbreak cairn sitting on the very edge of nothing!

There are, of course, other routes to the summit of this lonely hill – from Glen Achall near Ullapool or Strath Mulzie in the north, or from Gleann Beag in the south-east. The first three approaches involve a considerable walk-in, although mountain bikes can be useful, as they ease the initial forestry miles. It's something of a luxury to pick up your bike at the end of this long day, and virtually freewheel all the way back to Inverlael. The last time I used a bike I only turned the pedals twice in the whole descent. That certainly erased the painful memories of the ride up earlier in the morning.

81 Coigach and The Fiddler

Ardmair, just north of Ullapool, is a magnificent spot with its spit of white shingle beach curving gracefully out into the bay. The sanctuary of Isle Martin protects it from the Minch gales, and beyond, the Summer Isles float on their sea of green. But Ardmair's dominant feature is a landmark, a great wall of weathered Torridonian sandstone which dominates the northern shore of the bay, a relic of one of the most ancient land masses in the world. Ben Mor Coigach's protective cap of Cambrian quartzite has long since gone, like many of its neighbours, but this venerable relic still rises straight from the sea and lifts its head to almost 750m at its eastern extremity, a 1.5km long wall of buttresses and gullies.

While that seaward wall is impressive, it's really only a front, hiding an intricate, complex system of peaks, ridges, corries and lochans, a gem of a wilderness area which is unspoiled and challenging and one which begins to express itself as you drive further northwards on the A835.

Ben Mor Coigach, at 743m, is the highest summit, but the other main peak of the area, Sgurr an Fhidhleir rises to a sharp and dramatic point about 1.5km along a broad north-west ridge from Ben More. It's a high eyrie of a summit, the culmination point of a huge singular blade of rock, which rises from the bare moorland close to the reflective waters of Lochan Tuath. The traverse of these two hills brings together all the finer characteristics of a walk which blends sea and mountain in that distinctive combination which you only find in such places as the Skye and Rum Cuillin, and on one or two mainland mountains, notably Ladhar Bheinn in Knoydart. Indeed, the traverse of Ben Mor Coigach's long south-west ridge beyond Armair Bay could well be a high-level promenade to Tir nan Og, beyond the shimmering seas of the Celtic seaboard.

At Drumrunie junction on the A835 a minor road runs west towards Achiltibuie. As everyone else rushes off to climb Stac Pollaidh, just a few km along the road, park your vehicle and cross the river just east of Loch Lurgainn. Follow the right bank of the Allt Claonaidh as far as Lochan Tuath, which mirrors the mighty north-west prow of Sgurr an Fhidhleir, the peak of the fiddler. Walkers don't follow the prow: that's the domain of rock climbers who'll find a long and exposed climb of very severe standard, a

Route Summary

Cross the river just E of Loch Lurgainn and follow the S bank of the Allt Cloanaidh to Lochan Tuath. Climb a steep heather-filled gully immediately S of the prow of Sgurr an Fhidhleir to reach the bealach between the Fiddler and Ben Mor Coigach. Ascend Sgurr an Fhidhleir, return to the bealach and climb the grassy slopes of Ben Mor Coigach. Traverse the ridge, return to the summit and return to the Allt Claonaidh via Beinn Tarsuinn.

Map: OS Sheet 15

Access Point: Drumrunie to Achiltibuie road GR140067

Distance: 16km

Approx Time: 6-8 hours

Grade: Moderate hill walk

Translation: big hill of Coigach; peak of the fiddler

Pronunciation: byn mor coy-gach; skoor an fiddler

moderate grade which belies the dangers of loose rock and vegetated ledges. South of the prow, a prominent heather-filled gully climbs steeply up to the bealach between The Fiddler and Ben Mor Coigach in the south, and from there easy slopes lead to the summit of Sgurr an Fhidhleir itself, a stunning place with magnificent views.

Retrace your steps back to the broad bealach and climb the grassy slopes to Ben Mor Coigach itself. The south-west ridge towards Garbh Choireachan is well worth exploring. A succession of rocky towers and good sandy paths make this ridge an absolute delight with views out over the Summer Isles and across the Minch to Harris and Lewis. On a good day you'll see the Cuillin of Skye, the Torridons, An Teallach, the Beinn Dearg hills and of course that wonderful array of northern hills, from Inverpollaidh to Assynt.

From the summit of Ben Mor Coigach descend to the small bealach below Speicin Coinnich, and then down the steep slopes towards Beinn Tarsuinn. Continue over the summit and down steep, heathery slopes back to the Allt Claonaidh and the boggy path back to the road.

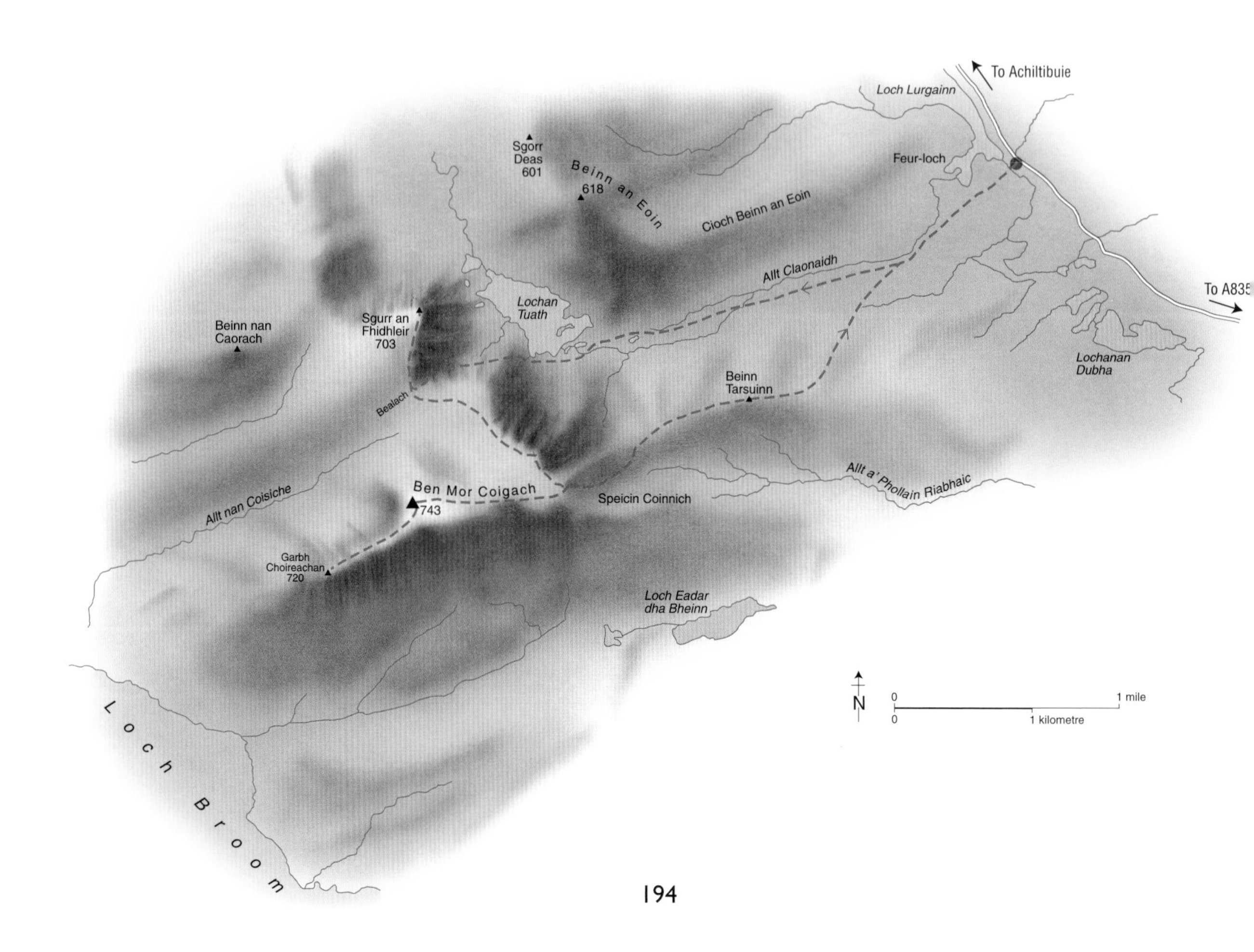

Cul Mor, Stac Pollaidh and Cul Beag across Achnahaird Bay from Rubha a' Chairn

82 The Rubha Mor of Achnahaird

North of Ullapool the road from Drumrunie to Achiltibuie, with Inverpollaidh on one side and the hills of Coigach on the other, is justly famed for its dramatic landscape, but as you approach the sea at Achnahaird, the grandeur softens and few can resist the shell-white sands, one of the finest beaches in the country. North and west of Achnahaird lies Rubha Mor, an arrowhead-shaped peninsula of rolling moorland, dramatic cliffs and remote, secretive bays. Several times I've wandered around the stunning coastline of the peninsula, enjoying the views across Enard Bay to the indented Lochinver coastline and the dramatic shape of Suilven, described by the eighteenth-century traveller Thomas Pennant as the 'Sugar-Loaf mountain'. It's a place to loiter during the hazy days of summer, playing at rock climbing on the sun-kissed sandstone cliffs at Reiff, or snoozing on one of the beaches, lulled by the song of gulls and the easy rhythm of the Atlantic swell.

South of the Rubha Mor peninsula and across the waters of Badentarbat Bay lie the Summer Isles where the great wildlife

Route Summary

From Achnahaird Bay follow the coastline N, past Camus Coille, to the northern point, Rubha Coigeach. Continue past and turn S towards Camus Eilean Ghlais. Beyond the bay cross a series of fields towards the cottages at Reiff. Cross the moor beyond the croft at Blair-buie, past Lochan Dubha and Loch a' Chaoruinn to the road just W of Brae of Achnahaird.

Map: OS Sheet 15

Access Point: Achnahaird Bay

Distance: About 16km

Approx Time: 4-6 hours

Grade: Moderate coastal walk

writer, Frank Fraser Darling, wrote his autobiographical book, *Island Years*. Just north of the crofting community at Reiff the sandstone cliffs of Camas Eilean Ghlais have become very popular with rock climbers. The cliffs are not particularly high, but they are steep and the rock is incredibly solid, offering marvellous sport in a magnificent coastal setting.

From the sands of Achnahaird Bay follow the coastline north keeping fairly close to the cliff edge. Inland, the rolling moorland is infested by pools and lochans many of which are haunted by the loon-like cry of the Great Northern Diver. In parts of Canada this wavering laugh-like sound is said to be the departing cry of dead Algonquin Indians. Continue north, avoiding the long indentations of various gullies and coves by detouring inland where necessary. Pass the Bay of the Woods at Camas Coille, although there are no trees there now, and follow the coastline to the northern point, Rubha Coigeach. Here the sandstone cliffs are at their most spectacular. Across Enard Bay to the north-east you can clearly see the pencil slim outline of the Stoer lighthouse and the gaunt upthrust of Suilven, thought locally to translate as Pillar Rock, despite the colourful description by Thomas Pennant.

Pass the northern point and turn south, avoiding Faochag Bay, the Bay of the Whelks, and on to Camus Eilean Ghlais. Beyond the bay, cross a series of sheep cropped fields towards the white-washed cottages of Reiff. You can continue south, then east on the narrow tarmac road all the way back to Achnahaird. A much more satisfying finish is to cross the untracked moorland beyond the croft at Blairbuie, passing Lochan Dubha and Loch a' Chaoruinn, to meet up with the road just west of Brae of Achnahaird.

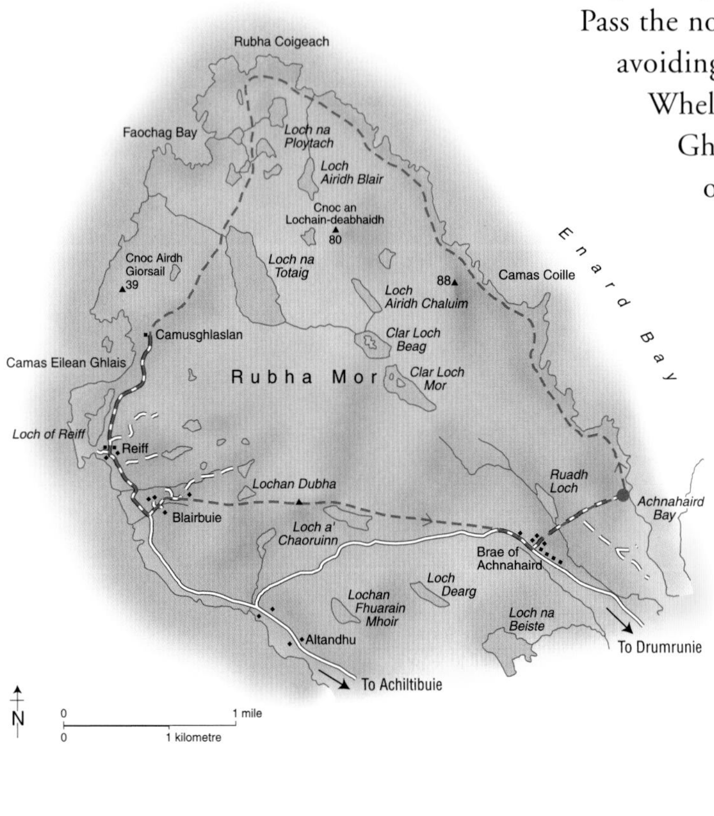

Stac Pollaidh from the south-east

83 Stac Pollaidh

Stac Pollaidh, 613m, is one of the most popular mountains in Scotland, largely because of its easy access and relatively low height. With something like 30,000 ascents every year it's beginning to suffer badly from erosion. So why include it in a book like this, encouraging even more people to climb its flanks?

Well, first of all I suspect Stac Pollaidh would fall within most people's hundred favourite walks, so it would seem churlish to exclude it because of its popularity, but more importantly I want to add my voice to that of Scottish Natural Heritage and the Footpath Trust, who are trying to encourage walkers to take an alternative route from the overused south facing one.

Following a public appeal and a grant of over a quarter of a million pounds from the Heritage Lottery Fund, the Footpath Trust has plans to develop another old footpath which runs round the western shoulder of Stac Pollaidh. This will, eventually, connect with the present footpath and so offer walkers a circular route around the mountain.

Route Summary

From the car park on the Drumrunie to Achiltibuie road, cross the road and take the obvious path which runs in a N direction up the hill. About half way up a track bears off to the right. Follow this track, traversing round the E shoulder of the hill to where a series of zigzags climb up to the prominent saddle from the N. To go to the summit follow the obvious path W over a series of sandstone pinnacles.
NB: Return to the road by your route of ascent.

Map: OS Sheet 15

Access Point: Car park on the Drumrunie to Achiltibuie road

Distance: 3km

Approx Time: 2-3 hours

Grade: Moderate hill walk / scramble

Translation: peak of the peat moss

Pronunciation: staak polly

SNH and the Footpath Trust have been upgrading the original ascent route which leads round the east shoulder of the mountain and approaches the summit from the north. This offers a safer and more enjoyable walk and doesn't take any longer than the obvious scramble up the south face, a route that has now become very loose and dangerous.

The Inverpolly National Nature Reserve car park is situated north of Loch Lurgainn on the minor road which runs from Drumrunie to Achiltibuie. Leave the car park, cross the road and follow the signposts and obvious path uphill towards the saddle on the summit ridge above. About halfway up the path branches; one section continues upwards (the section the Footpath Trust want people to avoid) while the other cuts off to the right, round the eastern end of the hill, to where a series of zigzags work their way up the north-east slopes of the hill to the saddle on the summit ridge.

The mountain's base rock is grey Lewisian gneiss, formed some 1500 million years ago. But the hill itself is predominantly red sandstone, laid down on top of the gneiss about 800 million years ago. The grinding ice age and subsequent weathering of frost and wind has worn down this sandstone tower into the ragged, spiky crest that is so familiar today. The saddle is the destination for the vast majority of walkers, as the summit of the hill lies to the west, along a well marked path which takes you over exposed teeth and pinnacles, with a scramble on the final rock tower which involves some awkward climbing.

Even if you don't go to the summit, the saddle offers wide views across much of the Wester Ross National Scenic Area. The hills of Coigach, Suilven, Canisp, Cul Mor and Cul Beag and the Inchnadamph mountains can all be seen from here. Red-throated divers, otters and golden eagles are among the wildlife that frequent the area.

Please don't be tempted to scree run down the south face of the hill back to the road. Return the way you came, allowing the dreadful scars on the southern slopes time to heal.

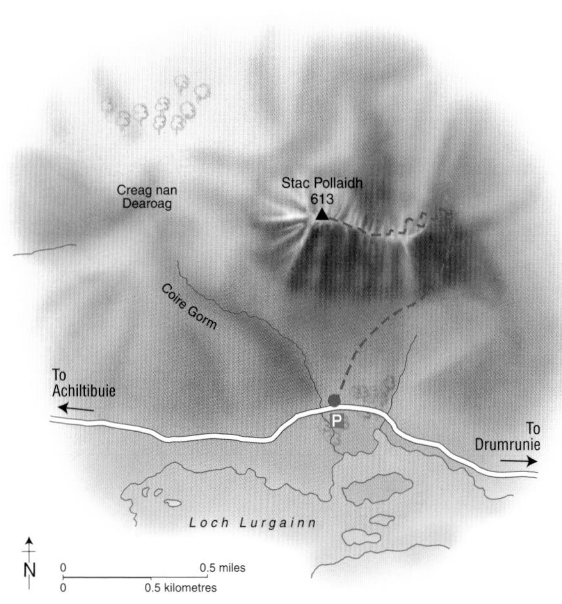

Inverpolly National Nature Reserve and Coigach from the summit of Suilven

84 Suilven

My first visit to Suilven was part of a three-day backpacking trip across the bare mattress of the Sutherland moors. We climbed Suilven from the east, then walked south to climb the Inverpollaidh twins, Cul Mor and Cul Beag. The first night was unforgettable. We watched from our loch-side camp as a riot of sunset colour lit up the surrounding hills in a pageant which was gloriously brash and provocative. The whole display was enacted in deafening silence, an experience which is as spiritually cleansing as anything can be. The waters of the loch before us were like glass, reflecting the long rising ridge of Canisp, a fine enough mountain in its own right but dominated by the Matterhorn spire of Suilven, the uncontested showpiece of Sutherland.

Suilven is chameleon-like, but rather than change its colour it changes its shape dramatically when seen from different angles, more so than any mountain I know. From Elphin in the east it appears as a fine conical peak, rising from its bedrock plinth of Lewisian gneiss, but from the west, from the Lochinver coast, its western sentinel, Caisteal Liath, forms a huge rounded bastion of quartzite-capped sandstone. From Stac Pollaidh, or Cul Mor in the south its shape changes again into a long, drawn-out sugarloaf, with an obvious depression in the middle, Bealach Mor, the only break in the fortress-like defences. The mountain is in fact a long broken ridge with three main summits, the western one of which,

Route Summary

From the bridge follow a path N then NW around the head of the Cam Loch. Continue on this path across high moorland, but before it descends to Lochan Fada strike out to the NW towards Suilven. Climb the mountain by either scrambling over Meall Beag or the easier option of ascending its Bealach Mor from the S. Descend via the Bealach Mor to the N, pass the outflow of Loch na Gainimh and follow the path which leads eventually to Lochinver.

Map: OS Sheet 15

Access Point: A835 Bridge over Ledmore River just N of Elphin GR229121

Distance: 25km

Approx Time: 8-10 hours

Grade: Strenuous hill walk

Translation: possibly from the Norse word for pillar

Pronunciation: sool-avin

Caisteal Liath, can be easily climbed by way of the Bealach Mor.
Suilven can be climbed from a number of different directions, from Inverkirkaig in the south-west; from Lochinver in the north, or from Elphin in the east, but my own preference is to be dropped off by car in Elphin, and picked up at the end of the day in Lochinver, a wonderful through-route of some 26km, a traverse which not only gives the opportunity to take in these deer haunted Sutherland moors, but climaxes on a superb scrambling ascent of the mountain's eastern prow, Meall Beag. This east-west traverse of Suilven is a day you'll never forget.

Just beyond a bridge over the Ledmore River, just north of Elphin, a stalker's path runs along the north shore of the Cam Loch. About half-way along the lochside, just beyond the crossing of the Abhainn a' Chroisg, the path begins to fade and its faint outline can be difficult to follow through the heather as it bears north to climb onto the long ridge of Meall na Braclaich. Once on the rounded crest of the ridge the route becomes clearer and the great spire of Suilven itself draws you on like a magnet. To the north, the long trench of Lochan Fada reflects the slopes of Canisp and to the south, across the waters of the Cam Loch and Loch Veyatie rises the craggy outline of Cul Mor.

It's a watery landscape haunted by the call of the black-throated diver, the loon-like echo that was thought by the Cree Indians of North America to be the sorrowful cry of dead warriors forbidden entry to their heaven. This is also the hunting ground of the golden eagle. I once watched a pair here drifting effortlessly in the thermals. Masters of the sky in search of prey.

As you approach Suilven its Matterhorn aspect gradually fades into something less portentous. The angle of its eastern slope lessens and it's with some relief that you realise that while still steep, it's eminently climbable. By threading together any number of series of ledges, you can scramble up to the broad summit of Meall Beag surprisingly easily, but don't relax too quickly – Suilven doesn't submit its crown quite so easily.

From Meall Beag the ridge narrows and you are greeted by a deep crack in the sandstone strata. Step across this fissure and continue until you reach a sudden and sheer drop with no obvious point of descent. This 30m cliff poses a very serious obstacle, but it can be turned by descending steep ground on the north side of the ridge to where a faint line can be found traversing westwards into the dank and gloomy, but welcome, bealach below Meall Mheadhonach. From this dripping recess a faint path takes a zigzag route up the steep slopes of Meall Mheadhonach from where more steep, rocky slopes eventually give way to grassy slopes dropping to the safety of the Bealach Mor. As if to offer some assurance, an ancient drystone wall crosses the ridge at this point, pointing the eventual descent line to the north down a steep gully: if a wall can be built down the gully, it shouldn't prove too difficult to scramble down!

Easy grassy slopes now lead to the summit of Caisteal Liath, a rounded dome of a place with breathtaking views of mountain, moor and sea. Enjoy the panorama of the mountains of Assynt, the delectable outline of Quinag, the mountains of Inverpollaidh and the coastal hills of Coigach. The descent route follows the wall down the northern gully of the Bealach Mor. Pass the western outflow of Loch na Gainimh to the stalker's path which crosses the Abhainn na Craich Airigh and continues down towards Glencanisp Lodge and the track to Lochinver.

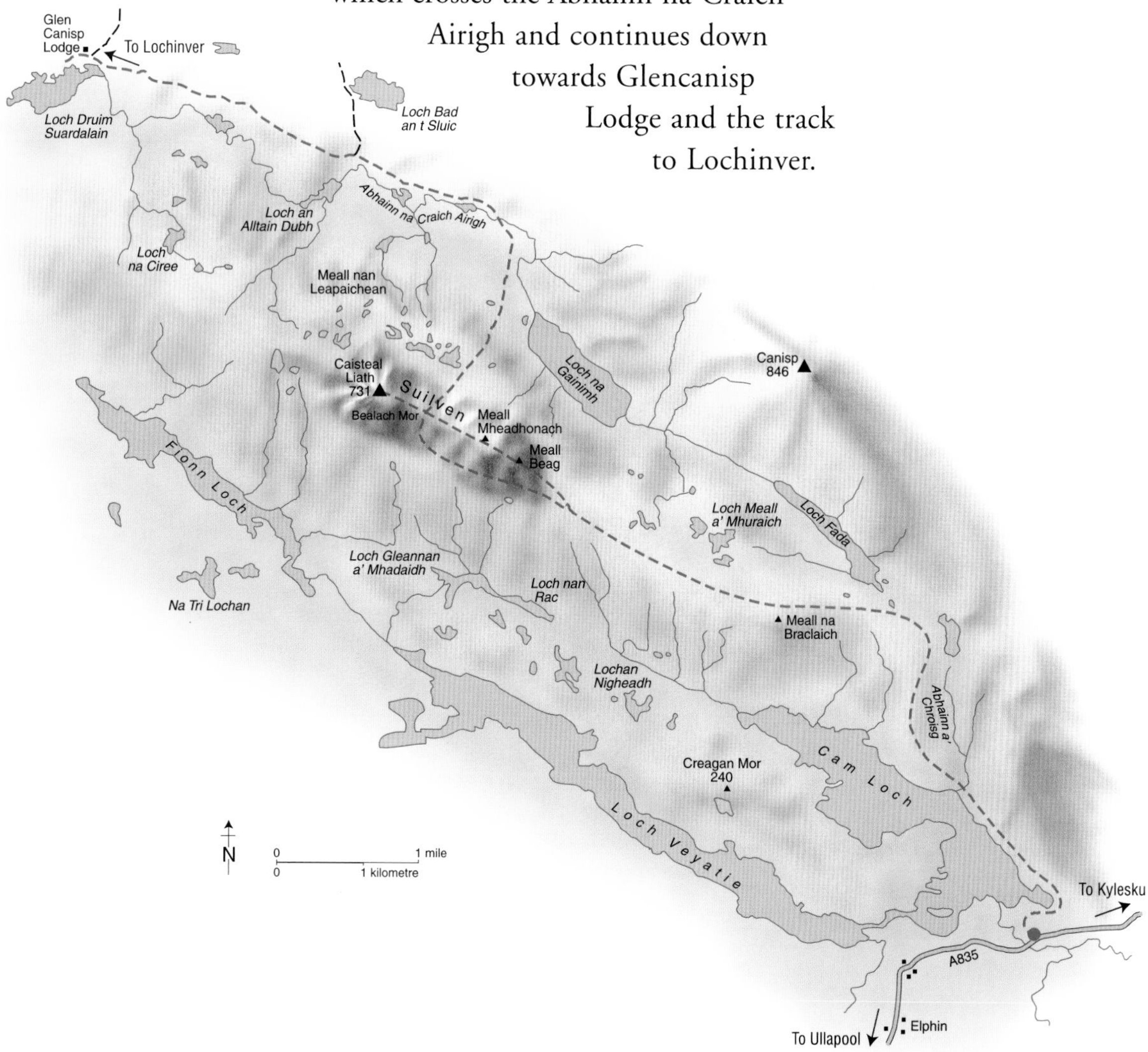

85 Sandwood Bay

Route Summary

Follow the signposted track, then the rough footpath from Blairmore to Sandwood Bay. Return via the cliff tops above Am Buachaille. Continue in a SW direction above the next bay until you meet the stream which issues from Loch a' Mhuillinn. Follow the stream S then E back to the loch and follow the track of your outward route back to Blairmore.

Map: OS Sheet 9

Access Point: Blairmore

Distance: 16km

Approx Time: 5-7 hours

Grade: Moderate coastal walk

Sandwood Bay lies several kilometres south of Cape Wrath, the most north-westerly point on the Scottish mainland. The bay itself boasts 1.5km of beach, backed by marram-grass sand dunes. North and south of the bay high sea-cliffs face the constant vagaries of the Minch and Atlantic gales. The hinterland is formed by Sutherland moors, dotted with lochans, remote and unwelcoming.

At the south-west end of the bar a 100m sea stack rises from its sandstone plinth. This is Am Buachaille, the Herdsman. Behind the beach and sequestered from it by the sand dunes lies Sandwood Loch, and sitting on the grassy hillside above it, the ruins of Sandwood Cottage.

There is a spirit abroad in Sandwood Bay, a spirit of place which is curiously atmospheric and compelling. There are those who claim it is the principal place in Scotland for mermaids: a local shepherd claims to have seen the figure of a woman on a rocky strand which runs out into the sea from the middle of the bay. A black-bearded sailor supposedly haunts the shores. Fishermen at sea have seen him marching over the marram-grass dunes, clad in a cap and dark-blue reefer jacket. Seton Gordon tells of walking here in the 1920s and of how astonished he was at the number of shipwrecks which littered the shore. He believed these were old vessels, lost on this coast before the building of the Cape Wrath lighthouse. He also wondered if Viking long-boats were buried in the sands: it was the Vikings who named this place Sand-Vatn or Sand Water.

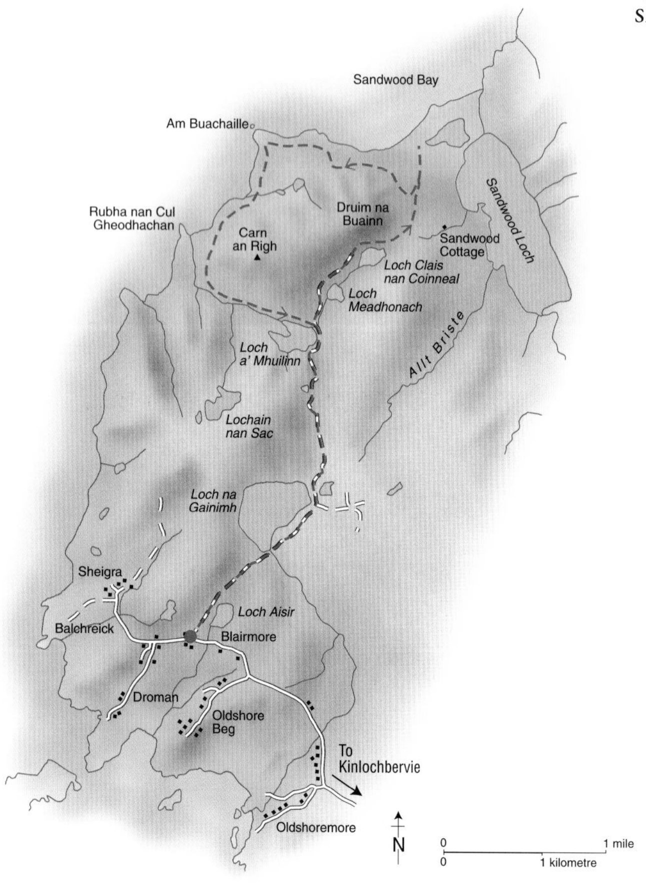

It isn't a long or difficult walk into Sandwood Bay. Take the Oldshoremore road beyond Kinlochbervie and drive to the tiny hamlet of Blairmore. Here a hand-painted sign by the roadside points out the route to Sandwood Bay, 6.5km away. A rough road goes half that distance, before it dwindles into a wet,

Sandwood Bay and Am Buachaille, Sutherland

peaty footpath. It would be very easy to dismiss the walk into Sandwood Bay as dull and boring: at first glance there is little but monotonous moorland, but there is always the brightness of wildlife to cheer things up: the chacking of wheatears, the music of the ubiquitous skylark, croaking ravens and perhaps even the haunting call of a black-throated diver from one of the myriad lochans. The plainness of the walk-in is a complete contrast to the bay itself, with its pale-yellow sand and white-fringed surf as it breaks on the shore. On a good day the vast sea will reflect the blueness of the sky and on an overcast day the waters will become brilliant green matching the verdant marram grass of the dunes.

As you drop down grassy slopes towards the bay you'll pass the remains of Sandwood Cottage, claimed at one time to have been the most isolated house in Scotland. Today it is largely used by anglers and walkers as a bothy. It is also reputedly haunted by the ghost of the black-bearded sailor!

You don't get any idea of the size of Sandwood Bay until you've crossed the barrier of sand dunes which sequester Sandwood Loch from the beach. It is immense, with an air of intense solitude. On my most recent visit, a thin mist hung in the air over the bay with the slim stack of Am Buachaille just shimmering from a flat sea. In the north the cliffs appeared to evaporate in various shades of grey towards Cape Wrath. I sat on the rocky strand for a long time, mesmerised by the gentle surge and suck of the waves. Ringed plovers paraded on the flat rocks and gulls hung in the still air.

Rather than return by the outward path, take to the sea-cliffs to the south of the bay, following the crumbling cliff edge. Pass Am Buachaille, with its fulmars on the red sandstone ledges like residents in a multi-storey block of flats. A well-worn sheep track runs south along the cliff edge and offers wide views down into the next cove, not a sandy one like Sandwood Bay but rocky and rough, the green seas glinting and contrasting with the black cliffs.

Follow the cliff edges south to the foot of this bay until you reach a fairly prominent stream. This flows from Loch a' Mhuilinn, close to the Blairmore track, your incoming route. It makes a fine round trip and no doubt your mind will be busy thinking up your next trip to Sandwood Bay. It's that sort of place.

86 Foinaven

Route Summary

From Lone cottage take the path which follows the Allt Horn to the high bealach between Foinaven, Arkle and Meall Horn. Each of these three summits can be gained from this bealach. To climb Foinaven continue N to Creag Dionard, the 778m spot height, where a broad ridge runs in a NW direction to another spot height at 806m. From here the summit ridge runs roughly NW then N to Ganu Mor, Foinaven's highest point. From the summit descend to the Allt Horn bealach where you have the option of climbing Arkle and Meall Horn before descending back to Lone.

Map: OS Sheet 9

Access Point: A838, GR298402

Distance: Foinaven only: 28km. Foinaven, Arkle and Meall Horn: 33km

I had never seen Foinaven look so commanding. This northern hill has been translated as 'the big wedge', and as I gazed out over the waters of Loch a' Chadh-Fi, a northerly arm of Loch Laxford, I could understand why it had been so named. Impressive in size, its western slopes are bulky and steeply rounded, and on this particular day, white with fresh, spring snow. The Cambrian quartzite flanks of what is probably the finest hill in this empty quarter of Northern Scotland are a delight to climb at any time of year.

In 1992, an Ordnance Survey re-survey had elevated the height of Foinaven to Munro status, but eventually the OS settled on a height just under the magical 3000ft (914m), and the tranquillity of Foinaven was assured, at least for a while. Several years on I met over a hundred people on the slopes of Foinaven, which would suggest that, Munro or not, the sheer character of this mountain attracts people. Its relative remoteness in distant Sutherland is probably more of a saving grace than the fact that it has avoided Munro height! Mind you, that busy day was probably exceptional. A ridge of high pressure had lingered over the north-west, bringing

Approx Time: 12-15 hours
Grade: Strenuous hill walk
Translation: white hill (big wedge)
Pronunciation: foy-nayven

with it joyous days of sun and blue skies and the white screes of Foinaven, and its near neighbour Arkle, sparkled like snow.

At the east end of Loch Stack, a track leaves the A838 Lairg to Laxford Bridge road, crosses over a bridge and runs to the old, suitably named cottage at Lone. From there a stalker's path runs north-eastwards up to a high bealach which connects three separate mountains: Arkle to the west, Foinaven to the north-west and Meall Horn to the east. It is an incredible spot, with steep western slopes dropping down to a rosary of mountain tarns which eventually merge with the lochan-splattered moorland south-east of Rhiconich, a landscape in which it is hard to tell whether it is a loch covered in islands, or a bog full of ponds. I was just glad I didn't have to walk through it.

Above the long glen that held the lochans, steep crags give way to a sinuous ridge winding above the two great corries of Arkle, An Garbh-choire and Am Bathaich. The summit sits high above, but I was more intent on Foinaven, whose southern top, Creag Dionard is only a couple of kilometres from the Bealach Horn.

Seeing a large group of walkers coming up beside the Allt Horn behind me, I struggled over the flat bog of the bealach and climbed the grassy, boulder-strewn slopes, keen to keep my solitude as long as possible. From Creag Dionard the views began

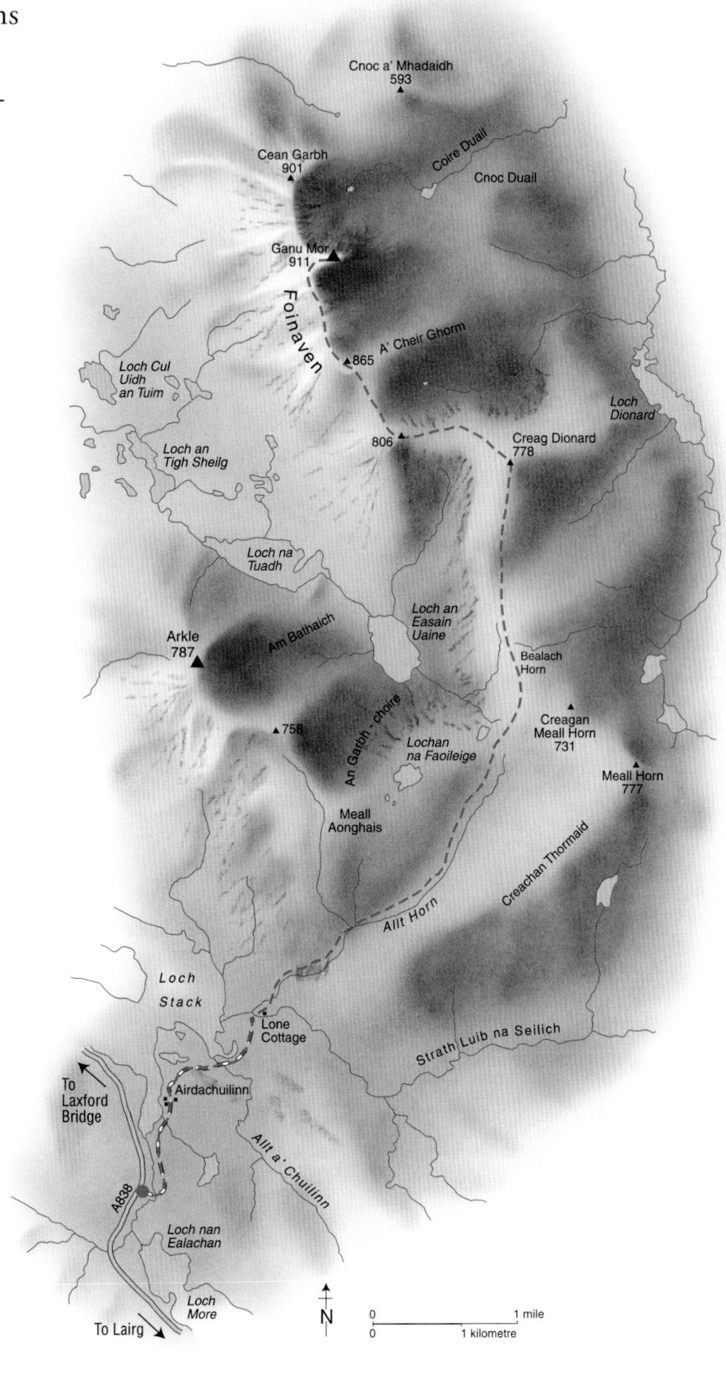

to open out, portraying the watery extravagance of this vast, northern corner of Scotland. Thrift and campion added colour to the upper screes as I turned westwards to the start of the summit ridge. A steep descent drops down loose, scree-covered slopes and suddenly the ridge narrows. A few ups and downs, a lot of scree and loose boulders and huge gaping corries falling away to the east – this wonderful ridge deserves several thousand words of heartfelt description, as does the view from the summit, Ganu Mor. As I approached the cairn I met several more walkers climbing from the north, and together we spent several minutes exclaiming in delight as we recognised hills and features all around us. Cape Wrath stands a few kilometres away to the north west, and we followed the panorama past Cranstackie and Beinn Spionaidh, Ben Hope, Ben Loyal and away in the blue distance, Morven in Caithness.

It was marvellous being amid such splendour, and the shared experience added to the day rather than detracted from it. Munro status or not, Foinaven will always be a popular hill, but will remain relatively free of the crowds because of its distance from the main centres of population. Having said that, I hope the Scottish Mountaineering Club, the arbiters of all things Munro, will never be tempted to promote it over the 3000ft Plimsoll line. It's good enough as it is!

87 Ben Hope

Route Summary

Leave the minor road S of Loch Hope where a signpost points out the route to Ben Hope. Follow the stream and head NE to make for an obvious break in the crags, which takes you onto a wide terrace above the escarpment. Turn N and follow the cliff edge which buttresses the mountain's summit.

Map: OS Sheet 9

Access Point: Roadside at GR 461478

Distance: 7km

Approx Time: 4-6 hours

Grade: Easy hill walk

Translation: hill of the bay

Pronunciation: byn hope

Go north from Ben Hope and it is downhill all the way to Iceland! The last time I stood on the summit of this, our most northerly Munro, my emotions were curiously mixed, exulting in the heady tonic of sea and mountain, yet at the same time removed and distant, as though I hadn't earned the right to be there at all. I'd gatecrashed someone's celebration, had invaded a hallowed privacy and I was uncertain of my role. My good friend Chris Townsend had just spent the previous 118 days climbing all the Munros and tops in Scotland, the first person to achieve such a feat, and Chris Brasher and I joined him for his last summit, Ben Hope, 927m above sea level.

Brasher, as usual, was in ebullient mood. Chris was quiet, no doubt reflecting on all the events that had brought him to this final destination, and I just felt awkward and uncomfortable. I think if I had been Chris I would have wanted to savour this final ascent, to tease out the moments of success before descending to normality, but, bless him, he tholed us with grace and dignity, even when we plied him with champagne and haggis. In the book which described his journey he wrote of that final summit: 'We reached the large summit cairn. I felt pleased, elated but somehow distant. I knew I'd finished but at the same time couldn't believe it. Surely I would go down, find somewhere to camp, then climb more hills the next day? Wouldn't I?'

I felt guilty and had to cast out that particular demon, destroy that particular shadow which, by association, would affect my memories of that particular hill. Ben Hope is far too fine a mountain to climb with a nagging remorse perched on your shoulder. So I went back to wander up its long southern ridge, alone, to make my peace with the mountain.

From the north Ben Hope appears as a crag-girt wedge, but is most often climbed from the south, where the western cliffs form a clear navigational aid. A signposted path leaves the road 1.5km or so north of the farm at Alltnacaillich, and takes a meandering route past a series of cascading waterfalls to steeper, craggier slopes. A sly line breaks through a breach-like weakness in the western escarpment to deliver you on the bare, stony, summit slopes. A well-worn footpath scours its way uphill, twisting and turning past the inevitable waymark cairns, one of the cancers of the modern hill game. But even the puerile works of homo constructus can't compete with the sense of isolation which eases off into the watery wilderness far below. The long and thin arm of Loch Hope leads the eye to the open sea, and to the east the multi-topped outline of Ben Loyal sings clearly of the wonder and fascination of mountains, no matter how far above or below any of man's perceived plimsoll lines. A gentle stroll across the stony, barren plateau leads to the summit cairn, and I could cast aside the shadows of that earlier visit and renew my relationship with the mountain on its own terms. This was my party, and I was no longer a stranger.

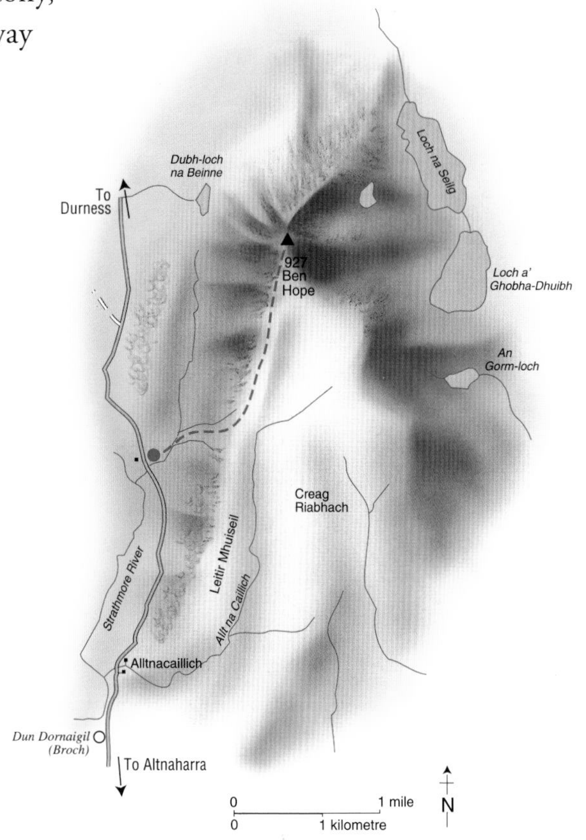

The Islands

Covering Arran, Jura, Mull, Rum and Skye, I've also described walks on Harris, Orkney, Shetland, and Kerrera, just off the coast south of Oban.

It's surprising how many of Scotland's islands are mountainous, or at least hilly, and I would claim that one mountain group, the Cuillin of Skye, makes up the finest mountain landscape we have. When you consider the subtle blend between mountain and seascape that is the Cuillin's finest characteristic, I would suggest we have, just off our west coast, one of the finest mountain ranges in Europe, if not the world. What the Cuillin lacks in worldly height terms, it makes up for in sheer, sublime magnificence. Magnificent too are the hills of the Cuillin of Rum and of course the wonderfully jagged ridges of Arran; I wonder how many walkers are also familiar with the delights of Jura, Mull, Harris, Orkney and Shetland?

There's a lifetime of walking on these islands alone, and amazingly, there are many, many others I haven't even visited yet. I suspect it would take several lifetimes to get to know them all.

THE WALKS

Marsco and the River Sligachan, Isle of Skye

Route Summary

Follow the road W from the pier, then a track, towards Cuilags hill. Where the track turns sharply right leave it for rough moorland and cross the outflow of Sandy Loch. Ascend slopes of Cuilags and continue for 1.6km to St John's Head. From here follow the cliffs for about 5km to Rora Head, passing the Old Man of Hoy. Continue along cliff tops before descending to Rackwick. From the village follow road E to where it crosses the river. Leave the road here and walk N by the river passing Berrie Dale on the left.

88 Hills of Hoy

The Old Man of Hoy is a 120m sandstone sea-stack which rises from the sea just off the west coast of the Orkney island of Hoy. (The name Hoy comes from the Norse for 'high'). It was first climbed by Rusty Baillie, Tom Patey and Chris Bonington in 1966 and later that year was the subject of what was the BBC's most expensive outside broadcast to date, when a team of climbers tackled the route for the cameras. Hoy itself is the second largest island in Orkney and offers the best walking possibilities.

A magnificent coastal walk follows the cliffs of Hoy from St John's Head south to Rora Head, passing above the famous Old Man of Hoy. This route suggests a circular itinerary, taking in the best of the coastal walking with a visit to the almost deserted village of Rackwick and a look at what is possibly the most

northerly natural woodland (rowan, aspen and birch) in Britain.

From Linksness Pier (daily ferry between Stromness and Hoy), follow the road, then a track, westwards towards Cuilags hill. After a short distance on the track, to where it turns sharply to the right, leave it for rough moorland and cross the outflow of Sandy Loch. It's an easy climb to the summit of Cuilags, at 433m the second highest hill on Hoy – Ward Hill is highest at 477m. From Cuilags' grassy summit the going is easy and level for 1.6km to St John's Head, a spectacular viewpoint above steep cliffs which fall to the crashing seas over 300m below, a place alive with the cries of whirling fulmars.

The Old Man of Hoy and St John's Head, Hoy, Orkney

From St John's Head a dramatic walk follows the unbroken cliffs for over 5km to Rora Head, passing above the wide bay presided over by the Old Man of Hoy. From Rora Head the route continues along the cliff tops before descending to the beach at Rackwick. Once a thriving fishing community, it now consists of no more than two or three crofts. Deserted cottages scatter the hillsides, but B&B can be found here if you ask, or you can find accommodation at Linksness.

Follow the road east from Rackwick to where it crosses the river. Leave the road here and head north beside the river passing Berrie Dale on the left – probably the most northerly natural woodland in the country. Continue north, cross the river and follow the western shore of Sandy Loch. Beyond the loch you'll meet the road you left earlier, which takes you back to the pier.

Before you leave the Stromness ferry check what time it will leave Hoy. Make sure you have enough time to complete the walk.

Continue N, cross the river and follow the W shore of Sandy Loch. Beyond the loch you'll meet the road you left earlier from where you return to the pier.

Map: OS Sheet 7
Access Point: Linksness Pier
Distance: About 19km
Approx Time: 6-8 hours
Grade: Moderate coastal walk

Muckle Flugga, the northernmost point of Great Britain, from Hermaness Hill, Unst, Shetland

Route Summary

Follow the signposted trail from the car park to the summit of Hermaness Hill. Descend in a NW direction to the clifftops. Follow them for about 2km S to Toolie where another waymarked route crosses the moorland to the Burn of Winnaswarta Dale and the outward path. Return to the car park.

Map: OS Sheet 1

Access Point: Car Park at GR612149

Distance: 8km

Approx Time: 3-5 hours

Grade: Moderate coastal walk

89 Hermaness, Shetland

The Shetland Islands consist of about 100 islands – less than a score are inhabited. Many are hilly, with dark moorlands contrasting with the deep greens of the valleys and cultivated coastal areas, their monotony relieved by innumerable lochans. The coastline is rugged with long winding sheltered inlets of the sea bordered by cultivated fields.

In June and July it is never really dark; indeed it is this long twilight, with its everchanging shadows that lingers longest in the memory. That, and the sound of a hundred thousand seabirds.

The highest hills of Unst, Hermaness Hill and Saxa Vord, are at the northernmost extremity – to either side of Burra Firth. They both have paths to their summits. Herma Ness is a bird sanctuary and Hermaness a National Nature Reserve since 1955, now managed by Scottish Natural Heritage.

A footpath runs north from the car park at the coastguard station on the west shore of the Burra Firth. The path climbs steadily, crosses the Burn of Winnaswarta Dale and then, skirting the east fringes of Sothers Brecks begins to climb the long south ridge of Hermaness Hill. There can be few hills of such lowly elevation, 200m, that can boast such a view. To the north, barely a kilometre away, lie the spectacular skerries and stack of Muckle Flugga; its summit crowned with a lighthouse, the northernmost inhabited point of the British Isles, and beyond it, by half a kilometre, is Britain's northernmost uninhabited island, Out Stack. It's sobering to consider that this lonely island, as much a part of Britain as Devon or Cornwall, is the same latitude as South Greenland!

Eastwards, across the waters of the Burra Firth, rises the highest hill on Unst, Saxa Vord at 280m. This hill is somewhat spoiled by a large RAF station with radar scanners and tracking installation, but it is manned by 800 people and no doubt provides employment for many of the islanders.

From Hermaness Hill, descend north-west to the top of the Herma Ness itself, and the beginning of a superb clifftop walk of over 2km to Toolie, where a waymarked route returns you to your earlier path, but first enjoy this coastal walk – bold headlands thrusting out into the ocean, rising to cliffs of over 150m. Lofty stacks with weird names – The Greing, Humla Stack, Clingra Stack and Flodda Stack, natural arches and deep caverns, and above all, the raucous cacophony of seabirds. The assault on the senses by the combination of the swirling waters below, the cries of 100,000 birds and the smell of guano is almost overwhelming.

There are several gannetries here on the Hermaness cliffs where over 10,000 pairs have built their nests. There are also puffins, 20,000 guillemots, 1500 razorbills, 2000 pairs of kittiwakes, over 100 pairs of shags and innumerable black guillemots.

As you leave the cliffs and cross the moorland again, you will no doubt be greeted by bonxies – great skuas – and possibly buzzed by them. About 60 per cent of the world's population breed here on these northern islands. Look out for other birds of the moorlands – red-throated divers, snipe, dunlin, golden plover and arctic skua. Hermaness is an ornithologists paradise.

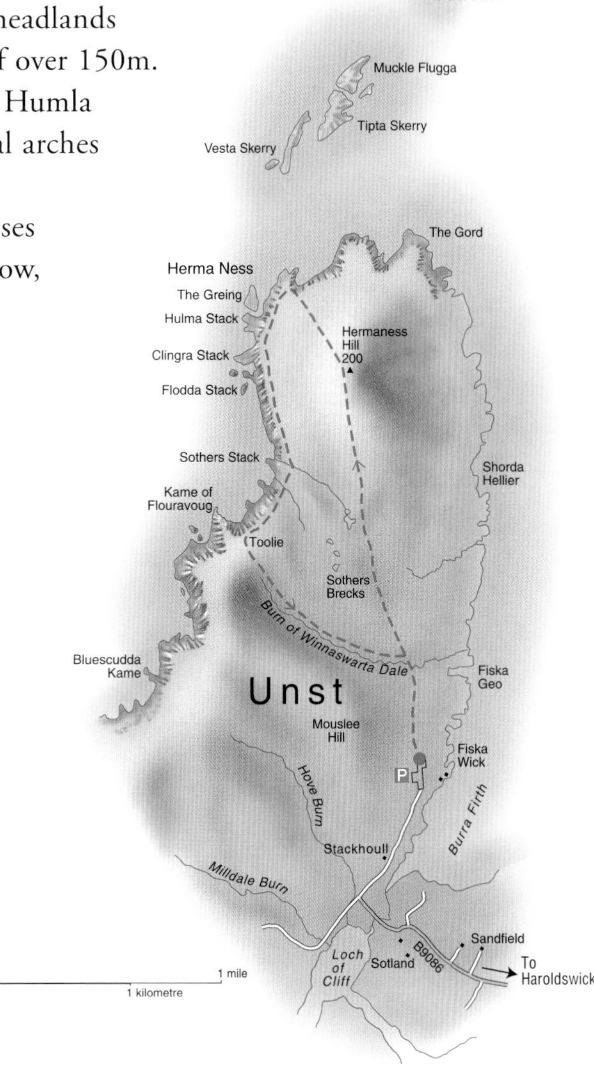

90 Clisham, Isle of Harris

Route Summary

From the bridge over the Maaruig River follow the slopes W to reach a col N of the Sron Carsaclett. Traverse the slopes in a NW direction to reach the S shoulder of Clisham. Follow this shoulder to the SE ridge which is then followed to the summit and trig point. Cross the ridge to Mulla-Fo-Dheas, and descend the S ridge of Tarsabhal back to the road.

Map: OS Sheet 14

Access Point: Bridge over the Maaruig River on the A859

Distance: 7km

Approx Time: 4-5 hours

Grade: Moderate hill walk

Translation: rocky cliff

Pronunciation: klee-sham

From the lonely shieling of the misty island,
Mountains divide us, and the wastes of seas,
Yet the blood is still strong, the heart is highland,
And we, in dreams, behold the Hebrides.

Stirring words to go through your mind as you see the hills of Harris appear through a heat haze over the Minch. The sea lay like quicksilver and the hills appeared like warts from the long flat peninsula that makes up Lewis.

This was my first visit to the Hebrides and I couldn't quite believe my luck. The Hebrides in a heat-wave, and now the old nostalgic songs of the Gaels could mean something. This looked like a place to leave you breathless with its beauty, and it wasn't long before I was breathless, for my first destination was the highest hill in Harris, An Cliseam or Clisham.

I'm tempted to call it a wee hill for it's only 799m but every metre has to be earned from sea-level. The whole area of North Harris is a wild mountainous place. Although they are generally regarded as two separate places, Harris and Lewis in fact make up one single island, the Long Island, the longest in the Outer Hebrides. There's also a wonderful sense of remoteness here, not surprising really when you consider that the only thing between here and north America is the archipelago of St Kilda, hanging on the very edge of the world. It didn't look as though there would be any distant views for me on this day though, as a thin haze hung over the islands.

Clisham is a well defined mountain, with a narrow ridge emanating off its summit towards some outliers, An t-Isean and Mulla-Fo-Dheas.

The Tarbert to Stornoway road gives convenient access and a bit of a start, about 150m above sea level. From a broad peaty shoulder the hill begins to take

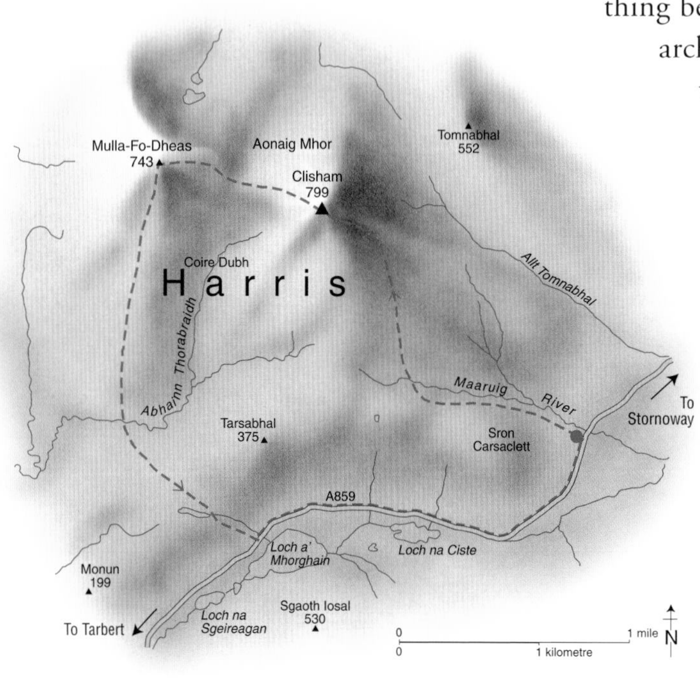

Clisham (An Cliseam), centre right, and Uisgnaval Mor from the south across Loch a Siar, Harris

shape until it represents a broad based pyramid whose south-east ridge offers an airy scramble on ancient Lewisian Gneiss.

I had read beforehand an account of a scramble on this hill by Seton Gordon who claimed it to be singularly devoid of bird life. He found grouse and meadow pipits and little else. I found grouse and meadow pipits too, but I also found golden plover. They were running round dirging away with that sad little call of theirs, a sound that emphasised the emptiness of these seldom trodden hills.

It's a straightforward climb to the top of Clisham via the shallow col north of Sron Carsaclett. I reached the summit trig point in a little over an hour which was too quick and too hot on such a summer day, but sense did eventually prevail and I dawdled on the rest of the ridge. The other hills of Harris, Uisgnaval Mor and Uisgnaval Beag stood out as shapely twins and beyond them the Nordic sounding Cleiseval and Ullaval, hills as remote as anything on the mainland. The ridge to Mulla-Fo-Dheas was a dream with interesting scrambling and some superb situations. Descend the south ridge of Mulla-Fo-Dhaes, skirting the south-west ridge of Tarsabhal, back to the road.

A pair of ravens kept me company, barking encouragement from time to time. All too soon it was time to creep down the rumbling screes and back to the glen. This was supposed to be a family holiday and the children wanted the white sands of a Hebridean beach, especially on a day like this.

91 Marsco, Isle of Skye

Route Summary
Follow the path S down Glen Sligachan for 3km. Follow the Allt na Measarroch to the Mam a' Phobuill, then climb S into Coire nan Laogh. Follow the E ridge of the corrie to the summit ridge, turn NW and follow the summit ridge to the cairn. Descend back to Glen Sligachan via the SE ridge and the Allt Am Fraoch-choire. Follow the footpath back to Sligachan.

Map: OS Sheet 32

Access Point: Sligachan Inn

Distance: 18km

Approx Time: 6-8 hours

Grade: Moderate hill walk

Translation: from the Norse meaning seagull rock

I climbed Marsco for the first time with Donnie Munro, the one-time lead singer with Runrig. We were making a television programme and I was a little surprised he had never been on the hill before, despite the fact he had recorded a song called Nightfall on Marsco. He was intrigued that it was a new hill for me too – he just assumed I had climbed everything.

At 736m Marsco falls below the Plimsoll line of both Corbett and Munro status, and that's maybe its saving grace. Its lack of elevation makes it a grand viewpoint for the higher hills that surround it, and its short and narrow summit ridge forms a grand circle vantage point for the superb spectacle of the Black Cuillin ridge across Glen Sligachan. Equally, the view to the south-east is dominated by the great notched ridge of Clach Glas and Bla Bheinn, a sight of Tolkienesque spires, gullies and rock walls, as dramatic as anything on Skye, the most sensationally scenic island of all.

Donnie and I were walking through from Sligachan to Elgol, taking in Marsco, Loch Coruisk, the Bad Step and Bla Bheinn *en route* in our televised three day trip, but Marsco is easily climbed in a day from Sligachan. Stand outside the historic Sligachan Inn where the great Dr Norman Collie, one of our finest Victorian mountaineers and explorers spent the last years of his life, and gaze south down the great U-shaped glen that separates the Red and the Black Cuillin. Beyond the Druim Ruaige face of Beinn Dearg Mhor, Marsco rises as a pyramid, its western ridge bulging out in a protuberance called Fiaclan Dearg, the red tooth. It's a bold mountain, dominating one of the finest views in Scotland. That, and that fact alone, makes it more than worthy of an ascent.

While Marsco can be climbed from the head of Loch Ainort in the east, I prefer this longer approach down Glen Sligachan. Here, in the shadow of the Black Cuillin, you are more aware of the hill's commanding position, and its individuality, rather than experiencing it as part of the long Red Cuillin ridge that runs from Bla Bheinn in the south to Glamaig in the north.

Follow the well used path down Glen Sligachan for about 3km to reach the Allt na Measarroch. A footpath follows the north bank of the burn and climbs steadily up to the grassy slopes of the Mam a' Phobuill, the pass of the people, which is the high point in an old route between the head of Loch Ainort and Glen Sligachan.

From the top of the pass climb grassy slopes southwards into Coire nan Laogh and then up the corrie's north-east ridge to a high col between the summit ridge and the hill's south-east top. From this shallow col the summit ridge tapers off to the north-west, gradually narrowing over 500m to a superbly narrow ridge which leads to the summit cairn and one of the finest views on Skye. Across the gulf of Glen Sligachan the sawtoothed ridge of the Black Cuillin simply takes the breath away, and to the south Bla Bheinn and Clach Glas leave you little chance of catching it again!

Once you've drunk your fill of Scotland's most amazing landscape, return to the col and descend the steep south-east ridge before dropping south into Am Fraoch choire. Follow the Allt nam Fraoch-choire down into Glen Sligachan where the footpath runs back over 7km to Sligachan.

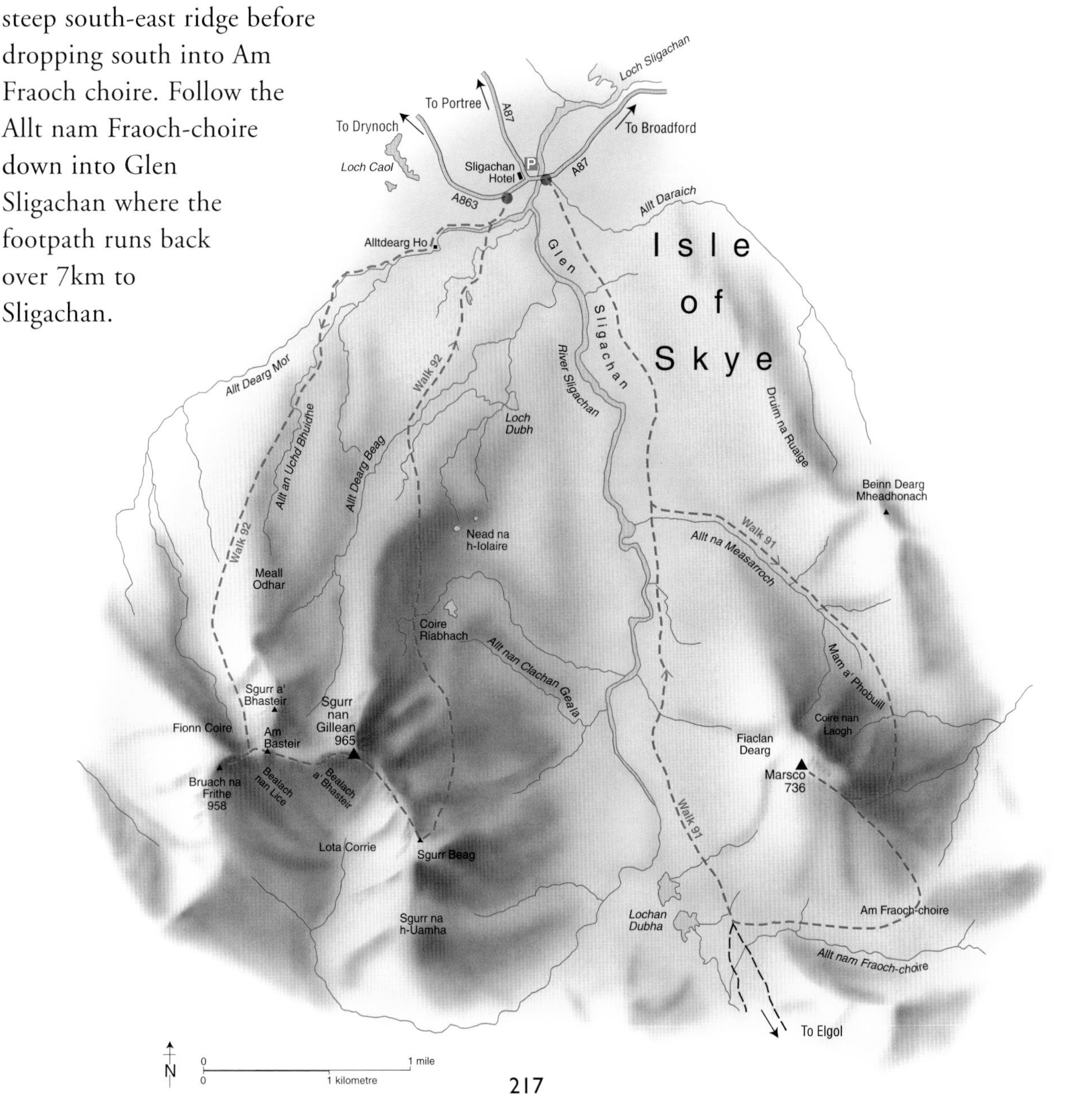

92 Sgurr nan Gillean, Isle of Skye

Route Summary

Walk up the Fionn Coire between Sgurr a' Bhasteir and Bruach na Frithe to reach the Cuillin ridge just W of the Bealach nan Lice (see map on p.217). Continue W to the summit of Bruach na Frithe. Return to the Bealach nan Lice and follow the scree path round the foot of Am Basteir to the Bealach a' Bhasteir. From here follow the E ridge of Am Basteir to an awkward scrambling descent, then continue on the ridge to the summit. Return to the Bealach a' Bhasteir and follow a gravelly path to the foot of Nicholson's Chimney which, after a steep scramble on good holds gives access to the W ridge of Sgurr nan Gillean. Climb this ridge to the summit. Descend the SE ridge and follow the well worn path back to Sligachan via Coire Riabhach.

Map: OS Sheet 32

Access Point: Sligachan

Distance: 16km

Approx Time: 6-8 hours

Grade: Strenuous and technical hill walk/scramble

Translation: peak of the young men

Pronunciation: skoor nan geelyan

Far, far distant, far on a horizon,
I see the rocking of the antlered Cuillin,
beyond the seas of sorrow, beyond the morass of agony,
I see the white felicity of the high-towered mountains.

The words of the great Gael, Sorley Maclean, and his 'antlered Cuillin' well describes those three great peaks which appear to form the portals of the Cuillin itself; Bruach na Frithe, Am Basteir and Sgurr nan Gillean.

We were making a television programme with ex-Runrig singer Donnie Munro. From the summit of Marsco and the long western ridge of Bla Bheinn, we had gazed in awe at the serrated edge of the Cuillin ridge, holding in its cusp the dark waters of Loch Coruisk. The best points to view the Cuillin are undoubtedly on these neighbouring Red Cuillin, or from Elgol in the south looking across Loch Scavaig. After a week of Cuillin gazing it was good to actually get to grips with the hills themselves.

One of our film crew members David, had never been to Skye before. At the first opportunity of some free time we drove to Sligachan and scampered up the length of the Fionn Coire between Sgurr a' Bhasteir and Bruach na Frithe, the dark walls of the mountains on either side of us pressing in as we climbed higher over seas of rock and boulder scree.

I was ahead of David when we reached the ridge, and wandered up towards the summit of Bruach na Frithe, probably the easiest of all the main Cuillin summits. When ten minutes passed I became rather concerned that David hadn't caught up. I shouldn't have worried – he was so amazed at the sight before him that it had literally stopped him in his tracks. Once he had recovered sufficiently he started photographing every peak and pinnacle in sight. He had never, in his own words, seen anything to compare with this view of the Cuillin ridge.

We had climbed Bruach na Frithe in quick time so we thought we'd take a look at Am Basteir too. Down into Lota Corrie we went looking for the route which led to the narrow crevice between the summit and its eponymous 'tooth', the great blade of rock that appears to stick out the side of Am Basteir. I descended this route several years ago and couldn't recall much about it, which was perhaps just as well, because it looked wet and greasy and

Sgurr nan Gillean, Cuillin Hills, Isle of Skye, from the north-west

uninviting. Undeterred, we climbed back through the Bealach na Lice and followed the screes which lead round the foot of Am Basteir to the Bealach a' Basteir, where the normal route climbs up a narrow ridge to the summit, dropping at one point into a narrow recess which calls for a fairly agile bit of scrambling.

Having climbed two summits it would have been a pity not to climb Sgurr nan Gillean as well, but I think David was a little concerned at our lack of equipment. All the other walkers we met were equipped with harnesses, slings, ropes and climbing helmets. But David had years of rock climbing experience behind him, so we went for it, relishing the big solid holds in Nicolson's Chimney and delighting in the narrow, steep and sinuous ridge crest that took us from there to the summit of the mountain. This has to be the finest mountain summit in the country, an airy crest thrown up by steep rocky slopes on all sides. It was no wonder Alexander Nicolson described it as 'the upheaval of Sgurr nan Gillean'. Before we began our long descent David summed up his day. He was thrilled that, at 51, he could still experience the best day in his life.

Bla Bheinn, Isle of Skye, from the north with Eigg and Rum in the distance

93 Bla Bheinn (Blaven), Isle of Skye

Bla Bheinn dwells in the shadow of its more illustrious neighbours, the Skye Cuillin, and while it lacks the sawtooth outline of the western ridge it has characteristics which gives it an independence which is surprising given the mystical reputation of the Cuillin. Dominating upper Loch Slapin, Blaven and Clach Glas, its eastern neighbour, are sequestered from the Cuillin by the dark gulf created by Glen Sligachan and Strath na Creitheach.

The most southerly of the Red Cuillin range, Bla Bheinn, 928m, offers a splendid viewpoint from which to gasp at the audacious outline of the Black Cuillin, and to appreciate the subtler curves of their pink-red neighbours. On a day of gusting winds and racing clouds I once struggled up the eastern ridge and broke the summit ridge skyline, just as the wind tore a great gash in the low clouds. Through that hole the sharp, tortured peaks of the Cuillin appeared, otherworldly and remote. It took me some moments to realise I could hear something other than the roar of the wind in my ears. It was the honking cacophony of geese, no doubt disorientated by the racing cloud and wind. I couldn't see them, but their music was clear, blending with the gusts into a natural melody that had me trembling in delight.

A marvellous sea and Cuillin-view route climbs Blaven from Camasunary up the hill's SSW ridge, a fine rocky scramble. The most popular route to the summit, through property now owned by the John Muir Trust, starts from the road near the head of Loch Slapin and follows the Allt na Dunaiche up and into Coire

Uaigneich. An often muddy footpath follows the north side of the stream weaving its way initially through some heather-covered moraines and a fine gorge. Further on tree-fringed cascades make a great foreground to the forbidding grey walls of Bla Bheinn, Chlas Glas and Sgurr nan Each. Beyond the falls, the path bends to the left and crosses the stream, steepening now as it takes more of a south-west line up heather, then grassy slopes and into Coire Uaigneich, the secret corrie, and a very different world.

Loch Fionna-choire lies like a sparkling diamond amid a world of chaos. Scree shoots and grey buttresses dominate and a line of man-built cairns march resolutely towards the horrid confines of the Great Scree Gully, beckoning walkers towards a miserable, scree-shifting scramble. Ignore the cairned route, kick the things down if you have the time, and instead turn to the right where a rough path takes a zigzag line up the southern slopes of the east ridge, before becoming clearer on the higher screes as it passes the top of the Great Prow which appears on the right. Reach a small top on the hill's eastern shoulder where the ridge becomes much more straightforward as it narrows and weaves gently to the left and then to the right. Buttresses intermittently bar the way, but pose little difficulty other than some mild scrambling before the ridge broadens out to where the summit trig point and cairn announces not only the top of Bla Bheinn, but the sudden and astonishing view across Glen Sligachan to the wondrous Cuillin.

The quickest descent, assuming you don't want to return the way you came, is to continue south along the summit ridge and down to an obvious bealach, the head of the Great Scree Gully. Although moving scree and rock can be awkward it's a lot easier descending this gully than climbing up it – a fairly rapid descent back to Coire Uaigneich. But a better descent is to head south from the south-west top which is reached from the col by a mild scramble, and then by following the broad south-east ridge to the upper slopes of Coire Uaigneich and the footpath back to Loch Slapin.

Route Summary

Leave the Elgol road and follow the path that runs alongside the north bank of the Allt na Dunaiche into Coire Uaigneich. Two craggy faces are split by a deepset scree filled gully, and both faces have routes to the summit ridge. Although the path becomes indistinct in places, turn NNW up a steep slope to the right of the obvious gully and up a distinct shoulder. Once this shoulder abuts on to the main ridge follow it in a WSW direction, along the rim of the ridge. As you climb closer to the summit dome there are one or two rocky obstacles to be scrambled over before more scree slopes lead to the summit. Descend S from the SW top, to the head of Coire Uaigneich.

Map: OS Sheet 32

Access Point: Head of Loch Slapin, GR562217

Distance: 6.5km

Approx Time: 4-6 hours

Grade: Moderate hill walk

Translation: possibly blue hill, or possibly warm hill

Pronunciation: blaa-vin

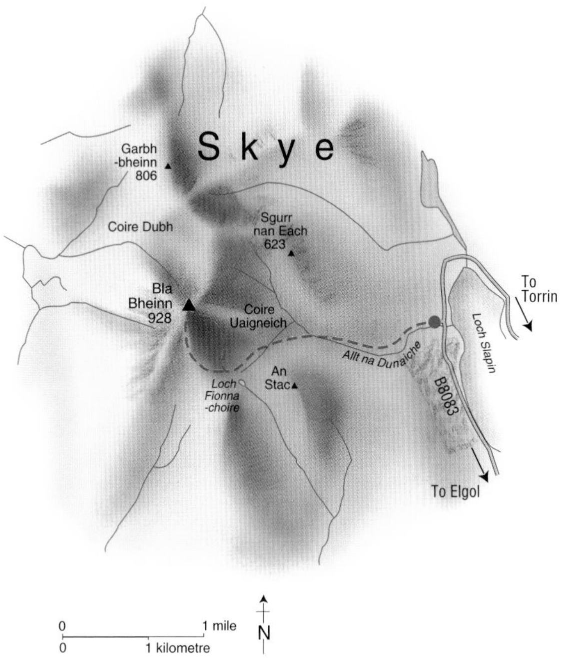

94 Boreraig and Suisinish – Skye's Deserted Villages

Route Summary

From Cill Chriosd on the Broadford to Torrin road, head back towards Broadford for a short distance, and turn onto a track on the right. Follow this track, then a narrow footpath across the hillside and over open moorland to its high point near Loch Lonachan. Now follow the Allt na Pairte all the way S to the coast at Boreraig. Take the shoreline path W to Suisinish. Another track now follows the shore of Loch Slapin N to Camus Malag, where it turns inland to meet up with the B8083 just E of Torrin. Follow the road back to Cill Chriosd.

Map: OS Sheet 32

Access Point: Opposite the ruins of Cill Chriod on the Broadford to Torrin road

Distance: 16km

Approx Time: 6-8 hours

Grade: Moderate coastal walk

Overlooking Loch Eishort on the Isle of Skye, the poignant beauty of Boreraig and Suisnish overshadow the tragic effects of the Highland Clearances. Both these villages were 'cleared' in the mid-nineteenth century, the inhabitants sent to Campbeltown from where they set sail for the New World on the Government ship *Hercules*. Many of them died from smallpox. Those who refused to go were burned out of their homes.

These deserted villages remind us of a time when the Highlands were much more densely populated than they are now. Today sheep browse the once fertile lands which supported generations of crofting families prior to that most shameful chapter of Scottish history – the Highland Clearances. This terrible period has its parallels in Bosnia and Rwanda, and has recently been described by one writer, David Craig, as ethnic cleansing.

The landowner of the time, Lord MacDonald, argued that the people had wasted good land, and it would be better for them, and the land, if they were removed. Once the people had gone, the lands were rented to flockmasters from the south. Fertile ground which had supported generations of crofters was used as grazing for sheep and now much of the landscape of the Highlands is denuded and degraded by the over-grazing of these woolly locusts and their antlered cousins. The terrible legacy of the clearances can be counted in more than just human terms!

A 16km walk visits these empty villages and rounds the point of Rubha Suisnish before following the rugged

Ruined croft at Boreraig looking towards Sleat across Loch Eishort, Isle of Skye

coast of Loch Slapin back to the start. Begin opposite the ruined church at Cill Chriosd (Christ's Church) on the Broadford to Torrin road. Walk back towards Broadford for a short distance, cross a cattle grid and turn onto a track on the right. Follow this track past a building to where a narrow footpath climbs to meet the course of a former narrow-gauge railway. Turn right onto this track, pass through an old marble quarry, and continue on the track as it runs across open moorland to its high point near Loch Lonachan. Follow the Allt na Pairte all the way south to the coast at Boreraig. Once you've explored the remains of the village, follow the path on the shoreline west to Suisinish, a marvellous situation above Rubha Suisnish where Lochs Eishort and Slapin meet.

The track, built by the Board of Agriculture early in the twentieth century to try and encourage the re-crofting of Suisinish, now follows the shore of Loch Slapin north with fine views across to the wonderful outline of Bla Bheinn and Clach Glas. Follow the track as far as the bay of Camus Malag to where it turns inland to meet up with the B8083 just east of Torrin. Follow the road past Loch Cill Chriosd back to the old church.

95 The Cuillin of Rum

The island has a fascinating history. In 1983 a mesolithic site was discovered in Kinloch, which was radio-carbon dated from burnt hazelnut shells to 8500 years ago. This suggests that Rum can boast the earliest known evidence of man in Scotland. Neolithic arrowheads have been found and there are remains of Iron Age forts and Bronze Age cairns. The place is steeped in antiquity and you could have a marvellous week here without even stepping onto a hill.

In 1869 the island was sold to the Campbells of Ballinby and then in 1886 to John Bullough, a wealthy industrialist. He built shooting lodges at Papadil and Harris and planted some 80,000 trees around Loch Scresort. On his death his son George inherited the island and built Kinloch Castle. George, by all accounts, was something of a character, importing granite from the Isle of Arran to build the castle and insisting that all the builders wear the kilt! The Bulloughs only remained in residence for a few months each year, and eventually Sir George's widow sold the island to the Nature Conservancy Council in 1957. The island is now a National Nature Reserve, administered by Scottish Natural Heritage. For many years the castle was run by the National Trust for Scotland as a hotel, but it is now closed, although there is simple bothy accommodation at the back of the castle. My first visit to Rum

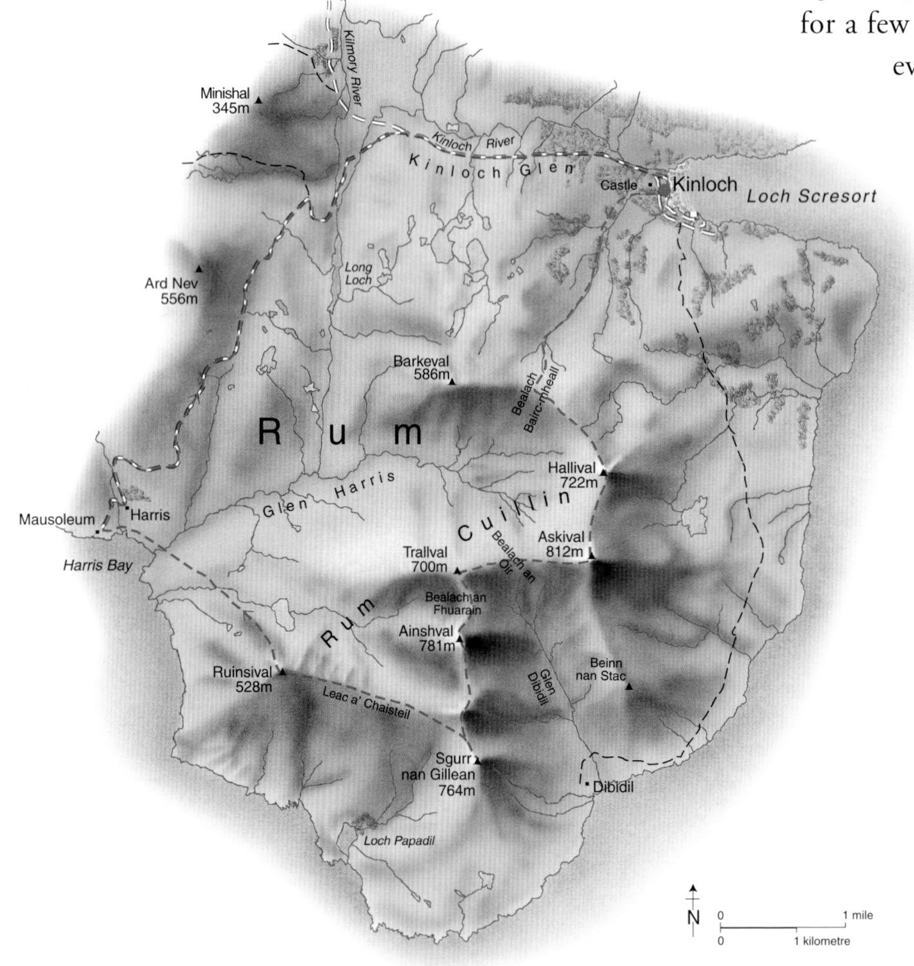

was with the photographer John Cleare. Over glasses of whisky with the island's chief warden we had learned that the whole traverse of the Rum Cuillin was a fairly demanding outing, over 32km of rough hill scrambling with a lot of ascent, and it had been suggested to us there were one or two places where a rope might be useful. We didn't have a rope with us, but didn't worry unduly, reckoning that we could probably avoid any real difficulties.

After a late breakfast the weather looked foul so we dithered for a while in Kinloch Castle, amazed at the treasures within this curious time capsule of the Hebrides. We eventually decided to go and it looked as though it would be a desperate outing as we battled against wind and rain on the hike up Coire Dubh, heading for the first of the hills, Hallival. Beyond Hallival, as we battled against the wind up the very narrow north ridge of Askival, the highest of the Rum Cuillin, we realised that the first major obstacle was immediately in front of us.

The ridge narrowed appreciably and beyond it a black tower blocked the way ahead. It looked menacing in the wind-torn mist and cloud, but as we scrambled closer we saw that a path led away around it to the east. Always one for a good tussle Cleare suggested we tackle it direct, and as he wanted to take a photograph he suggested I go first.

Like most similar situations the actual climb looked harder than it was. An easy step over the mauvais pas and a short scramble led me to the base of a 6m wall. A crack ran up the middle of it and the holds were good, and despite the exposure below it was an easy enough scramble.

The rest of the ridge was delightful, good scrambling on rough rock, and by the time we reached the summit the cloud had cleared and the sun appeared, illuminating magnificent views in every direction. Below our feet the Isle of Eigg stretched out on a sparkling sea and away to the north the neighbouring Cuillin of Skye dominated the horizon and captivated the eye. If the clearance of the weather wasn't enough reward for us the grunting of a raven drew our attention to a magnificent sight. Below us, a golden eagle was being mobbed and harassed by four ravens. The eagle appeared completely nonplussed though, and simply dropped a gear and accelerated away into the teeth of the wind, an amazing exhibition of power flying.

Route Summary

From Kinloch Castle follow the well used path in a SW direction beside the Allt Slugan a' Choilich towards Coire Dubh. From the headwaters of this stream continue S to the Bealach Bairc-mheall. From here climb Hallival, then follow the ridge to Askival. The Askival Pinnacle can be climbed on its W side by a moderately difficult scramble but this can be avoided by a traverse on the E side of the ridge. Descend W to the Bealach an Oir, then climb Trallval. Descend to Bealach an Fhuarain and climb the N ridge of Ainshval, avoiding the lower rocky section. Continue from Ainshval, over a subsidiary top to Sgurr nan Gillean. The summit is at the S end of the ridge. Return to Kinloch by traversing NW along the Leac a' Chaisteil and dropping N into Glen Harris where a bulldozed track takes you back to the start.

Map: OS Sheet 39

Access Point: Kinloch

Distance: 21km

Approx Time: 8-12 hours

Grade: Strenuous hill walk

Askival, Ainshval and Trallval from the summit of Hallival, Rum

As we dropped down the long craggy ridge of Askival I wished I had those eagle's wings, for we still had a long way to go and a lot of climbing to do. Trallval was the next top, a double peak with lush green grass on top of some superb crags, and then a big drop over rough rock and scree to the Bealach an Fhuarain. In front rose the magnificent peak of Ainshval, whose north ridge looked very intimidating indeed. It curved smoothly up to the summit but in its lower reaches it abutted onto a great white buttress. It turned out to be great sport threading a route up through those walls and cracks, real exploratory scrambling and then on up the tight ridge to the summit.

Not far now to the last top, Sgurr nan Gillean, and then the long walk back to Kinloch via the cottage and curious mausoleum at Harris. The Bulloughs had it built, a Greek-looking structure which I thought, from photographs, would be out of place. But it wasn't. With the sun lowering on the western horizon, the grass a verdant green and the sea a rich blue, we could have been strolling by the Aegean Sea rather than the Minch. This was the Bulloughs' Parnassus, and for the moment it was ours too.

96 Ben More of Mull

Ben More of the Isle of Mull was my final Munro, first time round. No matter the individual attributes of a mountain, no matter how fine or grand it may be, there is a special aura that permeates one's last Munro, a peculiar significance which lasts forever. And it was largely this significance that changed my attitude to Mull as an island.

I had no doubt in my mind that I had mistreated Mull – mistreated her badly, and I've yet to make up for my earlier cavalier attitude. I made the basic mistake of treating an entire island as a mountain, a mountain to be climbed, and to make matters worse I had climbed it in an attitude of triumphalism.

It had been an unholy, quick raid to a holy island, to climb the hill, enjoy a celebration meal in technicolour Tobermory and then flee the place. Previous visits were no less fleeting – quick drives through to Iona, day trips by ferry from Oban, and a quick climb of Sgurr Gaoith with Tommy Weir as landward relief during a windy boat trip of the Inner Isles.

More recently I've tried to make partial amends – a week-long stay to film a television documentary about a long walk through the island, which was great for seeing new parts of Mull, but unfortunately the technology that allows you to make such a film holds you apart from the heartbeat of the island – walkie-talkies, radio microphones, cameras, four-wheel drive vehicles and dammit, helicopters, ostensibly create a shield around you – aye, like a television screen, which prevents you from experiencing the very throb of the place.

Other than those collecting the island's only Munro, the Isle of Mull is curiously ignored by hill walkers, which is a pity for there are a couple of grand Corbetts and a lot of fine walking, albeit mostly on rough ground. If nothing else, Ben More is a taster of what the

Route Summary

Start at the foot of the Abhainn na h-Uamha and follow the south bank up the grassy Gleann na Beinne Fada to reach the col between Beinn Fhada and A' Chioch. Turn S and climb towards A' Chioch. Continue on the ridge over A' Chioch to Ben More. Descend by the broad NW ridge.

Map: OS Sheet 48

Access Point: Loch na Keal

Distance: 13 km

Approx Time: 6-8 hours

Grade: Moderate hill walk

Translation: big hill

Pronunciation: byn moar

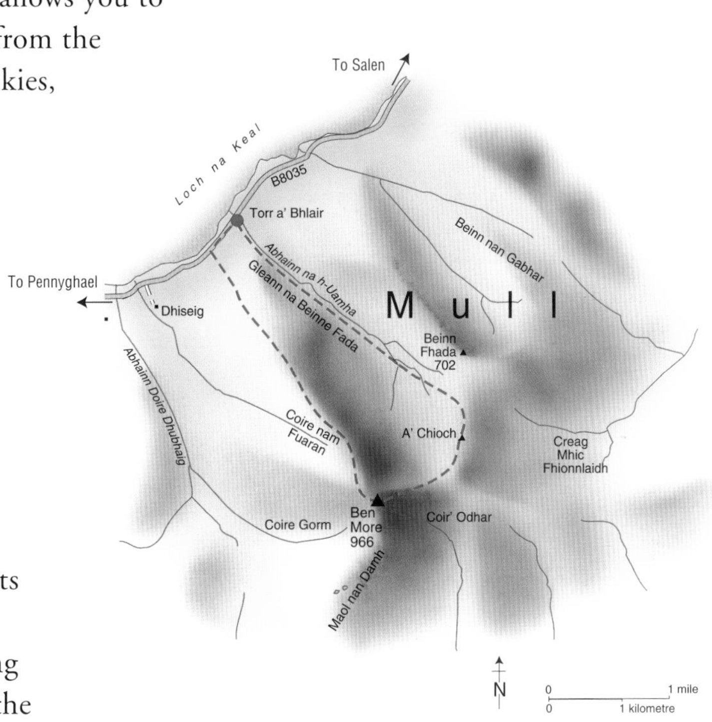

Ben More and Coire Gorm from the west, Isle of Mull

island has to offer. Perhaps another reason why walkers leave Ben More as their last Munro is to give them a chance to save up for it – it can be a costly weekend. Positioned near the west of the island it is a fair distance from the ferry at Craignure, and you either have to take a car on the ferry from Oban, and drive to the starting point, or take a local bus to Salen from where you still have an 11km walk to Loch na Keal. A bike would be useful, and cheaper to transport on the Oban/Craignure ferry!

From the roadside, the B8035, on the south-eastern shores of Loch na Keal, follow the lovely Abhainn na h-Uamha up the length of Gleann na Beinne Fada to the obvious col in the ridge between Beinn Fhada on your left and A' Chioch on your right. From the col turn south and climb steeper and rockier slopes to the summit of A' Chioch.

The route to Ben More continues to the south-west as a superb rocky ridge, involving a steep descent to the rock-girt bealach. Crags fall away to the north-west and there are a couple of big gaps in the slabby wall which can be easily avoided. A steeper, rocky scramble leads directly to the summit wind break of Ben More at 966m. This final climb to Ben More looks steep and difficult from the bealach but don't be discouraged; it's easier than it looks.

A word of warning – the summit rocks are magnetic, and compasses are notoriously unreliable. Best descent is down the broad and straightforward north-west ridge.

97 Below the Carsaig Arches

Mull is an island of surprises for the walker and one of its gems is the coastal walk from the tiny hamlet of Carsaig on the Ross of Mull to Carsaig Arches – one of the natural wonders of the island. The approach to the Carsaig Arches is the culmination of a glorious 6.5km walk below breathtaking cliffs haunted by feral goats and golden eagles.

On the shore about 3km beyond Carsaig lies the Nun's Cave. Tradition suggests that persecuted nuns were driven here from Iona during the Reformation. It's a large cave and according to an old account, it is capable of sheltering some 300 people. Carvings adorn the walls, mostly Celtic crosses, but it is difficult to make out those of antiquity from more modern graffiti. The oldest date that can be recognised is 1633 and there is a clear carving of a sailing ship. There is also the clear mark of a mason, and it's believed that stone used to build the Abbey Church on Iona was taken from this cave, indeed the quarrying here was worked from the Middle Ages right through until last century.

The Carsaig Arches are a natural wonder – a headland of columnar basalt with a sea cave which has eroded right through the rock like a tunnel. Close by, a tall, slender sea stack is pierced by another arch, and in between the great waves crash relentlessly. Beyond lies an enormous table of rock known as Leac na Leum, the slab of the leap.

Carsaig is a fairly isolated community and is reached by the hill road from Pennyghael on the south shores of Loch Scridain. From the pier a track runs west through the trees and follows the shore of Carsaig Bay. To the west of the bay the path becomes clear and here and there planks of wood have been laid out across muddy sections. Follow the path, sometimes along grassy terraces, at other times across the rocky shore below the steep, beetling cliffs of Sron nam Boc. Watch out for

Route Summary

From Carsaig pier a track runs W through the trees and follows the shore of Carsaig Bay. Follow the path below the cliffs of Sron nam Boc to the Nun's Cave. Continue on the coastal path to Malcolm's Point and the Carsaig Arches. A narrow track climbs up around a steep headland – the path is fairly exposed here – and then drops down to a secluded bay. The return route above the cliffs involves a scramble on loose rock up Binnein Ghorrie, the next obvious break in the line of cliffs, to reach the moorland above the shore and cliffs, or alternatively, return the way you came.

Map: OS Sheet 48

Access Point: Carsaig Pier

Distance: 13km

Approx Time: 5-7 hours

Grade: Moderate coastal walk

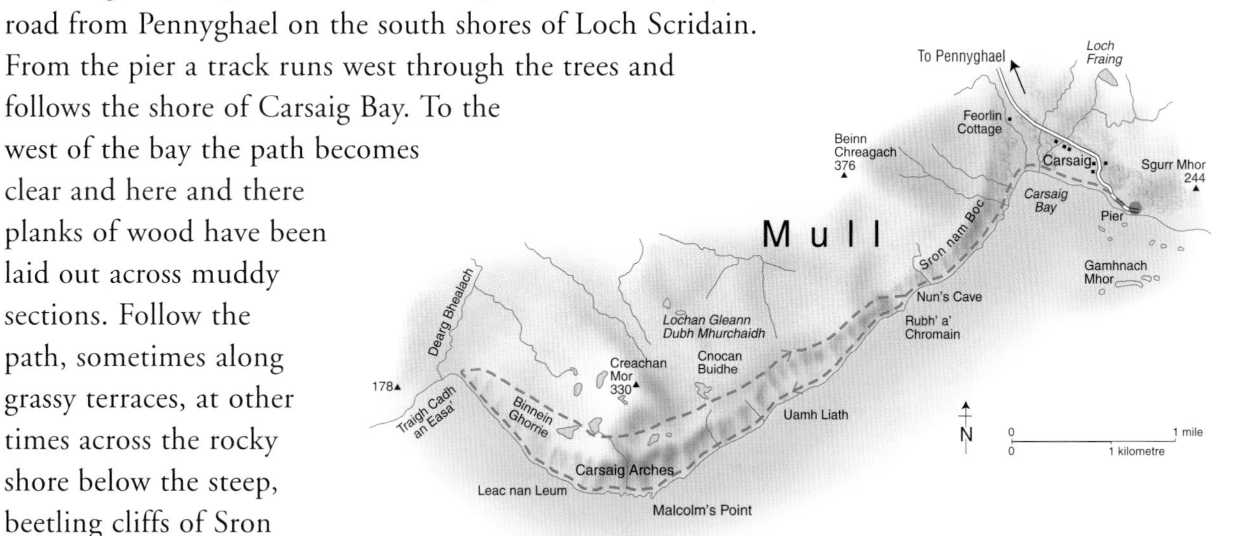

Carsaig Arches at Malcolm's Point, Ross of Mull

a curious Sphinx-like rock which stands guard over the hidden entrance to the Nun's Cave, or Uamh nan Cailleachan, the cave of the old women. A bank hides the entrance but you can't miss it, and it's worth spending some time looking for the ancient carvings.

From the cave it's about an hour's walk to Malcolm's Point and the Carsaig Arches. The coastline becomes increasingly wilder the further west you go with marvellous views back towards the lonely Garvellachs and out to the dim outlines of Jura, Islay and Colonsay. Suddenly the path crosses a tableland of rock to a deep inlet where the sea surges into the first of the two Carsaig Arches.

To the right a narrow track climbs up around a steep headland – this path is fairly exposed here – and then drops steeply down to a secluded bay where you can actually walk much of the way through the first arch. The other arch stands close by, a natural gateway through a tall and slim sea stack. The return route above the cliffs involves a scramble on loose rock up Binnein Ghorrie, the next obvious break in the line of cliffs, to reach the moorland above the shore and cliffs, or alternatively there's little lost in returning the way you came.

98 The Green Isle of Kerrera

Eight kilometres in length and tucked in close to Oban, the island of Kerrera is separated from the mainland by the Sound of Kerrera. Compared to Oban, Kerrera has a peaceful tranquillity and a lush greenness. It's a hilly little island, speckled with small crags.

It was on Kerrera that Alexander II of Scotland died of a fever in 1249 when trying to assert his rights in a district which at that time regarded Norway, not Scotland, as its mother-country.

At the southern end lies the ruined Gylen Castle, perched on a rocky headland and reached from Lower Gylen. A tunnel gives access through the castle to the headland beyond. Built in 1582 by the MacDougalls of Dunollie, Gylen Castle was destroyed in 1647 by General Leslie's troops who carried off the Brooch of Lorne, allegedly worn by Robert the Bruce in the fourteenth-century Battle of Dalrigh. The brooch was eventually purchased by General Duncan Campbell of Lochnell who presented it back to the MacDougalls.

Once you land from the ferry turn left below the Ferry House and follow the road south towards Horseshoe Bay and then past Dail Righ where Alexander II died. Continue past the Little Horseshoe Bay towards Upper Gylen. Just before you reach the farmhouse leave the track through a gate on the right and follow a track which leads to the ruins of Gylen Castle.

Follow the coast to Ardmore bay where the main track can be re-joined. Pass the old house at Ardmore and follow the old drove-road above Port Phadruig to Barnabuck. The route now weaves its way up over Am Maolan with superb views up and down the length of the Firth of Lorne. Follow the track gently downhill, past Balliemore, back to the ferry.

The passenger ferry crosses the Sound of Kerrera from a jetty 3km south-west of Oban on the Gallanach road. The ferry crossing takes about 5 minutes.

Route Summary

Cross to the island by ferry and turn left below the Ferry House. Follow the road S past Horseshoe Bay and the King's Field, towards Upper Gylen, and then Lower Gylen. Just before you reach the farmhouse leave the track through a gate on the left and follow another track which leads to the ruins of Gylen Castle. From here follow the coast to Armore bay where the main track can be re-joined. Pass the old house at Ardmore and follow the old drove-road above Port Phadruig to Barnabuck. Cross Am Maolan and follow the track gently downhill, past Balliemore, back to the ferry.

Map: OS Sheet 49

Access Point: Kerrera ferry on the Oban to Gallanach road

Distance: 12km

Approx Time: 4-6 hours

Grade: Easy coastal walk

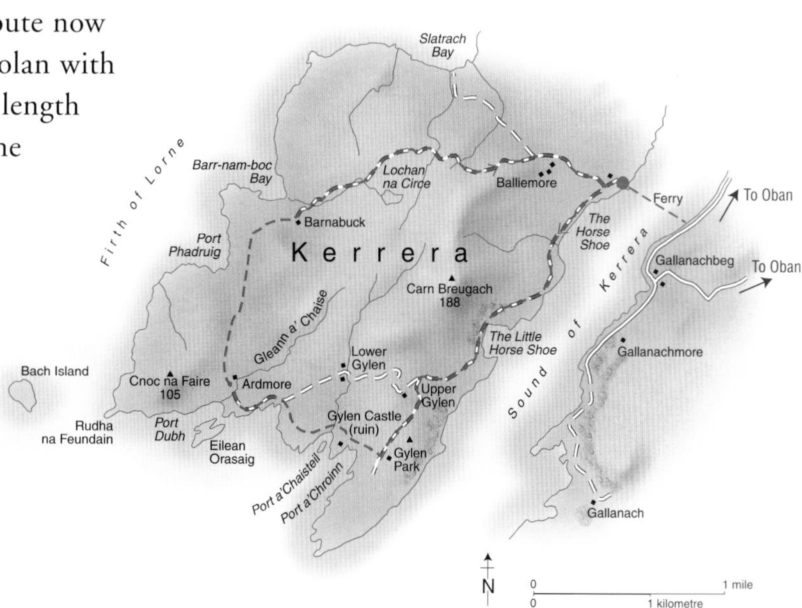

99 The Paps of Jura

Jura's Paps bunch together in the southern half of an island which is Highland in atmosphere, but lies on the same longitudinal line as Glasgow. The island, 45km long by 13km wide, is named after the Norse for deer island, and is said to support as many adders as it does deer!

The quartzite domes of the three Paps are split by low cols and surrounded by low-lying moorland, which is boggy underfoot. These are not easy hills and their traverse, including an add-on, Corra Bheinn, necessitates about 1650m of climbing in 16km. A big day by any standard.

The round begins at the bridge over the Corran River on the A846, the island's only road. Take an almost direct line to the head of Loch an t-Siob, aim right of a wood and across a shoulder, and down to the river east of the loch's outflow. From the head of the loch climb to the bealach left of the steep summit cone of Beinn a' Chaolais, then continue up steep quartzy rubble to the summit.

The route onwards starts easily enough on mossy ground, giving

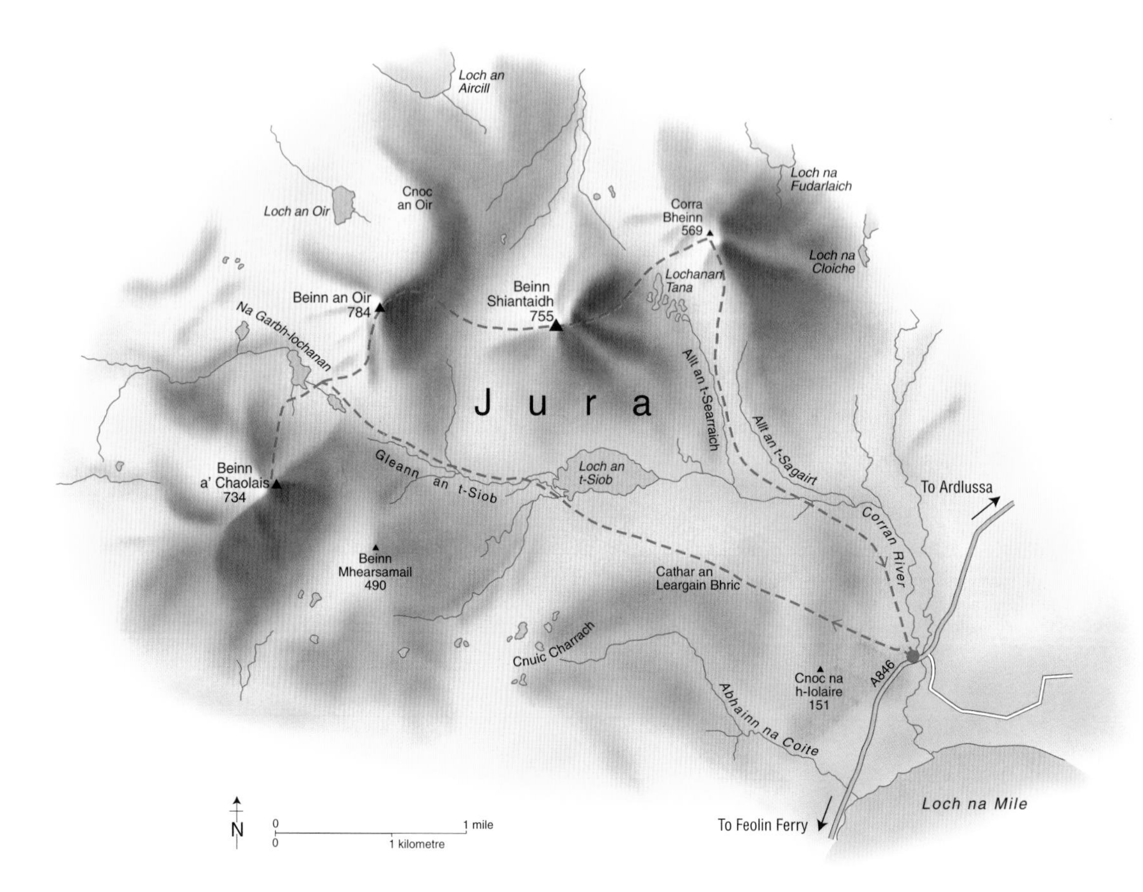

The Paps of Jura across the Sound of Jura from Knapdale, Argyll

a false sense of security. The descent becomes tricky on shifting unstable blocks. It feels like a long descent to the bealach and when you reach it, large quartzite blocks make the going difficult. It's almost a relief to get climbing again, up the scree covered slopes to emerge at the skyline. Follow a pleasant narrowing ridge to the summit. A causeway of stones continues north for a few hundred metres to the remains of some stone huts. There is some difference in opinion as to the origins of the huts and causeway. Some say they were built by observers who manned the summit during the Second World War. Others suggest they were created by Ordnance Survey workers during triangulation work in the nineteenth century. From the huts, descend right towards the bealach below Beinn Shiantaidh; steeper slopes lower down can be outflanked by following a grassy terrace down to the right.

The ascent of Beinn Shiantaidh's west ridge is comparatively pleasant with another narrowing ridge leading to the summit, and superb views over the north of the island towards Corryvreckan and the island of Scarba. Someone told me there was a box beside the cairn with an old visitor's book in it, but I couldn't find it. I did find the descent route, even though its line is far from obvious. A lower cairn marks the route. Keep to the right, picking up an indistinct path that weaves its way through the quartzite rocks and screes. The bealach below Corra Bheinn will be welcome, keeping well to the right of its little lochan.

The ascent of Corra Bheinn, a 'fourth' pap, is optional, but since it's less severe than the three Pap ascents it's worth it. Descend eastwards to a path that offers an easy route back to the road.

Route Summary

From the bridge over the Corran River cross the moorland below the eastern shoulder of Beinn Mhearsamail and take a direct line for Loch an t-Siob. Climb from the W end to the bealach between Beinn Mhearsamail and Beinn a' Chaolais. Steep slopes lead to the summit. Descend NE down difficult ground to another bealach. Climb the S ridge of Beinn an Oir then descend E before climbing Beinn Shiantaidh. Finally climb NNE to Corra Bheinn, then descend E to a footpath which can be followed SSW back to the road.

Map: OS Sheet 61

Access Point: The bridge over the Corran River

Distance: 16km

Approx Time: 6-8 hours

Grade: Strenuous hill walk

Caisteal Abhail and Cir Mhor from the north, with Goat Fell in the distance, Isle of Arran

100 Cir Mhor, Arran

As a youngster holidaying on the Clyde coast I would gaze across the waters of the Firth of Clyde at the 'sleeping warrior' outline of the Isle of Arran. This was another world, a highland landscape of mountains, rushing burns and vast seascapes, but it was to be another ten years before I set foot on the island.

I'll never forget the first view up Glen Sannox. Here was wildness in the extreme, a serrated skyline that terrified me, yet at the same time drew me onwards like a magnet. I wanted to climb everything in sight, but my companions, older and wiser than me, suggested we reserve our energies for the western side of the glen.

A bridge on the A841 crosses the River Sannox and some distance south of it a track leaves the road and passes a cottage to make its way up Glen Sannox. Soon afterwards another bridge crosses the river and a footpath makes its way across the moorland towards a broad, craggy ridge. This is the north-east shoulder of Suidhe Fhearghas, and it offers a good route to the main Caisteal Abhail ridge. Make the most of the rather eroded footpath approaching the rounded summit of Suidhe Fhearghas, for the character of this walk soon changes. Ahead lies Caisteal Abhail, and

Route Summary

Leave the road and follow a track, past a cottage, into Glen Sannox. Cross the bridge over the river and follow the path which makes for the NE shoulder of Suidhe Fhearghas. Climb to the summit ridge and follow this in a SW direction to the gap of the Ceum na Caillich. Drop down to the right to avoid the scrambling descent, then from the gap climb to the summit of Caisteal Abhail. Descend to the S, avoiding the crags on the right, to a bealach from which the steep NW ridge of Cir Mhor is climbed. Descend due E to The Saddle from where a steep path drops down in a NE direction into Glen Sannox.

its notorious Ceum na Caillich, the Witches Step.

The direct descent into the gap of the Witches Step is not the route to follow if you're not an experienced scrambler – far better to descend about 60m on the north side of the gap where a footpath takes you to the foot of the cleft. The scramble itself begins in a groove immediately right of the main summit boulder and lower down an exposed slab is the crux.

From the bottom of the cleft, some straightforward scrambling takes you over a succession of rock tors to the summit of Caisteal Abhail at 859m. Some paths on the south side of the ridge avoid the main scrambling difficulties. From the summit an awkward line of crags bar the way ahead, so retrace your steps a short way. On the right of the crags much more benevolent slopes sweep around the head of Glen Sannox to the foot of Cir Mhor. The ascent to the summit is easy, but the descent to The Saddle is steep and awkward, requiring scrambling and a lot of care on loose screes.

Unless you continue to Goat Fell, Arran's highest peak, the route now descends north-east from The Saddle into upper Glen Sannox. A steep footpath makes its way down through a band of cliffs to the upper reaches of Glen Sannox where a footpath follows the river back to the bridge which meets the outward track. Follow this back to the A841.

Follow the footpath on the N bank of the river all the way back to the bridge and the track to the road.

Map: OS Sheet 69

Access Point: South of the bridge over the River Sannox on the A841

Distance: 13km

Approx Time: 4-6 hours

Grade: Strenuous hill walk/scramble

Translation: big comb

Pronunciation: keer voar

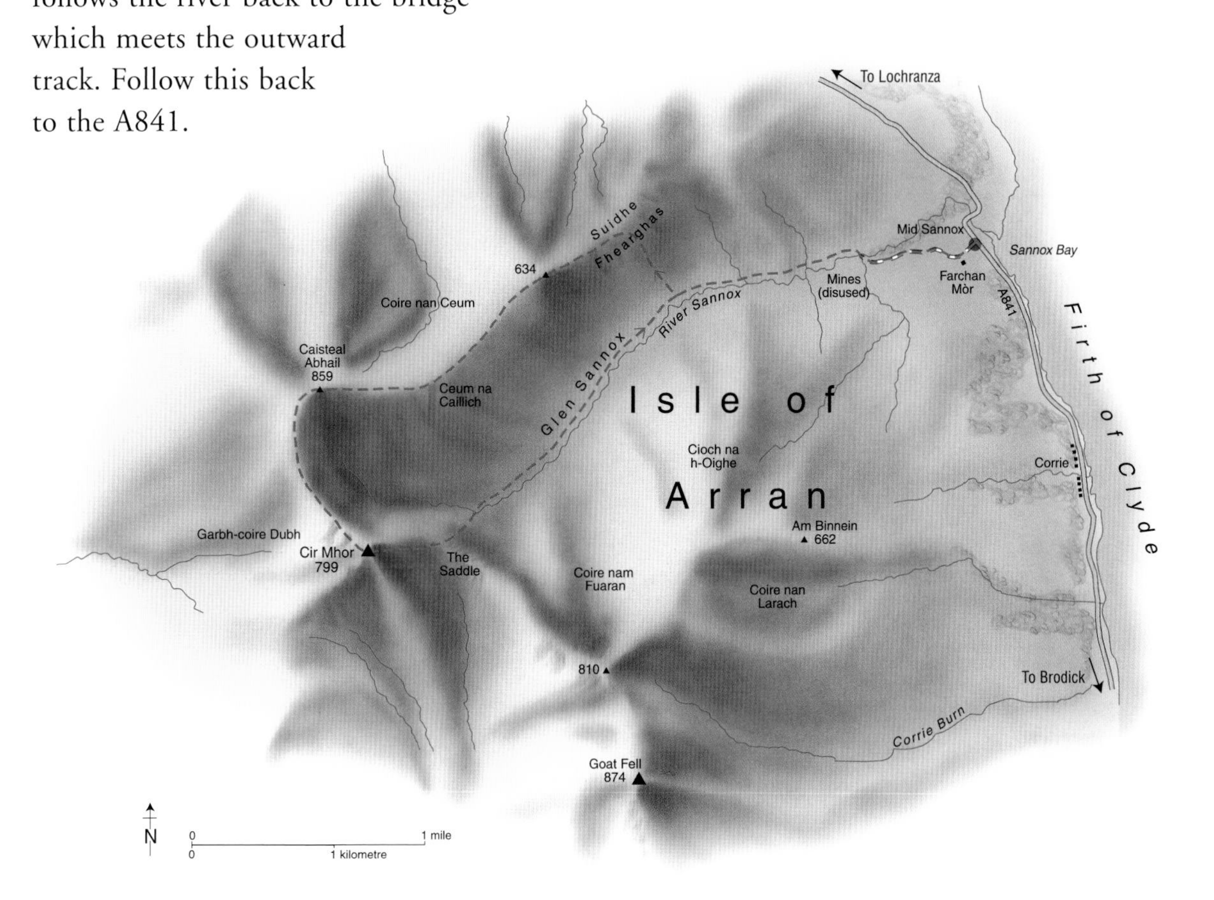

ACCESS

Despite the fact that Scotland has long boasted a large network of rights of way and that since time immemorial walkers have always enjoyed a *de facto* right to walk in the countryside and upland areas, a right enshrined in tradition, hideously unwelcoming signs began to appear on gates and fences warning the public to 'keep out'. Others notices warned of the consequences of trespass, choosing to ignore the fact that in all probability there was never any such thing in Scots law!

Some of the best barristers and law lords in the country have long been unable to agree on what constitutes Scottish access and in recent years there have been strong calls for a change in legislation to make it clear to everyone what their rights were.

Following on from devolution and the creation of a Scottish Parliament, a land reform agenda was set out by the Scottish Executive. This agenda was to include the creation of national parks in Scotland, in Loch Lomond and the Trossachs and in the Cairngorms.

Springing from that same land reform agenda, the Land Reform (Scotland) Act 2003 now gives the public statutory access rights to most land and inland water in Scotland. This new legislation arguably gives Scotland the best access provisions in Europe and means that walkers can climb hills, go for walks in the countryside and even cross farm land without threat. However, people only have these rights if they exercise them responsibly by respecting the privacy, safety and livelihoods of others as well as caring for the environment. Equally, land managers have to manage their land and water responsibly in relation to access rights.

In conjunction with the new access legislation, a Scottish Outdoor Access Code has been published (www.outdooraccess-scotland.com) to provide detailed guidance on the responsibilities of those exercising access rights and of those managing land and water. As such, the Code provides a practical guide to help everyone make the proper decisions about what best to do in everyday situations.

The Code is based on three key principles that apply equally to everyone:

- Respect the interests of other people. Act with courtesy, consideration and awareness. If exercising access rights, make sure you respect the privacy, safety and livelihoods of those working or living in the outdoors and other people enjoying the outdoors. If you are a land manager, respect people's use of the outdoors and their need for a safe and enjoyable visit.

- Care for the environment. If exercising access rights, look after the places you visit and leave the land as you find it. If managing the land, help maintain the natural and cultural heritage features that make the outdoors attractive to visit and enjoy.
- Take responsibility for your own actions. If exercising access rights, remember the outdoors is not risk-free and act with care at all times. If you are a land manager, act with care at all times for people's safety.

In essence, the legal do's and don'ts are provided for in the Act, and the advice as to what constitutes responsible behaviour is contained in the Scottish Outdoor Access Code.

The main places where the public doesn't have any access rights include houses and gardens, and non-residential buildings and associated land, land in which crops are growing (although you can walk round the margins of fields where crops are growing or have been sown), land next to a school and used by the school, sports or playing fields when these are in use and where the exercise of access rights would interfere with such use, land developed and in use for recreation and where the exercise of access rights would interfere with such use, golf courses (but you can cross a golf course provided you don't interfere with any games of golf), places like airfields, railways, telecommunications sites, military bases and installations, working quarries and construction sites; and visitor attractions or other places which charge for entry.

Many estates in Scotland are involved in deer stalking and ask hillwalkers to respect the stag shooting season which generally runs from about mid August to 20th October. Some estates may extend this season for a couple of weeks or so and one or two may begin slightly earlier. During this time there are many upland areas in Scotland that are unaffected by deer stalking, like those reserves operated by Scottish Natural Heritage and the National Trust for Scotland.

The Mountaineering Council for Scotland and Scottish Natural Heritage jointly operate a website (www.hillphones.info) and Hillphones system.

By using Hillphones intending visitors can obtain information about stalking and plan their outings accordingly. Recorded messages are updated by 8.00am each day and calls are charged at normal rates. Wherever possible, Hillphone messages contain a forecast of stalking activities for the next few days. It may help to have a map beside you when you call the Hillphone.

The service is supported by the Access Forum, and has been organised by the Mountaineering Council of Scotland, Scottish Natural Heritage and the participating estates. The service aims to improve communications between stag stalkers and hillwalkers and has been a huge success.

MOUNTAIN SAFETY

The majority of the walks described in this book venture onto what can often be a cruel and unforgiving landscape, and appropriate safety precautions should always be taken. Seasonal variations in the weather patterns on the Scottish hills are extremely fickle, and snow showers are not unusual in what we commonly shrug off as summer. I've personally experienced snow in every month of the year in the Cairngorms. Paradoxically, the winter months can also be 'unseasonal' and long, mild spells with not a lick of snow on the tops is not uncommon. The real danger is in the weather's propensity for quick and sudden change. That's when hillwalkers are generally caught out and those going to the high tops should have a good understanding of basic weather lore. At the very least we should go to the hills with a knowledge of the weather forecast for the next few days, and such forecasts are generally pretty accurate. These are available from newspapers, radio and television, and dedicated phone lines such as the Met Office's Weathercall, tel: 0871 200 3985, www.metoffice.com

West Highlands & Islands: 09014 722 075
Grampian & East Highlands: 09014 722 074
(Calls at publication cost 60p/min)

Most accidents on Scottish hills stem from poor navigation. It's when walkers become 'temporarily misplaced' that accidents are likely to happen because of confusion, fear or lack of care. Use of map and compass and navigational skills can be learned fairly quickly, but like any other skill efficiency only comes with practice. It worries me that many walkers are content to blindly follow a line of waymarked cairns up a mountain's flank. Such cairns are not only unsightly but environmentally damaging and should have no place on the Scottish hills. Surely following a compass bearing in misty weather is more reassuring and aesthetically satisfying than following a line of heaped stones?

As well as the appropriate map and compass, hillwalkers shouldn't set off without waterproofs and spare clothing, even in summer, and should carry emergency supplies such as food, a whistle and a torch. Scottish winter conditions are often Arctic in nature and just as severe as those experienced in higher European mountains. Such conditions must be treated with respect, and an ice axe, crampons, and specialist winter gear are essential, as is a good understanding of snow conditions and avalanche awareness. Please remember there is no such thing as Scottish winter hillwalking – in the normal conditions of a Scottish winter the activity is no less than mountaineering. So if you don't feel proficient as a mountaineer either stick to low-level routes or enrol on one of the excellent mountaineering courses that are available. Information on mountaineering clubs and how to get in touch with them can be found by writing to either of the following addresses:

The Honorary Secretary of the Mountaineering Council of Scotland
The Old Granary
West Mill Street
Perth PH1 5QP

sportscotland
Caledonia House
South Gyle
Edinburgh EH12 9DQ

It's not only the hillwalker who faces potential dangers – some of the low-level walks in this book involve river crossings, and streams which are completely benevolent one day, can, in wet weather, change into roaring torrents within 24 hours. My wife and I once walked from Kinloch Hourn to Barrisdale in Knoydart on a magnificent spring day with blue skies and sunshine. We were so enthralled by the scenery we didn't even notice the little burns we stepped over. Three days later, after a lot of mild, wet weather which melted the snow on the higher tops, we faced a real epic on our return journey. In places we had to struggle across thigh-deep torrents. One raging river just couldn't be crossed. We had to walk down to Loch Hourn and wade into the sea to bypass it!

Finally, let someone know where you are going and approximately when you will return. Every year rescue teams spend fruitless and frustrating hours searching for people in the wrong places, so write out a brief description of your route, and an estimated time of return, and leave it with a responsible person. The enjoyment of your walk will be heightened by the knowledge that if things should happen to go wrong, someone, somewhere, will know where to look for you. And next time you have a chance to donate to the Scottish Mountain Rescue Service, please don't hesitate to do so.

INDEX

Entries in **bold** indicate photographs